KU-443-529

THE ROUGH GUIDE TO

Mallorca

There are more than two hundred Rough Guide titles
covering destinations from Alaska to Zimbabwe
and subjects from Acoustic Guitar to Travel Health

Forthcoming travel guides include

The Algarve • The Bahamas • Cambodia • Caribbean Islands
Costa Brava • New York Restaurants • Bolivia • Zanzibar

Forthcoming reference guides include

Elvis • Online Travel • Internet Radio • Cult TV

Rough Guides Online
www.roughguides.com

Rough Guide Credits

Text Editor:	Matthew Teller
Series Editor:	Mark Ellingham
Editorial:	Martin Dunford, Jonathan Buckley, Jo Mead, Kate Berens, Ann-Marie Shaw, Paul Gray, Helena Smith, Judith Bamber, Orla Duane, Olivia Eccleshall, Ruth Blackmore, Geoff Howard, Claire Saunders, Gavin Thomas, Alexander Mark Rogers, Polly Thomas, Joe Staines, Richard Lim, Duncan Clark, Peter Buckley, Sam Thorne, Lucy Ratcliffe, Clifton Wilkinson, David Glen, Alison Murchie (UK); Andrew Rosenberg, Stephen Timblin, Yuki Takagaki, Richard Koss (US)
Online:	Kelly Cross, Anja Mutić-Blessing, Jennifer Gold, Audra Epstein, Suzanne Welles (US)
Production:	Susanne Hillen, Andy Hilliard, Link Hall, Helen Ostick, Julia Bovis, Michelle Draycott, Katie Pringle, Mike Hancock, Zoë Nobes, Rachel Holmes, Andy Turner
Cartography:	Melissa Baker, Maxine Repath, Ed Wright, Katie Lloyd-Jones
Picture Research:	Louise Boulton, Sharon Martins
Finance:	John Fisher, Gary Singh, Edward Downey, Mark Hall, Tim Bill
Marketing & Publicity:	Richard Trillo, Niki Smith, David Wearn, Chloë Roberts, Birgit Hartmann, Claire Southern (UK); Simon Carloss, David Wechsler, Kathleen Rushforth (US)
Administration:	Tania Hummel, Demelza Dallow, Julie Sanderson

Acknowledgements

Special thanks to Maria Peterson for tidying up so many loose ends and helping with the Spanish. Dave Robson for his advice on wine and George Scott for providing such fine lodgings at Binissalem. Ruth Rigby should also be credited for her help with Basics, and thanks also to Dominic Rigby, who contributed the section on Mallorca's birdlife. At Rough Guides, I am grateful to the redoubtable Gavin Thomas for hiking the hikes, and my hard-working, eagle-eyed editor, Matthew Teller. Thanks also to Gerrard Kennedy and Narrell Leffman for Basics research in the US and Australia; Helen Ostick for typesetting; Katie Lloyd-Jones for cartography; and Laurence Larroche for proofreading.

This third edition published June 2001 by Rough Guides Ltd, 62–70 Shorts Gardens, London WC2H 9AH.
Reprinted April 2002

Distributed by the Penguin Group:
Penguin Books Ltd, 80 Strand, London WC2R ORL
Penguin Putnam, Inc. 375 Hudson Street, New York, NY 10014, USA.
Penguin Books Australia Ltd, 487 Maroondah Highway, PO Box 257, Ringwood, Victoria 3134, Australia.
Penguin Books Canada Ltd, 10 Alcorn Avenue, Toronto, Ontario M4V 1E4, Canada.
Penguin Books (NZ) Ltd, 182–190 Wairau Road, Auckland 10, New Zealand.
Printed in England by Clays Ltd, St Ives PLC
Typography and original design by Jonathan Dear and The Crowd Roars.
Illustrations throughout by Edward Briant.

ISBN 1-85828-703-0

THE ROUGH GUIDE TO

Mallorca

Written and researched by
Phil Lee

ROUGH
GUIDES

Help us update

We've gone to a lot of trouble to ensure that this third edition of *The Rough Guide to Mallorca* is accurate and up-to-date. However, things inevitably change, and if you feel we've got it wrong or left something out, we'd like to know: any suggestions, comments or corrections would be much appreciated. We'll credit all contributions and send a copy of the next edition – or any other Rough Guide if you prefer – for the best correspondence.

Please mark letters "Rough Guide to Mallorca" and send to:
Rough Guides, 62–70 Shorts Gardens, London WC2H 9AH or
Rough Guides, 4th Floor, 345 Hudson St, New York, NY 10014.

Email should be sent to:
mail@roughguides.co.uk

Online updates about Rough Guide titles can be found on our website at www.roughguides.com

The Author

Phil Lee has been writing for the Rough Guides for over a decade. His other books in the series include Norway, Menorca, Canada, Brussels, Belgium & Luxembourg, Toronto and Holland. He lives in Nottingham, where he was born and raised.

Readers' letters

Many thanks to everyone who sent in helpful letters and emails on the last edition of the *Rough Guide to Mallorca and Menorca*: Mark Dorrington; Bettina Hartas Geary; Dinah Anderton; David Lee; Judith de Serra; Mel Greig; Mr & Mrs Chris Coakes; John Banfield; Ann Bamforth; Claire McGregor; Solna, Roger & Natasha Burnham; Barbara Mckiernan; Jean Sinclair; Joan Pozzoli; David Andersson; Lynette Brucks; John Fanshawe; Kathryn Drewitt; Roxane Smith; Helen Sandelands; Robbie Martzen; Paul Davies; Graeme Falconer; Ms E. Werenowska.

This book is dedicated to my dear mother, Lois Lee.

Rough Guides

Travel Guides • Phrasebooks • Music and Reference Guides

We set out to do something different when the first Rough Guide was published in 1982. Mark Ellingham, just out of University, was travelling in Greece. He brought along the popular guides of the day, but found they were all lacking in some way. They were either strong on ruins and museums but went on for pages without mentioning a beach or taverna. Or they were so conscious of the need to save money that they lost sight of Greece's cultural and historical significance. Also, none of the books told him anything about Greece's contemporary life – its politics, its culture, its people, and how they lived.

So with no job in prospect, Mark decided to write his own guidebook, one which aimed to provide practical information that was second to none, detailing the best beaches and the hottest clubs and restaurants, while also giving hard-hitting accounts of every sight, both famous and obscure, and providing up-to-the-minute information on contemporary culture. It was a guide that encouraged independent travellers to find the best of Greece, and was a great success, getting shortlisted for the Thomas Cook travel guide award, and encouraging Mark, along with three friends, to expand the series.

The Rough Guide list grew rapidly and the letters flooded in, indicating a much broader readership than had been anticipated, but one which uniformly appreciated the Rough Guides' mix of practical detail and humour, irreverence and enthusiasm. Things haven't changed. The same four friends who began the series are still the caretakers of the Rough Guide mission today: to provide the most reliable, up-to-date and entertaining information to independent-minded travellers of all ages, on all budgets.

We now publish 150 titles and have offices in London and New York. The travel guides are written and researched by a dedicated team of more than 100 authors, based in Britain, Europe, the USA and Australia. We have also created a unique series of phrasebooks to accompany the travel series, along with the acclaimed series of music guides, and a best-selling pocket guide to the Internet and World Wide Web. We also publish comprehensive travel information on our website: *www.roughguides.com*

Contents

Chapter 3 Northern Mallorca 160

Chapter 4 Eastern Mallorca 196

Part Three Contexts 235

Index 273

List of maps

MAP SYMBOLS

▬▬	Motorway	⌂	Monastery
═══	Main road	♜	Castle
───	Minor road	🏛	Stately home
⊞⊞⊞	Steps	🕴	Lighthouse
- - - -	Footpath	♨	Spring
▬▬▬	Pedestrianized road	�	Gardens
▪▪▪▪	Wall	▲	Mountain peak
━●━	Railway	◠	Cave
+++++	Tram line	⸫	Cliff
··········	Waterway	⋎	Viewpoint
— —	Ferry route	ⓘ	Tourist office
▬ ▬ ▬	Chapter division boundary	⊠	Post office
▪━▪━▪	International boundary	★	Bus stop/taxi stand
✕	Airport	⛽	Petrol station
P	Parking	◯	Stadium
◉	Accommodation	▬	Building
■	Restaurant	⊞	Church (town maps)
⚠	Campsite	░	Park
◆	Point of interest	⋰	Beach
‡	Church/cathedral (regional maps)	⬭	Saltpan

Introduction

Few Mediterranean holiday spots are as often and as unfairly maligned as **Mallorca**. The largest of the Balearic Islands, an archipelago to the east of the Spanish mainland which also comprises Menorca, Ibiza and Formentera, Mallorca is commonly perceived as little more than sun, sex, booze and high-rise hotels – so much so that there's a long-standing Spanish joke about a mythical fifth Balearic island called "Majorca" (the English spelling) which is inhabited by an estimated eight million tourists a year. However, this image, spawned by the helter-skelter development of the 1960s, takes no account of Mallorca's beguiling diversity.

Until well into the twentieth century, Mallorca was a sleepily agrarian backwater, left behind in the Spanish dash to exploit the Americas from the sixteenth century onwards. Mass tourism has reversed the island's fortunes since World War II, bringing the highest level of disposable income per capita in Spain, but the price has been profound social transformation and the disfigurement of tracts of the coastal landscape. However, the spread of development is surprisingly limited, essentially confined to the Bay of Palma, a thirty-kilometre strip flanking the island capital, and a handful of mega-resorts notching the east coast. Elsewhere, Mallorca is much less developed than many other parts of Spain.

Palma, Mallorca's capital and the Balearics' one real city, is a bustling, historic place whose grandee mansions and magnificent Gothic cathedral defy the expectations of many visitors. To the east of Palma stretches **Es Pla**, an agricultural plain that fills out the centre of the island, sprinkled with ancient and seldom-visited country towns. On either side of the plain are coastal mountains. In the west and to the north, the rugged **Serra de Tramuntana** hides beautiful cove beaches, notably Cala de Deià and Platja de Formentor, and deep sheltered valleys. The range is crisscrossed with footpaths and makes for ideal hiking country, particularly in the cooler spring and autumn. Tucked away here too are a string of picturesque villages, such as Orient and Fornalutx, and a pair of intriguing monasteries at

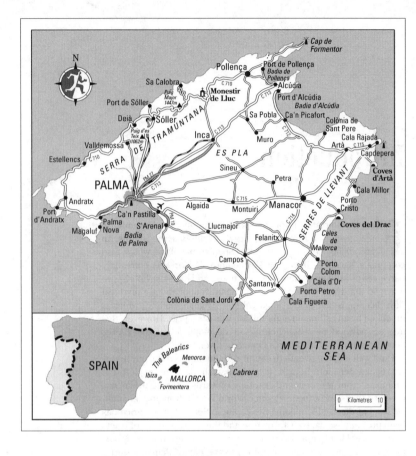

Valldemossa and Lluc. The gentler, greener **Serres de Llevant** shadow the coves of the east coast and culminate in the pine-clad headlands and medieval hill towns of the island's northeast corner. There's a startling variety and physical beauty to the land, which, along with the mildness of the climate, has drawn tourists to visit and well-heeled expatriates to settle here since the nineteenth century, including artists and writers of many descriptions from Robert Graves to Roger McGough.

Practicalities

Access to Mallorca is easy from Britain and northern Europe, with plenty of charter flights and complete package deals, some of which drop to absurdly low prices out of season or through last-minute booking. From mainland Spain, both ferries and flights are frequent and comparatively inexpensive. The island has one airport and one major ferry port, both on the outskirts of the capital, Palma. From here, the rest of Mallorca is within easy striking distance by car – it only takes a couple of hours to drive from one corner of the island to the other – and to a large extent by public transport too.

The main constraint for travellers is accommodation. From mid-June to mid-September rooms are in very short supply. If you go at this time, you're well advised to make a reservation several weeks, sometimes months, in advance or to book a package. Out of season, things ease up and you can idle round, staying pretty much where you want. Two or three weeks are sufficient to see most of the island;

Palma climate table

	J	F	M	A	M	J	J	A	S	O	N	D
Highest recorded temp (°C)	22	23	24	26	31	37	39	37	35	31	26	24
Average daily max. temp (°C)	14	15	17	19	22	26	29	29	27	23	18	15
Average daily min. temp (°C)	6	6	8	10	13	17	20	20	18	14	10	8
Lowest recorded temp (°C)	-3	-4	-1	1	5	8	12	11	4	1	1	-1
Average hours of sunshine per day	5	6	6	7	9	10	11	11	8	6	5	4
Average number of days with rain	8	6	8	6	5	3	1	3	5	9	8	9

on a shorter visit, head for Palma and the northwest coast. Bear in mind also that six of Mallorca's monasteries rent out renovated cells at inexpensive rates – it's well worth sampling at least one.

Climate

Spring and autumn are the ideal times for a visit, when the weather is comfortably warm, with none of the oven-like temperatures which bake the island in July and August. It's well worth considering a winter break too: even in January, temperatures are usually high enough during the day to sit out at a café in shirtsleeves. The island sees occasional rain in winter, however, and the Serra de Tramuntana mountains, which protect the rest of Mallorca from inclement weather and the prevailing northerly winds, are often buffeted by storms.

Basics

Getting there from Britain

The easiest and cheapest way to reach Mallorca from Britain is to fly, which takes a little over two hours nonstop from London, or two-and-three-quarter hours nonstop from Manchester. More arduous is the long drive to the east coast of Spain, where regular car ferries from Barcelona and Valencia depart for Palma; these same ports also offer a summertime catamaran service. If you do decide to drive, it's worth considering the ferries from the south coast of England direct to Spain: sailing from Plymouth to Santander, or Portsmouth to Bilbao, cuts many hours off the driving time through France. By train, reckon on 16 to 20 hours for the journey from London to Barcelona via Paris.

By air

Hundreds of aircraft, mostly **charter flights**, shuttle back and forth between Britain and Mallorca's one and only airport at Palma during the summer season and, although the charters are heavily subscribed by package-tour operators well in advance, there are usually spare seats for independent travellers after these package firms have taken their allocation. Excellent deals are available, with tickets averaging around £190 return for a scheduled flight, or as little as £80 return for a last-minute charter flight. As a general rule,

prices are at their highest during July and August. On these flight-only deals, waiting until the last minute to book won't gain you much advantage: you won't save much (if any) cash and you have to be prepared to fly from any UK airport at any time of the day or night.

As far as **scheduled flights** are concerned, your choices are limited to a handful of nonstop flights each day from the UK to Palma, or a few more daily services via Barcelona. A full fare on a scheduled flight to Palma is likely to cost more than twice the average charter price, but scheduled tickets on special offer or with certain restrictions can be reasonably good value, especially as the departure times of scheduled flights are often more sociable than those of charters.

In particular, it's well worth checking out the new breed of **low-cost airlines** for flights to Palma. These 'no frills' and often ticketless airlines will always be cheaper than the big carriers and are certainly competitive with the cheaper charter flights; they'll also often have more convenient flight times than charters and give you more choice as to when you fly. Given the restrictions on flight times on charter flights and the cost of the more open-ended scheduled flights, these flights can be the best option if you're planning a very long or very short stay. Booking your flight over the **Internet** can also reduce the cost: EasyJet, for example, knocks a few pounds off if you buy online instead of over the phone.

It's also worth considering buying a **package holiday** (see p.6), even if you've no intention of using the accommodation provided. Package prices – as little as £90 for a week – can be so low that they represent a reasonable deal for the flight alone.

Charter flights

There are frequent **charter flights** from almost all of Britain's airports to Palma during the summer, with flights operating throughout the year from the larger airports – Glasgow, Newcastle, Manchester, East Midlands, Birmingham, Luton, Stansted and Gatwick. For an idea of current prices and availability, contact any high street travel agent or try some of the websites listed on pp. 4-5. Otherwise,

AIRLINES IN BRITAIN

Air Europa, *www.air-europa.co.uk*
☎ 0870/240 1501.

Air 2000, *www.air2000.com* ☎ 0870/240 1402.

British Airways, *www.britishairways.com*
☎ 0845/773 3377; 146 New St, Birmingham; 32
Frederick St, Edinburgh; 64 Gordon St,
Glasgow; 156 Regent St, London W1; 41
Deansgate, Manchester.

British Midland, *www.britishmidland.com*
☎ 0870/607 0555.

EasyJet, *www.easyjet.com* ☎ 0870/600 0000.

Go, *www.go-fly.com* ☎ 0845/605 4321.

Iberia, *www.iberia.com* or *www.iberiaair-lines.co.uk* ☎ 0845/601 2854; 27 Glasshouse St,
London W1.

DISCOUNT FLIGHT AGENTS IN BRITAIN

Avro, Vantage House, 1 Weir Rd, London SW19
8UX ☎ 020/8695 4440 (*www.avro-flights.co.uk*). Flight-only agent, specializing in
charter flights.

Cheapflights, *www.cheapflights.co.uk* – UK
website which searches for the best fare bargains.

Dial-a-Flight, *www.dial-a-flight.com*
☎ 0870/333 4488. First-rate scheduled and
charter flight bargains with over-the-phone
booking and a useful online price search.

Expedia UK, *www.expedia.co.uk* – Microsoft's
venture into the Internet travel market, with a
'flight wizard' listing many (but not all) airline
options, plus its own special fares.

Flightline, *www.flightline.co.uk* ☎ 0800/036
0777 or ☎ 01702/715151. Another outfit offer-

ing online searches for cheap, mainly charter,
flights.

Lastminute.com, *www.lastminute.com* – the
best-known of the cheap flight websites, selling
everything from holidays to mobile phones.

North-South Travel, Moulsham Mill Centre,
Parkway, Chelmsford CM2 7PX
☎ 01245/608291. Friendly, competitive travel
agency, offering plenty of discount fares – with
the added bonus that profits are used to support projects in the developing world, especially
the promotion of sustainable tourism.

STA Travel, *www.statravel.co.uk* – London
call centre ☎ 020/7361 6145; Northern call centre ☎ 0161/830 4713; 86 Old Brompton Rd,
London SW7; 117 Euston Rd, London NW1; 38

good sources of last-minute bargains include
Teletext, local newspapers – the widest selection
of ads for London departures is invariably found in
the classified pages of the London listings maga-
zine *Time Out* or in the *Evening Standard* – and
the travel pages of the weekend broadsheets.
Otherwise, the operators and agents listed in the
box above are a good starting point. In particular,
both Avro, a specialist charter flight agent, and Air
2000, one of the largest charter airlines, offer
cheap deals and will provide you with information
about flights and prices direct. In terms of costs,
last-minute flight-only deals can cost as little as
£70 return.

The principal disadvantage of charter flights is
the **fixed return date** – a maximum of four
weeks from the outward journey. Some return
charters are, however, good value even if you
only use the outward half of the ticket, but for
more flexibility you'll probably want to buy a ticket for a scheduled flight.

Scheduled flights

With regard to **scheduled flights**, British Midland
operates nonstop services to Palma from
Heathrow (daily; 2hr 15min) and from **East
Midlands** (April–Oct 2–3 weekly; 2hr 30min), with
daily one-stop flights from **Glasgow** (5hr),
Edinburgh (5hr), **Leeds-Bradford** (4hr) and
Manchester (4hr); and once-weekly flights from
Teesside (4hr) and **Guernsey** (4hr). The low-cost
carrier EasyJet flies nonstop to Palma from **Luton**
(twice daily; 2hr 20min) and **Liverpool** (daily; 2hr
30min). Go, another low-cost carrier, flies nonstop from **Stansted** to Palma, as well as to
Barcelona (year-round) and Ibiza (late March to
late Oct). British Airways has between five and
seven flights a week nonstop to Palma from
Gatwick (2hr 30min), as well as one-stop flights
via Madrid from Heathrow, Gatwick and
Birmingham. Air Europa, an independent Spanish
carrier, flies nonstop to Palma up to six times a
week from Gatwick (2hr 15min), and as many

Store St, London WC1; 11 Goodge St, London W1; 30 Upper Kirkgate, Aberdeen ☎01224/658222; 38 North St, Brighton ☎01273/728282; 25 Queens Rd, Bristol ☎0117/929 4399; 38 Sidney St, Cambridge ☎01223/366966; 27 Forrest Rd, Edinburgh ☎0131/226 7747; 184 Byres Rd, Glasgow ☎0141/338 6000; 88 Vicar Lane, Leeds ☎0113/244 9212; 78 Bold St, Liverpool ☎0151/707 1123; 75 Deansgate, Manchester ☎0161/834 0668; 9 St Mary's Place, Newcastle ☎0191/233 2111; 36 George St, Oxford ☎01865/792800; over 40 branches including on university campuses in Birmingham, Bristol, Canterbury, Cardiff, Coventry, Durham, Glasgow, Leeds, London, Loughborough, Nottingham, Sheffield and Warwick. Worldwide specialists in low-cost flights and tours for students and under-26s, though other customers welcome. Also over 200 offices abroad.

Trailfinders, *www.trailfinders.co.uk* – 22 The Priory Queensway, Birmingham ☎0121/236 1234; 48 Corn St, Bristol ☎0117/929 9000; 254 Sauchiehall St, Glasgow ☎0141/353 2224; 1 Threadneedle St, London EC2 ☎020/7628 7628; 215 Kensington High St, London W6 ☎020/7937 5400; 58 Deansgate, Manchester ☎0161/839 6969. One of the best-informed and most efficient agents for independent travellers.

Travel Cuts, *www.travelcuts.co.uk* – 295a Regent St, London W1 ☎020/7255 1944; 229 Great Portland St, London W1 ☎020/7436 0459; 44 Queensway, London W2 ☎020/7792 3770. Specialists in budget, student and youth travel with a range of discount flights.

The Travel Bug, *www.travel-bug.co.uk* – 125 Gloucester Rd, London SW7 ☎020/7835 2000; 597 Cheetham Hill Rd, Manchester ☎0161/721 4000. Large range of discounted tickets; their website offers a flight price 'wizard' as well as a brochure request service.

Usit Campus, *www.usitcampus.co.uk* – national call centre ☎0870/240 1010; 541 Bristol Rd, Selly Oak, Birmingham ☎0121/414 1848; 61 Ditchling Rd, Brighton ☎01273/570226; 39 Queen's Rd, Clifton, Bristol ☎0117/929 2494; 5 Emmanuel St, Cambridge ☎01223/324283; 53 Forrest Rd, Edinburgh ☎0131/225 6111; 122 George St, Glasgow ☎0141/553 1818; 52 Grosvenor Gardens, London SW1 ☎020/7730 3402; 166 Deansgate, Manchester ☎0161/833 2046; 105 St Aldates, Oxford ☎01865/242067. Student/youth travel specialists with 51 branches, including in YHA shops and on university campuses all over Britain.

---

times again with a stop in Madrid (6hr). Spain's national carrier, Iberia, operates a one-stop service to Palma from Heathrow (twice daily, in 4hr via Barcelona or 5hr via Madrid) and Manchester (once daily, via Barcelona; 4hr 15min).

Another option is to fly to Barcelona and switch planes: BA has plenty of flights there – three times a day from Heathrow, twice a day from Gatwick and once a day from Manchester – and you can book a connecting flight from Barcelona to Palma through them too, but it may be cheaper to book the connection separately with Iberia. For more information on flights from the Spanish mainland, see p.18.

The lowest scheduled **fares** carry almost as many restrictions as charter tickets. British Midland's prices are typical; their full-fare return to Palma (with no restrictions) can cost over £500 from East Midlands. On the other hand, its restricted economy-class return fares begin at £150 in the off-season, increasing to £200 mid-

season, and £230 in the high season. Air Europa offers fares of around £140 return in summer, with offers reducing this to £120 out of high season. EasyJet – which issues no tickets, serves no inflight food and lets you sit anywhere you like on the plane – can be much cheaper. Their fares rise with demand, the cheapest prices being available only if you book early (two or three months in advance). As a guide, prices on EasyJet are generally around £50–£70 each way from Luton, and £60–£80 each way from Liverpool in mid-season. Their most up-to-date pricing information is available on the Internet, where you get a £5 reduction on the cost of a return ticket. Go, another ticketless airline, also costs both legs of the journey separately when fixing the ticket price, allowing you to dramatically vary the overall cost if you have some travel flexibility. A one-way trip to Palma can cost from around £50 to £120, but an average return journey works out at around £150.

Look out also for the **special offers** which the scheduled airlines sometimes run on their economy class tickets. Another option is Iberia's **open-jaw tickets**, whereby you fly to one Balearic island and return from another: London–Palma and Menorca–London costs around £270 in low season, £287 in high season. You can either make your own way by sea from Palma to Menorca, or pay an extra £37 to fly.

Packages

Few places on earth provide the **package tourist** with as many choices as Mallorca, but unfortunately for the island's reputation it's the ugly

---

Alternative Mallorca, 60 Stainbeck Rd, Leeds LS7 2PW ☎0113/278 6862 (*www.alternative-mallorca.com*). All-in and accommodation-only packages at a wide range of prices in lesser-known parts of Mallorca, as well as walking and climbing holidays.

Costa Cruises, 45–49 Mortimer St, London W1N 8JL ☎020/7323 3333. Worldwide cruises with a series of short-break trips in the Mediterranean.

First Choice, First Choice House, Peel Cross Rd, Salford, Manchester M4 2AN ☎0870/750 0001 (*www.first-choice.com*). The standard range of package holiday fare, with a flight-only booking option. Late holiday and flight offers on the website.

Freelance Holidays (Mallorca), 40b Grove Rd, Stratford upon Avon CV37 6PB ☎01789/297705 (*www.freelance-holidays.co.uk*). A wide variety of self-catering accommodation in beautiful locations, including both the Serra de Tramuntana and the central plain, Es Pla – the least commercialized part of the island.

Globespan, Colinton House, 10 West Mill Rd, Colinton Village, Edinburgh EH13 0NX ☎0870/556 1522 (*www.globespan.co.uk*). A range of inclusive holidays and flights, with last-minute bargains available online. Many of its properties are in and around Pollença. Globespan are also one of the few companies to offer guided walks. These are in the Pollença area, run for five months of the year (avoiding high summer and the depths of winter), last all day and vary in difficulty from the fairly easy to the comparatively strenuous. Guided walks are not included in the price of a holiday; they cost between 3000ptas/€18.03 and 4500ptas/€27.05 each per person.

Headwater, 146 London Rd, Northwich, Cheshire, CW9 5HH ☎01606/813333 (*www.headwater.com*). Classy walking and other activity holidays.

Ilkeston Co-op, 12 South St, Ilkeston, Derbyshire DE7 5SG ☎0115/932 3546. A wide range of package holidays, often at extraordinarily cheap prices, plus bargain-basement charter flights to both Mallorca and Menorca, especially from Birmingham and East Midlands airports.

The Individual Traveller's Spain, Manor Courtyard, Bignor, Pulborough, W. Sussex RH20 1QD ☎0870/077 3773 (*www.indiv-travellers.com*). Deluxe selection of farmhouses, villas, cottages and village houses. Several tasty offerings are near Pollença and there are others in the small towns of the central plain, Es Pla, especially Sineu.

Magic of Spain, 227 Shepherd's Bush Rd, London W6 7AS ☎0870/027 0480. Upmarket hotel and villa holidays, often in out-of-the-way places. Several lovely *fincas* too. Highly recommended.

Mundi Color, 276 Vauxhall Bridge Rd, London SW1V 1BE ☎020/7828 6021 (*www.mundicolor.es*). Small but well-chosen selection of classy and atmospheric hotels in popular resorts (Cala Fornells, Illetas) and less familiar spots like Banyalbufar. City breaks in Palma's better hotels too.

P&O Cruises, 77 New Oxford St, London WC1A 1PP ☎020/7800 2222 (*www.pocruises.com*). Cruises in mainly European waters, departing from Southampton.

Thomson, Greater London House, Hampstead Rd, London NW1 7SD ☎0870/550 2555 (*www.thomson-holidays.com*). One of the largest UK package-tour companies. Brochures on all manner of Mallorca holidays to suit most budgets are available at any high-street travel agent, including vacations in villas and apartments, family-owned hotels and luxury hotels, as well as city breaks in Palma.

high-rise hotels – along with the drunken antics of some of their clientele – that have grabbed most of the media attention. However, there are also plenty of countrified villas and apartments, genteel pensions and ritzy hotels on offer from companies such as Mundi Color, as well as walking holidays around the islands' lesser-known beauty spots.

High-street travel agents will help you trawl through a wide range of packages, some of which are excellent value. If the price is right, it can be worth booking a package simply for the flight: after all, there's no compulsion to stick around at your hotel for the full period of your holiday and it's handy to have your lodgings sorted out at least for a night or two at each end of your trip. Packages are especially worth considering at the height of the season when island accommodation can be very hard to find through independent means, and the last-minute deals advertised in travel agents' windows can work out almost cheaper than staying at home.

To give yourself a general idea of prices, you could start by looking at the Thomson brochures in any travel agent. Prices per person for seven nights in a self-catering **apartment** with pool access, including the return flight, start at around £250 in the low season and rise to £450 in July and August. Thomson's **hotel** holidays begin at about £400 for a week in a standard high-rise with half-board in May (£500 in August). By comparison, Alternative Mallorca offers a week's half-board in a medium-sized three-star hotel for £600 per person (£690 in high season) excluding flight, whereas a week at the five-star *Gran Hotel Son Net* at Puigpunyent will set you back at least £1300 all year round. The price of a **villa** for up to six people, with a private pool, starts at around £380 per person per week (£600 in high season), including flights and self-catering facilities.

Packaged **activity holidays** are another option, with **walking** an especially popular pastime. The best hiking is in the Serra de Tramuntana mountains of northwest Mallorca, and going with a guide makes sense as the available hiking maps are not wholly reliable. Headwater is one company specializing in this type of holiday. Their seven-night package (Feb–April & Sept–Nov only), which includes five guided walks, three-star hotel accommodation and flight, costs £570 in February, or £660 in September.

Cruises in the Mediterranean are becoming increasingly popular too, and often incorporate trips to one or more of the Balearics. Ferry operator P&O runs half-a-dozen cruises a year from Southampton which dock at Palma. Depending on the length of the voyage and status of the cabin, prices range from £2000 to around £8000. For example, their 16-night "Cradles of Civilisation" cruise in August, which calls in at Mallorca on the way to Athens and Crete, will cost you around £2500 per person in a twin room with en suite shower. The cruise specialist Costa operates four-night short break cruises in April, which incorporate a flight to Barcelona and then a cruise to Mallorca, Menorca and Genoa, from where you catch a flight home. In this case, a shared twin room with shower en-suite will cost around £700 per person.

By train

Travelling by **train** from London, it takes at least 16 hours to reach **Barcelona**, from where there are regular ferries to Palma. The first leg of the journey involves taking a **Eurostar** train from London Waterloo through the Channel Tunnel to Paris Gare du Nord. The easiest option on the second leg is the overnight **Talgo** service, which leaves Paris Gare d'Austerlitz daily at around 8.30pm and arrives at Barcelona Estació-Sants at around 8.30am, in good time to connect with ferry departures to Mallorca. In Barcelona, Estació-Sants station is around 4km from the ferry departure point, Estació Marítim, which is located at the foot of La Rambla in the heart of the city. To get from Estació-Sants to the ferry port, take metro line no. 3 to Drassanes. There are alternative trains to Barcelona from Paris Gare de Lyon which run via Narbonne, Montpellier or Latour, with some routings using the high-speed TGV trains, but even so it's a longer journey – around 19 hours. Another, cheaper, option is to reach Paris using the Dover–Calais ferry, though again this may increase the overall journey time to over twenty hours.

The **price** of a standard rail ticket from London to Barcelona via the Channel Tunnel – available from some travel agents, Rail Europe (see box on p.8) and major train stations – fluctuates with the season and in accordance with restrictions that are similar to those of an airline ticket. To get the cheaper fares, you need to be away on a Saturday night and book at least eight days in advance. An apex 'leisure' return fare in October from London to Barcelona via Paris using the

UK TRANSPORT INFORMATION

www.pti.org.uk

TRAIN INFORMATION

Eurostar, *www.eurostar.com* ☎ 0870/518 6186.
National Rail Enquiries, *www.nationalrail.co.uk* ☎ 0845/748 4950.
Rail Europe, *www.raileurope.co.uk* ☎ 0870/584 8848;
179 Piccadilly, London W1.

RENFE (Spanish railways), *www.renfe.es*
SNCF (French railways), *www.sncf.com*

BUS INFORMATION

Eurolines, *www.eurolines.co.uk* ☎ 0870/514 3219.
National Express, *www.gobycoach.com* ☎ 0870/580 8080.

Eurostar and Talgo trains within these restrictions costs £250 return for an adult or £200 if you're under 26; with both fares, you share a 4-berth 'cabin' on the Talgo. A similar route taking a fast train from Paris via Latour or Montpellier will cost around £200 return, £180 if you're under 26. It's recommended to book well in advance in summer. You can book your ticket via the SNCF web site – for delivery via Rail Europe – a maximum of three months and a minimum of ten days in advance.

By bus

The main **bus route** between Britain and north-eastern Spain connects London with Barcelona (from where you can reach Mallorca by ferry; see p.20), running via Calais, Perpignan and Girona. Bus services from Britain are operated by Eurolines, with departures from London's Victoria Coach Station three times a week. Eurolines also sell tickets that include through transport to London from around the UK; they have offices at all National Express bus terminals nationwide and also offer tickets through many travel agents. The return **fare** from London to Barcelona is £99; there's a **youth fare** (for under-25s) of £90 return.

The journey time is around 23 hours – long, but just about bearable if you take enough to eat, drink and read. There are stops for around twenty minutes every four to five hours, and the routine is also broken by the cross-Channel ferry (included in the cost of a ticket). It's useful to carry some French francs for buying coffees and snacks – although after January 2002 you can use euros in France and Spain and by July 2002

the franc and the peseta will both be no more. Buses arrive at the Barcelona-Sants bus terminal, close to the Estació-Sants train station and some 4km north of the ferry dock, which is in the town centre at the foot of La Rambla. To get from the train station to the ferry port, take metro line no. 3 to Drassanes.

By car

The traditional route **by car** to Spain involves taking a ferry across the Channel and driving through France, for which you should allow at least two days – unless, that is, you can share the driving and manage to travel nonstop. Other, speedier options are using the shuttle trains through the Channel Tunnel, or taking the longer ferry journey direct to Santander or Bilbao on the northern Spanish coast and driving from there.

For details of ferries from mainland Spain to Mallorca, see p.20.

Cross-Channel car ferries

You can book your vehicle onto a **cross-Channel ferry** through a travel agent or direct with whichever ferry company you select. A low-season return fare on P&O's **Dover–Calais** ferry costs from around £210 for a driver, passenger and average-sized car, increasing to over £250 in the summer. Dover–Calais is the obvious – and fastest – choice. However, unless you live in the southeast of England, you'd be better off avoiding London traffic and heading instead for one of the other south-coast ports in order to cross **to Normandy or Brittany**. Useful routings are Newhaven to Dieppe, and Portsmouth, Poole to

CROSS-CHANNEL INFORMATION

Brittany Ferries, *www.brittanyferries.co.uk*
☎0870/901 2400. Poole to Cherbourg;
Portsmouth to Caen and St Malo; Plymouth to
Roscoff. Also runs ferries to Santander from
Plymouth (March–Nov) or Portsmouth
(Dec–March).

Eurotunnel, *www.eurotunnel.com* ☎0870/535
3535. For car, motorbike or van travel through
the Channel Tunnel.

Ferrysavers, *www.ferrysavers.com* – discount
ferry ticket agents.

Hoverspeed, *www.hoverspeed.co.uk*
☎0870/524 0241. Twenty-four daily departures.
Dover to Calais and Oostende; Folkestone to
Boulogne; Newhaven to Dieppe.

P&O European Ferries,
www.poportsmouth.com ☎0870/242 4999.
Portsmouth to Cherbourg, Le Havre and Bilbao.

P&O Stena Line, *www.posl.com* ☎0870/600
0600. Dover to Calais.

Sea France, *www.seafrance.com* ☎0870/571
1711. Dover to Calais.

Le Havre, Caen or Cherbourg. This also means
you avoid traffic around Paris, and can cut down
considerably on driving time through France.
Check *www.seaview.co.uk* for details of ferry
companies and routings.

The Channel Tunnel

Eurotunnel operates shuttle trains for vehicles
through the Channel Tunnel 24 hours a day, carrying cars, motorcycles, buses and their passengers. The journey between Folkestone and
Coquelles, near Calais, takes about 35 minutes.
Using this drive-on/drive-off service, rather than a
cross-Channel ferry, cuts a couple of hours off the
driving time to Spain. At peak times, shuttle trains
run every fifteen minutes; during the night they
run every 45 minutes. **Fares** vary with the season
and the time of day you travel, with off-peak
returns beginning at around £200 from October
to March and increasing to £390 on July and
August weekends between 6am and 10pm. The
ticket covers the car and all its passengers. The
five-day limit on most return tickets means you
may be better off buying two singles (which are
generally half the price of a return).

Ferries to Spain

The direct car and passenger ferries from England
to northern Spain, although expensive, greatly
reduce the driving time to Barcelona – and
roughly halve the mileage. Brittany Ferries sail
from **Plymouth to Santander** more or less twice
weekly from March to mid-November, with a sailing time of 24 hours (outside these months, less
frequent sailings are from Portsmouth instead).
P&O's twice-weekly ferry service from
Portsmouth to Bilbao runs all year round and
takes 36 hours. From Santander it's about nine
hours' drive to Barcelona; from Bilbao about
eight.

Ticket prices vary enormously according to the
season and the number of passengers carried. As
an illustration, a return with Brittany Ferries would
cost around £400 for two adults and car in low
season, £700 in peak season, including pullman
seats for sleeping. Two-berth cabins are available
from £57 return in low season, £77 in high season. Tickets are best booked in advance, either
directly with the company or through any major
travel agent.

Getting there from Ireland

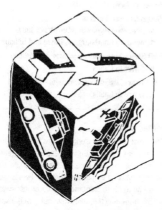

Charter flights are the cheapest and most obvious way to reach Mallorca from Ireland, but there is a limited range of scheduled flights too, mostly via Barcelona, though British Midland runs a service from both Dublin and Belfast via Heathrow, and EasyJet flies from Belfast via Luton. All flights land at Mallorca's one and only airport on the edge of Palma.

Charter flights

Summer **charter flights** direct to Mallorca are easy to pick up from either Dublin or Belfast. Prices are at their highest during August – reckon on around £280 return from Belfast, IR£380/€482.50 from Dublin – but drop a little in the months either side. If you're prepared to book at the last minute, you'll sometimes get a cheaper deal, though you won't necessarily get the departure date you want. Students – and anyone under 31 – should contact USIT, who generally have the best discounts.

As another option, you might find that taking a budget flight to London and then switching to a London–Palma charter flight will save you a few pounds. Major airlines aside, low-cost carriers to London include Ryanair (from Cork, Derry, Dublin, Kerry, Knock and Shannon to Stansted), Virgin Express (from Shannon to Gatwick), EasyJet (from Belfast International to Luton) and British European (from Belfast City to Gatwick and Stansted).

Alternatively, you could take a charter from Ireland to Barcelona, and then switch onto a domestic flight to Mallorca.

Scheduled flights and packages

Iberia have daily **scheduled flights** from Dublin to Palma via Barcelona, taking around four hours. The cheapest return fare costs around IR£240/€304.74 in July and August, but has several restrictions – you can't change your departure date and you can't extend your visit beyond a maximum of one month. The same ticket with-

---

AIRLINES IN IRELAND

Aer Lingus, *www.aerlingus.ie* – 46 Castle St, Belfast ☎ 0845/973 7747; 2 Academy St, Cork ☎ 021/432 7155; 40–41 O'Connell St and 13 St Stephen's Green, Dublin ☎ 01/844 4777; 136 O'Connell St, Limerick ☎ 061/474239.

British Airways, *www.britishairways.com* – Suite 1, Fountain Centre, College St, Belfast BT1 6ET ☎ 0845/773 3377; Republic reservations ☎ 1800/626747.

British European, *www.british-european.com* – UK ☎ 0870/567 6676.

British Midland, *www.britishmidland.com* – Suite 2, Fountain Centre, College St, Belfast ☎ 0870/607 0555; Nutley, Merrion Rd, Dublin ☎ 01/283 8833.

EasyJet, *www.easyjet.com* – UK ☎ 0870/600 0000.

Iberia, *www.iberia.com* – 54 Dawson St, Dublin ☎ 01/407 3017.

Ryanair, *www.ryanair.com* – UK ☎ 0870/156 9569; Dublin ☎ 01/609 7881.

Virgin Express, *www.virgin-express.com* – Shannon ☎ 061/704470.

TRAVEL AGENTS IN IRELAND

Aran Travel, Granary Hall, 58 Dominick St, Galway ☎091/562595 (*arantvl@iol.ie*). Well-informed and competitive holiday agent, with flight-only bargains.

Dial-a-Flight Ireland, 11 Warrington Place, Dublin 2 ☎01/617 7556. Scheduled and charter flight specialists.

Fahy Travel, 3 Bridge Street, Galway ☎091/563055 (*fahytrav@iol.ie*). Has a good selection of last-minute bargains.

Joe Walsh, 8–11 Baggot St, Dublin 2 ☎01/676 3053; 117 St Patrick St, Cork ☎021/427 7959. General budget fares agent.

Thomas Cook, *www.thomascook.com* – 11 Donegall Place, Belfast BT1 5AJ ☎028/9024 0833; 118 Grafton St, Dublin ☎01/677 1360. Package holiday and flight agent, with occasional discount offers.

Tom Mannion Travel, 71 O'Connell St, Ennis, Co. Clare ☎065/682 4211 (*www.travel.tmt.ie*). Discount flight agent, with online booking facilities.

Tony Roche Travel, Travel House, Walkinstown Cross, Dublin 12 ☎01/456 7311 (*www.trtravel.com*). Specialist in last-minute bookings.

Trailfinders, 4–5 Dawson St, Dublin 2 ☎01/677 7888. Competitive fares out of all Irish airports, as well as deals on hotels, insurance, tours and car rental worldwide.

Travelfinders, *www.travelfinders.com/ireland* – Internet-based bargain hunting travel agent.

Twohigs Travel, 8 Burgh Quay, Dublin ☎01/677 2666; 13 Duke St, Dublin ☎01/670 9750. Packages and flight agent.

Usit Now, *www.usitnow.com* – Fountain Centre, Belfast BT1 6ET ☎028/9032 4073; 19–21 Aston Quay, O'Connell Bridge, Dublin 2 ☎01/602 1600; 66 Oliver Plunkett St, Cork ☎021/427 0900; 16 Mary St, Galway ☎091/565177; Central Buildings, O'Connell St, Limerick ☎061/415064; 36 George's St, Waterford ☎051/872601. Ireland's main student and youth travel specialists.

out restrictions runs to about IR£400/€507.90 return all year. British Midland fly daily to Palma from Dublin and from Belfast, both via Heathrow; their Belfast–Palma flight costs around £420, considerably more than EasyJet's bargain fares from Belfast to Palma via Luton. Iberia operate a once-daily flight from Belfast to Barcelona via London, a route that's followed twice daily by British Airways. Watch out for special offers from the scheduled airlines, which can reduce fares by anything up to forty percent, and last-minute package deals, which can represent good value-for-money just for the flight.

A two-week **package holiday** to Mallorca (based on four people in a reasonably comfortable self-catering apartment) from Belfast costs about £350 per person in low season, rising to £500 high season; from Dublin, the same thing costs from about IR£300/€380.92 (low) to IR£640/€812.63 (high). You may well find you're routed via London, with an add-on fare for the connection from Ireland. If you wait until the last minute, you may be able to snatch up a package holiday for around IR£200/€253.95 from Dublin, with no obligation to use the accommodation on offer.

Getting there from the US and Canada

There are no direct flights from any part of North America to Mallorca. The nearest you'll get are Iberia's one- or two-stop flights from Los Angeles, New York, Chicago, Miami or Montréal to Palma via Madrid. Iberia offer competitive rates for their transatlantic flights, so they should be your first line of enquiry. The most obvious alternative is to search for the least expensive transatlantic fare offered by any airline to Madrid or Barcelona, from where an Iberia or Air Europa domestic flight will shuttle you across to Mallorca.

Shopping for tickets

Barring special offers, the cheapest of the airlines' published fares are usually **Apex** tickets, although these carry certain restrictions concerning the length of your stay (usually a maximum of one month, and including a Saturday night), and the latest date for payment for your ticket (usually 14 or 21 days before departure). You will also be penalized if you change your schedule. Some airlines offer youth or student fares to **under 26s**; a passport or driving licence are sufficient proof of age, though these tickets are subject to availability and can have eccentric booking conditions.

You might be able to cut costs further by going through a **specialist flight agent** – either a **consolidator**, who buys up blocks of tickets from the airlines and sells them at a discount, or a **discount agent**, who in addition to dealing with discounted flights may also offer special student and youth fares and a range of other travel-related services such as travel insurance, train passes, car rentals, tours and the like. Bear in mind, though, that penalties for changing your plans can be stiff. Remember too that these companies make their money by dealing in bulk – don't expect them to answer lots of questions. Some agents specialize in **charter flights**, which may be cheaper than anything available on a scheduled flight, but again departure dates are fixed and withdrawal penalties are high (check the refund policy). If you travel a lot, **discount travel clubs** are another option: their annual membership fee may be worth it for benefits such as cut-price air tickets and car rental.

Don't automatically assume that tickets purchased through a travel specialist will be cheapest; once you get a quote, check with the airlines and you may turn up an even better deal. Be advised also that the pool of travel companies is swimming with sharks – exercise caution and never deal with a company that demands cash up front or refuses to accept payment by credit card.

A further possibility is to see if you can arrange a **courier flight** to Madrid, although the hit-or-miss nature of these makes them most suitable for the single traveller who travels light and has a very flexible schedule. You get a discounted ticket in return for shepherding a parcel through customs and possibly giving up your baggage allowance. A couple of courier outfits are listed in the box. One more possibility is to look into tickets on the **Internet**. Some of the better websites for this are *www.cheaptickets.com*, *www.lowestfare.com*, and *www.travelzoo.com*. As always with the Web, there are some good deals out there, but you have to do a little investigative searching for the best bargains.

Air Europa, *www.air-europa.com* ☎ 1-800/327-1225. Flies five times a week from New York to Madrid, with flights on to Palma.

Air France, *www.airfrance.fr* – in the US ☎ 1-800/237-2747; in Canada ☎ 1-800/667-2747. Flies daily from New York, Chicago, Atlanta, Miami, San Francisco, Los Angeles, Washington DC, Toronto and Montréal to Paris, and then on to Madrid and Barcelona.

American Airlines/TWA, *www.americanair.com* ☎ 1-800/433-7300. Daily nonstop flights from Miami to Madrid, and weekly flights from New York to Madrid, as well as connecting flights from other major cities throughout the US.

British Airways, *www.britishairways.com* – in the US ☎ 1-800/247-9297; in Canada ☎ 1-800/668-1059. Flies daily from Montréal, Toronto and Vancouver plus 21 gateway cities in the US to London and on to Madrid and Barcelona.

Continental Airlines, *www.flycontinental.com* ☎ 1-800/231-0856. Daily flights from Newark to Madrid as well as connections from dozens of other major US cities.

Delta Airlines, *www.delta.com* ☎ 1-800/241-4141. Daily direct flights from New York to Madrid and Barcelona with connections from most other major North American cities.

Iberia, *www.iberia.com/ibusa* – in the US ☎ 1-800/772-4642; in Canada ☎ 1-800/423-7421. Flights from Los Angeles, New York, Chicago, Miami and Montréal to Palma via Madrid, plus special deals such as fly-drive. Helpful website.

Lufthansa, *www.lufthansa-usa.com* ☎ 1-800/645-3880. Flights from many US cities to Frankfurt and then on to Palma (as well as Madrid, Barcelona, Valencia and Bilbao).

Northwest/KLM, *www.nwa.com* ☎ 1-800/447-4747 or ☎ 1-800/374-7747. Flights from major US and Canadian cities to Madrid and Barcelona via Amsterdam.

Sabena, *www.sabena.com* ☎ 1-800/955-2000. Flights from East Coast and Midwest cities to Barcelona and Madrid via Brussels.

TAP Air Portugal, *www.tap-airportugal.pt* ☎ 1-800/221-7370. New York, Miami and Boston to Madrid and Barcelona via Lisbon.

Regardless of where you buy your ticket, the **fare** will, most likely, depend on season. As a general rule, you can expect fares to Spain to be highest from around mid-May to the end of September; they drop during the "shoulder" seasons (April to mid-May, October, and mid-December to mid-January); you'll get the best deals during the low season, November through March (excluding the weeks around Christmas and New Year). Remember that these seasonal boundaries can vary from airline to airline and from year to year, so if you want to make sure you're getting the best deal, always double check. Note that flying on weekends ordinarily adds around US$50/C$70 to the return fare; price ranges quoted in the following sections assume midweek travel and exclude taxes (around US$50/C$55).

From the US

The box below details leading airlines with services to Spain. On **Iberia**'s daily flights to Palma via Madrid, the Apex fare (maximum stay one month, payment 21 days before departure) from Los Angeles (12hr) is $1051 high season, $730 low season; from New York (8hr) $845 high, $571 low; from Chicago (9hr) $1075 high, $688 low; and from Miami (8hr) $927 high, $575 low. Travelling on any of these tickets, however, you can't break your journey in Madrid. If you want a stopover in mainland Spain, you'll need to purchase one ticket for the transatlantic leg and then a separate ticket for the onward flight to Mallorca. The price of an Iberia Apex fare to Madrid from Los Angeles is $895 ($765 low); from New York $999 ($571 low); from Chicago $812 ($538 low); and from Miami $927 ($575 low). You should also look out for special promotional offers.

Other companies worth investigating are **Lufthansa**, who currently quote a return New York–Palma via Frankfurt fare of $546 ($1238 high season), and **Delta**, whose non-stop low-season return special from New York to Barcelona costs just $447 ($1040 high season). The advantage of Barcelona as an intermediate destination is its proximity to Mallorca, with fre-

Air Brokers International, 150 Post St #620, San Francisco, CA 94108 ☎1-800/883-3273 or ☎415/397-1383 (*www.airbrokers.com*). Consolidator and specialists in RTW tickets.

Air Courier Association, 191 University Blvd #300, Denver, CO 80206 ☎1-800/282-1202 or ☎303/215-0900 (*www.aircourier.org*). Lowest courier fares to Europe.

Airtech, 588 Broadway #204, New York, NY 10017 ☎1-800/575-8324 or ☎212/219-7000 (*www.airtech.com*). Standby seat broker, courier agent and consolidator.

Council Travel, 205 E 42nd St, New York, NY 10017 ☎1-800/226-8624 or ☎888/COUNCIL or ☎212/822-2700 (*www.counciltravel.com*). Branches in San Francisco, Los Angeles, Boston, Chicago, Washington DC. Nationwide specialists in student travel.

Educational Travel Center, 438 N Frances St, Madison, WI 53703 ☎1-800/747-5551 or ☎608/256-5551 (*www.edtrav.com*). Student/youth and consolidator fares.

International Association of Air Travel Couriers, 8 South J St, PO Box 1349, Lake Worth, FL 33460 ☎561/582-8320 (*www.courier.org*). Courier flight broker.

STA Travel, 10 Downing St, New York, NY 10014 ☎1-800/777-0112 or ☎212/627-3111

(*www.sta-travel.com*). Branches in Los Angeles, Chicago, San Francisco, Philadelphia and Boston. Worldwide discount travel firm specializing in student/youth fares; also student IDs, travel insurance, car rental, train passes, and so on.

TFI Tours International, 34 W 32nd St, New York, NY 10001 ☎1-800/745-8000 or ☎212/736-1140. Consolidator.

Travac, 989 Sixth Ave, 16th floor, New York, NY 10018 ☎1-800/872-8800 or ☎212/563-3303 (*www.travac.com*). Consolidator and charter broker mostly to Europe. Has another office in Orlando.

Travel Avenue, 10 S Riverside #1404, Chicago, IL 60606 ☎1-800/333-3335 or ☎312/876-6866 (*www.travelavenue.com*). Discount travel company.

Travel Cuts, 187 College St, Toronto, ON M5T 1P7 ☎1-800/667-2887 or ☎416/979-2406 (*www.travelcuts.com*). Branches in Montréal, Vancouver, Calgary and Winnipeg. Canadian discount travel organization, specializing in youth fares.

UniTravel, 11737 Administration Drive #120, St Louis, MO 63146 ☎1-800/325-2222 (*www.flightsforless.com*). Consolidator.

quent onward Iberia flights to Palma costing anywhere between $93 and $178 round-trip.

From Canada

There's not much choice when it comes to flying direct from Canada to Spain, and less to Mallorca. Iberia operates the only service, from Montréal to Palma via Madrid three times a week. The Apex fare on this route is around C$1252 in high season, C$1008 in low. Fares are the same from Toronto as from Montréal, whilst from Vancouver expect to pay in the region of C$1880 (high), C$1390 (low). Travelling on these tickets, however, you can't break your journey in Madrid. If you want to stopover there, you'll need to purchase one ticket for the transatlantic leg and then a separate ticket for an onward flight to Mallorca. The price of an Iberia Apex fare to Madrid from Montréal or Toronto is around C$1015 (high season) or C$911

(low), and from Vancouver approximately C$1515 (high) or C$1275 (low). You should also check out other airlines through a discount agent such as STA. Travelling from Toronto to Mallorca, for instance, they may be able to route you through a European city such as London for a return fare of roughly C$1010 (high season) or C$823 (low).

Package deals in North America

North American travellers aren't spoiled for choice when it comes to tour operators offering **package deals** to Mallorca. Don't expect anything more than the basic air/hotel beach resort combo with a sightseeing tour thrown in and the option of reduced-rate car rental. The companies in the box have set packages available or will help you customize one of your own. As a very rough estimate of price, for a low-season six-night air-hotel package expect to pay upwards of US$1040.

Auto Europe ☎1-800/223-5555 (*www.auto
europe.com*). Air-hotel deals and car rental,
plus international mobile phone rentals.

Central Holidays, 120 Sullivan Ave, Englewood
Cliffs, NJ 07632 ☎1-800/227-5858 (*www.cen-
tralholidays.com*). Agents for the Iberia tour
department's "Discover Spain Vacations", offering escorted and independent tours.

EC Tours, 12500 Riverside Drive #210, Valley
Village, CA 91607-3423 ☎1-800/388-0877
(*www.ectours.com*). A variety of package tours.

Escapade Tours, c/o Isram World of Travel,
630 Third Ave, New York, NY 10017 ☎1-
800/356-2405 (*www.isram.com*). Package
trips.

International Gay Travel Association ☎1-
800/448-8550 (*www.igita.org*). Trade group
with lists of gay-owned or gay-friendly travel
agents, accommodations and other travel businesses.

M.I. Travel, 450 Seventh Ave #1805, New York,
NY 10123 ☎1-800/848-2314 or ☎212/967-6565.
Package and independent tours.

Petrabax Tours, 9745 Queens Blvd, Rego Park,
NY 11374 ☎1-800/634-1188 (*www.petrabax.
com*). Escorted tours, hotels, historic inns and
property rentals.

Saga Holidays, 222 Berkely St, Boston, MA
02116 ☎1-800/343-0273 (*www.sagaholidays.
com*). Group travel for seniors.

Getting there from Australia and New Zealand

There are no direct flights to any part of Spain
from Australia or New Zealand, but various airlines offer one-stop services to Madrid and
Barcelona. British Airways and Qantas via
London, KLM via Amsterdam, Alitalia via Milan,
Singapore Airlines via Singapore, and Thai
Airways via Bangkok all have reasonably frequent flights and competitive fares; Lauda Air's
connections via Vienna are less convenient but
are worth checking for special offers. From
Barcelona or Madrid there are regular direct
flights to Palma (see p.18).

Alternatively, it may be worth considering a
cheap flight to London, from where bargain fares
to Mallorca are generally easy to pick up (see
p.3). Any of the agents listed here can help with
deals to Spain or London, or ticket you right
through to Palma. **Booking ahead** as far as possible is the best way to secure the most reasonable prices.

Fares

Fares to Europe change according to the time of
year you travel. Mid-May to the end of August,
December, and the first half of January are the
high season; mid-January to the end of February,
October and November the low season; and the

AIRLINES IN AUSTRALIA AND NEW ZEALAND

Alitalia, *www.alitalia.it* – in Australia ☎02/9244 2400; in New Zealand ☎09/302 1452. Three connections a week to Madrid and Barcelona from Sydney and Melbourne via Milan.

British Airways, *www.britishairways.com* – in Australia ☎02/8904 8800; in New Zealand ☎09/356 8690. Daily flights from Sydney, Melbourne, Perth and Auckland to seven cities in Spain, via Bangkok or Kuala Lumpur and London; also daily from Brisbane via Singapore and London.

Iberia, enquiries through British Airways. No flights to Europe from Australasia, but easily the widest range of flights to Mallorca from London and other European destinations. Code-shares with JAL.

Japan Airlines (JAL), *www.japanair.com* – in Australia ☎02/9272 1111; in New Zealand ☎09/379 9906. Daily flights from Brisbane and Sydney, and several flights a week from Cairns and Auckland, to Madrid with either a transfer or overnight stop in Tokyo or Osaka.

KLM, *www.klm.com* – in Australia ☎1300/303 747; in New Zealand ☎09/309 1782. Three times a week from Sydney to Madrid or Barcelona via Amsterdam.

Lauda Air, *www.laudaair.com* – in Australia ☎1800/642 438 or ☎02/9251 6155; in New Zealand ☎09/308 3368. Three flights a week from Sydney and Melbourne to Barcelona, with a one-night stopover in Vienna.

Qantas, *www.qantas.com.au* – in Australia ☎13/13 13; in New Zealand ☎09/357 8900 or ☎0800/808767. Daily flights from major cities in Australia and New Zealand to Madrid with a transfer in London and either Singapore or Bangkok.

Singapore Airlines, *www.singaporeair.com* – in Australia ☎13/10 11 or ☎02/9350 0262; in New Zealand ☎09/303 2129 or ☎0800/808909. Twice a week from Melbourne and Sydney to Madrid via Singapore. Daily from Auckland to Madrid, with a one-night stopover in Singapore.

Thai Airways, *www.thaiair.com* – in Australia ☎1300/651 960; in New Zealand ☎09/377 3886 or ☎0800/100992. Three times a week from Brisbane, Cairns, Sydney and Auckland to Madrid via Bangkok.

TRAVEL AND DISCOUNT AGENTS IN AUSTRALIA AND NEW ZEALAND

Anywhere Travel, 345 Anzac Parade, Kingsford, Sydney ☎02/9663 0411 (*anywhere@ozemail.com.au*).

Budget Travel, 16 Fort St, Auckland, plus branches around the city ☎09/366 0061 or ☎0800/808040.

rest of the year the shoulder season. The lowest standard return fares to Spain are around A$1700/2300 (low/high season) from Australia, NZ$2000/2500 from New Zealand. To London, fares are only slightly different, if at all: around A$1400/2300 from Australia, NZ$2000/2500 from New Zealand.

Though they charge heavily for cancellations or alterations, **discount agents** generally offer better deals than the airlines themselves. Full-

Destinations Unlimited, 220 Queen St, Auckland ☎ 09/373 4033.

Flight Centres, *www.flightcentre.com.au* – In Australia: 82 Elizabeth St, Sydney, plus branches nationwide ☎ 02/9235 3522 (nearest branch ☎ 13 1600). In New Zealand: 350 Queen St, Auckland ☎ 09/358 4310, plus branches nationwide.

Northern Gateway, 22 Cavenagh St, Darwin ☎ 08/8941 1394 (*oztravel@norgate.com.au*).

STA Travel, *www.statravel.com.au* – In Australia: 855 George St, Sydney; 256 Flinders St, Melbourne; other offices in state capitals and major universities (nearest branch ☎ 13 1776, fastfare telesales ☎ 1300/360 960). In New Zealand: 10 High St, Auckland ☎ 09/309 0458, fastfare telesales ☎ 09/366 6673, plus branches in Wellington, Christchurch, Dunedin, Palmerston North, Hamilton and at major universities.

Student Uni Travel, 92 Pitt St, Sydney ☎ 02/9232 8444 (*sydney@backpackers.net*),

plus branches in Brisbane, Cairns, Darwin, Melbourne and Perth.

Thomas Cook, *www.thomascook.com.au* – In Australia: 175 Pitt St, Sydney ☎ 02/9231 2877; 257 Collins St, Melbourne ☎ 03/9282 0222; plus branches in other state capitals (nearest branch ☎ 13 1771, telesales ☎ 1800/801002). In New Zealand: 191 Queen St, Auckland ☎ 09/379 3920.

Trailfinders, 8 Spring St, Sydney ☎ 02/9247 7666; 91 Elizabeth St, Brisbane ☎ 07/3229 0887; Hides corner, Shield St, Cairns ☎ 07/4041 1199.

Travel.com.au, *www.travel.com.au* – 76 Clarence St, Sydney ☎ 02/9249 5444 or ☎ 1800/000447.

Usit Beyond, *www.usitbeyond.co.nz* – cnr Shortland St and Jean Batten Place, Auckland ☎ 09/379 4224 or ☎ 0800/788336, plus branches in Christchurch, Dunedin, Palmerston North, Hamilton and Wellington.

SPECIALIST TRAVEL AGENTS

European Travel Office (ETO), 122 Rosslyn St, West Melbourne ☎ 03/9329 8844; Suite 501, level 5, 89 York St, Sydney ☎ 02/9299 9177; 407 Great South Rd, Auckland ☎ 09/525 3074. Offers a selection of hotels in Mallorca from A$65 to A$108 twin share.

IB Tours, 1/47 New Canterbury Rd, Petersham, Sydney ☎ 02/9560 6932 (*www.ib-tours.com.au*). Has a range of tours, accommodation and car hire in Mallorca.

Ibertours, 1/84 William St, Melbourne ☎ 03/9670 8388 or ☎ 1800/500016 (*www.ibertours.com.au*). Palma city stays, including three nights' accommodation in a four-star hotel plus four days of car rental from A$458 to A$703 twin share. Also has individually tailored packages to Mallorca.

Silke's Travel, 263 Oxford St, Darlinghurst, Sydney ☎ 02/9380 6244 or ☎ 1800/807860 (*www.silkes.com.au*). Specially tailored packages for gay and lesbian travellers.

---

time students and those aged under 26 or over 60 may also be eligible for special fares, although availability tends to vary according to the season. Some useful discount agents are listed in the box, and others can be found in the travel sections of the major weekend newspapers. Also, of course, take a look on the Internet; *www.travel.com.au* offers discounted fares as does *www.sydneytravel.com* and plenty of others.

Getting there from the rest of Spain

Mallorca is easily reached by plane and ferry from mainland Spain as well as from the other Balearic islands of Menorca and Ibiza. Obviously, the main advantage of a flight is its speed: Barcelona to Palma, for example, takes just forty minutes, compared to the ferry trip of eight hours. By plane, there's also the advantage of a wider range of jumping-off points: regular scheduled flights link many of Spain's major cities with Palma, whereas ferry and catamaran links are confined to four departure ports – Barcelona, Valencia, Ibiza Town and Maó (on Menorca).

Ticket prices also favour aircraft travel: it is less expensive by ferry, but not by all that much, and certainly not enough to justify the extra time and trouble – unless, that is, you're in or near one of the departure ports anyway. The only situation in which the boat is a necessity is if you're taking your own vehicle over to Mallorca.

By air from mainland Spain

The vast majority of **scheduled flights** to Palma from the Spanish mainland are operated by the Iberia Regional/Air Nostrum partnership. The Iberia group has sales offices in every major Spanish city and most capital cities abroad. Seat availabil-ity isn't usually a problem and fares are very reasonable – a return flight to Palma from Madrid, for instance, costs 23,000ptas/€138.23, or from Barcelona 14,850ptas/€89.25. Iberia's one-way fares are normally roughly half the return fare, but buying a return to Mallorca can offer savings – a one-way flight Barcelona–Palma, for instance, costs just under 10,000ptas/€60.10, roughly two-thirds of the return fare. There are also a variety of excursion fares available at discounted prices; these special offers can be seen at the *www.airnostrum.es* or *www.iberia.com* websites.

It's sometimes possible to get a cheaper ticket on a **charter flight**. These are available in most major Spanish cities, but you may have to plod around local travel agents to find one – travel agents are listed in the Yellow Pages under *viajes agencias*. You could also try Spanair, the largest charter operator, whose website (*www.spanair.com*) is where you can search for flights and make reservations by email. Spanair is very competitive – reckon on 11,000ptas/€66.11 for a one-way trip from Madrid to Palma, 9000ptas/€54.09 one-way from Barcelona. Spanair also has a nationwide enquiry number (☎902 131 415) and an office at Palma airport (☎971 745 020).

IBERIA OFFICES AND DOMESTIC FLIGHT FREQUENCIES TO PALMA

In addition to their many mainland offices, the national carrier **Iberia** has a nationwide domestic flight reservation and information line in Spain on ☎902 400 500 (English spoken). The route frequencies and journey times given below cover nonstop flights to Mallorca unless otherwise specified.

Alicante Doctor Gadea 12 ☎965 218 613 (twice daily; 1hr 10min).

Barcelona Passeig de Gràcia 30 ☎934 013 387, and Plaça Espanya s/n ☎933 257 358 (10 daily; 40min).

Bilbao Ercilla 20 ☎944 241 935 (3 daily via Barcelona; 3hr).

Ibiza Town Passeig Vara de Rey 15 ☎971 302 580 (8 daily; 45min).

Madrid Velázquez 130 ☎915 878 787 or ☎915 874 747 (6–9 daily; 1hr 15min).

Maó (Menorca) Aeroport Menorca ☎971 369 016 (8 daily; 45min).

Palma (Mallorca) Avgda Joan March 8 ☎971 757 151.

Sevilla Avda. De la Buhaira 8 ☎954 988 208 (2–3 daily via Madrid; 3hr).

Valencia Paz 14 ☎963 527 552 (6 daily; 1hr).

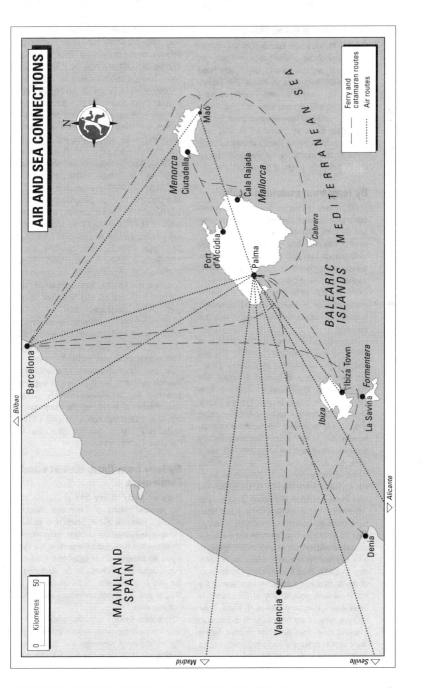

AIR AND SEA CONNECTIONS

N

MAINLAND SPAIN

△ Bilbao

Barcelona

Valencia

Denia

Madrid ▽

Seville ▽

△ Alicante

MEDITERRANEAN SEA

BALEARIC ISLANDS

Menorca
Ciutadella
Maó

Cala Rajada
Mallorca

Port d'Alcúdia
Palma

Cabrera

Ibiza
Ibiza Town
Formentera
La Savina

Ferry and catamaran routes
Air routes

0   Kilometres   50

By air from Ibiza or Menorca

Flying to Mallorca from Ibiza or Menorca couldn't be simpler. Iberia, which has a monopoly on inter-island flights, operates eight **scheduled flights** daily from Ibiza to Palma. The journey takes 45 minutes and costs around 10,350ptas/€62.21 one-way or 13,550ptas/€81.44 round-trip. From Menorca there are also eight daily flights of around 45 minutes, with prices about the same. There's usually no problem with seat availability, but you need to book ahead during the height of the season.

By ferry from mainland Spain

There are two companies running **car ferry and catamaran** services between mainland Spain and Mallorca: **Trasmediterranea** and the much smaller **Balearia**. Advance booking is strongly recommended on both car ferry and catamaran services throughout the summer. If you're taking a vehicle or need a cabin, book in advance year-round. **Tickets** can be purchased at the port of embarkation or in advance via both company's websites or Trasmediterranea's agents (see box opposite).

Trasmediterranea's principal car ferry routes to Palma are from **Barcelona** (2–4 daily; 8hr) and **Valencia** (6–7 weekly; 9hr). They also run car ferries from Barcelona to Ibiza (3–4 weekly; 9hr) and Menorca (3–8 weekly; 9hr) and from Valencia to Menorca (1 weekly; 17hr via Palma). There are no services between early December and the end of January. Trasmediterranea **catamarans** run to Palma from Barcelona (usually mid-June to mid-Sept, but sometimes Feb–Nov; 1 daily; 4hr 30min) and from Valencia via Ibiza (same frequency; 6hr 15min). Balearia car ferries run to Palma from Valencia (1 daily; 8hr) and from **Denia**, just south of Valencia (1 daily; 10hr).

Both ferry companies have complex **fare** structures that take into account the time of day of your trip, your accommodation on board and any accompanying vehicle as well as the length of your stay and the season in which you're travelling. That said, there's no difference in the price of ferries between the routes from any of the main mainland ports to any of the islands. In other words, everything else being equal, it will cost the same to get from Valencia to Palma as it will to travel from Barcelona to Ibiza. Setting aside special deals and packages, a return ticket is about twice as much as a single.

The price of a mid-season passenger fare on a Trasmediterranea ferry from either Barcelona or Valencia to Palma, Maó or Ibiza is currently 6920ptas/€41.68 one-way, 10,350ptas/€62.34 return. Taking a car on the ferry will cost at least 19,000ptas/€114.45; should you be travelling in a group, check out the car-plus-occupants deals that may work out cheaper. There are night-time sailings on most routes, when a **cabin** is extremely useful, especially if you're travelling with children. From either Barcelona or Valencia to Palma, Maó or Ibiza, the inclusive one-way cost of a single cabin starts at 23,090ptas/€139.09, a double cabin at 18,690ptas/€112.59 per person, a triple cabin at 14,790ptas/€89.09 per person, a four-berth cabin at 11,410ptas/€68.73 per person. On the same routes, the tariff for cars up to 2.4m long is 19,315ptas/€116.35, with caravans costing 42,705ptas/€257.25; motorbikes cost 3540ptas/€21.32 and bicycles are carried free. You might also consider Trasmediterranea's special all-in price for a car with up to four passengers. These packages start at around 47,000ptas/€283.13 one-way. By comparison, Balearia charges 6295ptas/€37.92 for the adult fare from Denia to Palma, with vehicles under 1.8m costing 18,350ptas/€110.54.

On the Trasmediterranea catamaran from Valencia to Palma (via Ibiza), a one-way adult passenger fare is 8990ptas/€54.15, standard class. Vehicles up to 6m long (the maximum permitted) and 1.8m high cost 19,315ptas/€116.35 each way. Prices are identical on the Barcelona–Palma catamaran route.

By ferry from Ibiza, Menorca and Formentera

There are plenty of ferry links to Mallorca from the nearby islands of Ibiza and Menorca, although Formentera has boats only to Ibiza. **Advance bookings** are strongly recommended on all services throughout the summer – all year if you are taking a vehicle (apart from the routes from Formentera). **Tickets** can be purchased at the port of embarkation or in advance on the Web or through Trasmediterranea's agents (see box opposite).

From **Ibiza Town**, Trasmediterranea runs a car ferry service three times weekly to Palma (4hr 30min); the adult passenger fare costs around 3540ptas/€21.28 for a one-way trip. Plying the

FERRY COMPANIES

Balearia, *www.balearia.com* ☎902 160 180.
Cape Balear de Cruceros *www.cape-balear.com* ☎971 818 517.
Iscomar *www.iscomar.com* ☎902 119 128.
Trasmediterranea, *www.trasmediterranea*
.com ☎902 454 645. Offices at: Barcelona

(Estació Marítim s/n); Ibiza Town (Estació
Marítim s/n); Madrid (c/Alcalá 61, CP 28014);
Maó (Muelle de Levante 30); Palma (Estació
Marítim 2); Valencia (Estació Marítim). Agents in
UK and Ireland: Southern Ferries, first floor, 179
Piccadilly, London W1V 9DB ☎020/7491 4968.

same route, Trasmediterranea catamarans (mid-June to mid-Sept 3 weekly; some spring and autumn sailings; 2hr 15min) charge about forty percent more, but also offer substantial discounts on day returns. Both the ferries and the catamarans charge 10,000ptas/€60.10 one-way in high season for cars up to 1.8m long. Balearia also runs car ferries between Ibiza Town and Palma (1 daily; 4hr 30min) with a tariff of 4500ptas/€27.05 per adult, and vehicles up to 1.8m at 14,300ptas/€85.95.

From **Menorca**, Trasmediterranea also operates one or two car ferries per week from Maó to Palma (6hr). Cape Balear de Cruceros operates a passenger-only catamaran service from Menorca's Ciutadella to Cala Rajada between one and three times daily (1hr 15min). A return

ticket costs 8000ptas/€48.08, a one-way ticket 4000ptas/€24.04. Iscomar car ferries run from Ciutadella to Port d'Alcúdia (1–2 daily; 3hr 30min) for 4400ptas/€26.44; vehicles up to 4.5m in length cost an additional 7800ptas/€46.88. Remember, however, that car rental firms on the Balearics do not allow their vehicles off their home island.

Formentera, the smallest of the inhabited Balearic Islands, has no airport and is linked by direct ferry and hydrofoil only with the island of Ibiza. Balearia runs both car ferries (8 daily; 1hr) and hydrofoils (mid-July to Sept 10 daily; 25min; no vehicles) between Formentera and Ibiza Town. The adult fare is 1250ptas/€7.51 one-way by ferry, 2085ptas/€12.53 one-way by hydrofoil. By ferry, a car costs 5000ptas/€30.05 each way.

Visas and red tape

Citizens of EU countries (and Norway and Iceland) need only a valid national identity card to enter Spain for up to ninety days. Since Britain has no identity card system, however, British citizens do have to take a passport. US, Australian, New Zealand and Canadian citizens don't need a visa, but do require a passport valid for the entire period of the visit – and can stay for up to ninety days. Visa requirements do change, however, and it is always advisable to check the current situation.

To **stay longer than ninety days**, EU nationals (and citizens of Norway and Iceland) can apply for a *permiso de residencia* (residence permit) from within Spain. You'll either have to produce proof that you have sufficient funds to be able to support yourself without working (reckon on 5000ptas/€30.05 per day), or a contract of employment (*contrato de trabajo*), or something to prove you are self-employed (for example as a teacher), which involves registering at the tax office. Other nationalities will either need to get a special visa from a Spanish consulate before departure (see box below for addresses); or can apply for one ninety-day visa extension, showing proof of sufficient funds, once in Spain. In Mallorca, further advice can be obtained from the various consulates listed in the box opposite; nationalities not listed should contact their representative in Madrid or elsewhere in Spain.

SPANISH EMBASSIES AND CONSULATES ABROAD

Australia 15 Arkana St, Yarralumla, Canberra, ACT 2600 ☎02/6273 3555; Level 24, 31 Market St, Sydney, NSW 2000 ☎02/9261 2433; 4th floor, 540 Elizabeth St, Melbourne, VIC 3000 ☎03/9347 1966.

Canada 74 Stanley Ave, Ottawa, ON K1M 1P4 ☎613/747-2252; 1 Westmount Square #1456, Montréal, PQ H3Z 2P9 ☎514/935-5235; Simcoe Place, 200 Front St #2401, PO Box 15, Toronto, ON M5V 3K2 ☎416/977-1661.

Ireland 17a Merlyn Park, Ballsbridge, Dublin 4 ☎01/269 1640.

New Zealand No representation.

UK 39 Chesham Place, London SW1X 8SB ☎020/7235 5555; Suite 1a, Brook House, 70 Spring Gardens, Manchester M2 2BQ ☎0161/236 1213; 63 North Castle St, Edinburgh EH2 3LJ ☎0131/220 1843. Visa information line ☎0900/160 0123.

USA 2375 Pennsylvania Ave NW, Washington, DC 20037 ☎202/728-2330 (*www.spainemb.org*); 545 Boylston St #803, Boston, MA 02116 ☎617/536-2506; 180 N Michigan Ave #1500, Chicago, IL 60601 ☎312/782-4588; 1800 Berins Drive #660, Houston, TX 77057 ☎713/783-6200; 5055 Wilshire Blvd #960, Los Angeles, CA 90036 ☎323/938-0158; 2655 Lejeune Rd #203, Coral Gables, Miami, FL 33134 ☎305/446-5511; 2102 World Trade Center, 2 Canal St, New Orleans, LA 70130 ☎504/525-4951; 150 E 58th St, New York, NY 10155 ☎212/355-4080; 1405 Sutter St, San Francisco, CA 94109 ☎415/922-2995.

FOREIGN EMBASSIES AND CONSULATES IN SPAIN

Australian Embassy, Pza Descubridor Diego de Ordas 3, 28003 Madrid ☎914 419 300, fax 914 425 362 (*www.embaustralia.es*). Consular offices in Barcelona ☎933 309 496 and Seville ☎954 220 971.

Canadian Embassy, Núñez de Balboa 35, 28001 Madrid ☎914 233 250, fax 914 233 251 (*www.canada-es.org*). Consular offices in Barcelona ☎932 150 704 and Malaga ☎952 223 346.

Irish Embassy, Ireland House, Paseo de la Castellana 46-4, 28046 Madrid ☎915 763 500, fax 914 351 677. Consular office in Mallorca: c/Sant Miquel 68a, 07002 Palma ☎971 719 244.

New Zealand Embassy, 3rd floor, Plaza de la Lealtad 2, 28014 Madrid ☎915 310 997, fax 915 230 171.

UK Embassy, Fernando el Santo 16, 28010 Madrid ☎917 008 200, fax 917 008 272 (*www.ukinspain.com*). Consular office in Mallorca: Consulado Británico, Plaça Major 3, D 07002 Palma ☎971 712 445, 971 712 085 or 971 716 048, fax 971 717 520.

USA Embassy, Serrano 75, 28006 Madrid ☎915 872 200, fax 915 872 303 (*www.embusa.es*). Consular office in Mallorca: Av. Jaume III 26, 07012 Palma ☎971 722 660, fax 971 718 755.

Insurance

As an EU country, Spain has free reciprocal health agreements with other member states. To take advantage, British and other EU citizens will need to complete self-certification form E111, available over the counter from main post offices. Treatment within this scheme is, however, only provided by practitioners within the Spanish health care system, the Instituto Nacional de la Salud, whereas most doctors on Mallorca are more accustomed to – or only deal with – private insurance work. Taking out your own travel insurance means you won't have to hunt around for a doctor who will treat you for free, and will also cover the cost of items not within the EU scheme's purview, such as dental treatment and repatriation on medical grounds. It will usually also cover your baggage and tickets in case of theft, as long as you get a report from the local police. Non-EU residents will need to insure themselves for all eventualities, including medical costs. For further details of what to do and where to go in a medical emergency, see the section on health (p.32).

A typical **travel insurance** policy usually provides cover for the loss of baggage, tickets and – up to a certain limit – cash or cheques, as well as cancellation or curtailment of your journey and medical costs. Most of them exclude so-called dangerous sports unless an extra premium is paid: in Mallorca this can mean horse-riding, windsurfing, skiing, trekking and mountaineering. Read the small print and benefits tables of prospective policies carefully, since coverage can vary wildly for roughly similar premiums. Many policies can be chopped and changed to exclude coverage you don't need – for example, sickness and accident benefits can often be excluded or included at will. If you do take medical coverage,

---

ROUGH GUIDE TRAVEL INSURANCE

Rough Guides now offer our own travel insurance, customized for our readers by a leading UK broker and backed by a Lloyds underwriter. It's available for anyone, of any nationality, travelling anywhere in the world, and we are convinced that this is the best-value scheme you'll find.

There are two main Rough Guide insurance plans – **Essential**, for effective, no-frills cover, starting at £11.75 for two weeks; and **Premier**, which is more expensive but has more generous and extensive benefits. Each can be supplemented with a "Hazardous Activities Premium" if you plan to indulge in sports considered dangerous, such as skiing, scuba-diving or trekking. Unlike many policies, the Rough Guides schemes are calculated by the day, so if you're travelling for 27 days rather than a month, that's all you pay for. You can alternatively take out annual multi-trip insurance, which covers you for all your travel throughout the year in Europe or worldwide (with a maximum of sixty days for any one trip).

For a policy quote, call the Rough Guide Insurance Line free on UK freefone ☎ 0800/015 0906, US freefone ☎ 1-866/220 5588. From elsewhere in the world dial your international access code followed by ☎ 441243/621046. Alternatively, *www.roughguides.com/insurance* can provide an online quote.

ascertain whether benefits will be paid as treatment proceeds or only after your return home, and whether there is a 24-hour medical emergency number. When securing baggage cover, make sure that the per-article limit – typically under £500 equivalent – will cover your most valuable possession. If you need to make a claim, you should keep receipts for medicines and medical treatment, and in the event you have anything stolen, you must obtain an official statement from the police. Bank and credit cards often have certain levels of medical or other insurance included and you may automatically get travel insurance if you use a major credit card to pay for your trip.

In the UK and Ireland, travel agents and tour operators are likely to require some sort of insurance when you book a package holiday. If you have a good all-risks home insurance policy it may cover your possessions against loss or theft even when overseas. Many private medical schemes such as BUPA or PPP also offer coverage plans for abroad, including baggage loss,

cancellation or curtailment and cash replacement as well as sickness or accident.

Americans and **Canadians** should also check that they're not already covered. Canadian provincial health plans typically provide some overseas medical coverage, although they are unlikely to pick up the full tab in the event of a mishap. Holders of official **student/ teacher/youth cards** are entitled to accident coverage and hospital in-patient benefits – the annual membership is far less than the cost of comparable insurance. **Students** may also find that their student health coverage extends during the vacations and for one term beyond the date of last enrolment. **Homeowners' or renters'** insurance often covers theft or loss of documents, money and valuables while overseas, though conditions and maximum amounts vary from company to company.

In **Australia** and **New Zealand**, travel insurance is put together by the airlines and travel agent groups (see box on p.16-17) in conjunction with insurance companies.

Travellers with disabilities

Despite its popularity as a holiday destination, Mallorca pays scant regard to its visitors who have disabilities: facilities lag way behind those of most other EU regions. That said, things are slowly improving. Hotels with wheelchair access and other appropriate facilities are increasingly common and attitudes are beginning to change. By law, all new pub-

---

CONTACTS FOR TRAVELLERS WITH DISABILITIES

Organización Nacional de Ciegos de España (ONCE), Plaça Bisbe Berenguer de Palou, Palma ☎971 469 311 (*www.once.es*). ONCE, the Spanish organization for the visually impaired, is active and influential, thanks in part to its huge lottery. It sells braille maps and can arrange trips. Write for details.

Spanish National Tourist Office (see box on p.28 for addresses). Publishes a fact sheet listing addresses and some accessible accommoda-

tion, but it's far from comprehensive.

Access-Able Travel Source, *www.access-able.com* – large international database of travel information for people with disabilities.

All go here, *www.allgohere.com* and **Everybody**, *www.everybody.co.uk* – both provide an online accessible airline directory as well as a guide to other useful information sites for travellers with disabilities.

UK AND IRELAND

Access Travel, 6 The Hillock, Astley, Lancs M29 7GW ☎01942/888844 (*www.access-travel.co.uk*). Private operator specializing in overseas holidays for wheelchair users, including Mallorca.

Disability Federation of Ireland, 2 Sandyford Office Park, Sandyford, Dublin 18 ☎01/295 9344. General information and advice.

Holiday Care Service, 2nd floor, Imperial Building, Victoria Rd, Horley, Surrey RH6 9HW ☎01293/774535 (*www.holidaycare.org.uk*). Information on all aspects of travel. Issues a

factsheet on Mallorca which includes detailed descriptions of wheelchair-accessible and other suitable hotels and apartments. Reservations service on ☎01293/773716.

RADAR, 12 City Forum, 250 City Rd, London EC1V 8AF ☎020/7250 3222, Minicom ☎020/7250 4119 (*www.radar.org.uk*). A good source of advice on holidays and travel abroad.

Tripscope, Alexandra House, Albany Road, Middx TW8 0NE ☎0845/758 5641 with Minicom (*tripscope@cableinet.co.uk*). Travel information for people with disabilities.

lic buildings in Spain are required to be fully accessible.

Flying to Mallorca may pose difficulties, although all the scheduled airlines concerned – including the main carrier, Iberia – will assist travellers with disabilities to some degree. If you're driving from the UK, the Brittany Ferries crossing from Plymouth to Santander offers good facilities, as do most of the cross-Channel ferries. On Mallorca itself, however, **transport** is a real problem, as buses and trains are not equipped for wheelchairs, and none of the islands' car rental firms has vehicles with adaptations – though at least the taxi drivers are usually helpful. Note also that the more remote roads along the coast and out in the countryside have very rough surfaces. Toilet facilities for people with disabilities are a rare sight.

USA AND CANADA

Directions Unlimited, 720 N Bedford Rd, Bedford Hills, NY 10507 ☎ 1-800/533-5343 (*www.directionsunlimited.org*). Tour operator specializing in custom tours for people with disabilities.

Jewish Rehabilitation Hospital, 3205 Place Alton Goldbloom, Chomedy Laval, PQ H7V 1R2 ☎ 450/688-9550 ext 226. Guidebooks and travel information.

Mobility International USA, PO Box 10767, Eugene, OR 97440; voice and TDD ☎ 541/343-1284 (*www.miusa.org*). Information and referral services, access guides, tours and exchange programmes. Annual membership $35 (includes quarterly newsletter).

Society for the Advancement of Travel for the Handicapped (SATH), 347 Fifth Ave, New York, NY 10016 ☎ 212/447-7284 (*www.sath.org*). Non-profit-making travel industry referral service that passes queries on to its members as appropriate.

Travel Information Service ☎ 215/456-9600. Telephone-only information and referral service for travellers with disabilities.

Twin Peaks Press, Box 129, Vancouver, WA 98666-0129 ☎ 360/694-2462 (*www.twinpeaks-press.com*). Publisher of the *Directory of Travel Agencies for the Disabled* ($19.95), which lists more than 350 agencies worldwide; *Travel for the Disabled* ($19.95); the *Directory of Accessible Van Rentals* ($9.95); and *Wheelchair Vagabond* ($14.95), loaded with personal tips.

AUSTRALIA AND NEW ZEALAND

ACROD (Australian Council for Rehabilitation of the Disabled), PO Box 146, Deakin West, ACT 2600 ☎ 02/6285 2440 (*www.acrod.org.au*); 24 Cabarita Rd, Cabarita ☎ 02/9743 2699. General travel information.

Disabled Persons Assembly, PO Box 27-524, Wellington 6035 ☎ 04/801 9100 (*www.dpa.org.nz*). Advice and general travel information.

Information and maps

The Spanish National Tourist Office (SNTO) produces and gives away a wide range of maps, pamphlets and special-interest leaflets on Mallorca. Contact, or better still visit, one of their offices before you leave home and stock up. In particular, try to get hold of the booklet listing all the Balearic Islands' hotels, *hostals* and campsites, as this is printed in Madrid and can be difficult to obtain on the island itself.

Tourist offices

The main provincial and municipal **tourist offices** in Palma (see p.71) will provide free maps of the town and the island, and leaflets detailing all

sorts of island-wide practicalities – from bus and train timetables to lists of car rental firms, ferry schedules and boat excursion organizers.

Outside Palma, many of the larger settlements and resorts have seasonal tourist offices (addresses are detailed in the guide). These vary enormously in quality, and while they are generally extremely useful for local information, they cannot be relied on to know anything about what goes on outside their patch.

Opening hours vary considerably, but the larger tourist offices are all open at least from Monday to Friday (8/9am–2/3pm). The smaller concerns operate from April or May to September or October, usually in the mornings only from Monday to Friday. We've given details of opening times throughout the guide, though in remoter spots you can't always rely on the officially posted hours.

Maps

For most visitors, the **maps** printed in this guide – supplemented by the free road and town maps issued by the tourist offices – will suffice, though if you're planning to explore the islands' nooks and crannies by bike or car, you'll need a more detailed road map. There are many alternatives, widely available from island newsagents, petrol stations, souvenir shops and bookshops. You shouldn't pay more than 600ptas/€3.61 for any of the road maps detailed below. If you buy supplementary maps,

---

SNTO OFFICES

www.tourspain.es

Australia and New Zealand c/o Spanish Tourism Promotions, 178 Collins St, Melbourne ☎03/9650 7377.

Canada 2 Bloor St West #3402, Toronto, ON M4W 3E2 ☎416/961-3131 (*www.docuweb.ca/SpaininCanada*).

UK 22–23 Manchester Sq, London W1M 5AP ☎020/7486 8077; 24hr brochure request line

☎0906/364 0630 (*www.tourspain.co.uk*).

USA 666 Fifth Ave, New York, NY 10103 ☎212/265-8822; Water Tower Place #915 East, 845 N Michigan Ave, Chicago, IL 60611 ☎312/642-1992; 8383 Wilshire Blvd #960, Beverly Hills, Los Angeles, CA 90211 ☎323/658-7188; 1221 Brickell Ave, Miami, FL 33131 ☎305/358-1992.

it's important to remember that all **roadsigns** and town and street signs on Mallorca have recently been translated into the local language, **Catalan**; Castilian (ie Spanish) maps are now obsolete. To ensure you're buying a Catalan map, unfold it and check out the spelling of Port de Pollença on Mallorca's north coast; if it reads "Puerto de Pollença", you've got an old, Castilian map. Just to confuse matters, however, some maps switch between the two languages for no apparent reason.

The best Catalan map of the island, entitled *Mallorca*, is published by the Ministerio de Obras Públicas (Ministry of Public Works). This accurately portrays the island's most important highways and principal byways, and provides topographical details too. It's not, however, as easy to get as most of its rivals − to buy it you'll need to consult a specialist map shop either before you go (see box on p.30) or in Mallorca. More easily available Catalan alternatives include the easy-to-follow *Collins Mallorca Holiday Map* (1:175,000), which usefully indicates distances between settlements, marks salient geographical features and provides a street plan and index of central Palma. In Mallorca, the largely Catalan *Mallorca and Palma* map (1:175,000) is a widely available and inexpensive local government publication equipped with a large-scale, indexed plan of Palma and brief descriptions of the city's tourist attractions. Its only drawbacks are the absence of topographical features and some waywardness when it comes to depicting the island's byroads.

Serious **hikers** are poorly provided for: there are no really reliable maps with walking trails marked. The IGN (Instituto Geográfico Nacional) issues **topographical maps** of the Balearics at 1:25,000 and 1:50,000, based on an aerial survey of 1979, but many minor roads and footpaths simply don't appear and even crags and cliffs are not always shown. As a precaution, some hikers cross-check IGN maps with their rather out-of-date predecessors, the Mapa Militar (military maps), published at the same scales. These maps are available from bookshops in Palma and Sóller, or more expensively from a few specialist suppliers overseas.

That said, Discovery Walking Guides Ltd, a UK company operated by David and Ros Brawn, is beginning to fill the cartographic void. They have already published a very competent 1:40,000 'Mallorca North & Mountains' map, covering most of the western coast, and a more general island map is in the offing. Most better UK bookshops, and some on Mallorca, sell their maps, or you can order them worldwide from Amazon (*www.amazon.com*).

Mallorca on the Internet

As yet, the **Internet** hasn't really taken off in Mallorca. Most sites emanating from the island are rudimentary and many are not regularly updated. Furthermore, the majority are only available in Castilian (Spanish) or Catalan, though you can get help in deciphering these from any Internet translation service − try *babelfish*. *altavista.com/translate.dyn* for Spanish translation.

Govern Balear
www.caib.es/kfcont.htm
The official site of the Balearic provincial government, and a well-presented source of general information. The tourist information section is presented in several languages, including English, and gives links to sites offering information on accommodation, eating and drinking, sports, and so on.

Mallorca Cycling − Tourist Guide
www.baleares.com/tourist.guide/cycling
Details of eight different cycle routes on the island, from 70km to 320km. Routes are designed to avoid busy roads and to provide sections on the flat as well as steep climbs. In several languages, including English.

Mallorca Highway
www.malhigh.com
Expat heaven, this site hosts private ads from German and English expatriates. Useful and amusing in equal measure.

Spanish Meteorological Institute Weather Information
www.inm.es/wwb
Daily weather forecasts for the whole of Spain.

Palma de Mallorca City Council
www.a-palma.es/eng_index.htm
If you manage to navigate through the occasionally distant and complex Internet path to reach this site, it's surprisingly useful, providing

MAP OUTLETS

UK AND IRELAND

London Daunt Books, 83 Marylebone High St,
W1M 3DE ☎020/7224 2295, and 193
Haverstock Hill, NW3 4QL ☎020/7794 4006;
National Map Centre, 22–24 Caxton St, SW1H
0QU ☎020/7222 2466 (*www.mapsnmc.co.uk*);
Stanfords, 12–14 Long Acre, WC2E 9LP
☎020/7836 1321 (*www.stanfords.co.uk*); The
Travel Bookshop, 13–15 Blenheim Crescent,
W11 2EE ☎020/7229 5260 (*www.thetravel-
bookshop.co.uk*).

England Blackwell's Map and Travel Shop, 53
Broad St, Oxford OX1 3BQ ☎01865/792792
(*www.bookshop.blackwell.co.uk*); Heffers Map
and Travel, 20 Trinity St, Cambridge, CB2 1TJ
☎01223/586586 (*www.heffers.co.uk*); The Map
Shop, 30a Belvoir St, Leicester, LE1 6QH
☎0116/247 1400; Newcastle Map Centre, 55
Grey St, Newcastle, NE1 6EF ☎0191/261 5622
(*www.newtraveller.com*); Stanfords, 29 Corn
St, Bristol, BS1 1HT ☎0117/929 9966
(*www.stanfords.co.uk*); Waterstone's, 91

Deansgate, Manchester M3 2BW ☎0161/837
3000 (*www.waterstones-manchester-deans-
gate.co.uk*).

Scotland John Smith and Sons, 26 Colquhoun
Ave, Glasgow, G52 4PJ ☎0141/221 7472
(*www.johnsmith.co.uk*); James Thin Melven's
Bookshop, 29 Union St, Inverness, IV1 1QA
☎01463/233500 (*www.jthin.co.uk*).

Ireland Easons Bookshop, 40 O'Connell St,
Dublin 1 ☎01/873 3811 (*www.eason.ie*); Fred
Hanna's Bookshop, 27–29 Nassau St, Dublin 2
☎01/677 1255; Hodges Figgis, 56–58 Dawson
St, Dublin 2 ☎01/677 4754 (*www.hodgesfig-
gis.com*); Waterstone's, Queens Building, 8
Royal Ave, Belfast BT1 1DA ☎028/9024 7355,
and 7 Dawson St, Dublin 2 ☎01/679 1415, and
69 Patrick St, Cork ☎021/427 6522.

Stanfords in London is the UK's largest
map sellers, and operates a mail order
service by phone, fax or email.

USA

Chicago Rand McNally, 444 N Michigan Ave, IL
60611 ☎312/321-1751
(*www.randmcnally.com*).

Los Angeles and around Distant Lands, 56 S
Raymond Ave, Pasadena, CA 91105 ☎626/449-
3220 (*www.distantlands.com*); Map Link, 30 S
La Petera Lane, Unit #5, Santa Barbara, CA
93117 ☎805/692-6777 (*www.maplink.com*).

New York Complete Traveler, 199 Madison Ave,
NY 10016 ☎212/685-9007; Rand McNally, 150
E 52nd St, NY 10022 ☎212/758-7488;
Traveler's Choice, 22 W 52nd St, NY 10019
☎212/941-1535 (*tvlchoice@aol.com*).

San Francisco Bay Area Book Passage, 51
Tamal Vista Blvd, Corte Madera, CA 94925
☎415/927-0960 (*www.bookpassage.com*);

detailed street maps, public transport information and "where to go" and "what's on" guides.
Primarily in Spanish, but English sections too,
though some of the translations are not complete.

Consell de Mallorca
www.cim.net
One of the best presented sites produced by the
island, but virtually indecipherable as it's in
Catalan only. It has a useful events page
Novetats, although there's a certain element of
guesswork involved in the translation.

Complete Traveler, 3207 Fillmore St, San Francisco, CA 94123 ☎415/923-1511; Phileas Fogg's, #87 Stanford Shopping Center, Palo Alto, CA 94304 ☎1-800/533-FOGG (*www.foggs.com*); Rand McNally, 595 Market St, San Francisco, CA 94105 ☎415/777-3131; Sierra Club Bookstore, 730 Polk St, San Francisco, CA 94110 ☎415/977-5653 (*www.sierraclubbookstore.com*).

Seattle Elliott Bay Book Company, 101 S Main St, WA 98104 (☎206/624-6600; *www.elliottbaybook.com*).

Vermont Adventurous Traveler Bookstore, PO Box 64769, Burlington, VT 05406 ☎1-800/282-3963 (*www.AdventurousTraveler.com*).

Washington DC ADC Map and Travel Center, 1636 I St NW, DC 20006 ☎202/628 2608; Travel Books & Language Center, 4437 Wisconsin Ave NW, DC 20016 ☎1-800/220-2665.

Rand McNally (*www.randmcnally.com*) has dozens of stores across the US; call ☎1-800/333-0136 (ext 2111) for the address of your nearest store and for mail-order maps.

CANADA

Montréal Ulysses Travel Bookshop, 4176 St-Denis, PQ H2W 2M5 ☎514/843-9447 (*www.ulysses.ca*).

Ottawa World of Maps, 1235 Wellington St, ON K1Y 3A3 ☎613/724-6776 (*www.worldofmaps.com*).

Toronto Open Air, 25 Toronto St, ON M5R 2C1 ☎416/363-0719.

Vancouver World Wide, 552 Seymour St, BC V6B 3J5 ☎604/687-3320 (*www.itmb.com*).

AUSTRALIA

Adelaide The Map Shop, 6 Peel St ☎08/8231 2033.

Brisbane Worldwide Maps and Guides, 187 George St ☎07/3221 4330.

Cairns Walkers Bookshop, 96 Lake St ☎07/4051 2410.

Melbourne Mapland, 372 Little Bourke St ☎03/9670 4383.

Perth Perth Map Centre, 1/884 Hay St ☎08/9322 5733.

Sydney Travel Bookshop, Shop 3, 175 Liverpool St ☎02/9261 8200.

NEW ZEALAND

Auckland Specialty Maps, 46 Albert St ☎09/307 2217.

Christchurch Mapworld, 173 Gloucester St, Christchurch ☎03/374 5399 (*www.mapworld.co.nz*).

Health

No inoculations are required for Mallorca and the only blights to your holiday are likely to be a possible upset stomach or ferocious hangover. To avoid the former, wash fruit and avoid *tapas* dishes that look like they were cooked last week. Many islanders also refrain from consuming mayonnaise during the summer.

If you should fall ill, for minor complaints it's easiest to go to a **farmàcia** – there are plenty of them and they're listed in the Balearic Islands' Yellow Pages (although we provide details of several pharmacies in the main towns). Pharmacists are highly trained, willing to give advice (often in English), and able to dispense many drugs which would be available only on prescription in many other countries. Most keep usual shop hours (Mon–Fri 9am–1pm & 4–7pm, Sat 9am–1pm), but in Palma some open late and at weekends, and a rota system means at least one is open 24 hours a day. The rota is displayed in the window of every pharmacy, or you can check at reception in one of the better hotels. Outside the towns, you'll find a *farmàcia* in most of the larger villages, though there's not much chance of late-night opening or of an English-speaking pharmacist unless you're staying in a resort area.

In more serious cases you can get the address of an **English-speaking doctor** from your consulate, hotel, local *farmàcia* or tourist office. If you're seeking free treatment under the EU health scheme, double-check that the doctor is working within the Spanish health care system (the Instituto Nacional de la Salud), or you'll be liable for all costs. Even within the EU agreement, you still have to pay forty percent of **prescription charges** (senior citizens are exempt). Most private insurance policies also don't cover prescription charges – their "excesses" are usually greater than the cost of the medicines. All **dentists** are private – you'll pay around 6000ptas/€36.06 to get a cavity filled. A comprehensive list of *dentistas* can be found in the Yellow Pages, or ask at your hotel or *hostal* reception.

In medical **emergencies**, phone the **Creu Roja** (Red Cross), which operates the island's main ambulance service, on ☎ 202220. If you're reliant on free treatment within the EU health scheme, try to remember to make this clear both to the ambulance staff and, if you're whisked off to hospital, to the medic you subsequently encounter. You should hand over a photocopy of your E111 on arrival at hospital, or else you may be mistaken for a private insurance job and billed accordingly. Hospital charges can be as much as 14,000ptas/€84.14 per visit.

Condoms no longer need to be smuggled into Spain as they did during the Franco years. They're available from most *farmàcias*, and from all sorts of outlets in the resorts, such as bars and vending machines – thankfully, since a recent survey of 18- to 30-year-old visitors to the island found that the average time between arrival and first sexual contact was 3hr 42min.

Costs, money and banks

In terms of food, wine and transport, Mallorca remains a budget destination for northern Europeans, North Americans, Australians and New Zealanders. However, Balearic hotel prices have increased considerably over the last few years, so independent travellers on any kind of budget will have to plan their accommodation carefully and, in summer, when vacant rooms are scarce, reserve well in advance. Another serious expense may be partying: nightclubs can relieve you of thousands of pesetas in the space of a few hours.

Precise costs for places to stay are given in the guide, and you should consult the box on p.39 for general guidelines on accommodation prices. On average, if you're prepared to buy your own picnic lunch, stay in inexpensive *hostals* and hotels, and stick to the cheaper bars and restaurants, you could get by on around £20–25/US$30–35 a day per person. If you intend to stay in three-star hotels and eat at quality restaurants, then you'll need more like £50/$75 a day per person, with the main variable being the cost of your room – and bear in mind that room prices rise steeply as the season progresses. On £80/$120 a day and upwards, you'll be limited only by your energy reserves, unless you're planning to stay in a five-star hotel, in which case this figure won't even cover your bed. **Eating out** is excellent value, and even in a top-notch restaurant in Palma a superb meal will only set you back around £17/US$25 – though, of course, you may pay well over the odds for food and drink in the tourist resorts. As always, if you're travelling alone you'll spend much more than you would in a group of two or more – sharing rooms saves a lot of money.

One other cost is **IVA**, a seven percent sales tax (VAT) levied on most goods and services. Check in advance to see if IVA is included in the price of your bigger purchases; otherwise, especially in more expensive hotels and restaurants, you may be in for a bit of a shock.

THE EURO

On January 1, 1999, eleven EU countries – Austria, Belgium, Finland, France, Germany, Ireland, Italy, Luxembourg, the Netherlands, Portugal and Spain – irrevocably fixed their exchange rates to a new currency, **the euro** (€), which will gradually take over as the single currency for all of them and Greece, which joined in late. In Spain, as in the other eleven countries, euro notes and coins will be issued in January 2002 and will circulate in tandem with pesetas for two months. From March 2002, the euro will be the only legal currency in Spain. Even beforehand, throughout 2001, you can get travellers' cheques in euros, and you will not be charged commission for changing euros in any of the twelve countries in the euro zone (also known as **"Euroland"**). Neither will you be charged for changing from any of the old currencies to any other (French francs to Spanish pesetas, for example). After the switchover, you'll be able to hand in the old currencies at any bank and get an equivalent amount of euros commission-free.

The three remaining EU countries – Sweden, the UK and Denmark (the last of which voted in October 2000 to stay out of the euro zone) – may or may not join the twelve at some later point. The issue has become a political hot potato all over Europe, and the advent of the euro in 2002 will be watched closely.

Money and the exchange rate

Pending the introduction of the euro in 2002 (see box on p.33), the Spanish currency is the **peseta**. **Coins** come in denominations of 1, 5, 10, 25, 50, 100, 200 and 500 pesetas (indicated in this book as "ptas"); **notes** as 1000, 2000, 5000 and 10,000 pesetas. The **exchange rate** for the Spanish peseta at the time of writing was around 260 to the British pound, 210 to the Irish pound, 175 to the US dollar, 120 to the Canadian dollar, 100 to the Australian dollar and 80 to the NZ dollar.

As of March 2002, the Spanish currency will become the **euro** (€), made up of 100 cents. One euro has been fixed in perpetuity to be exactly 166.386ptas. Until euro prices on Mallorca find their own level, we've given all prices in this book in pesetas and an exact equivalent in euros and cents. Needless to say, you may find euro prices in 2002 and afterwards differing slightly from our quoted equivalents.

You can take into Spain as much money as you want in any form, although amounts over five million pesetas (€30,050.61) must be declared. Departing Spain, sums over one million pesetas (€6010.12) have to be declared.

Travellers' cheques and plastic money

One reliable way to carry your funds is in **travellers' cheques**. The usual fee for their purchase is one percent of face value. Make sure to keep the purchase agreement and a record of cheque serial numbers safe and separate from the cheques themselves. In the event that cheques are lost or stolen, the issuing company will expect you to report the loss forthwith. Consequently, when you buy your travellers' cheques, ensure you have details of the company's emergency contact numbers or the address of their local office. Most companies claim to replace lost or stolen cheques within 24 hours. American Express cheques are sold through most North American, Australasian and European banks, and they're the most widely accepted cheques in Spain. When you cash your cheques in Mallorca, guard against outrageous **commissions** (they should be around 400–500ptas/€2.40–3.01 per transaction). If commission is waived, make sure that you're not being fobbed off with a drastically worse exchange rate in recompense.

Most **plastic cards** – Visa, Mastercard, as well as other British and US bank cards – can also be used for withdrawing cash from **cash dispensers** (**ATMs**) in Spain (which often give English-language options). Check with your bank to find out about these reciprocal arrangements. Make sure you have a personal identification number (PIN) that's designed to work overseas. **Credit cards** are particularly useful for car rental, cash advances (though these attract a high rate of interest from the date of withdrawal) and hotel bills. American Express, Visa and Mastercard are all widely accepted on Mallorca.

Changing money

Spanish **banks** and **savings banks** have branches in all but the smallest of Balearic towns, and nearly all of them will change foreign currency and travellers' cheques (albeit with occasional reluctance for the more obscure brands). The Banco de Bilbao, Banco March, Banco de Crédito Balear and Banco de Santander are four of the most widespread banks, while Sa Nostra and La Caixa are the biggest savings banks on the islands. Most give cash advances on credit cards.

Banking hours are generally Monday to Friday 9am–2pm, plus Saturday (except in summer) 9am–1pm. Outside these hours, most major hotels and many travel agents will change money at less generous rates and with variable commissions, as will the many **exchange kiosks** that are concentrated in the tourist areas. Legally, exchange rates must be on public display.

Wiring money

Having money **wired** from home is always expensive, and should be considered a last resort. One option is to have your own bank send the money through; for that you need to nominate a receiving bank in Mallorca. Any local branch will do, but those in Palma will probably be more familiar with the process. Naturally, you need to confirm the co-operation of the local bank before you set the wheels in motion back home. The sending bank's fees are geared to the amount being transferred and to the urgency of the service you require. In the UK, for instance, standard transfers, taking two or three days, attract a charge of around £15 for the first £10,000, or £25 or so for larger amounts, whilst the same-day service costs about £20 or £36 respectively. The receiving bank charges a commission too – expect a 2000ptas/€12.02 charge on amounts up to about £400.

Money can also be wired via **Moneygram** with the funds available for collection within minutes of transmission. The appropriate call centre (see box) will advise on the banks and agents in Mallorca to which money can be wired. In the UK, branches of Thomas Cook and American Express as well as larger post offices operate as Moneygram agents – and will also advise on where the money can be sent. Charges depend on the amount. In the UK, it costs £33 to send £500, or £80 to send £2000. In the US, charges are $65 to send $1000, or $130 to send $3000.

MONEYGRAM CALL CENTRES	
Australia	☎ 1800/230100.
Canada	☎ 1-800/933-3278.
Ireland	☎ 00800/6663 9472.
New Zealand	☎ 0800/262263.
UK	☎ 0800/018 0104.
US	☎ 1-800/543-4080.

Getting around

On Mallorca you're spoiled for choice when it comes to transport. There's a reliable bus network between all the major settlements, a multitude of taxis, a plethora of car rental firms (which keeps prices down to a minimum, especially off-season), plenty of bicycles and mopeds to rent, as well as a couple of minor train lines. Distances are small and consequently the costs of travel low, whether in terms of petrol or the price of a ticket. It's only 110km from Andratx in the west to Cala Rajada in the east, and from Palma on the south coast to Alcúdia on the north shore is a mere 60km.

Buses

Mallorca has an extensive network of **bus services** linking Palma, the main city, with most of the villages and resorts of the coast and interior. These main bus routes are supplemented by more intermittent local services between smaller towns and between neighbouring resorts. Ticket **prices** are reasonable: the one-way fare from Palma to Colònia de Sant Jordi is, for instance, 640ptas/€3.85 and from Palma to Cala Rajada 890ptas/€5.35. Only Palma is large enough to have its own public transit system, with a multiplicity of bus services linking the city centre with the suburbs and beach resorts that surround it – see p.110 and p.118 for more on this – though the larger resorts all have some form of local transport, either bus or electric mini-train.

On all island bus services, destinations are marked on the front of the bus. Passengers enter the bus at the front and buy tickets from the driver, unless they've been bought in advance at a bus station. Bus stops are mostly indicated with the word *parada*. A confusing variety of bus companies operate the various routes on Mallorca, but a composite timetable is readily available from most tourist offices.

On the whole buses are reliable and comfortable enough, the only significant problem being that many country towns and villages do not have a bus station or even a clearly marked *parada*, which can be very confusing, as in some places buses leave from the most obscure parts of town. Remember also that bus services are drastically reduced on **Sundays** and **holidays**, and it's best not even to consider travelling out in the sticks on these days. The Catalan words to look out for on timetables are *diari* (daily), *feiners* (workdays, including Saturday), *diumenge* (Sunday) and *festius* (holidays).

Trains

Mallorca has two small sections of electrified **train track**, with narrow-gauge trains travelling through the mountains from Palma to Sóller (28km), and across the flatland of the interior from Palma to Inca (29km). Each line has its own station in Palma, alongside each other on Plaça Espanya. Neither train is as fast as the bus, but the trip to Sóller takes you through some of Mallorca's most magnificent scenery. The line to Inca, however, passes through some of its most tedious. The standard return fare from Palma to Sóller is 760ptas/€4.57 and to Inca 500ptas/€3.01.

Taxis

The excellence of the islands' bus services means it's rarely necessary to take a **taxi**, though they are a fast and easy way of reaching your resort from the airport and, perhaps more importantly, of getting back to your hotel after a day's hiking. In the latter case, you should arrange where you want to be picked up before you set out – there's no point wandering round a tiny village hoping a taxi will show up. Throughout Mallorca, the taxis of each town and resort area have their own livery: Palma taxis, for example, are black with a cream-coloured roof and bonnet (hood). Local journeys are all metered, though there are supplementary charges for each piece of luggage and for travel at night and on Sundays. For longer journeys there are official prices, which are displayed at the island's airport and at some taxi stands and tourist offices. Naturally, you're well advised to check the price with the driver *before* you get going. Fares are reasonable, but not inexpensive: the journey from the airport to downtown Palma, a distance of around 11km, will cost you in the region of 2200ptas/€13.22, while the fare from Palma airport to Port d'Andratx (37km) is about 5200ptas/€31.25.

Driving and vehicle rental

Getting around on public transport is easy enough, but you'll obviously have a great deal more freedom if you have **your own vehicle** and, predictably, most of the more secluded (and attractive) beaches have no public transport provision. Major roads are generally good, though back roads are very variable – unpaved minor roads are particularly lethal after rain. Traffic is generally well-behaved (even if Spain does have one of the highest incidences of traffic accidents in Europe), but noisy, especially in Palma, where the horn is used as a recreational tool as well as an instrument of warning. **Fuel** (*gasolina*) comes in four grades. Different companies use different brand names, but generally *Super Plus* is 98-octane fuel, selling at about 155ptas/€0.93 per litre; *Super* is 96-octane, selling at about 145ptas/€0.87 per litre, and almost always without lead (*sense plom*); while *Mezcla*, or *Normal*, is low-grade 90-octane, available for about 130ptas/€0.78 per litre. Diesel (*gasoleo* or *gasoil*) costs about 120ptas/€0.72 per litre. Mallorca is well supplied with petrol stations; a few are open 24 hours a day, seven days a week, though most close around 9pm or 10pm and on public holidays.

Most foreign **driving licences** are honoured in Spain – including all EU, US and Canadian ones – but an **International Driver's Licence** (available at minimal cost from your home motoring organization) is an easy way to set your mind at rest. If you're bringing your own car, you must have adequate insurance, a green card (available from your insurers or motoring organization), and a **bail bond**, a document to be shown to the police if you're involved in anything but the most trivial of accidents. Without a bail bond, the police will almost certainly imprison you and impound your vehicle pending an accident investigation. Extra insurance coverage for unforeseen legal costs is also well worth having, as is an appropriate **breakdown** policy from a motoring organization. In the UK, for example, the RAC and AA charge about £110 for a year's Europe-wide breakdown cover, with all the appropriate documentation, including green card and bail bond, provided. Note, however, that rates vary depending on the age of the vehicle and increase if you're towing anything.

Throughout the Balearics speed **limits** are posted: the maximum on urban roads is 60kph, on other roads 90kph, on motorways 120kph. On the main highways speed traps are fairly frequent. If you're stopped for any violation, the Spanish police can (and usually will) levy a stiff on-the-spot fine of up to 10,000ptas/€60.10 before letting you go on your way, their draconian instincts reinforced by the fact that few tourists are likely to appear in court to argue the case. Most **driving rules** and regulations are pretty standard: seat belts are compulsory, "Stop" signs mean exactly that, and drink-driving will land you in big trouble. A single, unbroken white line in the middle of the road means **no overtaking**, even if the rule is frequently ignored; note also that drivers often sound their horns when overtaking. You yield to traffic coming from the right at all junctions, whether or not there's a give way sign; and be prepared for road signs that give very little, if any, warning of the turning you might require. On major trunk roads, turnings that take vehicles across oncoming traffic are being phased out and replaced by semi-circular minor exits that lead round to traffic lights on the near side of the major road. Finally, drivers do not have to stop (and usually don't) at zebra crossings, which merely indicate a suitable pedestrian crossing place: if you come to an abrupt stop at a crossing, as you might do elsewhere, the pedestrians will be amazed and someone may well crash into your rear end.

Car rental

There are scores of companies offering **car rental** (still rendered in Castilian as *coches de alquiler*), their offices thronging the islands' resorts, larger towns and airports. Most of the major international players have outlets and dozens of small companies make up the remainder. Several addresses are given in the Palma "Listings" on p.106, and comprehensive lists are available from the tourist office. To rent a car, you'll have to be 21 or over (and have been driving for at least a year), and you'll probably need a credit card – though some places will accept a hefty deposit in cash and some smaller companies simply ignore all the normal regulations. However, no car rental firm will allow you to transport their vehicles from one Balearic island to another. If you're planning to spend much time driving on rougher tracks, you'll probably be better off with a moped, or even a four-wheel drive vehicle (about thirty percent more expensive than the average car and available from larger rental agencies).

Rental **charges** vary enormously: out-of-season costs for a standard car can come down to as little as 2000ptas/€12.02 per day with unlimited mileage; in July and August, by comparison, the same basic vehicle could set you back 6000ptas/€36.06 a day (though weekly prices are slightly better value, and special rates operate at the weekend). The big companies all offer competitive rates, but you can often get a better deal through someone in contact with local vehicle rental firms, such as Holiday Autos. If you choose to deal directly with smaller, local companies, proceed with care. In particular, check the policy for the excess applied to claims, and ensure that it includes a bail bond (see opposite), collision damage waiver or CDW (applicable if an accident is your fault) and, in general, adequate levels of financial cover. **Fly-drive** deals are well worth investigating. In Britain, for example, Iberia offer Avis cars from around £100 a week in the low season, £170 in high season (including unlimited mileage, CDW, bail bond, insurance and VAT), as long as you book your flight with them.

Moped rental

Mopeds (scooters) are a popular means of transport, especially for visiting remoter spots, and are widely available. Prices start at about 2000ptas/€12.02 per day, including insurance and crash helmets, which must be worn. Be warned, however, that the insurance often excludes theft – always check with the company first. You will generally be asked to show some kind of driving licence (particularly for mopeds over 50cc), and to leave a deposit on your credit card, though most places will accept cash as an alternative. We've listed names and addresses of rental companies throughout the guide where most appropriate; tourist offices will provide comprehensive lists of suppliers.

Cycling

Cycling can be an inexpensive and flexible way of getting around Mallorca, and of seeing a great deal of the countryside that would otherwise pass you by. In general terms, you have to be pretty fit to tackle the steep hills of the northern part of the island, but the central plain Es Pla is fairly easy going and, with the exception of the main arterial roads, there is little traffic. The Spanish are keen cycling fans, which means that you'll be well received and find reasonable facilities, while cars will normally hoot before they pass – though this can be alarming at first. Mallorca's main tourist office in Palma (see

CAR RENTAL AGENCIES

UK

Autos Abroad ☎0870/066 7788; *www.autosabroad.co.uk*

Avis ☎0870/606 0100; *www.avisworld.com*

Budget ☎0800/181181; *www.go-budget.co.uk*

Europcar ☎0845/722 2525; *www.europcar.co.uk*

National ☎0870/536 5365; *www.nationalcar-europe.com*

Hertz ☎0870/844 8844; *www.hertz.co.uk*

Holiday Autos ☎0870/400 0000; *www.holidayautos.com*

Suncars ☎0870/500 5566; *www.suncars.com*

Thrifty ☎01494/751600; *www.thrifty.co.uk*

REPUBLIC OF IRELAND

Avis ☎01/605 7555; *www.avis.com*

Budget ☎1850/575757; *www.budget.ie*

Europcar ☎01/614 2800; *www.europcar.ie*

Hertz ☎01/676 7476; *www.hertz.co.uk*

Holiday Autos ☎01/872 9366; *www.holidayautos.com*

NORTH AMERICA

Alamo ☎1-800/522-9696; *www.goalamo.com*

Auto Europe in US ☎1-800/223-5555; in Canada ☎1-888/223-5555; *www.autoeurope.com*

Avis in US ☎1-800/331-1084; in Canada ☎1-800/272-5871; *www.avis.com*

Budget ☎1-800/527-0700; *www.budget.com*

Dollar ☎1-800/800-6000; *www.dollar.com*

Enterprise ☎1-800/325-8007; *www.enterprise.com*

Europe by Car ☎1-800/223-1516; *www.europebycar.com*

Hertz in US ☎1-800/654-3001; in Canada ☎416/620-9620; *www.hertz.com*

National ☎1-800/CAR-RENT; *www.nationalcar.com*

Thrifty ☎1-800/367-2277; *www.thrifty.com*

AUSTRALIA

Avis ☎13/6333; *www.avis.com*

Budget ☎1300/362848; *www.budget.com*

Dollar ☎1800/358008; *www.dollarcar.com.au*

Hertz ☎1800/550067; *www.hertz.com*

National ☎13/1908; *www.nationalcarrental.com.au*

Thrifty ☎1300/367227; *www.thrifty.com.au*

NEW ZEALAND

Apex ☎0800/105055; *www.southern.co.nz*

Avis ☎09/526 2800; *www.avis.com*

Budget ☎0800/652227; *www.budget.com*

Hertz ☎0800/655955; *www.hertz.com*

National ☎09/537 2582; *www.nationalcar.co.nz*

Thrifty ☎09/309 0111; *www.thrifty.co.nz*

p.71) produces a free specialist leaflet, the *Guía del Ciclista* (in Spanish only), which details suggested itineraries and indicates distances and levels of difficulty. On the Internet, the **Mallorca Cycling Tourist Guide** (*www.baleares.com/tourist.guide/cycling*) outlines eight different cycle routes, from 70km to 320km, in several languages including English.

Renting a bike costs anywhere between about 900ptas/€5.41 and 1300ptas/€7.81 a day for an ordinary bike (4500ptas/€27.05 to 6500ptas/€39.07 per week), or about thirty percent more for a mountain bike. Renting is straightforward as there are dozens of suppliers (there's usually one at every resort) and tourist offices will provide a list or advise you of the nearest outlet; we've also listed a few in the guide.

Getting your own bike to Mallorca should present few problems. Most **airlines** are happy to take them as ordinary baggage provided they come within your weight allowance (though it's sensible to check first: crowded charter flights may be less obliging). You'll have to deflate the tyres to avoid explosions in the unpressurized hold and turn the handlebars sideways. **Ferries** from the mainland (and between the Balearic islands) transport bikes for free or at minimal cost. Bike **parts** can often be found at auto repair shops or garages – look for Michelin signs – and there are bike shops in Mallorca's larger towns.

Accommodation

Although package-tour operators have a stranglehold on thousands of hotel rooms, villas and apartments in Mallorca, reasonably priced rooms are still available to the independent traveller, even though options are severely limited at the height of the season. Off season you should be able to get a simple, medium-sized double room with shower and sink for around 3500ptas/€21.04, whereas in August the same room, if available, can set you back as much as 5000ptas/€30.05 – though this still compares reasonably well with much of the rest of Europe. You can, however, comfortably spend 10,000ptas/€60.10 and upwards in hotels with three or more stars – some of them being very firmly in the super-luxury class.

Vacant rooms are at their scarcest from late June to early September, when **advance reservations** are strongly recommended. Most hoteliers speak at least a modicum of English, so visitors who don't speak Catalan or Spanish can usually book over the phone, but a confirmation letter or

---

ACCOMMODATION PRICE CODES

After each accommodation entry in this book you'll find a symbol that corresponds to one of nine price categories. These categories represent the minimum you can expect to pay for a **double room** in high season; for a single room, expect to pay around two-thirds the price of a double. The only ① options are youth hostels, where you'll get a dorm bed, and the monasteries.

Note that in the more upmarket *hostals* and *pensions*, and in anything calling itself a hotel, you'll pay a **tax** (IVA) of seven percent on top of the room price.

① Under 3000ptas/
    Under €18.03
	④ 6000–8000ptas/
	    €36.06–€48.08
		⑦ 14,000–20,000ptas/
		    €84.14–€120.20

② 3000–4000ptas/
    €18.03–€24.04
	⑤ 8000–10,000ptas/
	    €48.08–€60.10
		⑧ 20,000–25,000ptas/
		    €120.20–€150.25

③ 4000–6000ptas/
    €24.04–€36.06
	⑥ 10,000–14,000ptas/
	    €60.10–€84.14
		⑨ Over 25,000ptas/
		    Over €150.25

fax is always a good idea. In Mallorca the easiest place to get a room is Palma, with Sóller lagging not far behind, but don't forget the five monasteries on the island that offer accommodation – they're a good bet for vacancies, even in high summer.

It's often worth **bargaining** over room prices, especially outside peak season and at fancier hotels, since the posted tariff doesn't necessarily mean much. Many hotels have rooms at different prices, and tend to offer the more expensive ones first. Most places also have rooms with three or four beds at not a great deal more than the double-room price, which represents a real saving for small groups. On the other hand, people travelling alone invariably end up paying over the odds. We've detailed where to find places to stay in most of the destinations listed in the guide, from the most basic of rooms to luxury hotels, and given a price range for each (see box on p.39). We've also indicated where an establishment closes over the winter – though this is fairly unusual.

Fondas, casas de huéspedes, pensions, hostals and hotels

The one thing all travellers to Mallorca have to get to grips with is the elaborate diversity of types of places to stay – though in practice the various categories often overlap. The least expensive places are **fondas**, **casas de huéspedes** and **pensions** (*pensiones* in Castilian), further categorized with either one or two stars. Establishments in these categories are few and far between in the Balearics, and the distinctions between them blurred, but in general you'll find food served at *fondas* and *pensions* (some will rent rooms on a meals-inclusive basis only), while *casas de huéspedes* – literally "guesthouses" – are often used as long-term lodgings. Confusingly, the name of many *pensions* does not follow their designation: lots of *pensions* call themselves *hostals* and vice versa. As a result, the name isn't always a reliable guide to the establishment's price, though the

sign outside usually is (see box).

Slightly more expensive are **hostals** (*hostales* in Castilian) and **hostal-residencias**, categorized from one to three stars. A one-star *hostal* generally costs about the same as a *pensió*. Many *hostals* offer good, functional rooms, often with a private shower. The *residencia* designation means that no meals other than breakfast are served.

Moving up the scale, **hotels** are also star-graded by the authorities, from one to five stars. One-star hotels cost no more than three-star *hostals* (sometimes less), but three-star hotels cost a lot more, and at four or five stars you're in the luxury class with prices to match. There are also a handful of *hotel-residencias*, where the only meal provided is breakfast.

It's safe to assume that bedrooms in a hotel will be adequately clean and furnished, but in the lower categories you're well advised to ask to see the room before you part with any money. Standards vary greatly between places in the same category (even between rooms in the same *hostal*) and it does no harm to check that there's hot water if there's supposed to be, or that you're not being stuck at the back in an airless box. Note that bathrooms in many *pensions* and *hostals* (some hotels too) will have only showers, not bath tubs.

By law, each establishment must display its room rates, and there should be a card on the room door showing the prices for the various seasons. If you think you're being overcharged, take up your **complaint** first with the management; you can usually produce an immediate resolution by asking for one of the *hojas de reclamaciones* (complaints forms) that all places are obliged by law to keep. The threat of filling in a form is usually in itself enough to make the proprietor back down.

Monasteries

In recent times Mallorca's **monasteries** have become severely underpopulated and six of them now let out empty cells to visitors of both

---

sexes. They all have delightful settings either in the hills or on hilltops and the majority are dotted across the centre of the island. The six are: the Santuari de Sant Salvador near Felanitx (see p.221); the Ermita de Nostra Senyora de Bonany near Petra (see p.204); the Ermita de Nostra Senyora del Puig outside Pollença (see p.173); the Monastir de Nostra Senyora de Lluc (see p.164); the Santuari de Nostra Senyora de Cura on Puig Randa near Algaida (see p.201); and the Ermita de Sant Miquel outside Montuiri (see p.202). There's an increasing demand for this simple, cheap form of accommodation so, although it's possible just to turn up and ask for a room, you'd be well advised to either phone ahead or, if your Spanish isn't good enough, get the local tourist office to make a reservation on your behalf. For a double room, you can expect to pay around 3000ptas/€18.03 at most of these monasteries, though it's a little more at Lluc (3900ptas/€23.44) and Sant Miquel (10,000ptas/€60.10), the most visited and commercialized of the six. Reasonably priced food is usually available, but check arrangements when you book.

Youth hostels

There are only two **youth hostels** (*albergues juveniles*) on Mallorca – one near Palma, the other outside Alcúdia. The former is open all year, the latter from April to September. Both tend to be block-booked by school groups, so unless you reserve a bed well in advance you shouldn't rely on either as a viable source of inexpensive accommodation. At both, the price of a bed is about 1400ptas/€8.41 (or 1800ptas/€10.82 if you're over 26) and you'll need a sheet sleeping bag. The hostels are operated by international organization Hostelling International (HI) and they expect you to have a membership card, available either from your home hostelling organization or buyable on the spot at minimal cost. Specific details of each hostel are given in the guide.

Fincas

Many of Mallorca's old stone **fincas** (farmhouses) have been snaffled up for use as second homes, and some are now leased by the owners to package-tour operators for the whole or part of the season – Individual Traveller's Spain (see p.6) has one of the best selections. Out of the tour operators' main season, these *fincas* often stand idle – ask around the villages of the northwest coast to see if someone's prepared to rent one out informally. At any time of the year, though preferably **well in advance** of your holiday, it's worth approaching the Associació Agroturisme Balear, Avgda Gabriel Alomar i Villalonga 8a–2a, 07006 Palma (☎971 721 508, fax 971 717 317, *agroturismo@mallorcanet.com*), which issues a booklet detailing most of the finest *fincas* and takes bookings. Although some form part of a working farm, others are very luxurious and situated in remote, beautiful spots. They're also not cheap: prices range from 6000ptas/€36.06 to 12,000ptas/€72.12 per person per night, and a minimum length of stay of anything between two nights and two weeks is often stipulated.

Camping

There are two official **campsites** (*càmpings*) on Mallorca: the *Sun Club Picafort*, beside the main road between Port d'Alcúdia and Ca'n Picafort, and the *Club San Pedro* (June to mid–Sept), outside the village of Colònia de Sant Pere, at the east end of the Badia d'Alcúdia (Bay of Alcúdia). Both are Class 1C campsites occupying seaside locations, but whereas the first is well-maintained and smart, the second badly needs an overhaul. Each has about five hundred pitches taking tents, trailer caravans and motor caravans, and a comprehensive range of facilities, including a food shop, laundry room, swimming pool, bicycle and pedalo rental, bars and restaurants and all sorts of sports amenities. *Sun Club Picafort* is very popular and heaves with campers in the summer, when it's best to make a reservation well ahead of time. Prices and specific details of each site are given in the relevant chapters.

Camping rough is legal, but not encouraged, and has various restrictions attached. Spanish regulations state that you're not allowed to camp "in urban areas, areas prohibited for military or touristic reasons, or within 1km of an official campsite". What this means in effect is that you can't camp on resort beaches (though there is some latitude if you're discreet), but you can camp out almost anywhere in the countryside, providing you act sensitively and use some common sense. Whenever possible, ask locally first and/or get the permission of the landowner.

Eating and drinking

Traditional Balearic food, which has much in common with Catalan food, is far from delicate, but its hearty soups and stews, seafood dishes and spiced meats can be delicious. In common with other areas of Spain, this regional cuisine has, after many years of neglect, experienced something of a renaissance, and nowadays restaurants offering *Cuina Mallorquína* are comparatively commonplace and should not be missed. Neither should a visit to one of the islands' many pastry shops (*pastisserias*), where you'll find the sweetest of confections and the Balearics' gastronomic pride and joy, *ensaimadas* (spiralled flaky pastries).

The distinction between **cafés** (or *cafeterias*) and **restaurants** is blurred. Most serve both light snacks and full meals, with the best deals often appearing as the *menú del día* (menu of the day). At either end of the market, however, the differences become more pronounced: in the more expensive restaurants, there is usually a *menú del día*, but the emphasis is on à la carte; by contrast, the least expensive cafés serve up only simple snacks, and in their turn are often indistinguishable from the **bars**, also known as *cellers* or *tavernas*. Before the tourist boom, these snacks always consisted of traditional dishes prepared as either *tapas* (small snacks) or *racions* (larger ones). Today, it's often chips, pizzas and sandwiches, but in Palma there's still a lively

tapas scene, allowing you to move from place to place sampling a wide range of local specialities.

Opening hours vary, but as a general rule cafés and *tapas* bars open from around 9am until at least early in the evening, many until late at night. Restaurants are open from around noon until 2, 3 or sometimes 4pm, before reopening in the evening from around 6 or 7pm until 10 or 11pm. Those restaurants with their eye on the tourist trade often stay open all day and can be relied upon on Sundays, when many local spots close. There's rarely any need to **reserve** a restaurant table in Mallorca – for the few places where it's advisable, we've given the establishment's phone number.

In this section, we've generally given the **Catalan** names for food and drink items, since Catalan is Mallorca's first language. Most restaurants, cafés and bars have **multilingual menus** that include English, but out in the countryside, in the cheaper cafés and restaurants, there may only be a Catalan menu – or maybe no menu at all, in which case the waiter will rattle off the day's dishes in Catalan. Occasionally, though, the menu may be in **Castilian** (ie Spanish), and Castilian is also used or understood by almost all restaurant staff. Bearing all this in mind, we've given Castilian names alongside Catalan ones wherever it's useful.

Breakfast, snacks and sandwiches

For **breakfast** you're best off in a bar or café. Some *hostals* and most hotels will serve a basic "continental" breakfast, but it's generally less expensive and more enjoyable to go out. A traditional Balearic breakfast (or lunch) dish is *pa amb tomàquet* (*pan con tomate* in Castilian) – a massive slice of bread rubbed with tomato, olive oil and garlic, which you can also have topped with ham – washed down with a flagon of wine. *Pa amb oli* (bread rubbed with olive oil) arrives in similar style, but dispenses with the tomato. If that sounds like gastric madness, other breakfast

COMMON FILLINGS FOR BOCADILLOS		
Catalan	**Castilian**	**English**
Butifarra	*Butifarra*	Catalan sausage
Cuixot dolç	*Jamón York*	Cooked ham
Formatge	*Queso*	Cheese
Llom	*Lomo*	Loin of pork
Pernil salat	*Jamón serrano*	Cured ham
Salami	*Salami*	Salami
Salxitxó	*Salchichón*	Sausage
Tonyina	*Atún*	Tuna
Truita	*Tortilla*	Omelette
Xoriç	*Chorizo*	Spicy sausage

standbys are *torradas* (*tostadas*; toasted rolls) with oil or butter and jam, and *xocolata amb xurros* (*chocolate con churros*) – long, fried tubular doughnuts that you dip into thick drinking chocolate. Most places also serve *ou ferrat* (*huevo frito*; fried egg) and cold *truita* (*tortilla*; omelette), both of which make an excellent breakfast.

Coffee and **pastries** (*pastas*), particularly croissants and doughnuts, are available at some bars and cafés, though for a wider selection of cakes you should head for a *pastisseria* (pastry shop) or *forn* (bakery), which have an excellent reputation, as in the rest of Spain. These often sell a wide array of appetizing baked goods besides the obvious bread, croissants and *ensaimadas*. For ordering coffee see p.51.

Some bars specialize in **sandwiches** (*bocadillos*), both hot and cold, and as they're usually outsize affairs in French bread they'll do for breakfast or lunch. In a bar with *tapas* (see below), you can have most of what's on offer put in a sandwich, and you can often get them prepared – or buy the materials to do so – at grocery shops as well. Menorcan cheese (*formatge*) is popular throughout Mallorca; the best is hard with a rind, similar to British cheddar.

Tapas and racions

Tapas are small snacks, three or four chunks of fish, meat or vegetables, cooked in a sauce or served with a dollop of salad, which traditionally used to be provided free with a drink. These days you have to pay for anything more than a few olives, but a single helping rarely costs more than 200–350ptas/€1.20–€2.10 unless you're somewhere very flashy. **Racions** (*raciones* in Castilian)

are bigger portions of the same, served with bread and usually enough in themselves to make a light meal; they cost around 450–650ptas/€2.71–€3.91. (Make it clear when ordering whether you want a *ració* or just a *tapa*.) The more people you're with, of course, the better: half-a-dozen or so different dishes can make a varied and quite filling meal for three or four people.

One of the advantages of eating *tapas* in bars is that you are able to experiment. Most places have food laid out on the counter, so you can see what's available and order by pointing without necessarily knowing the names; others have blackboards (see the lists on p.44).

Cafeterias and restaurants

Regular meals are usually eaten in a *cafeteria* or *restaurant*, though the distinction between the two, particularly at the cheaper end of the market, is often very blurred. In similar fashion, cafeterias blend seamlessly into café-bars and bars, almost all of which serve at least some food. That said, the average price of an average meal in an average establishment does slide down the scale from restaurant to cafeteria to café-bar to bar. At a **cafeteria** offering something like egg, steak or chicken and chips, or *calamars* and salad, a meal will generally cost in the region of 500–900ptas/€3.01–€5.41, excluding drink, whereas the price of a main course at a good quality restaurant averages about 1500ptas/€9.02. Restaurants run from simple formica-table and checked-tablecloth affairs to expense-account palaces. Many have a daily set menu – the **menú del día** – which is usually on

TAPAS AND RACIONS

CATALAN	CASTILIAN	ENGLISH
Anxoves	Boquerones	Anchovies
Bollit	Cocido	Stew
Calamars	Calamares	Squid, usually deep-fried in rings
Calamars amb tinta	Calamares en su tinta	Squid in ink
Cargols	Caracoles	Snails, often served in a spicy/curry sauce
Cargols de mar	Berberechos	Cockles (shellfish)
Calamarins	Chipirones	Whole baby squid
Carn amb salsa	Carne en salsa	Meat in tomato sauce
Croqueta	Croqueta	Fish or chicken croquette
Empanada petita	Empanadilla	Fish or meat pasty
Ensalada russa	Ensaladilla	Russian salad (diced vegetables in mayonnaise)
Escalibada	Escalibada	Aubergine (eggplant) and pepper salad
Faves	Habas	Broad beans
Faves amb cuixot	Habas con jamón	Beans with ham
Fetge	Hígado	Liver
Gambes	Gambas	Prawns
Musclos	Mejillones	Mussels (either steamed, or served with diced tomatoes and onion)
Navallas	Navajas	Razor clams
Olives	Aceitunas	Olives
Ou bollit	Huevo cocido	Hard-boiled egg
Pa amb tomàquet	Pan con tomate	Bread, rubbed with tomato and oil
Patates amb all i oli	Patatas alioli	Potatoes in garlic mayonnaise
Patates cohentes	Patatas bravas	Fried potato cubes with spicy sauce and mayonnaise
Pilotes	Albóndigas	Meatballs, usually in sauce
Pinxo	Pincho moruno	Kebab
Pop	Pulpo	Octopus
Prebes	Pimientos	Sweet (bell) peppers
Ronyons amb xeres	Riñones al jerez	Kidneys in sherry
Sardines	Sardinas	Sardines
Sípia	Sepia	Cuttlefish
Tripa	Callos	Tripe
Truita espanyola	Tortilla española	Potato omelette
Truita francesa	Tortilla francesa	Plain omelette
Tumbet	Tumbet	Pepper, potato, pumpkin and aubergine (eggplant) stew with tomato purée
Xampinyons	Champiñones	Mushrooms, usually fried in garlic
Xoriç	Chorizo	Spicy sausage

offer alongside the à la carte menu, though some of the more basic places might only serve a menú del día. This consists of three or four courses, including bread, wine and service, and usually costs 900–1400ptas/€5.41–€8.41, quite a bit more in glitzy restaurants and at seaside resorts.

In all but the most rock-bottom establishments it's customary to leave a small **tip**; the amount is up to you, though ten to fifteen percent of the bill is sufficient. Service is normally included in a *menú del día*. The other thing to take account of is **IVA**, a sales tax of seven percent, which is either included in the given prices (in which case it should say so on the menu) or added to your bill at the end.

Menu items

In terms of cuisine, *restaurants*, *cafeterias* and bars in Mallorca, especially in the resort areas, are reliant on the tourist industry and many ignore the strong flavours of traditional Balearic and Spanish food for the blandness of pizzas, hamburgers and pastas, or else dish up a hotch-potch of sanitized local favourites such as omelettes, paella and grilled meats. However, there are still plenty of places – highlighted in the guide – where the food is more distinctive and flavoursome. Fresh **fish and seafood** can be excellent, though it's almost always expensive: much of it is imported, despite the local fishing industries around the Balearics and on the Catalan coast. Nevertheless, you're able to get hake, cod (often salted) and squid at very reasonable prices, while fish stews and rice-based *paellas* are often truly memorable. **Meat** can be outstanding too, usually either grilled and served with a few fried potatoes or salad, or – like ham – cured or dried and served as a starter or in sandwiches. Veal is common, served in great stews, while poultry is often mixed with seafood (chicken and prawns) or fruit (chicken/duck with prunes/pears).

Vegetables rarely amount to more than a few chips or boiled potatoes with the main dish, though there are some splendid vegetable concoctions to watch out for, such as *tumbet* (pepper, potato, pumpkin and aubergine/eggplant stew with tomato purée). It's more usual to start your meal with a **salad**, either a standard green or mixed affair, or one of the islands' own salad mixtures, which come garnished with various vegetables, meats and cheeses. **Dessert** in the cheaper places is nearly always fresh **fruit** or *flam*, the local version of *crème caramel*; look out also for *crema catalana*, with a caramelized sugar coating (the Catalan version of *crème brûlée*), and *músic*, dried fruit-and-nut cake.

Vegetarian and vegan options

If you eat fish but not meat you'll relish a stay on Mallorca – the range of seafood is magnificent. The *menú del día* nearly always features a fish dish, and there are plenty of vegetable and egg dishes, as well as fruit, to be going on with. Even out in the country, you'll often find trout on the menu. If you're a **vegetarian**, however, your diet will be a little more limited. Palma has a couple of vegetarian restaurants (see p.100) and most of the resorts are accustomed to having vegetarian guests, but elsewhere the choice isn't so great and is essentially confined to large salads, fried eggs and chips or omelettes.

If you're a **vegan**, you'll no doubt come prepared to cook your own food at least some of the time. However, some restaurant salads and vegetable dishes are vegan – like *espinacs a la Catalana* (spinach, pine nuts and raisins) and *escalivada* (aubergine/eggplant and peppers) – but they're few and far between. Fruit and nuts are widely available, and most pizza restaurants will serve you a vegetarian pizza without cheese: ask for *vegetal sense formatge* (in Castilian, *vegetal sin queso*).

For vegetarian and vegan **shopping**, use the markets – where you can buy ready-cooked lentils and beans, and pasta – or look out for shops marked *Aliments regim* (*dietética* in Castilian), which sell wholefoods, soya milk and desserts, and so on.

If you're a **vegetarian**, try in Catalan *"Sóc vegetarià/ana – es pot menjar alguna cosa sense carn?"* (I'm a vegetarian – is there anything without meat?). In Castilian, that's *"Soy vegetariano/a – hay algo sin carne?"* Alternatively, you may be better understood if you simply resort to the Catalan *"No puc menjar carn"* (I can't eat meat).

Wine

Wine (*vi* in Catalan, *vino* in Castilian) is the invariable accompaniment to every meal and is, as a rule, inexpensive. In bars, cafés and budget restaurants, it may be whatever comes out of the barrel – either red (*negre/tinto*), white (*blanc/blanco*) or rosé (*rosada/rosado*) – or the house bottled special (ask for *vi/vino de la casa*). In a bar, a small glass of wine will generally cost anything from 50ptas/€0.30 to 100ptas/€0.60;

BALEARIC DISHES AND SPECIALITIES

Many of the specialities that follow come from the Balearics' shared history with Catalunya. The more elaborate fish and meat dishes are generally only found in fancier restaurants.

PASTRIES (*PASTAS*)

Cocaroll	Pastry containing vegetables and fish
Ensaimada	Flaky spiral pastry with fillings such as *cabello de ángel* (sweetened citron rind)
Panades sobrasada	Pastry with peas, meat or fish

SOUP (*SOPA*)

Carn d'olla	Mixed meat soup	*Sopas mallorquínas*	Vegetable soup, sometimes with meat and chickpeas (*garbanzos*)
Escudella	Mixed vegetable soup		
Sopa d'all	Garlic soup		

SALAD (*AMANIDA*)

Amanida catalana	Salad with sliced meat and cheese
Escalivada	Aubergine/eggplant, pepper and onion salad
Esqueixada	Dried cod salad with peppers, tomatoes, onions and olives

STARTERS

Entremesos	Starter of mixed meat and cheese
Espinacs a la Catalana	Spinach with raisins and pine nuts
Fideus a la cassola	Baked vermicelli with meat
Llenties guisades	Stewed lentils
Pa amb oli	Bread rubbed with olive oil, eaten with ham, cheese or fruit
Samfaina	Ratatouille-like stew of onions, peppers, aubergine/eggplant and tomato
Truita (d'alls tendres; de xampinyons; de patates)	Omelette/tortilla (with garlic; with mushrooms; with potato). Be sure you're ordering omelette (*tortilla*), not trout (*truita*)!

RICE DISHES

Arròs negre	"Black rice", cooked with squid ink
Arròs a banda	Rice with seafood, the rice served separately
Arròs a la marinera	Paella: rice with seafood and saffron
Paella a la Catalana	Mixed meat and seafood paella, sometimes distinguished from a seafood paella by being called *Paella a Valencia*

MEAT (*CARN*)

Albergínies en es forn	Aubergines/eggplants stuffed with grilled meat
Botifarra amb mongetes	Spicy blood sausage with white beans
Conill (all i oli)	Rabbit (with garlic mayonnaise)
Escaldum	Chicken and potato stew in an almond sauce
Estofat de vedella	Veal stew
Fetge	Liver
Fricandó	Veal casserole

Frito mallorquín	Pigs' offal, potatoes and onions cooked with oil
Mandonguilles	Meatballs, usually in a sauce with peas
Perdius a la vinagreta	Partridge in vinegar gravy
Pollastre (farcit; amb gambas; al cava)	Chicken (stuffed; with prawns; cooked in sparkling wine)
Porc (rostit)	Pork (roast)
Sobrasada	Finely minced pork sausage, flavoured with paprika

FISH (*PEIX*) AND SHELLFISH (*MARISC*)

Bacallà (amb samfaina)	Dried cod (with ratatouille)
Caldereta de llagosta	Lobster stew
Cloïsses	Clams, often steamed
Espinagada de Sa Pobla	Turnover filled with spinach and eel
Greixonera de peix	Menorcan fish stew, cooked in a pottery casserole
Guisat de peix	Fish and shellfish stew
Llagosta (amb pollastre)	Lobster (with chicken in a rich sauce)
Lluç	Hake, either fried or grilled
Musclos al vapor	Steamed mussels
Pop	Octopus
Rap a l'all cremat	Monkfish with creamed garlic sauce
Sarsuela	Fish and shellfish stew
Suquet	Fish casserole
Tonyina	Tuna
Truita	Trout (sometimes stuffed with ham, *a la Navarre*)

SAUCES AND COOKING TERMS

Salsa mahonesa	Mayonnaise
Allioli	Garlic mayonnaise
Salsa romesco	Spicy tomato and wine sauce to accompany fish (from Tarragona)
A la planxa/a la brasa	Grilled
Fregit/frit	Fried
Farcit	Stuffed/rolled
Guisat	Casserole
Rostit	Roast

DESSERTS (*POSTRES*)

Arròs amb llet	Rice pudding
Crema Catalana	Crème caramel, with caramelized sugar topping
Gelat	Ice cream
Mel i mató	Curd cheese and honey
Postres de músic	Cake of dried fruit and nuts
Turrón	Almond fudge
Xurros	Deep-fried doughnut sticks (served with hot chocolate)
Yogur	Yoghurt

Continues over

VEGETABLES *(VERDURES/LLEGUMES)*

Albergínies	Aubergines/Eggplants	*Patates*	Potatoes
Cebes	Onions	*Pèsols*	Peas
Concombre	Cucumber	*Tomàquets*	Tomatoes
Espàrrecs	Asparagus	*Xampinyons*	Mushrooms
Mongetes	Beans	(also *bolets, setes*)	
Pastanagues	Carrots		

FRUIT *(FRUITA)*

Plàtan	Banana	*Poma*	Apple
Maduixes	Strawberries	*Préssec*	Peach
Meló	Melon	*Raïm*	Grapes
Pera	Pear	*Taronja*	Orange
Pinya	Pineapple		

in a restaurant prices start at around 250ptas/€1.50, and even in the poshest of places you'll be able to get a bottle of house wine for under 2000ptas/€12.02. If you're having the *menú del día*, house wine will be included in the price – you'll get a third- to a half-litre per person.

All Mallorca's more expensive restaurants, its supermarkets, and some of the cheaper cafés and restaurants carry a good selection of Spanish wines. The thing to check for is the appellation **Denominació d'Origen (DO)**, which indicates the wine has been passed as being of sufficiently high quality by the industry's watchdog, the Instítuto Nacional de Denominaciónes d'Origen (INDO). Over forty regions of Spain currently carry DO status, including the north central region that produces Spain's most famous and widely distributed red wine, **Rioja**. Even though there's now a profusion of reds being produced all over the country, it's hard to match Rioja for reliability and finesse. The wines are generally made of the *tempranillo* and *garnacha* grapes and are classified according to their age. At one end of the scale, *joven* indicates a young, inexpensive, straightforward wine which has spent no time in wood. Wines labelled *con crianza* (with breeding) or *reserva* have received respectively moderate and generous ageing in oak casks and in the bottle. At the top of the scale, in both price and quality, are the *gran reserva* wines, which are only produced in the best years and which have to spend at least two years in the

cask followed by three in the bottle before being offered for sale. The names to look for in red Rioja include **Martínez-Bujanda**, **Tondonia** and **Monte Real**.

The region of **Navarra** also produces excellent wine using similar techniques and grape varieties at a fraction of the price of Rioja. The labels to watch for here are **Chivite** and **Señorío de Sarría**. Around Barcelona, the region of **Penedès** was long renowned for its heavy and coarse red wines, responsible for countless hangovers. These days, things have improved and the produce of firms like **Torres** and **Masía Bach** have already established a solid reputation. Nevertheless, it's the reds of the **Ribera del Duero** region, 120km north of Madrid, which have attracted most recent attention, with wines such as **Protos**, **Viña Pedrosa** and **Pesquera** offering the smooth integration of fruit and oak that is the hallmark of good Spanish wine.

Spain's **white wines** have not enjoyed the same reputation as the reds. Traditionally, they tended to be highly alcoholic and over-oaked. Spain's best white, the **Rioja Blanca** made by **Marqués de Murrieta**, descends from this tradition, but it offers a smooth-tasting marriage of oak and lemony fruit. The demands of the export market have recently led to new approaches to white wine-making, and the result has been clean, fruity and dry wines that tend to be competent rather than memorable. The best of this style has to be **Marqués de Riscal Blanco** from Rueda, just south of Valladolid.

SOME COMMON CATALAN AND CASTILIAN FOOD TERMS

CATALAN	CASTILIAN	ENGLISH
Pa	Pan	Bread
Mantega	Mantequilla	Butter
Formatge	Queso	Cheese
Ous	Huevos	Eggs
Oli	Aceite	Oil
Pebre	Pimienta	Pepper
Sal	Sal	Salt
Sucre	Azúcar	Sugar
Vinagre	Vinagre	Vinegar
All	Ajo	Garlic
Arròs	Arroz	Rice
Fruita	Fruta	Fruit
Verdures/Llegumos	Verduras/Legumbres	Vegetables
Esmorzar	Desayunar	to have breakfast
Dinar	Almorzar	to have lunch
Sopar	Cenar	to have dinner
Menú	Carta	Menu
Ampolla	Botella	Bottle
Got	Vaso	Glass
Forquilla	Tenedor	Fork
Ganivet	Cuchillo	Knife
Cullera	Cuchara	Spoon
Taula	Mesa	Table
El compte	La cuenta	The bill/check

Spain's growing reputation for **sparkling wine** has been built on the performance of two producers, Freixenet and Codorniú, which hail from a small area west of Barcelona. Local grape varieties are used and the best examples, known as **cava**, are made by the same double-fermentation process as is used in champagne production.

Drinking

You'll do most of your everyday **drinking** – from morning coffee to nightcap – in a **bar** or **café** (between which there's little difference). Very often, you'll eat in here too, or at least snack on some *tapas*. Bars situated in old wine cellars are sometimes called *cellers* or *tavernas*; a *bodega* traditionally specializes in wine. In Palma you also have the choice of drinking in rather more salubrious surroundings in the so-called *bars modernos* – designer bars, for want of a better

description. Some of these are extraordinarily chic and stylish, sights in their own right, but their drinks are invariably expensive. Locals hang out for hours while imbibing very little.

Bar **opening hours** are difficult to pin down, but you should have little trouble in getting a drink somewhere in Palma until 2am or perhaps 3am. Elsewhere you're OK until at least 11pm, sometimes midnight. The islands' nightclubs tend to close by 2am or 3am. Some bars close on Sundays and don't expect much to be happening in the resorts out of season.

Sherry, brandy, gin and beer

Fortified wines and spirits in the Balearics are those you can find throughout Spain. The classic Andalucian wine, **sherry** – *vino de Jerez* – is served chilled or at room temperature, a perfect drink to wash down *tapas*. The main distinctions are between *fino* or *jerez seco* (dry sherry),

MALLORCAN WINE

Wine production has flourished in the Balearics since classical times. In the nineteenth century, sweet "Malvasia" – wine similar to Madeira – was exported in great quantity, until the vineyards were devastated by **phylloxera**, whose root-eating activities changed the course of Spanish wine history in the late nineteenth century. The small yellow phylloxera aphid, about 1mm long, was indigenous to eastern North America. It first appeared in Spain in 1878, carried either in soil or on agricultural tools and footwear, and in the space of twenty years it destroyed Spain's existing vine stock and made thousands bankrupt. Indeed, vine cultivation never re-established itself on Ibiza or Menorca, and, with the best will in the world, Mallorcan wines, produced from newly imported vines, were long regarded as being of only average quality.

In the last few years, however, a concerted effort has been made to raise the standards of Mallorcan wine-making, driven on one side by the tourist industry and on the other by the realization among local producers that the way forward lay in exporting wine that matched international standards. This meant new methods and new equipment. Mallorca's leading wine is **Binissalem**, from around the eponymous village northeast of Palma. Following vigorous local campaigning, it was justifiably awarded its Denominació d'Origen credentials in 1991.

Red Binissalem is a robust and aromatic wine made predominantly of the local *mantonegro* grape. It is not unlike Rioja, but it has a distinctly local character, suggesting cocoa and strawberries. The best producer of the wine is **Franja Roja**, who make the **José Ferrer** brand – well worth looking out for, with prices starting at around 350ptas/€2.10 per bottle, or 1200ptas/€7.21 for the superior varieties. Red Binissalem is widely available throughout Mallorca, and the Franja Roja Bodega, c/Conquistador 103, Binissalem, welcomes visitors by prior appointment (☎971 511 050).

White and rosé Binissalem struggle to reach the same standard as the red. However, the **Binissalem Blanco** made by **Herederos de Ribas** is a lively and fruity white that goes well with fish. Also around the island are various country wineries making inexpensive and unpretentious wine predominantly for local consumption, such as the **Muscat Miguel Oliver** or the **Celler Son Calo**. The best places to sample these local, coarser wines is in the *cellers* and bars of the country towns of the interior – we've recommended several in the guide.

If you're visiting in late September, you can catch Binissalem's **Festival of the Grape Harvest** (Festa d'es Verema), which takes place during the week leading up to the last Sunday of the month. Saturday is the best day, with a procession of decorated floats and a good deal of free wine. On a more sedate level, Palma's **Food Week** (Setmana de Cuina Mallorquína) takes place in the middle of May all over the centre of town, with stalls featuring the cuisine and wine of the island.

The best selection of wines in Mallorca is at Palma's **El Centro del Vino y del Cava**, c/Bartomeu Rossello-Porcel 19 (☎971 452 990).

---

amontillado (medium), and *oloroso* or *jerez dulce* (sweet), and these are the terms you should use to order. In mid-afternoon – or even at breakfast – many islanders take a *copa* of **liqueur** with their coffee. The best, certainly to put *in* your coffee, is **coñac**, excellent Spanish brandy, mostly from the south and often deceptively smooth. If you want a brandy from Mallorca, try the mellow, hard-hitting Suau, and from Catalunya, look for Torres. Other good brands include Magno, Veterano and Soberano. Most other spirits are ordered by brand name, too, since there are generally cheaper Spanish equivalents for standard imports. Larios **gin** from Málaga, for instance, is about half the price of Gordons, but around two-thirds the strength and a good deal rougher. The

Menorcans, who learnt the art of gin-making from the British, still produce their own versions, in particular the waspish Xoriguer. Always specify *nacional* to avoid getting an expensive foreign brand.

Almost any **mixed drink** seems to be collectively known as a *cuba Libre* or *cubata*, though strictly speaking this should refer only to rum and Coke. For mixers, ask for orange juice (*suc de taronja* in Catalan), lemon (*llimona*) or tonic (*tònica*).

Cervesa, pilsner-type beer (more usually seen in Castilian as *cerveza*), is generally pretty good, though more expensive than wine. The two main brands you'll see everywhere are San Miguel and Estrella, though keep an eye out in Palma for draught *cerveza negra* – black fizzy beer with a bitter taste. Beer generally comes in 300ml bottles or, for a little bit more money, on tap: a small glass of draught beer is a *cana*, a larger glass a *cana gran*. Equally refreshing, though often deceptively strong, is **sangría**, a wine-and-fruit punch which you'll come across at *festas* and in tourist resorts.

Soft drinks

Soft drinks are much the same as anywhere in the world, but one local favourite to try is *orxata* (*horchata* in Castilian) – a cold milky drink made from tiger nuts. Also, be sure to try a *granissat*, or iced fruit-squash; popular flavours are *granissat de llimona* or *granissat de café*. You can get these drinks from **orxaterias** and from **gelaterias** (ice cream parlours; *heladerías* in Castilian).

Although you can drink the **water** almost everywhere, it usually tastes better out of the bottle. Inexpensive *aigua mineral* comes either sparkling (*amb gas*) or still (*sense gas*).

Coffee and tea

Coffee – served in cafés, bars and restaurants – is invariably espresso, slightly bitter and, unless you specify otherwise, served black (*café sol*). A slightly weaker large black coffee is called a *café americano*. If you want it white ask for *café cortado* (small cup with a drop of milk) or *café amb llet* (*café con leche* in Castilian) made with hot milk. For a large cup ask for a *gran*. Black coffee is also frequently mixed with brandy, cognac or whisky, all such concoctions termed *carajillo*; a liqueur mixed with white coffee is a *trifásico*. **Decaffeinated** coffee (*descafeinat*) is increasingly available, though in fairly undistinguished sachet form.

Tea (*te*) comes without milk unless you ask for it, and is often weak and insipid. If you do ask for milk, chances are it'll be hot and UHT, so your tea isn't going to taste much like the real thing. Better are the **infusions** that you can get in most bars, such as mint (*menta*), camomile (*camamilla*) and lime (*tiller*).

DRINKS

CATALAN	CASTILIAN	ENGLISH
	ALCOHOL	
Cervesa	*Cerveza*	Beer
Vi	*Vino*	Wine
Xampan/Cava	*Champán/Cava*	Champagne/Sparkling wine
	HOT DRINKS	
Café	*Café*	Coffee
Café sol	*Café solo*	Espresso
Café amb llet	*Café con leche*	White coffee
Descafeinat	*Descafeinado*	Decaff
Te	*Té*	Tea
Xocolata	*Chocolate*	Drinking chocolate
	SOFT DRINKS	
Aigua	*Agua*	Water
Aigua mineral	*Agua mineral*	Mineral water
(amb gas)	*(con gas)*	(sparkling)
(sense gas)	*(sin gas)*	(still)
Llet	*Leche*	Milk
Suc	*Zumo*	Juice
Orxata	*Horchata*	Tiger nut drink

Post, phones and email

The Spanish postal system is efficient if not especially speedy, and there are post boxes liberally distributed across the island. Public phone booths are common too, though you may have to hunt around a bit in the smaller villages. Cybercafés are a rarity.

Post

There are **post offices** (*correus*) in every town in Mallorca and many of the villages, the majority handily located on or near the main square. Opening hours are usually Monday to Friday 9am–2pm, though the main post office in Palma is open through the afternoon and on Saturday mornings too. All post offices close on public holidays.

Outbound post is slow but reasonably reliable, with letters or cards taking a week or ten days to reach Britain and Ireland, up to two weeks to North America, and about three weeks to Australasia. You can buy **stamps** (*segells*) at tobacconists (look for the brown and yellow *tabac* or *tabacos* sign) and at scores of souvenir shops as well as at post offices. Post boxes are yellow, and on those where you have a choice of slots, pick the flap marked *províncies i estranger* or *altres destinos*. Postal rates are inexpensive, with postcards and small letters attracting two tariffs: one to anywhere in Europe; the other worldwide.

Inbound post is fairly reliable. You can send letters to any post office by addressing them "Poste Restante", followed by the surname of the addressee (preferably underlined and in capitals), and then the name of the town followed by "Mallorca, Spain". To collect, take along your passport or identity card. If you're expecting post and your first enquiry produces nothing, ask the clerk to check under all of your names: letters are often filed under first or middle names.

Phones

You can make domestic and international **phone** calls with equal ease from Spanish public phones, which generally work well. Alternatively, many bars have pay phones for public use. Most hotel rooms have phones, though there's always an exorbitant surcharge for their use.

The majority of public phones take coins, credit cards and phonecards, which are available in several denominations, from 1000ptas/€6.01 upwards, from most newsagents and tobacconists. Most public phones display instructions in several languages including English along with a list of Spanish area codes and some international country codes. Mallorca's Yellow Pages is a useful source of information and includes an introductory section and index in English. Within Spain, the **ringing tone** is long, whereas **engaged** (busy) is shorter and rapid. On pickup, the standard Spanish response to a call is to the point: *digáme* (speak to me).

For international calls on a coin-phone, you're best off shovelling in at least 300ptas/€1.80 to ensure a connection – and make sure you have a good stock of coins on hand if you're intending to have a conversation of any length.

International and domestic **rates** are slightly cheaper after 10pm and before 8am, and after 2pm on Saturday and all day Sunday. Precise costs are detailed in the Yellow Pages. Making a **collect** or **reverse-charge call** (*cobro revertido*) can be a bit of a hassle, especially if your Spanish – the language in which the phone company conducts its business – is poor. It's

PHONING TO AND FROM MALLORCA

Spanish phone numbers no longer have area codes – all nine digits must be dialled, even when calling within the same area. All Mallorca phone numbers begin with ☎971, but this is not an area code; it's an inseparable part of the complete nine-digit number.

USEFUL TELEPHONE NUMBERS

Directory enquiries ☎003 European operator ☎008 International operator ☎025

PHONING ABROAD FROM MALLORCA

Dial the international access code 00 followed by:

– to the UK: 44, then area code (minus the 0) then number.

– to Ireland: 353, then area code (minus the 0) then number.

– to the US or Canada: 1, then area code, then number.

– to Australia: 61, then area code (minus the 0), then number.

– to New Zealand: 64, then area code (minus the 0), then number.

PHONING MALLORCA FROM ABROAD

Dial your international access code:

– from the UK, Ireland or New Zealand: 00

– from the US or Canada: 011

– from Australia: 0011

Then dial **34 for Spain**, followed by the nine-digit number.

best to call the international operator for advice on ☎025.

If you have a **mobile phone**, it's worth asking your supplier if it can be used in Mallorca – most British BT Cellnet phones, for example, provide good coverage – and be sure to get them to lift the international bar code (if there is one) before your trip.

Email

Sending and receiving your **email** on Mallorca is becoming increasingly easy. In Palma and several of the larger resorts there are internet cafés of some description and many of the more expensive hotels have facilities to connect in their rooms. We've given addresses of internet cafés in the guide where appropriate.

The Media

English-language newspapers and magazines are widely available in Mallorca, and most hotel (if not *hostal*) rooms have satellite TV.

Newspapers and magazines

British and other European newspapers, as well as *USA Today* and the *International Herald Tribune*, are all widely available in the resort areas and larger towns of Mallorca. These are supplemented by a ragbag of locally produced English papers and journals, the most informative of them being the *Majorca Daily Bulletin*.

Of the **Spanish newspapers**, the best two are *El País* – liberal, and the only one with much serious analysis or foreign news coverage – and its rival, *El Mundo*, a left-of-centre broadsheet. Other national papers include *ABC*, solidly elitist with a hard moral line against abortion and divorce, and the equally conservative *La Vanguardia*. Printed in Catalan, *Avui* is the chief nationalist paper, but its main competitor, the Catalan *El Diari de Barcelona*, is more liberal. On the Balearics, there are several rather modest local papers, of which *Ultima Hora* and *Diario de Mallorca* are the most substantial.

Amongst a plethora of glossy **magazines**, Spain's most interesting offering is *Ajo Blanco*, a monthly from Barcelona with an eclectic mix of politics, culture and style. The more arty and indulgent *El Europeo*, a massive quarterly publication from Madrid, can also be worth a browse.

And, of course, Spain is the home of *Hola* – the original of *Hello*.

TV and radio

In general, Spaniards love their **TV** and consequently you'll catch more of it than you might expect sitting in bars and cafés. On the whole it's hardly riveting stuff, the bulk being a mildly entertaining mixture of kitsch game shows and foreign-language films and TV series dubbed into Spanish. Soaps are a particular speciality, either South American *culebrones* ("serpents" – they go on and on), which take up most of the daytime programming, or well-travelled British or Australian exports, like *EastEnders* (*Gent del Barri*) and *Neighbours* (*Veins*). Sports fans are well catered for, with regular live coverage of football (soccer) and basketball matches; in the football season, you can watch one or two live matches a week in many bars. The number of TV stations is increasing all the time, but the two main national channels are TVE1 and TVE2, and you'll also spot the Catalan TVE3 and Canal 33.

BBC World Service radio broadcasts in English virtually 24 hours a day on 648kHz medium wave. It also broadcasts on short wave, on 3.955, 6.195, 9.410 and 12.095MHz, among others. The *Majorca Daily Bulletin* and other local English newspapers detail the BBC's frequencies and broadcasting schedules.

Opening hours and public holidays

Although there's been some movement towards a northern European working day in Mallorca – especially in Palma and the major tourist resorts – most shops and offices still close for a siesta of at least two hours in the hottest part of the afternoon. There's a lot of variability, but basic working hours are generally Mon–Fri 9am–1pm & 4–7pm, Sat 9am–1pm; notable exceptions are the extended hours operated by the largest department stores, some important tourist attractions and most tourist/souvenir shops.

Museums and churches

Almost without exception, **museums** take a siesta, closing between 1pm and 3pm, while many close on Mondays and some on Saturdays and Sundays too. Don't be surprised if the official opening times of the less-visited museums are disregarded. Admission charges are usually in the region of 300ptas/€1.80, irrespective of the size of the collection or the quality of the exhibits.

Palma Cathedral, arguably Mallorca's key sight, attracts an entrance fee of 500ptas/€3.01, but other **churches** are almost always free. They gen-

erally open every weekday and sometimes at the weekend, but nearly all close for a two- or three-hour siesta. That said, the less significant churches are often kept locked, opening (if at all) only for worship in the early morning and/or the evening (around 6–9pm). In these cases, either time your visit to coincide with the Mass, or find someone with a key. This is not as difficult as it sounds, since a sacristan or custodian almost always lives nearby, and someone will know where to direct you. You're often expected to give a small donation.

Public holidays

Public holidays – as well as scores of local festivals (see box on p.57) – may well disrupt your travel plans at some stage. There are ten Spanish national holidays each year and these are supplemented by, in Mallorca, five more holidays. The island's resorts are generally oblivious to public holidays, but elsewhere almost all businesses and shops close, and it can prove difficult to find a room. Similarly, vacant seats on planes and buses (which are in any case reduced to a skeleton service) are at a premium.

PUBLIC HOLIDAYS	
January 1	New Year's Day (*Año Nuevo*)
January 6	Epiphany (*Reyes Magos*)
March 19	St Joseph's Day (*Sant Josep*)
Good Friday	(Castilian *Viernes Santo*; Catalan *Divendres Sant*)
May 1	Labour Day (*Día del Trabajo*)
Corpus Christi	(early or mid-June)
June 24	St John's Day (*Sant Joan*, King Juan Carlos's name-day)
June 29	St Peter and St Paul (*Sant Pere i Sant Pau*)
July 25	St James's Day (*Santiago*)
August 15	Assumption of the Virgin (*Asunción*)
October 12	Discovery of America Day (*Día de la Hispanidad*)
November 1	All Saints (*Todos los Santos*)
December 6	Constitution Day (*Día de la Constitución*)
December 8	Immaculate Conception (*Inmaculada Concepción*)
December 25	Christmas Day (Castilian *Navidad*; Catalan *Nadal*)

Festivals, the bullfight and football

It's hard to beat the experience of arriving in a town to discover the streets decked out with flags and streamers, a band playing in the square and the entire population out celebrating the local *festa* (in Castilian, *fiesta*). Everywhere in Mallorca takes at least one day off a year to devote to partying. Usually it's the local saint's day, but there are celebrations, too, of harvests, deliverance from the Moors, of safe return from the sea – any excuse will do.

Each festival is different, with a particular local emphasis, but there is always music, dancing, traditional costume and an immense spirit of enjoyment. The main event of most *festas* is a parade, either behind a revered holy image or a more celebratory affair with fancy costumes and *gigantones*, giant carnival figures that rumble down the streets to the delight, or terror, of children.

Although these *festas* take place throughout the year – and it's often the obscure and unexpected event which proves to be most fun – **Holy Week** (*Setmana Santa*) stands out, its passing celebrated in many places with magnificent processions.

The box opposite gives the highlights of Mallorca's festival year. For information about less prominent festivals, try local tourist offices. Remember that although outsiders are nearly always welcome at a *festa*, you will have difficulty finding a room, and should try to book your accommodation well in advance.

The bullfight

In recent years the popularity of the **bullfight** (*los toros*) has declined across Spain, though it was never as big a deal in Catalunya and the Balearics as elsewhere. Yet Mallorca does have two main rings – one in Palma, the other in Muro – which still attract large crowds. The spectators turn up to see the *matadores* dispatch the bulls cleanly and with "artistic merit", which they greet with thunderous applause and the waving of handkerchiefs. A prolonged and messy kill will get the audience whistling in derision. Some Spaniards do, of course, object to the whole spectacle, but opposition is not widespread and if Spaniards tell you that bullfighting is controversial, they are more likely to be referring to new refinements to the "sport", especially the widespread but illegal shaving down of bulls' horns. The horns are as sensitive as fingernails a few millimetres in, and paring them down deters the animals from charging and affects their balance, thereby reducing the danger to the *matador*.

Whether you attend a bullfight, obviously, is down to you. If you spend any time in Mallorca during the season (there are eight or nine bullfights between March and October), you may well encounter *los toros* on a bar TV, and that will probably make up your mind. Many neutrals are particularly offended by the use of horses: padded up for protection, the horses are repeatedly charged by the bulls, which clearly terrifies them – though they can't make their feelings heard as their vocal chords have been cut out.

Each highly stylized bullfighting programme, or **corrida**, begins with a procession to the accompaniment of a *paso doble* by the band. Leading the procession are two *algauziles* or "constables", on horseback and in traditional costume,

MALLORCA'S FESTIVAL CALENDAR

JANUARY

16 The *Revetla de Sant Antoni Abat* (Eve of St Antony's Day) is celebrated by the lighting of bonfires (*foguerons*) in Palma and several of Mallorca's villages – especially Sa Pobla and Muro, where the inhabitants move from fire to fire, dancing round in fancy dress and eating *espinagades*, traditional eel and vegetable patties.

17 *Beneides de Sant Antoni* (Blessing of St Antony). St Antony's feast day is marked by processions in many of Mallorca's country towns, notably Sa Pobla and Artà, with farmyard animals herded through the streets to receive the saint's blessing and protection against disease.

19 *Revetla de Sant Sebastià*. Palma has more bonfires, singing and dancing for St Sebastian.

20 *Festa de Sant Sebastià*. This feast day is celebrated in Pollença with a procession led by a holy banner (*estenard*) picturing the saint. It's accompanied by *cavallets* (literally "merry-go-rounds"), two young dancers each wearing a cardboard horse and imitating the animal's walk. You'll see *cavallets*, which are of medieval origin, at many of the island's festivals.

FEBRUARY

Carnaval Towns and villages throughout the island live it up during the week before Lent with marches and fancy dress parades. The biggest and liveliest are in Palma, where the shindig is known as *Sa Rua* (the Cavalcade).

MARCH/APRIL

Setmana Santa (Holy Week) is as widely observed as it is everywhere else in Spain. On **Maundy Thursday** in Palma, a much venerated icon of the crucified Christ, *La Sang*, is taken from the eponymous church on the Plaça del Hospital (off La Rambla) and taken in procession through the city streets. There are also solemn **Good Friday** (*Divendres Sant*) processions in many towns and villages, with the more important taking place in Palma and Sineu. Most holy of all, however, is the Good Friday *Davallament* (The Lowering), the culmination of Holy Week in Pollença. Here, in total silence and by torchlight, the inhabitants lower a figure of Christ down from the hilltop Oratori to the church of Nostra Senyora dels Àngels. During Holy Week there are also many *romerias* (pilgrimages) to the island's holy places, with one of the most popular being the climb up to the Ermita Santa Magdalena, near Inca. The Monestir de Lluc, which possesses Mallorca's most venerated shrine, is another religious focus during this time, with the penitential trudging round its Camí dels Misteris del Rosari (The Way of the Mysteries of the Rosary).

MID-MAY

The *Festa de Nostra Senyora de la Victòria* in Port de Sóller features mock battles between Christians and infidels in commemoration of the thrashing of a band of Arab pirates in 1561. Lots of booze and firing of antique rifles into the air.

JUNE

Corpus Christi At noon in the main square of Pollença an ancient and curious dance of uncertain provenance takes place – the *Ball de les Àguiles* (Dance of the Eagles) – followed by a religious procession.

JULY

15–16 *Día de Virgen de Carmen*. The day of the patron saint of seafarers and fishermen is celebrated in many coastal settlements – principally Palma, Port de Sóller, Colònia de Sant Pere, Porto Colom and Cala Rajada – with parades and the blessing of boats.

Last Sunday The *Festa de Sant Jaume* in Alcúdia celebrates the feast day of St James with a popular religious procession followed by all sorts of fun and games – folk dances, fireworks and the like.

AUGUST

2 *Mare de Déu dels Àngels*. Moors and Christians battle it out again, this time in Pollença.

20 *Cavallet* (see above) dances in Felanitx.

Continues over

Throughout August International Festival at Pollença, including art and sculpture exhibitions and chamber music.

SEPTEMBER

Second week In Alaró, the *Nativitat de Nostra Senyora* (Nativity of the Virgin) is honoured by a pilgrimage to a hilltop shrine near the Castell d'Alaró.

OCTOBER

Third Sunday *Festa d'es Butifarra* (Sausage

Festival). Of recent origins, this festival follows on from tractor and automobile contests held in the village of Sant Joan. It features folk dancing and traditional music as well as the eating of specially prepared vegetable pies (*coca amb trampó*) and sausages (*berenada de butifarra*).

DECEMBER

Christmas (*Nadal*) is especially picturesque in Palma, where there are Nativity plays in the days leading up to the 25th.

followed by the three *matadores*, who will each fight two bulls, and their personal teams, each comprising two mounted assistants – *picadores* – and three *banderilleros*. At the back are the mule teams who will drag off the dead bulls. The picadores stab pikes into the beast's withers to soften it up and the process is continued by the *banderilleros*, who stick beribboned and sharpened sticks into the bull in preparation for the *matador*, who kills the animal off.

Tickets for *corridas* cost 2000ptas/€12.02 and up – much more for the prime seats and prestigious fights. The cheapest seats are *gradas*, the highest rows at the back, from where you can see everything that happens without too much of the detail; the front rows are known as the *barreras*. Seats are also divided into *sol* (sun), *sombra* (shade) and *sol y sombra* (shaded after a while), though these distinctions have become less relevant as more and more bullfights start later in the day, at 6pm or 7pm, rather than the traditional 5pm. The *sombra* seats are more expensive, not so much for the spectators' personal comfort as for the fact that most of the action takes place in the shade. On the way in, you can rent **cushions**: two hours sitting on concrete is not much fun. Beer and soft drinks are sold inside.

If you want to know more about the **opposition to bullfighting**, contact Spain's Anti-Bullfight Campaign, *ABC International*, c/Bailén 164, local 2 interior, 08037 Barcelona (*www.intercom.es/adda*).

Football

To foreigners, the bullfight is easily the most celebrated of Spain's spectacles. In terms of popular support in modern Spain, however, it ranks far below **fútbol** (football/soccer). For many years, the country's two dominant teams have been Real Madrid and FC Barcelona, and these have shared the League title and Cup honours with repetitive regularity. Both teams are in Division 1 – *la Primera Liga* – of Spain's four-division League (Divisions 1, 2A, 2B and 3), and play alongside the excellent Palma-based Real Club Deportivo Mallorca. **Real Mallorca**, as they're known (☎971 221 221, *www.rcdmallorca.es*), are easily the Balearics' best team, winning the Spanish Cup in 1998, finishing third in the Primera Liga in 1999 and progressing the same year to the final of the European Cup Winners' Cup – which they lost after a late goal 2-1 to Italian club Lazio. They're still riding high, and boast a hefty complement of exciting world-class players. They play in the Son Moix stadium, just to the north of Palma city centre beyond the Via Cintura on Camí dels Reis, and a visit to a match is good fun, the crowd noisy, enthusiastic and usually good-humoured. The season runs from early September to April with a short Christmas break; most matches are on Sunday afternoons, and tickets, which are available at the turnstiles, cost between 3000ptas/€18.03 and 9000ptas/€54.09. A good way behind Real Mallorca, in Division 3, come **Atlético Baleares**, who are also based in Palma and play in the Estadi Baleares, near the Via Cintura.

Trouble, the police and sexual harassment

Many northern European expatriates love Mallorca for its lack of crime – with good reason. In the island's villages and small towns petty crime is unusual, and serious offences, from burglary to assault and beyond, extremely rare. Of the three larger towns, only Palma presents any problems, mostly low-key stuff such as the occasional fight and minor theft; commonsense precautions are normally enough to keep you out of any trouble.

However, you should also be aware that some of the late-night bars of the seedier resorts are commonly colonized by noisy and aggressive male tourists. In this regard, S'Arenal and Magaluf have the worst reputations, but it's more a question of which bar you're in, rather than the resort you're staying at. If you've accidentally dropped into a rough house, get out while the going is good.

If for some reason you do have dealings with the Spanish police, remember that, although they are polite enough in the normal course of events, they can be extremely unpleasant if you get on the wrong side of them. At all times, keep your cool.

Avoiding trouble

Almost all the problems tourists encounter in the Balearics are to do with **petty crime** – pickpocketing and bag-snatching – rather than more serious physical confrontations, so it's as well to be on your guard and know where your possessions are at all times. Sensible **precautions** include: carrying bags slung across your neck and not over your shoulder; not carrying anything in pockets that are easy to dip into; making photocopies of your passport, airline ticket and driving licence; leaving passports and tickets in the hotel safe; and noting down travellers' cheque and credit card numbers. When you're **looking for a hotel room**, never leave your bags unattended. If you have a **car**, don't leave anything in view when you park. Vehicles are rarely stolen, but luggage and valuables left in cars do make a tempting target. At **night** in Palma, avoid unlit streets, don't go out brimming with valuables, and try not to appear hopelessly lost.

Thieves often work in pairs and, although theft is far from rife on Mallorca, you should be aware of certain **ploys**, such as: the "helpful" person pointing out "birdshit" (shaving cream or something similar) on your jacket, while someone else relieves you of your money; the card or note you're invited to read on the street to distract your attention; the move by someone in a café for your drink with one hand (the other hand is in your bag as you react to save your drink); and if you're studying postcards or papers at stalls, watch out for people standing unusually close.

What to do if you're robbed

If you're robbed, you need to **go to the police** to report it, not least because your insurance company will require a police report. Don't expect a great deal of concern if your loss is relatively small – and expect the process of completing forms and formalities to take ages. In the unlikely event that you're **mugged** or otherwise threatened, *never* resist, and try to reduce your contact with the robber to a minimum. Either just hand over what's wanted, or throw money in one direction and take off in the other. Afterwards, go straight to the police, who will be more sympathetic and helpful on these occasions – tourism is, after all, the islands' economic lifeblood. Many police officers speak English.

The police

General Franco created a **police force** of labyrinthine complexity and since his death political parties of all persuasions have dodged the fundamental reorganization that is really needed. The reason is simple: no one wants to take them on.

There are three main types of police in Spain: the Guardia Civil, the Policía Nacional and the Policía Municipal, all of them armed. Dressed in green uniforms, the **Guardia Civil** police the highways and the countryside, but they are generally regarded as being officious and best avoided. Even now, many Spaniards are deeply suspicious of them, remembering their enthusiastic support of Franco and the unsuccessful coup led by one of their colonels, Tejero, when he held the parliament hostage in February 1981. They have, however, had their sails trimmed in recent years – improbably, they've even assumed some environmental responsibilities – and the loathed tricorn hat has been abandoned except for ceremonial occasions. In fairness, the Guardia Civil have attempted to improve their image, launching what (almost) amounts to a charm offensive; recent tourists' reports of their attitude have been favourable. A second police force, the brown-uniformed **Policía Nacional**, have made a better fist of the transition to democracy despite their disagreeable origins as Franco's brutal security police, the Policía Armada; they were even instrumental in Tejero's failure. They are mainly seen in Palma, armed with submachine guns and guarding key installations or personnel. They are also used to control crowds and demonstrations and – despite their democratic credentials – are not known for their sensitivity. Consequently, if you do need the police, and above all if you're reporting a serious crime, you're usually better off seeking out the more sympathetic **Policía Municipal**, who wear blue uniforms. The problem is that this force only operates in the towns, and so in the countryside you'll usually have no choice but to throw yourself on the tender mercies of the Guardia Civil, who are inclined to resent the suggestion that any crime exists on their turf. Indeed, you may end up feeling as if you're the one who stands accused.

Offences

Should you be **arrested** on any charge, you have the right to contact your consulate in Palma (see p.23 for the addresses). Unfortunately, many consulates are notoriously reluctant to get involved, though most are required to assist you to some degree if you have had your passport stolen or lost all your money. If you've been detained for a drugs offence, don't expect any sympathy or help. You also ought to be aware of a couple of **offences** that you might commit unwittingly.

In theory, you're supposed to carry some kind of **identification** at all times, and the police can stop you in the streets and demand it. In practice they're rarely bothered if you're clearly a foreigner.

Nude bathing or **unauthorized camping** (see p.41) are activities more likely to bring you into contact with officialdom, though a warning to cover up or move on is more likely than any real confrontation. Topless tanning is commonplace at all the resorts, but in country areas, where attitudes are more traditional, you should take care not to upset local sensibilities.

Sexual harassment

Spain's macho image has faded in the post-Franco years and these days there are few parts of Mallorca where foreign women, travelling alone, are likely to feel threatened, intimidated, or attract unwanted attention. The tendency of Spaniards to move around in mixed crowds, filling central bars, clubs and streets late into the night, also helps to make you feel less exposed. If you are in any doubt as to your safety, flag down a taxi (there are plenty of them) and escape.

The major tourist **resorts** have their own artificial holiday culture, which has much to do with sex. The men (of all nationalities) who hang around in nightclubs and bars here pose a no greater or lesser threat than similar operators at home, though the language barrier makes it harder to know who to trust. Amongst Spaniards, "*déjame en paz*" (leave me alone) is a fairly standard rebuff.

The **remoter parts** of the island's interior can pose problems for women too. In some areas you can walk for hours without seeing a soul or coming across an inhabited farm or house. It's rare that this poses a threat — help and hospitality are much more the norm — but you are certainly more vulnerable and local men are less accustomed to women being on their own.

Finding work

Unless you've some particular skill and have applied for a job advertised in your home country, the only real chance of long-term work in Mallorca is in language schools. However, there is much less work about than in the boom years of the early 1980s — schools are contracting rather than expanding — and you'll need to persevere if you're to come up with a rewarding position. To give yourself any kind of chance, you'll need some sort of recognized qualification, like a TEFL (Teaching English as a Foreign Language) or ESL (English as a Second Language) certificate.

Teaching and language work

Finding a **teaching** job is mainly a question of pacing the streets, stopping in at every language school around and asking about vacancies. For the addresses of schools, look in the Yellow Pages under *academias*. The best time to try is in the second half of September when the schools know how many replacement teachers they need. Reputable schools will require you to have undergone at least a one-month intensive teacher training course and to give a demonstration lesson. If you intend to stay in Mallorca for any length of time, you'll need a *permiso de residencia* — see "Visas and red tape" p.22.

Other options are to try advertising **private lessons** (better paid, but harder to make a living at) in the local press or, if you speak good Spanish, **translation work**, most of which will be business correspondence — look in the Yellow Pages under *traducciones*. If you intend doing translation work, you'll usually need access to a PC and a fax machine.

Temporary work

If you're looking for **temporary work**, the best chances are in the **bars and restaurants** of the larger resorts. This may help you have a good time but it's unlikely to bring in much money; the low pay (often from British bar owners) reflects your lack of official status. If you turn up in spring and are willing to stay through the season you might get a better deal — and this is also true if you're offering some special skill like windsurfing. Occasionally there are jobs on offer at **yacht marinas**, scrubbing down and servicing the boats of the well-heeled; just turn up and ask around, but don't be too hopeful.

Directory

ADDRESSES These are usually abbreviated to a standard format – "c/Bellver 7" translates as Bellver Street (*carrer*) no. 7. *Plaça* means square. "Plaça Rosari 5, 2è" means the second floor at no. 5. "Passeig d'es Born 15, 1–C" means suite C, first floor, at no. 15. "s/n" (*sense número*) indicates a building without a street number. In Franco's day, most avenues and boulevards were named after Fascist heroes and, although the vast majority were redesignated years ago, there's still some confusion in remoter spots. Another source of bafflement can be house numbers: some houses carry more than one number (the by-product of half-hearted reorganizations), and on many streets the sequence is impossible to fathom.

CHILDREN Most *hostals*, pensions and hotels welcome children and many offer rooms with three or four beds. Restaurants and cafés almost always encourage families too. Many package holidays have child-minding facilities as part of

the deal. For babies, food seems to work out quite well (some places will prepare food specially) though you might want to bring powdered milk – babies, like most Spaniards, are pretty contemptuous of the UHT stuff generally available. Disposable nappies and other basic supplies are widely available in the resort areas and the larger towns.

ELECTRICITY The current is 220 volts AC, with standard European-style two-pin plugs. Brits will need an adaptor to connect their appliances, North Americans both an adaptor and a 220-to-110 transformer.

LAUNDRIES Although there's the occasional self-service laundrette (usually rendered in Castilian as *lavandería automática*), mostly you'll have to leave your clothes for a full and somewhat expensive laundry service. A dry-cleaner is a *tintorería* (also Castilian).

TIME Spain is one hour ahead of the UK, six hours ahead of Eastern Standard Time, nine hours ahead of Pacific Standard Time, nine hours behind Australian Eastern Standard Time and eleven hours behind New Zealand – except for brief periods during the changeovers made in the respective countries to and from daylight saving. In Spain, the clocks go forward an hour on the last Sunday of March and back an hour on the last Sunday of October.

TOILETS Public toilets, which are rare, are averagely clean but almost never have any paper; it's best to carry your own. They're commonly referred to as *los servicios* or *el lavabo*. The usual signs are, for "Ladies", *Dones* or the Castilian *Damas* and, for "Gentlemen", *Homes* or the Castilian *Caballeros*. You may also see the potentially confusing *Señoras* (Women) and *Señores* (Men).

The Guide

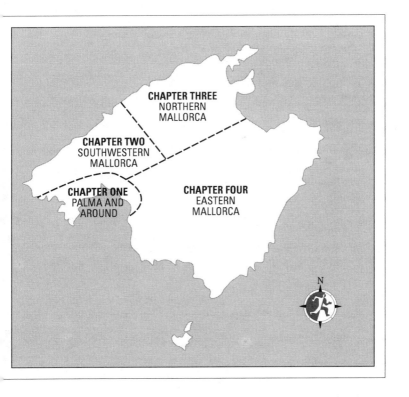

Chapter 1

Palma and around

P ALMA is an ambitious city. In 1983 it became the capital of one of Spain's newly established autonomous regions, the Balearic Islands, and since then it has shed the dusty provincialism of yesteryear, developing into a go-ahead and cosmopolitan commercial hub of 325,000 people. The new self-confidence is plain to see in the city centre, a vibrant and urbane place of careful coiffures and well-cut suits, which is akin to the big cities of the Spanish mainland and a world away from the heaving tourist enclaves of the surrounding bay. There's still a long way to go – much of suburban Palma remains obdurately dull and somewhat dilapidated – but the centre now presents a splendid ensemble of lively shopping areas, mazy lanes and refurbished old buildings, all enclosed by what remains of the old city walls and their replacement boulevards. This geography encourages downtown Palma to look into itself and away from the sea, even though its harbour – now quarantined by the main highway – has always been the city's economic lifeline.

The Romans were the first to recognize the site's strategic value, establishing a military post here, but real development came with the Moors who made their **Medina Mayurka** a major seaport protected by no fewer than three concentric walls. Jaume I of Aragón captured the Moorish stronghold in 1229 and promptly started work on the **cathedral**, whose mellow sandstone still towers above the waterfront, presenting from its seaward side – in the sheer beauty of its massive proportions – one of Spain's most stunning sights.

As a major port of call between Europe and North Africa, Palma boomed under both Moorish and medieval Christian control, but its wealth and prominence came to a sudden end with the Spanish exploitation of the New World: from the early sixteenth century, Madrid looked west across the Atlantic and Palma slipped into Mediterranean obscurity. One result of its abrupt decline has been the preservation of much of the **old town**, the narrow, labyrinthine streets and high-storeyed houses of which are at their most beguiling behind the cathedral. This district possesses few specific sights, but it's a delightful place to wander, especially as an ambitious renova-

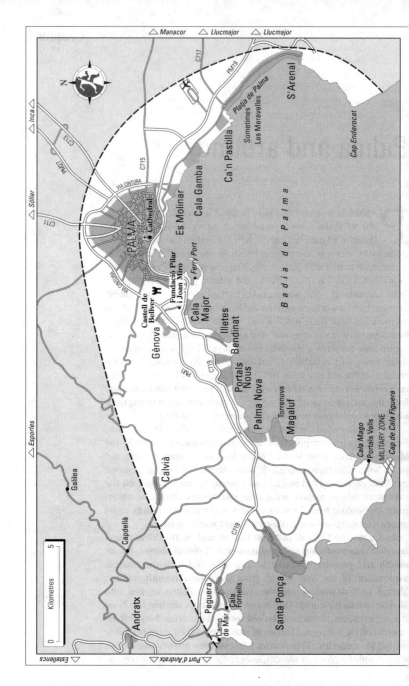

tion programme is rapidly returning the area to its old elegance. The pick of Palma's other historic attractions are the fourteenth-century **Castell de Bellver** and the heavyweight Baroque of the **Basílica de Sant Francesc**.

Yet for most visitors, Palma's main appeal is its sheer vitality: at night scores of excellent **restaurants** offer the best of Spanish, Catalan and Mallorcan cuisine, while the city's **cafés** buzz with purposeful chatter. Palma also boasts **accommodation** to match most budgets, making it a splendid base from which to explore the island. In this respect, the city is far preferable, at least for independent travellers, to the string of resorts along the **Badia de Palma** (Bay of Palma), where nearly all the accommodation is block-booked by tour operators. If you are tempted by a cheap package, it's as well to bear in mind that the more agreeable of the resorts lie to the west of the city, where a hilly coastline of rocky cliffs and tiny coves is punctuated by mostly small, sandy beaches. Development is ubiquitous, but **Cala Major** is of interest as the home of an excellent museum and the former studio of Joan Miró; well-to-do **Illetes** has several excellent hotels and a couple of lovely cove beaches; and pint-sized **Cala Fornells** has a fine seashore setting and a pair of good hotels, with the spacious sandy shoreline of family-oriented **Peguera** in easy reach. Places to avoid include the massive villa complex of **Santa Ponça**, lager-swilling **Magaluf**, **Camp de Mar**, set in an attractive wooded bay fringed by a good beach but currently in the throes of a massive expansion, and all the resorts to the east of Palma. Here the pancake-flat shoreline is burdened by a seamless band of skyscrapers stretching from **Ca'n Pastilla** to **S'Arenal** – behind what is, admittedly, one of the island's longest and most impressive beaches, the **Platja de Palma**.

Arrival

Mallorca's gleaming international **airport** is 11km east of Palma, immediately behind the resort of Ca'n Pastilla. It has one enormous terminal, which handles both scheduled and charter flights, with separate floors for arrivals (below) and departures (above). Both floors have airport **information desks** – a good job, as the airport can be very confusing: signage is below par and the layout is unnecessarily complicated (and the butt of many local jokes). On the arrivals floor, a flotilla of **car rental** outlets jostle for position by the luggage carousels. Beyond, through the glass doors, is the main arrivals hall, which has 24-hour **cash dispensers** (ATMs) and **currency exchange** facilities. Here, also, is a provincial **tourist office**, with public transport timetables, taxi rates, maps and general island information (Mon–Sat 9am–2pm & 3–8pm, Sun 9am–2pm). The tourist office has lists of hotels and *hostals*, but will not help arrange **accommodation** and neither will most of the package-tour travel agents scattered

Arrival

around about the main arrivals hall. An exception, however, is the extremely helpful Prima Travel ☎971 789 322, fax 971 789 318 (*www.prima-travel.com, accommodation@prima-travel.com*), who have a good selection of hotels, apartments and villas – and its employees either are English or speak the language well.

For full details of accomm-odation in Palma see p.72.

If you're collecting someone from the airport by car, there's a free five-minute stop zone, plus an enormous if slightly confusing **car park**. When you arrive, grab a ticket from the machine at the car park entrance; before departure, take the ticket to one of the pay machines, which allow you twenty minutes' grace to find your vehicle and leave. The airport is linked to the city and the Bay of Palma resorts by a busy highway (*autopista*) which shadows the shoreline from S'Arenal in the east to Palma Nova and Magaluf in the west.

The least expensive way to reach Palma from the airport is by **bus** #17 (daily, every 15min 6am–9.30pm & every 30min 9.30pm–1.30am; 300ptas/€1.80). These leave from the main entrance of the terminal building – just behind the taxi rank – and reach the city's inner ring road near the foot of Avinguda Gabriel Alomar i Villalonga, at the c/Joan Maragall junction. They then head on to Plaça Espanya, on the north side of the centre, before continuing west to the Passeig Mallorca and then south to the top of Avinguda Jaume III. There are frequent stops along the way. A **taxi** from the airport to the city centre will set you back about 2000ptas/€12.02; taxi rates are controlled and a list of island-wide fares is available from – or displayed in the window of – the provincial tourist office in the arrivals hall.

Arrival by ferry

For details of ferries and flights to Mallorca from the Spanish mainland and nearby islands, see p.18.

The Palma **ferry terminal** is about 4km west of the city centre. Its two passenger terminals are 160m apart, with Terminal 2 ferries operated by Trasmediterranea and Terminal 3 ones by Balearia. Transport to the city is straightforward. **Bus** #1 (175ptas/€1.05) leaves hourly from outside Terminal 2 to the Plaça de la Reina and the Plaça Rei Juan Carles I, at either end of the Passeig d'es Born, and then continues to the Plaça Espanya. It operates from 7.40am to 8.30pm, but beware of reduced services on Sundays and holidays. There are also **taxi** ranks outside each of the ferry terminal buildings; the fare to the city centre is about 600ptas/€3.61.

Orientation, city transport and information

Almost everything of interest in Palma is located in the city centre, a roughly circular affair whose southern perimeter is largely defined by the cathedral and the remains of the old city walls, which in turn abut the coastal motorway and the harbour. The city centre's landward limits are determined by a zigzag of wide boulevards built beside or in place of the old town walls – **Avinguda de la Argentina** and **Avinguda Gabriel Alomar i Villalonga** connect with the coastal motorway, thereby completing the circle. The **Via Cintura**, the ring road around the suburbs, loops off from the coastal motorway to create a much larger, outer circle.

Orientation, city transport and information

The city centre itself is crossed by four interconnected avenues: **Passeig d'es Born**, **Avinguda Jaume III**, **c/Unió** (which becomes **c/Riera** at its eastern end) and **Passeig de la Rambla**. Your best bet is to use these four thoroughfares to guide yourself round the centre – Palma's jigsaw-like side streets and squares can be very confusing. Central Palma is about 2km in diameter, roughly thirty minutes' walk from one side to the other. If you're in a hurry, take a **taxi**: fares are reasonable and there are ranks outside all the major hotels.

City transport

To reach the city's outskirts, take the **bus**. City buses are operated by **EMT** (Empresa Municipal de Transports) and almost all their services pass through **Plaça Espanya**, linking the centre with the suburbs and the nearer tourist resorts. In the city centre, each EMT bus stop sports a large route map with timetable details. Tickets, available from the driver, cost 175ptas/€1.05 per journey within the city limits, a few pesetas more for the resorts. At present, there are no day passes or any other bargain arrangement, but there are (vague) plans to begin one sort of scheme or another. When it is up and running, tickets will be sold at most newsagents and tobacconists (look for the brown and yellow *tabacs* or *tabacos* signs). EMT have an information kiosk on Plaça Espanya and an enquiry line in Spanish and Catalan on ☎971 711 393.

For details of the delightful train journey to Sóller see p.123.

Island-wide buses are operated by several other companies. In the future, they will all be based in the brand-new **bus station** that is currently under construction a couple of hundred metres north of the Inca train station along c/Marqués de La Fontsanta. In the meantime – probably until 2002 – buses leave from the side streets surrounding **Plaça Espanya**. Amongst various services, those operated by Bus Nord Balear to Valldemossa, Deià, Sóller and Port de Sóller depart from outside the *Bar La Granja*, c/Arxiduc Lluis Salvador 1; you can get timetables at the bar, but you can only buy your ticket from the driver. Buses to Alcúdia, Sineu and Cala d'Or leave from the bus-stops on c/Marqués de La Fontsanta at c/Margarita Camairi, whilst buses to Pollença, Lluc and Porto Cristo leave from the stops on c/Miquel Marqués, just off c/Marqués de La Fontsanta. For other destinations, ask at the Plaça Espanya tourist information office (see p.71). Timetable information for all island-wide services is available in Spanish and Catalan on ☎971 176 970.

Frequencies and journey times of buses and trains are on p.118.

The island's two tiny **train stations** adjoin the northeast side of Plaça Espanya, each with its own line – one to Inca, the other to Sóller.

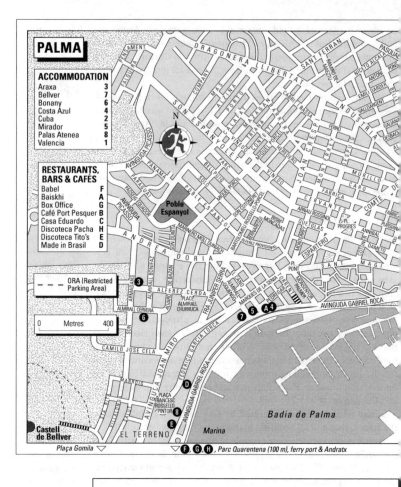

Parking in Palma

Trying to find a **car parking space** in downtown Palma can be a nightmare – you're well advised to leave your vehicle on the city's outskirts, especially for visits of more than an hour or two. If you're staying downtown, choose a hotel with a car park. Parking in the city centre requires an **ORA ticket** on weekdays 9.30am–1.30pm and 5–8pm, and on Saturdays 9.30am–1.30pm. At other times – when the centre is slightly less congested – parking is free. Tickets are readily available from ORA parking meters but, although the cost is minimal (50ptas/€0.30 for 30min, 140ptas/€0.84 for 90min), the longest-lasting ticket only provides an hour-and-a-half's parking – and fines are immediate and steep. Note also that if the time allowed overlaps into a free period, your ORA ticket is still valid when restricted time begins again.

THE GUIDE: CHAPTER 1

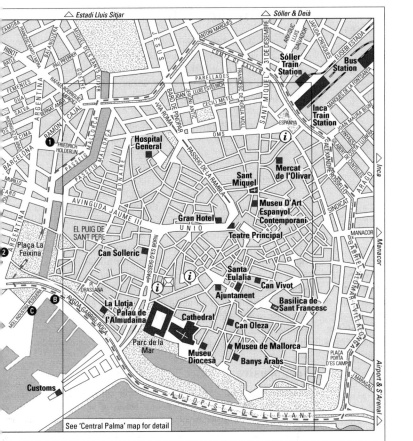

Information

The **provincial tourist office** is just off the Passeig d'es Born at Plaça de la Reina 2 (daily 9am–8pm; ☎971 712 216), while the main **municipal office** is at c/Sant Domingo 11, in the subway at the end of c/Conquistador (Mon–Fri 9am–8pm, Sat 9am–2pm; ☎971 724 090). Both provide city- and island-wide information, dispensing free maps, accommodation lists, bus schedules, ferry timetables, lists of car rental firms, boat trip details and all sorts of special-interest leaflets, including the useful *Artesanía*, which lists specialist suppliers of everything from pottery and pearls to books and handicrafts. A second municipal tourist office, located a few metres from the Inca train station on the northeast edge of Plaça Espanya, offers a similar service (Mon–Fri 9am–8pm, Sat 9am–1pm; ☎971 754 329).

Accommodation

There are about twenty *hostals* and thirty hotels dotted around
Palma, but demand for **accommodation** still tends to outstrip supply
from the middle of July through to late August. If you haven't got a
reservation and you're travelling during this period, you should
either phone around or contact Prima Travel, who specialize in last-
minute accommodation and have an office at the airport (see p.68).
At other times of the year, things are much easier: you could select
somewhere from our recommendations and contact them direct, or
get the official list of all the city's accommodation from one of the
city's three tourist offices – though note that they will not help you
book a room.

The bulk of Palma's **budget accommodation** is in the centre and,
fortunately enough, this is by far the most engaging part of the city;
the immediate suburbs are quite unprepossessing. There's a cluster
of places along the narrow, cobbled side-streets off the Passeig d'es
Born and – rather less appetizingly – around the Plaça Espanya. The
most convenient concentration of **smarter hotels** is on the Passeig
Mallorca, a particularly attractive portion of the inner ring road
where two sections of old city wall run down the middle of the boulevard on either side of an ancient watercourse. Another cluster is to
the west of the centre, overlooking the waterfront along Avinguda
Gabriel Roca. Note that in summer, some places insist on a minimum
stay of two or three nights.

*The nearest
youth hostel is
in the resort of
Sometimes, a
25-minute bus
ride from town
– see p.110.*

Inexpensive

Hostal Apuntadores, c/Apuntadors 8 ☎971 713 491 (*apuntadores@jet.es*).
Appealingly laid-back, youthful one-star *hostal* in an old house down a
cramped and bustling side street off Passeig d'es Born. Rooms are simple but

---

Accommodation price codes

All the accommodation prices in this book have been coded using the categories below, which correspond to each establishment's **least expensive
double room** in high season, excluding special offers. For a full explanation of these codes, see p.39.

        ① Under 3000ptas/Under €18.03
        ② 3000–4000ptas/ €18.03–€24.04
        ③ 4000–6000ptas/€24.04–€36.06
        ④ 6000–8000ptas/€36.06–€48.08
        ⑤ 8000–10,000ptas/€48.08–€60.10
        ⑥ 10,000–14,000ptas/€60.10–€84.14
        ⑦ 14,000–20,000ptas/€84.14–€120.20
        ⑧ 20,000–25,000ptas/€120.20–€150.25
        ⑨ Over 25,000ptas/Over €150.25

---

adequate with washbasins but not showers. Next door to the *Ritzi* (see below).
③.

Hostal-residencia Bonany, c/Almirall Cervera 5 ☎971 737 924. Faded one-star *hostal* on a quiet residential street about 3km west of the city centre, close to Castell de Bellver. Take bus #3, #4 or #21 from Plaça Espanya and get off at the start of Avgda Joan Miró. Closed Nov–March. ③.

Hostal-residencia Cuba, c/Sant Magí 1 ☎971 738 159, fax 971 403 131. Twenty attractive, well-appointed rooms in a beautifully restored *Modernista* stone house of 1904 with a pretty little tower and balustrade and a rooftop sun terrace. Overlooks the harbour and the bottom of busy Avgda Argentina. ④.

Hostal-residencia Monleón, Passeig de la Rambla 3 ☎971 715 317. Gloomy and slightly battered *hostal* in an old-fashioned 1950s building at the foot of La Rambla; often has vacancies when others don't. ③.

Hostal-residencia Pons, c/VI 8 ☎971 722 658. Simple rooms in a lovely old house with a courtyard and house plants. In the old part of town, near the Passeig d'es Born. ③.

Hostal-residencia Regina, c/Sant Miquel 77 ☎971 713 703. Ten frugal rooms above some shops in this plain, two-storey modern building bordering a main commercial street to the north of the old part of town. ③.

Hostal Ritzi, c/Apuntadors 6 ☎971 714 610. Spartan one-star rooms in an ancient and well-tended five-storey house off the Passeig d'es Born. Of the 17 rooms, those with their own shower cost about 1000ptas more than those with a washbasin. ②.

Hostal-residencia Terminus, c/Eusebi Estada 2 ☎971 750 014 (*terminus@mail.cinet.es*). Two-star establishment by the train station, with a quirk-ily old-fashioned foyer and fairly large, frugal but still comfortable rooms. ③.

Hostal-residencia Valencia, c/Ramon i Cajal 21 ☎971 733 147. Modern thir-ty-room *hostal* on the northern edge of the city centre. Spruce, almost anti-septic rooms, some with balconies overlooking the street. ④.

Moderate

Hotel Araxa, c/Alférez Cerdá 22 ☎971 731 640, fax 971 731 643. Attractive three-storey modern hotel with pleasant gardens and an outdoor swimming pool. Most rooms have balconies. In a quiet residential area about 2km west of the centre, not far from the Castell de Bellver: take bus #3, #4 or #21 from Plaça Espanya or bus #4 or #21 from Plaça de la Reina and get off at the west end of c/Marqués de la Sènia, just before the start of Avgda Joan Miró. ⑥.

Hotel-residencia Born, c/Sant Jaume 3 ☎971 712 942, fax 971 718 618 (*hborn@bitel.es*). This delightful hotel has an excellent downtown location and occupies a refurbished mansion with big wooden doors and a lovely court-yard where you can have breakfast under the palm trees. The rooms, most of which face onto the courtyard, are comfortable if a little plain. It's a popular spot, so try to book early if you're visiting in summer. ⑦.

Hotel Cannes, c/Cardenal Pou 8 ☎971 726 943. Recently renovated in brisk modern style, this fifty-room two-star hotel is located in a residential neigh-bourhood near Plaça Espanya, close to the principal shopping areas. ⑥.

Hotel Costa Azul, Avgda Gabriel Roca 7 ☎971 731 940, fax 971 731 971 (*costa@arrakis.es*). Standard high-rise, popular with package tours, with bal-conied rooms overlooking the bay. ⑦.

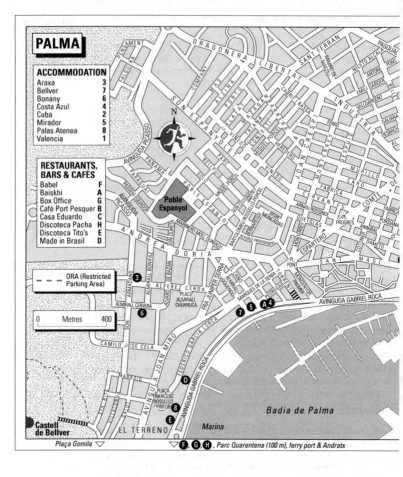

ACCOMMODATION

Araxa	3
Bellver	7
Bonany	6
Costa Azul	4
Cuba	2
Mirador	5
Palas Atenea	8
Valencia	1

RESTAURANTS, BARS & CAFÉS

Babel	F
Baiskhi	A
Box Office	G
Café Port Pesquer	B
Casa Eduardo	C
Discoteca Pacha	H
Discoteca Tito's	E
Made in Brasil	D

— — — ORA (Restricted Parking Area)

0 Metres 400

Plaça Gomila ▽   ▽ **F**, **G**, **H**, *Parc Quarentena (100 m), ferry port & Andratx*

Hotel-residencia **Palladium**, Passeig Mallorca 40 ☎971 713 945, fax 971 714 665. Proficient three-star hotel offering spick-and-span accommodation in a modern tower overlooking the handsome Passeig Mallorca. ⑦.

Hotel **Sol Jaime III**, Passeig Mallorca 14 ☎971 725 943, fax 971 725 946. Agreeable three-star with smart modern rooms, mostly with balconies. Front rooms overlook the Passeig Mallorca. Very reasonable prices. ⑦.

Expensive

Hotel-residencia **Almudaina**, Avgda Jaume III 9 ☎971 727 340, fax 971 722 599 (*almudaina@bitel.es*). Dapper modern rooms overlooking one of Palma's busiest streets, right in the centre. Very Spanish. ⑨.

Hotel **Bellver**, Avgda Gabriel Roca 11 ☎971 735 142, fax 971 731 451. Well-maintained high-rise chain hotel with smart, spacious rooms decorated in stan-

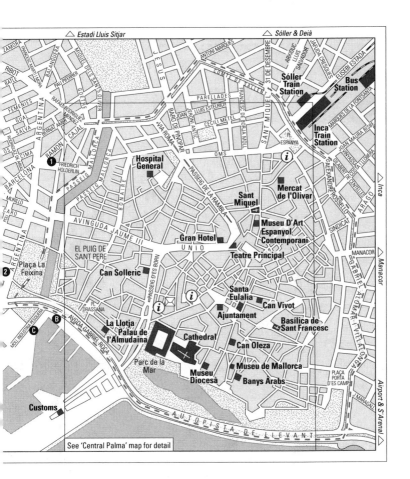

dard modern style, but with some original 1960s fittings – lots of wood and a touch of élan. Most rooms have balconies, either overlooking the harbour or (less appealingly) the city. Located a 15-minute walk west of the city centre. Popular with Spanish conventions and wedding parties. ⑧.

Hotel Mirador, Avgda Gabriel Roca 10 ☎971 732 046, fax 971 733 915. Flanked by much larger and higher hotels down by the waterfront, ten minutes' walk to the west of the city centre, this unassuming, slightly old-fashioned four-star hotel is popular with Spanish business folk. Considering its bayside location, room rates are quite reasonable. ⑧.

Hotel-residencia Palacio Ca Sa Galesa, c/Miramar 8 ☎971 715 400, fax 971 721 579 (*www.palaciocasagalesa.com*). Charmingly renovated seventeenth-century mansion set amongst the narrow alleys of the oldest part of town, a couple of minutes' walk from the cathedral. There's also an indoor heated swimming pool and fine views of the city from the roof terrace. Just

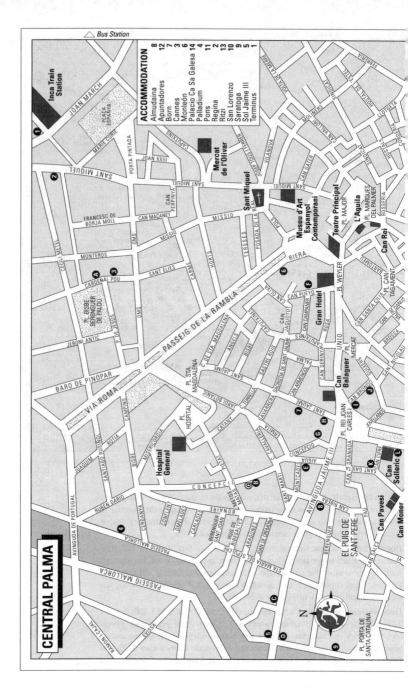

CENTRAL PALMA

△ Bus Station

Inca Train Station

ACCOMMODATION	
Almudaina	8
Apuntadores	12
Born	7
Cannes	3
Monleón	6
Palacio Ca Sa Galesa	14
Palladium	4
Pons	11
Regina	2
Ritzi	13
San Lorenzo	10
Saratoga	9
Sol Jaime III	5
Terminus	1

JOAN MARCH

PLAÇA ESPANYA

MARIE CURIE

PORTA PINTADA

SANT MIQUEL

JOAN XXIII

Mercat de l'Olivar

PORTA PINTADA

FRANCESC DE BORJA MOLL

CECILI METEL

CAN MAÇANET

CAN PERPINYÀ

MONTEROS

OMS

SANT ELIES

MISSIO

TERESES

POUS

MONTS

CARME

Sant Miquel

Museu d'Art Espanyol Contemporani

Teatre Principal

PL MAJOR

L'Aguila

PL MARQUES DEL PALMER

BOSSERIA

Can Rei

CARDENAL POU

PL BISBE BERENGUER DE PALOU

JERONI ANTIC

P. DE JESÚS

OMS

RIERA

PL WEYLER

Gran Hotel

PL CAN TAGAMENT

BARO DE PINOPAR

PASSEIG DE LA RAMBLA

VIA ROMA

PL STA MAGDALENA

PL HOSPITAL

Hospital General

CAN SERINYA

UNIO

PL MERCAT

Can Balaguer

SANT JAUME

PL REI JOAN CARLES I

CONCEPCIO

AVINGUDA DE PORTUGAL

PASSEIG MALLORCA

CONCEPCIO

AVINGUDA JAUME III

Can Solleric

Can Pavesi

Can Moner

EL PUIG DE SANT PERE

N

PL PORTA DE SANTA CATALINA

PASSEIG MALLORCA

RAMON LLULL

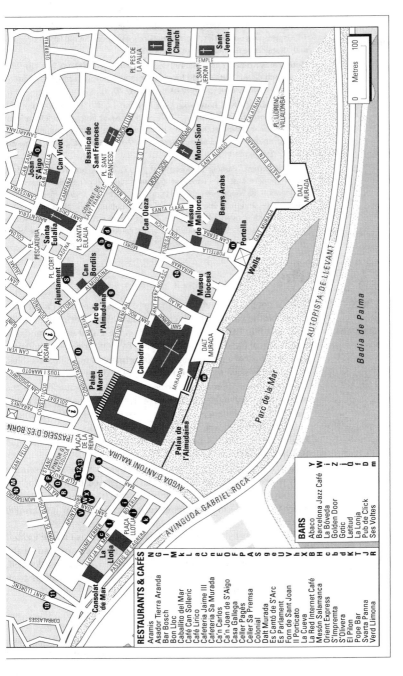

RESTAURANTS & CAFÉS

Aramis	N
Asador Tierra Aranda	G
Bar Bosch	I
Bon Lloc	M
Caballito del Mar	L
Café Can Solleric	K
Café Lírico	a
Cafeteria Jaime III	C
Cafeteria Sa Murada	n
Can Carlos	e
Can Joan de S'Aigo	O
Casa Gallega	F
Celler Pagès	P
Celler Sa Premsa	A
Colonial	S
Dalt Murada	g
Es Cantó de S'Arc	e
Es Parlament	U
Forn de Sant Joan	V
Il Porticato	h
La Cueva	X
La Red Internet Café	B
Mesón Salamanca	H
Orient Express	c
S'Imprenta	b
S'Olivera	d
El Pilon	K
Pope Bar	T
Svarta Panna	J
Verd Llimona	R

BARS

Abaco	Y
Barcelona Jazz Café	W
La Bóveda	i
Golden Door	j
Gòtic	o
Latitud	f
La Lonja	D
Pub de Click	m
Ses Voltes	

twelve luxurious and tastefully furnished rooms and suites. Opened in the 1980s, this was one of the first deluxe hotels to occupy an old island mansion and its success set something of a trend. ⑨.

Hotel Palas Atenea, Avgda Gabriel Roca 29 ☎971 281 400, fax 971 451 989. Classy and classic 1960s-style foyer leads to attractively furnished, comfortable rooms with balconies overlooking the bay. ⑧.

Hotel-residencia San Lorenzo, c/Sant Llorenç 14 ☎971 728 200, fax 971 711 901 (*sanlorenzo@fehm.es*). Delightful four-star hotel set in a luxuriously modernized seventeenth-century mansion, with a rooftop swimming pool. Located among the ancient side streets west of the Passeig d'es Born. Six rooms only, so reservations are essential. ⑧.

Hotel Saratoga, Passeig Mallorca 6 ☎971 727 240, fax 971 727 312. A bright, modern hotel in a smart, seven-storey block. It occupies a handy central location, its rooms are neat and trim, with marble floors and plenty of cupboard space, and there is a rooftop café and swimming pool. Most rooms have balconies either overlooking the boulevard or an interior courtyard, which comes complete with an outside pool and terrace. The only carp is the beds, which are a tad too light and insubstantial. ⑧.

The City

There's not much argument as to where to start a tour of Palma – it's got to be the **cathedral**, which dominates the waterfront from the crest of a hill. Palma's other landmark is the **Palau de l'Almudaina** next door, an important royal residence from Moorish times and now the repository of a mildly engaging assortment of municipal baubles, though successive modifications have robbed the building of much of its character. Spreading northeast behind the cathedral are the narrow lanes and ageing mansions of the most intriguing part of the **old town**. A stroll here is a pleasure in itself and, tucked away among the side streets, there are two good diversions: the **Museu de Mallorca**, the island's most extensive museum, and the Baroque **Basílica de Sant Francesc**.

North of the old town lies the heart of the early twentieth-century city, where the high-sided tenements are graced by a sequence of flamboyant buildings in the **Modernista** style (the Spanish, and especially Catalan, form of Art Nouveau), particularly on and around **Plaça Weyler**.

West of the city centre, you should consider a visit to the **Castell de Bellver**, an impressive hilltop castle, and perhaps also to the much less interesting **Poble Espanyol**, which comprises detailed, scaled-down reproductions of important and typical buildings from every region of Spain.

The cathedral

Legend has it that when the invasion force of Jaume I of Aragón and Catalunya stood off Mallorca in 1229, a fierce gale threatened to sink the fleet. The desperate king promised to build a church dedicated to the Virgin Mary if the expedition against the Moors was successful. It was, and Jaume fulfilled his promise, starting construction work the next year. The king had a political point to make too – he built his cathedral, a gigantic affair of golden sandstone, bang on top of the Great Mosque, inside the Almudaina, the old Moorish citadel. The Reconquest was to be no temporary matter.

As it turned out, the **cathedral** (*La Seu* in Catalan) was five hundred years in the making. Nonetheless, although there are architectural bits and bobs from several different eras, the church remains essentially Gothic, with massive exterior buttresses – its most distinctive feature – taking the weight off the pillars within. The whole structure derives its effect from sheer height, impressive from any angle but startling when viewed from the waterside esplanade.

The doors and bell tower

The finest of the cathedral's three doors is the **Portal del Mirador** (Lookout Door), which overlooks the Bay of Palma from the south facade. Dating from the late fourteenth century, the weathered Mirador features a host of Flemish-style ecclesiastical figurines set around a tympanum where heavily bearded disciples sit at a Last Supper. In contrast, the west-facing **Portal Major** (Great Door), across from the Almudaina, is a neo-Gothic disaster, an ugly reworking – along with the sixty-metre-high flanking turrets – of a far simpler predecessor that was badly damaged in an earthquake of 1851.

On the north side is a third door, the **Portal de l'Almoina**, decorated in a simple Gothic design of 1498. Up above rises the solid squareness of the **bell tower** (closed to the public), an incongruous, fortress-like structure that clearly did not form part of the original design. When the largest of the bells, the 5700-kilo N'Eloi, was tolled in 1857, it shattered most of the cathedral's windows.

The interior

You **enter** the cathedral on the north side through its museum (Mon–Fri 10am–5.30pm, Sat 10am–1.30pm; Nov–March Mon–Fri closes 3pm; 500ptas/€3.01). The majestic proportions of its **interior** are seen to best advantage from the western end, from the Portal Major. In the central **nave**, fourteen beautifully aligned, pencil-thin pillars rise to 21m before their ribs branch out – rather like fronded palm trees – to support the single-span, vaulted roof. The nave, at 44m high, is one of the tallest Gothic structures in Europe and its 121-metre length is of matching grandeur. This open, hangar-like construction, typical of Catalan Gothic architecture, was designed to make the high altar visible to the entire congregation, and to express the mystery of the Christian faith, with kaleidoscopic floods of light filtered in through the **stained-glass windows**. Most of the original glass was lost long ago, but recent refurbishment has returned several windows to their former glory and, now that many others have been un-bricked and cleaned, the cathedral has re-emerged from the gloom imposed by Renaissance, Baroque and neo-Gothic architects. There are seven rose windows, the largest of which crowns the triumphal arch of the apse at the east end and boasts over 1200 individual pieces of glass; providing the sun is out, it's best seen in the morning. The cathedral's designers also incorporated a specific, carefully orchestrated artifice: twice a year, at 6.30am on Candlemas and St Martin's Day, the sun shines through the stained glass of the eastern window onto the wall immediately below the rose window on the main, western facade.

Gaudí's restoration

The first attempt to return the church to something like its original splendour was made at the beginning of the twentieth century when an inspired local bishop commissioned the *Modernista* Catalan architect **Antoni Gaudí** to direct a full-blown restoration. At the time, Gaudí was renowned for his fancifully embellished metalwork, and his functionalist extrapolation of Gothic design was still evolving. This experimentation led ultimately to his most famous and extravagant opus, the church of the Sagrada Família in Barcelona, but here in Palma his work was relatively restrained – though still deeply controversial. Indeed, certain Catholic dignitaries took the aesthetic hump over the revamp and when, in 1926, a Barcelona tram flattened Gaudí they must have thought their prayers had been answered.

Gaudí worked on Palma's cathedral intermittently between 1904 and 1914, during which time he removed the High Baroque altar and shifted the ornate choir stalls from the centre of the cathedral, placing them flat against the walls of the presbytery. The new high altar, a medieval alabaster table of plain design, was then located beneath a phantasmagorical giant **baldachin**, suspended from the roof. This wrought-iron canopy, the flowing lines of which are enhanced by hanging lanterns, is supposed to symbolize the Crown of Thorns; it's not a great success, though to be fair, Gaudí never had time to complete it so it's impossible to say what the final version would have looked like.

Other examples of Gaudí's distinctive workmanship are dotted around the cathedral. The **railings** in front of the high altar are twisted into shapes inspired by Mallorcan window grilles, while the wall on either side of the **Bishop's Throne**, at the east end of the church, sports ceramic inlays with brightly painted floral designs. Yet Gaudí's main concern was to revive the Gothic tradition by giving light to the cathedral. To this end he introduced **electric lighting**, bathing the apse in bright artificial light and placing lamps and candelabra throughout the church. This was all very innovative: at the time, no choir had ever before been removed in Spain and electric lighting was a real novelty. The artistic success of the whole project, though, was undeniable, and it was immediately popular with the congregation. Like the rest of his work, however, it did not bring Gaudí much international acclaim: it was only in the 1960s that his techniques were championed and copied across western Europe, and that his crucial role in the development of modernism was finally acknowledged.

The chapels

The aisles on either side of the central nave are flanked by a long sequence of chapels, dull affairs for the most part, dominated by dusty Baroque altars of gargantuan proportions and little artistic merit. The exception, and the cathedral's one outstanding example of the Baroque, is the **Capella de Corpus Christi**, at the head of the aisle to the left of the high altar. Begun in the sixteenth century, the chapel's tiered and columned altarpiece features three religious scenes, cramped and intense sculptural tableaux of – from top to bottom – *The Temptations of St Anthony, The Presentation of Jesus in the Temple* and *The Last Supper*. Just across from the chapel is a massive stone pulpit that was moved here by Gaudí, a makeshift location for this excellent illustration of the Plateresque style. Dated to 1531, the pulpit's intricate floral patterns and bustling Biblical scenes cover a clumsy structure, the upper portion of which is carried by telamons, male counterparts of the more usual caryatids.

Though you can't get to the **Capella de la Trinidad** (Trinity Chapel) today – it's at the east end of the church directly behind the high altar – this tiny chapel is also of interest. Completed in 1329, it accommodates the remains of Jaume II and Jaume III, two notable medieval kings of Mallorca. Initially, the bodies were stored in a tomb that operated rather like a filing cabinet, allowing the corpses to be venerated by the devout. They were viewed in 1809 by the first British traveller to write an account of a visit to Mallorca, the unflappable Sir John Carr, who calmly observed that "considering the monarchs had been dead for five hundred years... they were in a state of extraordinary preservation." This gruesome practice was finally discontinued at the start of the twentieth century, and alabaster sarcophagi now enclose the royal bones.

For more on Jaume II and Jaume III, see p.241.

The Museu de la Catedral

The ground floor of the bell tower and two adjoining chapterhouses have been turned into the **Museu de la Catedral** (same times and ticket as cathedral) in order to accommodate an eclectic mixture of ecclesiastical treasures. The first room's most valuable exhibit, in the glass case in the middle, is a gilded silver monstrance of extraordinary delicacy, its fairy-tale decoration dating from the late sixteenth century. On display around the walls are assorted chalices and reliquaries and a real curiosity, the portable altar of Jaume I, a wood and silver chessboard with each square containing a bag of relics.

The second room is mainly devoted to the Gothic works of the **Mallorcan Primitives**, a school of painters who flourished on the island in the fourteenth and fifteenth centuries, producing strikingly naive devotional works of bold colours and cartoon-like detail. The work of two of the school's leading fourteenth-century practitioners is displayed here, the so-called **Master of the Privileges**, whose love of minute detail and warm colours reveals an Italian influence, and the **Master of Montesión**, who looked to his Catalan contemporaries for his sense of movement and tight draughtsmanship. Later, the work of the Mallorcan Primitives shaded into the new realism of the Flemish style, which was to dominate Mallorcan painting throughout the sixteenth century. **Joan Desi's** (unlabelled) *Panel of La Almoina* (c. 1500) illustrates the transition – it's the large panel showing St Francis, complete with stigmata, at the side of Christ. In terms of content, look out for the tribulations of **St Eulalia**, whose martyrdom fascinated and excited scores of medieval Mallorcan artists. A Catalan girl-saint, Eulalia defied the Roman Emperor Diocletian by sticking to her Christian faith despite all sorts of ferocious tortures, which are depicted in ecstatic detail here in a large, unlabelled panel painting by the Master of the Privileges. Ultimately she was burnt at the stake and, at the moment of her death, white doves flew from her mouth.

More works by the Mallorcan Primitives are displayed at the Museu de Mallorca – see pp.86–88.

The third and final room, the **Baroque chapterhouse**, is entered through a playful Churrigueresque doorway, above which a delicate Madonna is overwhelmed by lively cherubic angels. Inside, pride of place goes to the High Baroque altar, a gaudy, gilded affair surmounted by the Sacred Heart, a gory representation of the heart of Jesus that was very much in vogue during the eighteenth century. Some imagination went into the designation of the reliquaries displayed round the room: there's a piece of the flogging post, three thorns from Christ's crown and even a piece of the gall and vinegared sponge that was offered to the crucified Jesus. Of more appeal are a pair of finely carved, Baroque crucifixes, each Christ a study in perfect muscularity swathed in the flowing folds of a loincloth.

The Museu Diocesà

There are several more Mallorcan Primitive works in the **Museu Diocesà** (in Castilian, *Museo Diocesano*; April–Oct Mon–Fri 10am–1pm & 3–8pm, Sat & Sun 10am–1.30pm; Nov–March Mon–Fri 10am–1pm & 3–6pm, Sat & Sat 10am–1pm; 300ptas/€1.80). The museum is on c/Mirador immediately behind the cathedral – keep going straight past the Portal del Mirador – and is situated within the Bishop's Palace, a mostly seventeenth-century structure built around an expansive courtyard presided over by a statue of the Sacred Heart. It has only two rooms, beginning with a tiny antechamber in which is displayed a **panel painting** by the Master of Bishop Galiana, whose crisp draughtsmanship was very much in the Catalan tradi-

tion. This particular painting is an intriguing work, a didactic car-
toon-strip illustrating the life of St Paul, who is shown with his Bible
open and sword in hand, a militant view of the church that must have
accorded well with the preoccupations of the powerful bishops of
Mallorca. Look out also for the way the artist portrays the conversion
on the road to Damascus, with Saul/Paul struck by a laser-like beam
of light.

Beyond, in the main room, there are all sorts of bits and pieces,
including a selection of **majolica tiles**, the heavy-duty jasper **sar-
cophagus** built to house the remains of King Jaume II in the eighteenth century, and some spectacularly unsuccessful religious sculptures. In addition, two cabinets are packed with shiny, metallic-glaze
pottery of Moorish and Mudéjar design, rare survivors dating from
the fourteenth to the eighteenth century. Two **paintings** stand out
here too, the earlier being the *Passion of Christ*, by an unknown
artist dubbed the Master of the Passion of Mallorca. Dated to the end
of the thirteenth century, the panel painting follows a standard format, with a series of small vignettes outlining the story of Christ, but
the detail is warm and gentle: the Palm Sunday donkey leans forward, pushing his nose towards a child; one of the disciples reaches
out across the Last Supper table for the fish; and two of Jesus' disciples slip their sandals off in eager anticipation during the washing of
the feet. By contrast, Alonso de Sedano's sixteenth-century
Crucifixion is a sophisticated work of strong, deep colours within a
triangulated structure. Up above is the blood-spattered, pale-white
body of Christ, while down below – divided by the Cross – are two
groups, one of hooded mourners, the other a trio of nonchalant
Roman soldiers in contemporary Spanish dress.

*For more on
majolica, see
p.166.*

The Palau de l'Almudaina

Opposite the cathedral entrance stands the **Palau de l'Almudaina**,
originally the palace of the Moorish *walis* (governors) and later of
the Mallorcan kings (April–Sept Mon–Fri 10am–6.30pm, Sat
10am–2pm; Oct–March Mon–Fri 10am–2pm & 4–6pm, Sat
10am–2pm; 450ptas/€2.71; free on Wed to EU citizens showing
their passport). The present structure, built around a central courtyard, owes much of its appearance to Jaume II (1276–1311), who
spent the last twelve years of his life in residence here. Jaume converted the old fortress into a lavish palace that incorporated both
Gothic and Moorish features, an uneasy mixture of styles conceived
by the Mallorcan Pedro Selva, the king's favourite architect. The two
most prominent "Moorish" attributes are the fragile-looking outside
walls, with their square turrets and dainty crenellations, and the delicate arcades of the main loggia, which is readily viewed from down
below on the waterside esplanade.

Once Mallorca was incorporated within the Aragonese kingdom,
the Palau de l'Almudaina became surplus to requirements, though it

The audioguide, issued free at the ticket desk, gives plenty of background detail to the exhibits in several languages including English.

did achieve local notoriety when the eccentric Aragonese king Juan I (1387–1395) installed an alchemist in the royal apartments, hoping he would replenish the treasury by turning base metal into gold. (He was unsuccessful.) Today, the palace serves a variety of official functions, housing the island's legislature, its military – whose camera-shy guards stand outside one of the entrances – and a series of state apartments kept in readiness for visiting dignitaries and the king, which is presumably why those exhibits that are labelled carry Castilian inscriptions. When the king or some other bigwig is in residence, parts of the palace are usually cordoned off.

The palau

The self-guided tour of the palau begins with a series of medieval corridors and rooms that are almost entirely devoid of ornamentation, but things picks up in the **Salón de Consejos** (Hall of Councils; Room 5), where the walls sport a group of admirable Flemish **tapestries**, fifteenth- and sixteenth-century imports devoted to classical themes. Amongst them is a Roman Triumph, a blood-curdling war scene, and, best of the lot, the suicide of Cleopatra, showing a particularly wan-looking queen with the guilty asp slithering discreetly away. Moving on, the **Comedor de Oficiales** (Officers' Mess; Room 6) possesses a handful of **Flemish genre paintings**, fine still-life studies including one by the seventeenth-century Antwerp-based artist Frans Snyders – there's no label, but it's the painting with the man, the woman, the cat and several carcasses. Snyders was a contemporary of Rubens and odd-jobbed for him, painting in the flowers and fruit on many of his canvases. Beyond, there are charming views across the city from the outside **terraza** (terrace, Room 9), which holds a small formal garden, and then it's inside again for the **Sala de Guardia** (Hall of Guards; Room 10), where there are several dire eighteenth-century Spanish tapestries. Crude and inexact, these are in striking contrast to the Flemish tapestries exhibited elsewhere, but by then Spain had lost control of the Netherlands and the Spanish court was obliged to move on from its traditional supplier. In 1725, the Spanish king founded a tapestry factory in Madrid, but its products – as demonstrated here – were poor and there must have been some aesthetic gnashing of teeth when the Spanish court took delivery. Pressing on, the **Baños árabes** (Arab Baths; Room 11) are a rare survivor from Moorish times, comprising three stone-vaulted chambers, one each for cold, tepid and hot baths. Enough remains to see how this sophisticated set-up worked and why the Christian kings who supplanted the Moors adopted them lock, stock and barrel.

Palma also has another, less intact Arab bath house – see p.86.

After the Arab Baths, you move into the central courtyard, from where the Escalera Real (Royal Staircase; Room 13), installed by Philip II, leads up to the **state apartments** that fill out the palace's upper level. These apartments are really rather sterile, but there are several splendidly ornate Mudéjar wooden ceilings and a series of

Palma Cathedral

Mime artist, Palma

Palma

Renaissance courtyard, Palma

The Palma–Sóller train

Modernista facade, Palma

Baker's sign, Palma

Stone houses, Fornalutx

Valldemossa

Plaça Major, Palma

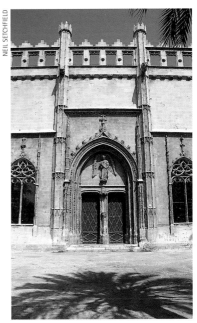

La Llotja, Palma

Monastery church, Valldemossa

Castell de Bellver, Palma

Lluc Monastery

fine Brussels tapestries, notably a magnificent seventeenth-century *Siege of Carthage* covering the back wall of the **Salón Gótico** (Gothic Hall; Room 20).

The last room here is the **Despacho de Su Majestad el Rey** (Office of the King; Room 21) after which you emerge back in the courtyard for the final part of the tour, the **Capilla de Santa Ana** (Chapel of St Anne; Room 22). Still used for army officers' masses and weddings, the chapel is an attractive, largely fourteenth-century Gothic structure, though the delicate marble carving above the entrance is Romanesque in style, a deliberate use of what was then an archaic tradition. The three figures above the door are, in the middle, the Virgin Mary, with saints Anne and Joachim to either side. The interior, with its vaulted and embossed ceiling, is decidedly intimate, almost cosy, a suitable home for the Chapel of St Praxedis, which, with its medieval effigy and reliquary, is devoted to a much venerated local saint.

The city walls and the Parc de la Mar

A flight of steps leads down from between the cathedral and the Palau de l'Almudaina to a handsomely restored section of the **Renaissance city walls**, whose mighty zigzag of bastions, bridges, gates and dry moats once encased the whole city. They replaced the city's **medieval walls**, portions of which also survive – look back up from the foot of the steps and a large chunk is clearly visible beneath and to either side of the cathedral. Constructed of sandstone blocks and adobe, the earlier fortifications depended for their efficacy on their height, with a gallery running along the top from which the defenders could fire at the enemy. By the middle of the fifteenth century, however, the development of more effective artillery had shifted the military balance in favour of offence, with cannons now able to breach medieval city walls with comparative ease. The military architects of the day soon evolved a new design in which walls were built much lower and thicker to absorb cannon shot, while four-faced bastions – equipped with artillery platforms – projected from the line of the walls, providing the defenders with a variety of firing lines. The whole lot was protected by a water-filled **moat** with deep, sheer sides. The costs of re-fortifying the major cities of western Europe were astronomical, but every country joined in the rush. In Palma, the Habsburgs ordered work to start on the new (Renaissance) design in the 1560s, though the chain of bastions was only completed in 1801.

From the foot of the steps below the cathedral, a wide and pleasant **walkway** travels along the top of the Renaissance walls, providing fine views of the cathedral and an insight into the tremendous strength of the fortifications. Heading west, the walkway leads to the tiered gardens of a small Moorish-style park, which tumble down to the foot of Avinguda d'Antoni Maura, an extension of the tree-lined Passeig d'es

Born (see p.93). In the opposite direction – east from the steps below the cathedral – the walkway passes above the planted palm trees, concrete terraces and ornamental lagoon of the **Parc de la Mar**, an imaginative and popular redevelopment of the disused land that once lay between the walls and the coastal motorway. Indeed, it has proved so popular that the municipality are considering shoving the road underground so that they can extend the park to the seashore. Wall and walkway zigzag along the south side of old Palma before fizzling out at Plaça Llorenç Villalonga. After a couple of minutes, you'll pass above the double **Portella gateway**, the outer portal of which carries the Bourbon coat of arms above its arch; you can come off the walkway here, going down either of two wide stone ramps to reach the foot of c/Portella. From here, it's a few metres to the Banys Àrabs, located amongst the narrow lanes at the southern end of the old town alleys.

Cafeteria Sa Murada, in the mini-square at the bottom of c/Portella, is a good spot for a drinks break – see p.101.

The old town

The medina-like maze of streets at the back of the cathedral constitutes the heart of the **old town**, which extends north to Plaça Cort and east to Avinguda Gabriel Alomar i Villalonga. Long a neglected corner of the city, the district is now being refurbished, an ambitious and massively expensive project that's slowly restoring its antique charms. The area's general appearance is its main appeal, and you can spend hours wandering down narrow lanes and alleys, loitering in the squares, gawping at Renaissance mansions and peering up at imposing Baroque and Gothic churches. As targets for your wanderings, aim for the district's two finest churches – the **Església de Santa Eulàlia** and the **Basílica de Sant Francesc** – plus the city's most extensive museum, the **Museu de Mallorca**.

The Banys Àrabs (Arab Baths)

Leaving the city wall walkway at the Portella gate, you'll find yourself in the old town at the foot of c/Portella. North of the gate, take the first turning right for the **Banys Àrabs**, c/Can Serra 7 (daily: April–Nov 9.30am–8pm; Dec–March 9.30am–7pm; 200ptas/€1.20). One of the few genuine reminders of the Moorish presence, this tenth-century brick *hammam* (bath house) consists of a small horseshoe-arched and domed chamber which was once heated through the floor. The arches rest on stone pillars, an irregular bunch thought to have been looted from the remains of the island's Roman buildings.

The baths are reasonably well preserved, but if you've been to the baths in Girona or Granada, or even those in the Palau de l'Almudaina (see p.84), these are anticlimactic; the lush garden outside, with tables where you can picnic, is perhaps nicer.

The Museu de Mallorca

Close by on c/Portella is the **Museu de Mallorca** (April–Sept Tues–Sat 10am–2pm & 5–8pm, Sun 10am–2pm; Oct–March

Tues–Sat 10am–1pm & 4–6pm, Sun 10am–2pm; 300ptas/€1.80; free on Sat afternoon & Sun). The museum occupies Can Aiamans, a rambling Renaissance mansion whose high-ceilinged rooms are a delightful setting for an enjoyable medley of Mallorcan artefacts, the earliest dating from prehistoric times, fleshed out by a superb assortment of Gothic paintings. Be warned, though, that the labelling of exhibits is very patchy: sometimes there's a Castilian or Catalan tag, but often there's nothing at all.

The collection begins on the **ground floor**, behind and to the right of the entrance, with half a dozen rooms filled with all sorts of bits and pieces retrieved from old buildings and archeological digs. Highlights include a selection of exquisite Arab and Moorish jewellery, inscribed Arab funerary tablets, and some beautiful, highly decorated wooden panelling that is representative of Mudéjar artistry. Retracing your steps, cross the courtyard and pop into the room at the foot of the stairway to look at a few old documents and one of the most atrocious paintings imaginable, *The Sacking of the City of Troy* by Miquel Bestard (c. 1590–1633), its figures dreadfully executed and the red of the flames thoroughly unconvincing. Fortunately, relief is near at hand, just up the stairs in the first of a couple of rooms devoted to the **Mallorcan Primitive** painters. On display in this first room are works by the Masters of Bishop Galiana, Montesión and Castellitx and, best of the lot, a panel painting entitled *Santa Quiteria*, whose precisely executed, lifelike figures – down to the wispy beard of the king – are typical of the gifted Master of the Privileges. In the same room, there's also a curious thirteenth-century work of unknown authorship dedicated to St Bernard, with the saint on his knees devotedly drinking the milk of the Virgin Mary.

For more on the Mallorcan Primitives, see p.82.

Beyond a room of religious statues and carved capitals, the second room of Gothic paintings is distinguished by a sequence of works by **Francesc Comes** (1379–1415), whose skill in catching the subtle texture of skin echoes his Flemish contemporaries and represents a softening of the early Mallorcan Primitives' crudeness. In his striking *St George*, the saint – girl-like, with typically full lips – impales a lime-green dragon with more horns than could possibly be useful. One of the last talented exponents of the Mallorcan Gothic, the **Master of the Predellas** – most probably a certain Joan Rosató – is well-represented by his Bosch-like *Life of Santa Margalida*, each crowd of onlookers a sea of ugly, deformed faces and merciless eyes. The work outlines the life of Margaret of Antioch, one of the most venerated saints in medieval Christendom. During the reign of the Roman Emperor Diocletian (284–305 AD), she refused to marry a pagan prefect and was consequently executed after being tortured with extravagant gusto. As if this weren't enough, she also had to resist more metaphysical trials: Satan, disguised as a dragon, swallowed her, but couldn't digest her holiness, so his stomach opened up and out she popped unharmed. This particular tribulation made Margaret the patron saint of pregnant women.

The ensuing rooms display the stodgy art of the Counter-Reformation, though Palma's own Miquel Bestard makes a second, much more successful appearance in his whopping *Feeding of the Five Thousand*. Miraculously, Jesus feeds the hungry crowd from a meagre supply of loaves and fishes, but the subtext is much more revealing: Bestard's crowds are well-behaved and respectful of authority – just what the Catholic hierarchy had in mind.

The museum's **top floor** holds a mildly engaging assortment of nineteenth- and early twentieth-century paintings by foreign artists once resident in Mallorca. There's also a neat sample of works by Mallorca's own **Juli Ramis** (1909–1990), whose striking style is well illustrated by his oil-on-fabric *Tres Cavalls* (Three Horses) and the radiant blues of *Tardor en blau* (Blue Autumn). A native of Sóller, Ramis left the island when he was nineteen to spend the next sixty years abroad, travelling widely and becoming acquainted with some of the leading artistic lights of his day, notably Picasso in the 1930s. Ramis mixed his styles, but was essentially an Expressionist with Surrealistic leanings. He returned to Mallorca in the last years of his life and died in Palma.

Also on this floor is a room of *Modernista* fittings and furnishings, mostly retrieved from shops and houses that have since been demolished. Of particular interest are the charming wall tiles manufactured at the island's **La Roqueta** works. The pottery was in production for just twenty years (1897–1918), but this coincided with the vogue for the *Modernista* pieces in which La Roqueta excelled. For once, the labelling here is quite good.

Mansions in Palma

Most of medieval Palma was destroyed by fire, so the patrician **mansions** that characterize the old town today generally date from the reconstruction programme of the late seventeenth and early eighteenth centuries. Consequently they were built in the fashionable Renaissance style, with columns and capitals, loggias and arcades tucked away behind outside walls of plain stone three or four storeys high, and are surprisingly uniform in layout. Entry to almost all of these mansions was through a great arched **gateway** that gave onto a rectangular courtyard around which the house was built. Originally, the **courtyard** would have been cheered by exotic trees and flowering shrubs, and equipped with a fancy stone and ironwork well-head, where visitors could water their horses. From the courtyard, a stone **exterior staircase** led up to the main public rooms – with the servants' quarters below and the family's private apartments up above.

Very few of these mansions are open to the public, and all you'll see for the most part is the view from the gateway – the municipality have actually started to pay people to leave their big wooden gates open. Several have, however, passed into the public domain, the Can Aiamans, now the home of the Museu de Mallorca, being the prime example. Others worth making a detour to see are Can Bordils, Can Oleza, Can Vivot (see opposite) and Can Solleric (p.93). Of these, only the last is open to the public.

Continuing on up the hill from the Museu de Mallorca, c/Portella leads to c/Morey where, at no. 9, you'll find the **Can Oleza**, a sixteenth-century mansion closed to the public with a cool and shaded courtyard embellished by a handsome balustrade and a trio of Ionic columns. Just up the street, it's worth detouring left along c/Almudaina for a peek at the chunky remains of the old east gate, the **Arc de L'Almudaina** – a remnant of the Moorish fortifications – and to see the renovated **Can Bordils**, one of the city's oldest private mansions, at no. 9.

Overshadowing the square at the top of c/Morey is the **Església de Santa Eulalia** (Mon–Fri 7am–12.30pm & 5.45–8.30pm, Sat 7am–1pm & 4.30–8.45pm, Sun 8am–1pm & 6.30–8.30pm), which was built on the site of a mosque in the mid-thirteenth century. It took just 25 years to complete and consequently possesses an architectural homogeneity that's unusual for ecclesiastical Palma, though there was some later medieval tinkering, and nineteenth-century renovators added the belfry and remodelled the main (south) facade. The church is typically Gothic in construction, with a yawning nave originally designed – as in the cathedral – to give the entire congregation a view of the high altar. The bricked-up windows of today keep out most of the light and spoil the effect, but suggestions that they be cleared have always been ignored. Framing the nave, the aisles accommodate twelve **chapels**, one of which – the first chapel on the right – sports a delightful Gothic panel painting in the finely observed Flemish style. In kitsch contrast, the other chapels are standard-issue Baroque, though they pale into insignificance when compared with the hourglass-shaped **high altarpiece**, a flashy Baroque extravagance of colossal proportions. This holy ground witnessed one of the more disgraceful episodes of Mallorcan history. During Easter week, 1435, a rumour went round that Jewish townsfolk had enacted a blasphemous mock-up of the Crucifixion. There was no proof, but the Jews were promptly robbed of their possessions and condemned to be burnt at the stake unless they adopted Christianity. The ensuing mass baptism was held here at Santa Eulalia.

Just west of the Plaça Santa Eulalia lies the fetching Plaça Cort (see p.92), whilst around the back of the church, at c/Can Savella 2, is the eighteenth-century **Can Vivot**, an especially opulent mansion, with a spacious main courtyard of red marble columns, graceful arches and a slender staircase. The house itself is closed to the public.

See p.82 for more on St Eulalia.

The sociable Ca'n Joan de S'Aigo, *behind Santa Eulalia at c/Can Sanç 10, is a good place for coffee and an ensaimada (flaky pastry).*

The Basílica de Sant Francesc

A short walk east of the Plaça Santa Eulalia along c/Convent de Sant Francesc is the **Basílica de Sant Francesc** (daily 9.30am–12.30pm & 3.30–6pm; closed Sun afternoon; 100ptas/€0.60), a domineering pile that occupies the site of the old Moorish soap factory. Built for the Franciscans towards the end of the thirteenth century, the original church was a vast Gothic edifice which benefited from royal patronage after Jaume II's son, also named Jaume, became a member of the order in 1300. Subsequent Gothic remodellings replaced the initial wooden ceiling with a single-span, vaulted stone roof of imposing dimensions and added stately chapels to the nave and apse. The Basílica became the most fashionable church in medieval Palma and its friars received handsome kickbacks for entombing the local nobility within its precincts. Increasingly eager to enrich themselves, the priests came to compete for possession of the corpses, while the various aristocratic clans vied with each other in the magnificence of their sarcophagi. These tensions exploded when a clansman, a certain Jaume Armadams, had a jug of water emptied over his head on All Saints' Day, 1490. The congregation gathered to pray before the tombs of the dead, went berserk and over three hundred noblemen fought it out in the nave before the priests finally restored order. The scandal caused the Basílica to be closed for several decades.

In the seventeenth century the church was badly damaged by lightning, prompting a thoroughgoing reconstruction which accounts for most of its present-day appearance. The main **facade** which dates from this period, displays a stunning severity of style with its great rectangular sheet of dressed sandstone stretching up to an arcaded and balustraded balcony. The facade is pierced by a gigantic rose window of Plateresque intricacy and embellished by a **Baroque doorway**, the tympanum of which features a triumphant Virgin Mary engulfed by a wriggling mass of sculptured decoration. Above the Madonna is the figure of St George, and to either side and below are assorted saints – look out for the scholar and missionary Ramon Llull, who is shown reading a book. The strange statue in front of the doorway of a Franciscan monk and a young Native American celebrates the missionary work of **Junipero Serra**, a Mallorcan priest despatched to California in 1768, who subsequently founded the cities of San Diego, Los Angeles and San Francisco.

For more on Junipero Serra, see p.203.

The church's interior, approached through a trim Gothic cloister is disappointingly gloomy – too dark, in fact, to pick out all but the most obvious of its features. However, you can push a switch to light the monumental **high altar** – it's on the right-hand side near the door to the sacristy. The altar is a gaudy Baroque affair featuring balustrades, lattice-work and clichéd figurines beneath a monk-made *St George and the Dragon.* Less overblown are the rolling scrolls and trumpeteer-angel of the eighteenth-century **pulpit** on the wall of the nave, and the ornate Gothic-Baroque frontispiece of the nearby organ. The first chapel on the left of the ambulatory shelters the **tomb of Ramon Llull**, whose bones were brought back to Palma after his martyrdom in Algeria in 1315. Considering the sanctity of the man's remains, it's an odd and insignificant-looking affair, with

Ramon Llull

The life of **Ramon Llull** (1235–1315) – a figure beloved of Catholic pro-
pagandists – was an exercise in redemption following carnal excess. As a
young man, Llull was an ebullient rake in the retinue of the future Jaume
II. His sexual adventures were not impeded in the least by his marriage,
but they ground to a dramatic halt when, having pursued Ambrosia de
Castillo, the woman of his immediate desire, into the church of Santa
Eulalia on horseback, she revealed to him her diseased breasts. A deeply
shocked Llull devoted the rest of his life to the Catholic faith, becoming a
fearless missionary and dedicated scholar of theology, philosophy and
alchemy. Exemplifying the cosmopolitan outlook of thirteenth-century
Mallorca, Llull learnt to read, write and speak several languages including
Arabic, and travelled to France, much of Spain and North Africa. He also
founded a monastery and missionary school on **Puig Randa**, 35km east of
Palma, where he spent ten years in seclusion and wrote no fewer than 250
books and treatises. It was Llull's scholarship that attracted the attention
of his old friend Jaume II, who summoned him to court in 1282. With royal
patronage, Llull then established a monastic school of Oriental languages
near Valldemossa, where he trained his future missionary companions.
Llull was killed on his third evangelical excursion to Algeria in 1315, his
martyrdom ensuring his subsequent beatification.

*The site of
Llull's mission-
ary school on
Puig Randa is
now occupied
by the
Santuari de
Nostra Senyora
de Cura – see
p.201.*

Llull's alabaster effigy set in the wall to the right of the chapel altarpiece at a disconcertingly precarious angle.

The Templar chapel

Follow c/Ramon Llull east from the basilica and you'll soon spy the
large and distinctive fortified **gateway** at the end of the street. Dating
from the thirteenth century, the gateway once marked the entrance to
the compound of the **Knights Templar**, a military order founded to
support the Crusades. The knights established bases right across the
Mediterranean and this was one of the more important – though they
were soon to be dispossessed. The order was rich and secretive, its
independence resented by the papacy and just about every secular
ruler in Europe. In 1312, following trumped-up charges of heresy, sorcery and bestiality, the pope disbanded the order and their Palma compound passed into the hands of the Hospitallers of St John, a rival
knightly order. The Knights Hospitallers struggled on until 1802 when
the Spanish king disbanded them and confiscated their property.

An alley leads through the gateway to the only other surviving part
of the military compound, the **Templar chapel** (in theory open
Mon–Fri 9.30am–1pm & 3.30–7pm, Sat 9.30am–1pm), whose
Gothic and Romanesque features were extensively remodelled in the
1880s. Inside, the gloomy nave is divided into three bays with ribbed
vaulting and a wooden ceiling over the atrium. The Romanesque
side-chapels in the entrance area are perhaps the church's most
diverting feature, all slender columns, rounded arches and intense
foliate and geometric decoration.

Plaça Sant Jeroni and around

Doubling back to the gateway, turn left along c/Temple and it's a couple of minutes' walk to **Plaça Sant Jeroni**, which is a pretty little piazza set around a diminutive water fountain. The severe stone walls of a former convent, now a college, dominate one side of the square, while the **Església de Sant Jeroni** fills out another. The church façade is mostly a plain stone wall, but it does sport an elaborate doorway, a swirl of carved foliage and some cheeky gargoyles. The tympanum portrays the story of Sant Jeroni (St Jerome) in the desert – a well-known tale in which the saint endures all sorts of tribulations and temptations, but still sticks true to the faith. Sant Jeroni also appears just above the gate, his head displayed between two heraldic lions, and inside, where – amongst several Mallorcan Primitive paintings – there is Pere Terrencs' lively *Sant Jeroni*. The paintings are, indeed, the highlight of the interior, a seventeenth-century affair with heavy stone vaulting and a whopping organ (but the church is, unfortunately, rarely open to the public).

St Jerome (342–420), a Croatian, lived much of his life in Bethlehem. He is known for making the first translation of the Bible from Hebrew into Latin and for resisting devilish temptations as a desert hermit.

From the square, c/Seminari and then c/Monti-Sion cut west to pass the **Església de Monti-Sion** (most likely to be open Mon–Fri 7–8.30am), whose thundering facade is a hectic heap of angels and saints, coats of arms and wriggling foliage. Below the figure of the Virgin, look out for a strangely inconclusive representation of the Devil – half-sheep, half-dragon. Beyond the church, c/Monti-Sion leads to a crossroads: turn right along c/Pare Nadal to reach the Basílica de Sant Francesc (see p.89); keep dead ahead and the twisting side streets will deliver you onto c/Cadena, a short distance from Plaça Cort.

Plaça Cort

With its elegant nineteenth-century facades, bustling **Plaça Cort** was named after the various legal bodies – both secular and religious – which, once upon a time, were concentrated here. Along with much of the rest of Spain, Mallorca possessed a truly byzantine legal system until the whole caboodle was swept away and rationalized during the Napoleonic occupation. On one side, the square is dominated by the **Ajuntament** (Town Hall), a debonair example of the late Renaissance style. Pop in for a look at the grand and self-assured foyer, which mostly dates from the nineteenth century, and the six folkloric *gigantones* (giant carnival figures) stored here – four in a corner, the other two tucked against the staircase.

From Plaça Cort, it's a pleasant five-minute stroll to the Passeig d'es Born via c/Sant Domingo, which weaves downhill lined by an attractive ensemble of nineteenth-century town houses with wrought-iron grilles and stone balconies. Alternatively, a short walk from Plaça Cort along c/Palau Reial brings you to the cathedral.

Along and around the Passeig d'es Born

Distinguished by the stone sphinxes at its top and bottom, the **Passeig d'es Born** has been the city's principal promenade since the early fifteenth century, when the stream that ran here was diverted following a disastrous flash flood. Nowadays, this leafy avenue is too traffic-congested to be endearing, but it's still at the heart of the city and in the immediate vicinity are some of Palma's most fashionable bars and restaurants.

At no. 27, overlooking the *passeig*, is the fine Italianate loggia of **Can Solleric** (Tues–Sat 10.30am–1.45pm & 5.30–9pm, Sun 10am–1.45pm; free), a lavish mansion of heavy wooden doors, marble columns and vaulted ceilings built for a family of cattle and olive oil merchants in 1763. Recently restored, the house now displays temporary exhibitions of modern art.

From **Plaça de la Reina**, the tiny, leafy square at the foot of the Passeig d'es Born, a wide and elegant flight of steps, the **Costa de la Seu**, leads up beneath the spiky walls of the Palau de l'Almudaina to the cathedral (see p.78). At the foot of the steps is another noteworthy mansion, the **Palau March**, a heavyweight affair whose arcaded galleries, chunky columns and large stone blocks were erected in the 1930s in the general style of the city's earlier Renaissance mansions. It was built for the Mallorcan magnate and art collector **Joan March** (1880–1962), who became the wealthiest man in Franco's Spain by skilfully reinvesting the profits he made from his control of the government monopoly in tobacco – though his enemies always insisted that it was smuggling that really made him rich. Most of the Palau March is not open to the public, but a few rooms have been turned into the **Biblioteca Bartomeu March Servera** (Mon–Fri 9.30am–2pm; free), one of several privately funded libraries dotted round the city.

You can view the art collection of the March family at the Banca March – see p.96.

South of Plaça de la Reina, **Avinguda d'Antoni Maura** runs down to the wide breakwater that marks the start of Palma harbour. The avenue takes its name from **Antoni Maura** (1853–1925), a Mallorquin who served as prime minister of Spain four times between 1903 and 1921. An outstanding orator and extraordinarily forceful personality, Maura was a conservative who opposed universal suffrage as "the politics of the mob", preferring a limited franchise and a constitution which gave power to the middle classes, as long as they marched to the tune of the church and the crown. To give the man some credit, his conservatism with regard to universal suffrage – which was in place from 1887 – was prompted by Spain's particular circumstances. In a backward, largely agrarian society, most Spaniards were largely indifferent to national issues and power was concentrated in the hands of district bosses, or *caciques*, who would bring out the vote for any candidate provided they were guaranteed control of political patronage. Some bosses ruled by intimidation, others by bribery, but the end result was a dense mixture of charity and jobbery, dubbed *caciquismo*, that made national government well-nigh impossible. Maura struggled against this chicanery, and his assertive nationalism was quite enough for Franco to have this avenue named after him.

El Puig de Sant Pere

The ancient neighbourhood of **El Puig de Sant Pere** (St Peter's Mount) covers the area west of the Passeig d'es Born and north to Avinguda Jaume III. Here, the narrow lanes and alleys shelter another sprinkling of patrician mansions, though most of the old houses were divided up into apartments years ago to cater for the district's sailors, dockers and fishermen. Again, it's the general flavour of the area that appeals rather than specific sights, but it's still worth seeking out two late Renaissance facades on c/Sant Feliu. At no. 8 is **Can Moner**, where the ornate doorway sports telamons, cherubs and cornucopia, whilst no. 10, **Can Pavesi**, offers a mythical beast with its tongue stuck right out.

Palma's best cybercafé, La Red, is at c/Concepció 5 – see p.107.

There's a gruesome story behind the name of a lane off nearby c/Estanc. **Mà del Moro**, "the hand of the Moor", harks back to Ahmed, an eighteenth-century slave who murdered his master in a house on this alley. Ahmed was executed for the crime, and his hand chopped off and stuck above the doorway of the house where the murder was committed.

Avinguda Jaume III

At the top of Passeig d'es Born, the sturdy shop and office blocks of **Avinguda Jaume III**, dating to the 1940s, march west towards the Passeig Mallorca. It's here you'll find some of the island's chicest clothes shops as well as downtown's biggest department store, El Corte Inglés. There's something very engaging about the avenue – a jostle of beshorted tourists and besuited Spaniards – and the web of ancient alleys immediately to the north is another attractive corner of the city, all high stone walls and dignified old mansions focused on c/Concepció.

East along c/Unió to Plaça Weyler and La Rambla

Eastwards from the top of the Passeig d'es Born runs **c/Unió**, a new if rather unimaginative appellation – it means "unity" – for a street Franco had previously named after General Mola, one of the prime movers of the Nationalist rebellion of 1936. Mola was killed in a plane accident during the Civil War, possibly to Franco's relief. Hitler, for one, thought that Mola was the more competent, remarking that his death meant that "Franco came to the top like Pontius Pilate in the Creed." **Can Balaguer**, the Renaissance mansion at c/Unió 3, has imposing doors and a grand cobbled courtyard. It is now used to display the work of local artists under the auspices of the city's art society, the Círculo de Bellas Artes; some of the work is very good, but don't expect a bargain.

A few metres further east along c/Unió is tiny **Plaça Mercat**, the site of two identical *Modernista* buildings, commissioned by a wealthy baker, Josep Casasayas, in 1908. Each is a masterpiece of flowing, organic lines tempered by graceful balconies and decorated with fern-leaf and butterfly motifs. Just down the street, on **Plaça Weyler**, stands a further *Modernista* extravagance, the magnificent **Gran Hotel** of 1903. Recently scrubbed and polished, the facade boasts playful arches, balconies, columns and bay windows enlivened with intricate floral trimmings and brilliant polychrome ceramics inspired by Hispano-Arabic designs. The interior houses a café-bar, a good art bookshop and the spacious **art gallery** of the Fundació La Caixa, the cultural arm of the savings bank, which organizes an excellent and wide-ranging programme of exhibitions (Tues–Sat 10am–9pm, Sun 10am–2pm; free). The permanent collection is confined to a large sample of the work of the Catalan impressionist Hermen Anglada-Camarasa, who produced dozens of evocative Mallorcan land- and seascapes during his sojourn on the island from 1914 to 1936.

There's another excellent example of *Modernismo* across the street from the Gran Hotel in the floral motifs and gaily painted wooden doorway of the **Forn des Teatre** (theatre bakery) at Plaça Weyler 9. A few metres away looms the Neoclassical frontage of the **Teatre Principal** – the city's main auditorium for classical music, ballet and opera – whose tympanum sports a fanciful relief dedicated to the nine Muses of Greek mythology.

At the theatre, the main street – now c/Riera – does a quick about-face to join the **Passeig de la Rambla**, whose plane trees shelter Palma's main flower market. The two statues at the foot of the boulevard, representing Roman emperors, were placed here in 1937 in honour of Mussolini's Italy – one set of Fascists tipping their municipal hats to another.

Plaça Major and around

On both sides of the Teatre Principal, steep flights of steps lead up to **Plaça Major**, a large pedestrianized square built on the site of the former headquarters of the **Inquisition** (see box on p.97). The square, a rather plain affair with a symmetrical portico running around its perimeter, once housed the fish and vegetable market, but nowadays it's popular for its pavement cafés.

On the south side of Plaça Major lies the much smaller **Plaça Marquès del Palmer**, a cramped setting for two fascinating *Modernista* edifices. The more dramatic is **Can Rei**, a five-storey apartment building splattered with polychrome ceramics and floral decoration, its centrepiece a gargoyle-like face set between a pair of winged dragons. The facade of the adjacent **L'Àguila** building is of similar ilk, though there's greater emphasis on window space, reflecting its original function as a department store.

To the south, the shopping area in between Plaça Marquès del Palmer and Plaça Cort remains one of the more agreeable parts of Palma. Its old-fashioned air is distilled from the three- and four-storey buildings that flank its main streets – principally pedestrianized c/Jaume II – embellished with an abundance of fancy iron-grilled balconies.

The Museu d'Art Espanyol Contemporani and around

Running north from Plaça Major, c/Sant Miquel is another popular and pleasant shopping street. Here, at no. 11, the **Banca March** occupies a fine Renaissance mansion whose *Modernista* flourishes date from a tasteful refurbishment of 1917. The building has two entrances, one to the bank, the other to the upper-floor **Museu d'Art Espanyol Contemporani** (Mon–Fri 10am–6.30pm, Sat 10am–1.30pm; 500ptas/€3.01), which features part of the contemporary art collection of the March family. Over fifty works are displayed, each by a different Spanish artist of the twentieth century, the intention being to survey the Spanish contribution to modern art. The theme is further developed by temporary exhibitions. The earliest piece, Picasso's *Tête de Femme* (1907), is of particular interest as it's one of the first of the artist's works to be influenced by the primitive forms that were to propel him, over the following decade, from the re-creation of natural appearances into abstract art. Miró and Dalí are also represented, and there's a substantial selection of work by the Spanish Cubist Juan Gris, but the bulk of the collection is remorselessly modern and hard to warm to, especially the allegedly "vigorous" abstractions of both the El Paso (Millares, Saura, Feito, Canogar) and the Parpalló (Sempere, Alfaro) groupings of the late 1950s.

For more on the March family, see p.93.

It's worth continuing a few metres up along c/Sant Miquel from the museum to the **Església Sant Miquel** (Mon–Sat 8am–1.30pm & 5–7.30pm, Sun 10am–1.30pm & 5.30–7.30pm). The sturdy exterior of this church, the result of all sorts of architectural meddlings, hides a gloomy barrel-vaulted nave and rib-vaulted side chapels. The poorly lit high altarpiece, a Baroque classic with a central image celebrating St Michael, showcases the intricate work of Francesc Herrara, a much-travelled Spanish painter of religious and genre subjects known for his purposeful compositions and tangy realism.

West along the harbourfront

The various marinas, shipyards, fish docks and ferry and cargo terminals that make up Palma's **harbourfront** extend west for several kilometres from the bottom of Avinguda d'Antoni Maura to the edge of Cala Major (see p.111). The harbour is at its prettiest at this eastern end and it's here that a cycling and walking path skirts the seashore, with boats to one side and bars, restaurants, apartment blocks and the smart hotels of the Avinguda Gabriel Roca – sometimes, confusingly, dubbed the Passeig Marítim – on the other.

The Spanish Inquisition

In 1478, mindful of his need for their military support, the pope granted Spain's Isabella I and Fernando V the right to establish their own **Inquisition**. It was much appreciated. The dual monarchs realised that the Catholic faith was the most powerful force binding a fragmented Spain together and they were sure the Inquisition would both consolidate the church's position and buttress their own. Installed in Castile in 1480 and in Aragón and Catalunya – including the Balearics – seven years later, the Inquisition began its work with the **Jews**. During the Middle Ages, the Jews had played a leading role in Spain's cultural and economic life and were generally treated with tolerance. This began to change in the late fourteenth century when many Spaniards became increasingly resentful of the Jews' commercial clout, and others resented the Jews' role as rent collectors for the big landowners. In 1391, anti-Semitic riots broke out across much of Spain – including Mallorca – and many Jews, in fear for their lives, hastily submitted to baptism. These new Christians were subsequently called **conversos**. In the event, though, baptism merely staved off disaster. The riots continued – like the disturbance in Palma in 1435 (see p.242) – and matters came to a head after the capture of Spain's last Moorish kingdom, Granada, in 1492. Flush with military success but short of cash, Fernando and Isabella **expelled** from Spain all those Jews who had not turned Christian – about 120,000 – and confiscated their property, leaving the remaining *conversos* isolated and vulnerable.

Following the Reformation, the Inquisition turned its gaze onto the **Protestants**, though in truth there were very few of them – only two thousand were indicted in Spain in the whole of the sixteenth century. Nevertheless, despite the limited nature of the Protestant threat, the Inquisition was profoundly influential. Most Spaniards regarded it as a bastion against heresy and, acting in this spirit, the Inquisitors kept all progressive thought at bay. Thus, whereas much of Europe was convulsed by disputation, Spain sank into ritual and dogma with the threat of the Inquisition in the background: in Palma few potential heretics could ignore the louring presence of its headquarters, plonked on a hill overlooking the city (now occupied by Plaça Major). Furthermore, by its very processes the Inquisition created an atmosphere of **fear** and **mistrust**. The Inquisitors acted on charges of heresy brought to them by the public, but these accusations were often frivolous or motivated by personal enmity. Worse still, even the most orthodox Catholic could not be sure of acquittal. The Inquisitor's examinations were often so theologically complex and long-winded that the danger of self-condemnation was ever-present – under torture, many would confess to anything and everything.

Opposed by reforming clerics in the eighteenth century and increasingly ignored by the state, the Inquisition gradually lost influence. It was finally **abolished** during the Napoleonic occupation of Spain in 1808. Fifteen years later, in 1823, the headquarters of the Inquisition in Palma was demolished.

Specific highlights, aside from a couple of attractive gardens, include the **Poble Espanyol**, a glib attempt to reproduce highlights of Spanish architecture, and the impressively sited hilltop **Castell de Bellver** overlooking the harbour.

Café Port Pesquer, *just east of the fish dock, has an attractive terrace bar on the waterfront –* *see p.101.*

Sa Llotja

The first harbourfront landmark is the fifteenth-century **Llotja**, th
city's former stock exchange (Tues–Sat 11am–2pm & 5–9pm, Su
11am–2pm; free). This carefully composed late Gothic building, wit
its four octagonal turrets, slender columns and tall windows, nov
hosts frequent and occasionally excellent exhibitions. It also boast
a series of fierce-looking gargoyles and a muscular angel – appropr
ately the Guardian Angel of Commerce – above the front door. Nex
door, the distinguished **Consolat de Mar** was built in the 1660s t
accommodate the Habsburg officials who supervised maritim
affairs in this part of the empire. Today, as the home of the presiden
Some of the Balearic Islands, it's closed to the public, but the outside i
exhibitions at worth a second look for its pair of crusty old cannons and elegan
Sa Llotja have Renaissance gallery. The forlorn-looking gate in between the tw
admission fees buildings – the **Porta Vella del Moll** – originally stood at the end c
and non- Avinguda d'Antoni Maura, where it was the main entrance into th
standard city from the sea, but was moved here when portions of the town wa
opening hours. were demolished in the 1870s.

To the Jardins La Quarentena

At the foot of **Avinguda Argentina** – opposite the jetties where th
fishing boats come in – is a pleasant terraced park, whose trees
lawns and flower beds step north to Plaça La Feixina. The park abut
both the walled watercourse which once served as the **city moat** an
the sheer **bastion** that anchored the southwest corner of th
Renaissance city wall, the only blot being the whopping **colum**
erected by Franco in honour – as they say – of those Balearic sailor
who were loyal to the Fascist cause.

The best views Continuing west from the foot of Avinguda Argentina, it's a furthe
of the harbour fifteen or twenty minutes' walk along the palm-lined esplanade to th
are from the next worthwhile objective, the delightful **Jardins La Quarentena**, :
Castell de leafy little park whose cool and shaded terraces, with their aromati
Bellver – see trees and shrubs, clamber up the hillside from the harbourfront.
opposite.

The Poble Espanyol

A couple of kilometres west of the old town, and reachable by EM
bus #5 from Plaça Espanya – the nearest stop is on Avinguda Andre
Doria – is the **Poble Espanyol** (Spanish Village; daily: April–Nov
9am–8pm; Dec–March 9am–6pm; 800ptas/€4.81). This kitsch, pur
pose-made tourist attraction was built between 1965 and 1967, wit
Francoist intentions apparent in its celebration of everythin
Spanish. Walled like a medieval city, the village contains accurat
reproductions of about twenty old and important buildings, such a
Barcelona's Palau de la Generalitat, Seville's Torre del Oro, a seg
ment of Granada's Alhambra, El Greco's house in Toledo, and th
Ermita de San Antonio in Madrid. These are woven round the vi
lage's streets and squares, where you'll also find craft workshops

souvenir shops, restaurants and bars. It's all a bit daft – and school parties swamp the place – but it's an easy way of introducing yourself to Spanish architecture.

The Castell de Bellver

Boasting superb views of Palma and its harbour from a wooded hilltop some 3km west of the city centre, and 1km southwest of the Poble Espanyol, is the **Castell de Bellver** (April–Sept Mon–Sat 8am–8pm, Sun 10am–7pm; Oct–March Mon–Sat 8am–7pm, Sun 10am–5pm; 275ptas/€1.65; free on Sun, when the castle museum is closed). Take **bus #3** or **#21** from Plaça Espanya or bus **#4** or **#21** from Plaça de la Reina to Plaça Gomila, which leaves a steep one-kilometre walk up the hill. If you're driving, turn off Avinguda Joan Miró (one-way west) onto the circuitous c/Camilo José Cela to reach the castle.

This handsome, strikingly well-preserved fortress was built for Jaume II at the beginning of the fourteenth century. Of canny circular design, the castle's immensely thick walls and steep ditches encircle a central **keep** that incorporates three imposing towers. In addition, an overhead, single-span **stone arch** connects the keep to a massive, freestanding tower, built as a final refuge. To enhance defence, the walls curve and bend and the interconnecting footbridges are set at oblique angles to each other. It's all very impressive – and looks well-nigh impregnable – but the castle was also intended to serve as a royal retreat from the summer heat, and so the austere outside walls hide a commodious, genteel-looking **circular courtyard**, surrounded by two tiers of inward-facing arcades that once belonged to the residential suites. The whole construction is ingenious, incorporating many skilful touches: the flat roof, for example, was designed to channel every drop of rainwater into a huge underground cistern.

Improvements in artillery, however, soon rendered the fortress obsolete, and it didn't last long as a royal residence either. As early as the 1350s the keep was in use as a prison, a function it performed until 1915. More recently, the castle interior has been turned into a **museum** with a series of modest exhibits tracking through the history of the city on the ground floor and a much more enjoyable miscellany of Roman sculpture upstairs. The Roman artefacts were collected by **Cardinal Antonio Despuig** (1745–1817), a local antiquarian and ecclesiastical bigwig, who bequeathed his collection to the city. The stone busts and effigies of Roman dignitaries are fairly routine, but there are some exquisite alabaster pieces too – including a sensuous sleeping woman, half-in and half-out of her toga. The problem is that there is no labelling at all, so unless you're a classical expert it's impossible to know quite what you're looking at.

After you've explored the castle, you can wander through the pine-scented woods that surround it. There's a network of **footpaths**, but no signs.

Cardinal Despuig's old country home, Raixa, south of Sóller, has terraced gardens open to the public – see p.132.

Eating and drinking

Eating well in Palma is less pricey – or can be – than anywhere else in Mallorca. Inexpensive **cafés** and **tapas bars** are liberally distributed around the city centre, with a particular concentration in the side streets off the Passeig d'es Born and Avinguda d'Antoni Maura. Many downtown cafés are up and running by 9am, but with most visitors eating breakfast at their hotel there's not the demand for early-morning places you might expect in a big city. On the other hand, for light lunches and snacks (*tapas*) you're spoiled for choice. You can chomp away in chic modernist surroundings, or join the crowds in simple formica and wallpaper diners where the food more than compensates for the decor – and then there's everything in between.

In Palma's cafés and restaurants, multilingual menus (in English, German, Catalan and Castilian) are commonplace.

There's not much distinction between *tapas* bars and **restaurants**, as many of the former serve full meals as well as snacks – and, of course, put a couple of *tapas* together and you've got a full meal anyway. Indeed, the differences often have more to do with appearance than food: if you've got a tablecloth, for instance, you're almost certainly in a restaurant. Opening times vary enormously, but many places close one day a week – usually Sunday or Monday, but sometimes only out of season – and the majority take a siesta from about 3pm or 4pm to 7pm or, in the case of smarter joints, 8pm.

Many of Palma's restaurants and *tapas* bars are geared up for the tourist trade, especially those along the harbourfront and amongst the side streets off Avinguda d'Antoni Maura. It is, however, foolish to be snooty about them, as some serve delicious food and are popular with Spaniards as well. If you venture a little further into the city centre, you'll discover more exclusively local haunts, some offering the finest of Catalan and Spanish cuisine. A smattering of restaurants specialize in ethnic foods such as Swedish and Indian, and there's a vegetarian café-restaurant too.

At all but the most expensive of places, 4000ptas/€24.04 will cover the cost of a starter and main course, as well as a bottle of wine – though you can expect prices to be jacked up in the summer.

Cafés and tapas bars

Bar Bosch, Plaça Rei Joan Carles I. One of the most popular and inexpensive *tapas* bars in town, the traditional haunt of intellectuals and usually humming with conversation. At peak times you'll need to be assertive to get served.

Bon Lloc, c/Sant Feliu 7. One of the few vegetarian café-restaurants on the island, centrally situated off the Passeig d'es Born. Informal atmosphere and good food at low prices. Open Mon–Sat 1–4pm.

Café Can Solleric, Passeig d'es Born 27. Attached to the art gallery of the same name (see p.93), this modern bar, with its brisk furnishings and fittings, is a fashionable spot – and especially popular when football is on the TV. However, there is no food to speak of and the tiny pavement area is only any good if you're indifferent to the rush of the traffic.

Café Lirico, Avgda d'Antoni Maura 6. Most of Palma's downtown cafés have been modernized, but not this one – its large mirrors, imitation marble and weatherbeaten clientele are reminiscent of Spanish cafés of yesteryear. Not much in the way of food.

Café Port Pesquer, Avgda Gabriel Roca s/n. Bright and breezy, gleamingly new café on the harbourfront a few minutes' walk west of Avgda d'Antoni Maura, overlooking the jetty where the fishing boats come in. The open-air terrace bar is a good spot to soak up the evening sun.

Cafeteria Jaime III, Avgda Jaume III 20. Popular with office workers and shoppers, this brisk modern café serves up a good line in snacks – try their *pa amb oli* (bread rubbed with olive oil) and smoked ham.

Cafeteria Sa Murada, in between the two sets of city walls at the foot of c/Portella. Tasty snacks with the emphasis on traditional Mallorcan dishes. If you've been walking the old town, this is a good spot to soak up the sun from the relative quiet of a pedestrianized mini-plaza.

Ca'n Joan de S'Aigo, c/Can Sanç 10. A long-established coffee house with wonderful, freshly baked *ensaimadas* (spiral pastry buns) for just 100ptas/€0.60 and fruit-flavoured mousses to die for. Charming decor too, from the kitsch water fountain to the traditional Mallorcan green-tinted chandeliers. It's on a tiny alley near Plaça Santa Eulalia – take c/Sant Crist and its continuation c/Canisseria, and turn right. Closed Tues.

Colonial, c/Palau Reial s/n. Mallorcans aren't really into the American-led coffee craze, but this spick-and-span modern café, a couple of doors down from the Ajuntament (Town Hall), prepares its brews from all sorts of coffee beans and offers a variety of infusion teas and a few *tapas* too.

Es Cantó de S'Arc, c/Morey 6. Smart café-restaurant just off Plaça Santa Eulalia with charmingly antique furnishings and fittings. A wide-ranging menu includes pizza and traditional Mallorcan dishes with main courses averaging around 1000ptas/€6.01. The *menú del día* at 950ptas/€5.71 is excellent and usually features either Catalan or Castilian favourites. Closed Sun.

La Cueva, c/Apuntadors 9. Small and busy *tapas* bar, one of several on this street, with a rack of liquors behind the bar and hocks of meat hanging up in front. Reasonable prices; tasty food.

Mesón Salamanca, c/Sant Jaume 3. In a glossily refurbished, warren-like town house off Avgda Jaume III, this establishment has a ground-floor wine bar offering tasty *tapas* from 1000ptas/€6.01 and up; it's much better than the stuffy restaurant upstairs.

Orient Express, c/Llotja de Mar 6, beside Sa Llotja. Idiosyncratic café-restaurant with an interior like the inside of a railway carriage. Salads are its speciality; you'll have to wait for a seat at lunchtime.

S'Impremta, c/Morey 2. Amiable neighbourhood café-restaurant offering a delicious range of *tapas* plus a great-value *menú del día* for 1000ptas/€6.01. Closes 5.30pm.

El Pilon, c/Can Cifre 4. Vibrant, cramped and crowded *tapas* bar on a side-street off the north end of Passeig d'es Born serving all manner of Spanish and Mallorcan dishes at very reasonable prices. Bags of atmosphere.

Pope Bar, c/Apuntadors 10. With its gaggle of bars and cafés, c/Apuntadors heaves with tourists throughout the summer, but somehow this little *tapas* bar has remained remarkably unaffected. There's no glitz and gloss here, but instead the bar – overlooked by fading soccer pennants and photos – is stocked with authentic *tapas* dishes at bargain-basement prices, from just 400ptas/€2.40 per portion.

Verd Llimona, c/Montenegro 7. This modern café-bar, with its plain but fashionable decor, is noted for its old-time snacks – try the *pa amb oli* (bread rubbed with olive oil) – and as a late-night drinking den.

Restaurants

Aramis, c/Montenegro 1 ☎971 725 232. One of the new breed of Spanish restaurants, reflecting the islanders' prosperity and European outlook. The decor here is smart and very nouveau, though the restaurant is lodged within an old stone mansion on a sidestreet off Passeig d'es Born. The menu is imaginative and international – ravioli and pumpkin, steamed hake and so forth. Main courses cost 2500–3500ptas/€15.03–€21.04.

Asador Tierra Aranda, c/Concepció 4, off Avgda Jaume III ☎971 714 256. A high-class, fairly formal carnivore's paradise in an old mansion: meats either grilled over open fires or roasted in wood-fired ovens, with suckling pig and lamb a speciality. Closed at lunchtime; open from 8pm.

Baiskhi, Avgda Gabriel Roca 8 ☎971 736 806. A hit with the locals, this excellent Indian restaurant is both smart and cosy, with flower petals scattered here and there, Indian paintings and music. There's no choice as such, just a set menu of several courses for 4000ptas/€24.04. The food is outstanding.

Caballito del Mar, across the plaza from Sa Llotja at Passeig Sagrera 5 ☎971 721 074. There was a time when this trim little restaurant was generally regarded as the best seafood place in town. It doesn't seem so outstanding today – for a start, the vegetables tend to be overcooked – but there's still an extensive range of fish to choose from. The *daurada amb sal al forn*, or *dorada à la sal* (sea bream baked in salt) remains excellent. Main courses average around 2500ptas/€15.03.

Ca'n Carlos, c/Aigua 5 ☎971 713 869. Charming, family-run restaurant featuring exquisite Mallorcan cuisine that takes in dishes such as cuttlefish and snails. The menu isn't extensive, but everything is beautifully and imaginatively prepared and there's a daily special as well as a fish of the day. Main courses average around 1800ptas/€10.82. The furnishings and fittings are smart and cheerfully modern. It's situated near the bottom of c/Aigua, a narrow side street off Avgda Jaume III. Open for lunch and from 8pm.

Casa Eduardo, Moll Industria Pesquera 4 ☎971 721 182. Spick-and-span restaurant located upstairs in one of the plain modern buildings beside the fish dock. There's an enjoyable view of the harbour, but the real treat is the fresh fish – a wonderful range, all simply prepared. The first-rate *menú del día* costs around 2500ptas/€15.03. It's about five minutes' walk west along the harbourfront from Avgda d'Antoni Maura; the fish dock is just before Avgda Argentina. Closed Sun and Mon.

Casa Gallega, c/Can Pueyo 6 ☎971 714 377. Long-established place offering quality Galician cuisine, particularly seafood. There's a downstairs *tapas* bar and a more formal restaurant upstairs. It's just north of Plaça Weyler, down the side street beside the Gran Hotel.

Celler Pagès, off c/Apuntadors at c/Felip Bauza 2 ☎971 726 036. Traditional Mallorcan food in a tiny, inexpensive restaurant near Passeig d'es Born. Easygoing atmosphere, though stifling hot in the summer. Main courses are 1000–1700ptas/€6.01–€10.22. Closed Sun.

Celler Sa Premsa, Plaça Bisbe Berenguer de Palou 8 ☎971 723 529. Justly popular restaurant with delicious seafood cooked in traditional Mallorcan style. A five-minute walk west of the Plaça Espanya. Old bullfighting photos and posters adorn the walls amidst a pot-pourri of dusty bygones; you'll probably share a table with other diners. Prices are surprisingly low – as little as 1800ptas/€10.82 per person for a three-course meal. Closed Sun year-round, and also closed Sat in July & Aug.

Dalt Murada, c/Sant Roc 1 ☎971 714 464. Café-restaurant specializing in Mallorcan cuisine. It occupies part of an attractively renovated Renaissance mansion a couple of minutes' walk north of the cathedral. The *tapas* are tasty and there's a shaded terrace where you can take a leisurely break from wandering the streets of the old town – but in the evenings it's heads down for a full restaurant meal. Reservations are advised.

Es Parlament, c/Conquistador 11 ☎971 726 026. All gilt-wood mirrors and chandeliers, this old and polished restaurant specializes in paella. The tasty and reasonably priced *menú del día* is recommended too. A favourite hangout of local politicians and lawyers. Closed Sun.

Forn de Sant Joan, c/Sant Joan 4 ☎971 728 422. Smart and extremely popular Catalan restaurant near Sa Llotja, one of several busy spots on this narrow alley. Fine fish dishes for around 2200ptas/€13.22, *tapas* from 950ptas/€5.71.

Il Porticato, c/Ramon Llull 8 ☎971 718 749. Well away from the tourist trail, this cosy bar-restaurant with pastel-painted walls and slick, modernist furniture offers tasty Italian cuisine. Pizzas from 850ptas/€5.11; pastas from 1000ptas/€6.01.

S'Olivera, c/Morey 5 ☎971 712 935. This appealingly smart restaurant, with its antique bygones dotted round the walls, is situated just off Plaça Santa Eulalia. A first-rate range of *tapas*, at around 600ptas/€3.61 per portion, plus quality Spanish cuisine and a good-value lunchtime *menú del día*.

Svarta Pannan, c/Can Brondo 5 ☎971 721 039. Comfortable Swedish restaurant conveniently close to Plaça Rei Joan Carles I. The food isn't remarkable, but makes a refreshing change; go for the seared salmon.

Specialist food and drink shops

Many Palma shops and most supermarkets carry a reasonable range of Spanish **wines**, and some also carry Balearic vintages. One of these is Vins, Plaça Cort 7 ☎971 726 819, while another, even better choice lies a couple of kilometres west of the centre off Avgda Andrea Doria: El Centro del Vino y del Cava, c/Bartomeu Rosselló-Porcel 19 (Mon–Fri 9am–1.30pm & 4.30–8pm, Sat 9am–1.30pm; ☎971 452 564). Amongst the city's specialist food shops, Colmado Santo Domingo, c/Sant Domingo 1, is a tiny, old-fashioned store packed with hanging **sausages** and local fruit and veg, and Colmado Colom, just down the street, is similar; both are in the city centre in the subway adjoining c/Conquistador. Palma has lots of good cake and **pastry** shops (*pastelerías*), including Forn des Teatre, Plaça Weyler 9, and the excellent Forn Fondo, c/Unió 15. The biggest department store in the city centre, El Corte Inglés, Avgda Jaume III 15 (Mon–Sat 10am–10pm), has a substantial **food and drink** section in its basement.

For details of Palma's markets, see p.107.

Nightlife and entertainment

Most of the cafés and *tapas* bars listed above are quite happy just to
ply you with drink, making the distinction between them and the
bars we've listed below somewhat artificial. Nonetheless, there is a
cluster of lively **late-night bars** – mostly with music as the backdrop
rather than the main event – amongst the narrow and ancient side
streets backing onto Plaça Llotja. Alternatively, a number of more
modish bars are strung along Avinguda Gabriel Roca in the vicinity
of the Jardins La Quarentena. Indeed, Avinguda Gabriel Roca, with
its ritzy hotels and apartment blocks, hums at night with locals hop-
ping between the bars comparing fashion notes. The suburb of El
Terreny, also west of the centre, below the Castell de Bellver, has a
clutch of late-night bars too, but the district has gone downhill since
its days as the trendiest part of Palma. It now features topless "enter-
tainment", sex shops and a scattering of **gay** bars (for which, see
p.107).

   Clubs (*discotecas*) are not Palma's forte, but there are one or two
of some merit on Avinguda Gabriel Roca. They're rarely worth investigating until around 1am and entry charges will rush you anything
between 500ptas/€3.01 and 1000ptas/€6.01, depending on the
night and what's happening. The doorstaff often operate an informal
dress code of one sort or another – if you want to get in, avoid beach
gear and (heaven forbid) white trainers.

   Traditionally, Palma has had little to offer in terms of **performing
arts**, but matters are on the mend. The grand nineteenth-century
Teatre Principal, Plaça Weyler 16 (☎971 725 548), has been resus-
citated and now features classical concerts and opera, whilst the
revamped Teatre Municipal, Passeig Mallorca 9B (☎971 739 148),
has a more varied programme of contemporary drama, classic films,
dance and ballet.

Late-night bars

Abaco, just off c/Apuntadors at c/Sant Joan 1 ☎971 715 974. Inhabiting a
charming Renaissance mansion, this is easily Palma's most unusual bar, with an
interior straight out of a Busby Berkeley musical: fruits cascading down its stairway, caged birds hidden amid patio foliage, elegant music and a daily flower bill
you could live on for a month. Drinks, as you might imagine, are extremely
expensive (cocktails cost as much as 2000ptas/€12.02) but you're never hurried
into buying one. It is, however, too sedate to be much fun if you're on the razzle.

Babel, Avgda Gabriel Roca 31. Small, fast, lively little late-night bar near the
Jardins La Quarentena. Pop and techno.

Barcelona Jazz Café Club, c/Apuntadors 9. Groovy little spot on one of the
busiest streets in town. Jazz, blues and Latin sounds. Metres from the corner
of c/Sant Joan.

Box Office, Avgda Gabriel Roca 31. Hip and popular bar near the Jardins La
Quarentena.

La Bóveda, c/Boteria 3, off Plaça Llotja. Classy, fashionable bar, one of several on this short alley, with long, wide windows and wine stacked high along the back wall. Be prepared to queue to get in – or come early.

Golden Door, c/Apuntadors 3. With the flavour of a 1970s disco – mirror ball and all – this slick bar-cum-club has a mixed gay and straight clientele. Open until 4am.

Gotic, Plaça Llotja 4. Tiny bar redeemed by its candle-lit patio/pavement tables, which nudge out across the piazza, adding a touch of romance.

Latitud, c/Felip Bauza 8, off c/Apuntadors. Tiny, upbeat bar, playing jazz, blues and sometimes classical music.

La Lonja, opposite Sa Llotja. A popular, well-established haunt, with revolving doors and pleasantly old-fashioned decor; the background music caters for (almost) all tastes. *Tapas* too.

Made in Brazil, Avgda Gabriel Roca 27. Alarming tropical decor in this pocket-sized club-cum-bar on the city-centre side of Jardins La Quarentena. Great Latin sounds and cocktails.

Pub de Click, Passeig Mallorca s/n. This is Palma's last-chance saloon – the sort of place you end up in when you've (almost) forgotten where you are. The green and yellow paintwork is marginally frightening, but as for the rest it bears an uncanny resemblance to a works canteen. Open 7pm to 4am every day of the week. At the top of c/Avgda Jaume III.

Ses Voltes, Parc de la Mar. Open-air spot which often has live acts – pop, jazz and rock to varying standards.

Clubs

Discoteca Pacha, Avgda Gabriel Roca 42 ☎971 455 908. Loud, popular and raucous housey disco with a dance floor and a couple of bars inside and another bar outside in the garden. A ten-minute walk west of the Jardins La Quarentena, and 800m east of the ferry terminal. Admission 2500ptas/€15.03.

Discoteca Tito's, Plaça Gomila 3 ☎971 730 017. With its stainless steel and glass exterior, this long-established nightspot looks a bit like something from a sci-fi film set. Outdoor lifts carry you up from Avgda Gabriel Roca (the back entrance) to the dance floor, which pulls in huge crowds from many countries – or you can go in through the front entrance on Plaça Gomila. The music (anything from house to Top 40) lacks conviction, but it's certainly loud. The Avgda Gabriel Roca entrance is just on the city centre side of the Jardins La Quarentena. Admission 3000ptas/€18.03.

Listings

Airlines Air Berlin ☎901 116 402; Air France, Avgda Jaume III 16 ☎971 715 900 or ☎901 112 266; British Midland, Avgda Joan Miró 16 ☎971 453 112, or airport ☎971 789 477; EasyJet ☎902 299 992; Iberia, Avgda Joan Miró 8 ☎971 756 718, or airport ☎971 743 042; Lufthansa, Plaça Rosari 5, 3è ☎971 213 612; Spanair, airport ☎971 260 060.

Airport information ☎971 789 000.

Banks There are plenty of banks on and around the Passeig d'es Born and Avgda Jaume III. Banco de Crédito Balear has branches at Avgda Jaume III 27,

Listings

and Plaça Espanya 1; Banca March at Plaça Rei Joan Carles I 5, and c/San Miquel 30; Banco Santander at c/Jaume II 18, and c/Bonaire 4. There are also British banks, with Lloyds TSB at Passeig Mallorca 4 and Barclays sharing the premises of the Banco de Crédito Balear at Avgda Jaume III 27. The two biggest savings banks, which also handle currency exchange, have branches all over the city. La Caixa has a handy downtown branch at Passeig d'es Born 23; for Sa Nostra go to Avgda Jaume III 18. There are 24-hour cash machines dotted round the city too.

Beaches The closest beach to the city centre is the narrow strip of sand next to the *autopista* just beyond Avgda Gabriel Alomar i Villalonga. Swimming is not, however, recommended here as the water is too polluted. Instead most locals make the half-hour trip on bus #15 east to the Platja de Palma (see p.110).

Bike shops Bimont, Plaça Progrés 19 ☎971 731 866, runs a bicycle repair service and is one of about twelve city shops to sell bikes, the biggest outlet being Ciclos Mallorca, c/Joan Alcover 23 ☎971 467 616. You can't rent bikes anywhere, but you can rent mopeds/scooters from RTR Rental, Avgda Joan Miró 340 ☎971 702 775.

Books and maps El Corte Inglés, Avgda Jaume III 15, sells a small and rather eccentric assortment of English-language books from Ken Follett to Anne Frank. It also has a modest selection of Mallorca guidebooks and maps. Librería Fondevila, near the Teatre Principal at Costa de Sa Pols 18 (Mon–Fri 9.45am–1.30pm & 4.30–8pm, Sat 9.45am–1.30pm; ☎971 725 616), doesn't do much better when it comes to novels and guidebooks, but it does have a fairly good selection of general maps of Mallorca. In addition, it has a reasonably comprehensive selection of IGN hiking maps. Palma has one specialist map shop, the Casa del Mapa, c/Sant Domingo 11 (Mon–Fri 9am–2pm; ☎971 225 945), with a fairly comprehensive selection of IGN hiking maps as well as various maps of the island and Palma.

Bullfights Palma's bullfighting ring, Plaça de Toros ☎971 755 245, is a few blocks northeast of the Plaça Espanya along c/Reina Maria Cristina. Get tickets and details from travel agents and hotel receptions.

Buses Details of all major Mallorcan bus services are available from all the city's tourist offices (see p.71). For information on EMT city buses, call ☎971 711 393 or visit the kiosk on Plaça Espanya. Information on buses island-wide is on ☎971 176 970 (in Spanish and Catalan).

Car rental Mallorca's airport heaves with car rental companies and so does Palma, where there's a concentration – including many small concerns – along Avgda Gabriel Roca. Amongst the big companies, there's Atesa-National, Avgda Gabriel Roca 25 ☎971 456 762, or airport ☎971 789 896; Avis, Avgda Gabriel Roca 16 ☎971 730 720, or airport ☎971 789 187; Betacar, Avgda Gabriel Roca 20 ☎971 455 144, or airport ☎971 789 135; Hertz, Avgda Gabriel Roca 13 ☎971 734 737, or airport ☎971 789 670. The tourist office will supply a complete list of rental companies.

Consulates Belgium, Passeig d'es Born 15 ☎971 724 786; Germany, Passeig d'es Born 15 ☎971 722 371; Ireland, c/Sant Miquel 68A ☎971 719 244; Netherlands, Sant Miquel 36 ☎971 716 493; Norway, c/Unió 2 ☎971 710 809; Sweden, c/Unió 2 ☎971 722 381; United Kingdom, Plaça Major 3 ☎971 712 445; USA, Avgda Jaume III 26 ☎971 725 051.

Doctors and dentists In the resort areas and in Palma most hotel receptions will be able to find an English-speaking doctor or dentist. For complete lists

look under *metges* (Castilian *médicos*) or *clíniques dentals* (*clínicas den-*
tales) in the Yellow Pages.

Email and Internet *La Red* cybercafé, c/Concepció 5, just off Avgda Jaume III
☎971 713 574 (*www.laredcafe.com*) has fifteen PCs as well as fax machines
and scanners. Good sounds, plus snacks and drinks too. Mon–Fri 11am–1am,
Sat & Sun 4pm–midnight; access is 850ptas/€5.11 per hour.

Emergencies ☎112.

Ferries Palma's tourist offices have ferry schedules and tariffs. Tickets can be
purchased at travel agents or direct from the offices of the two ferry lines down
at the ferry port, about 3.5km west of the city centre along Avgda Gabriel
Roca. At Terminal 2 is Trasmediterranea ☎902 454 645, which operates ferries to Maó on Menorca, Ibiza, Barcelona and Valencia; and a couple of minutes' walk away at Terminal 3 is Balearia ☎902 160 180, with services to
Valencia, Ibiza and Dénia. For more on ferry routes from the mainland, see
p.20. For details of transport to and from Palma's ferry terminal, see p.68.

Films Teatro Cine Rialto, c/Sant Feliu 3, presents mainstream Spanish films
plus international blockbusters, usually dubbed.

Gay scene Palma's gay bars and clubs are concentrated in the El Terreny district, just west of the city centre below the Castell de Bellver. Among several
popular spots dotted along the first part of Avgda Joan Miró are the *Status
Pub*, at no. 38; the *Yuppi Club*, no. 106; and *Flesh*, no. 68. The Ben Amics
organization, c/Impremta 1, 1è, runs an information line (Mon–Fri 7–9pm;
☎971 723 058) and produces a bimonthly newssheet that's available free at
most gay venues.

Hospital Hospital General, Plaça Hospital 3 ☎971 212 000.

Laundry There's a downtown self-service laundry, Lavandería Self Press, at
c/Annibal 14, off Avgda Argentina (☎971 730 643).

Libraries There's a quaint municipal library inside the Ajuntament (Town Hall)
on Plaça Cort (Mon–Fri 8.30am–8.30pm, Sat 9am–1pm). The city also has several privately funded libraries-cum-reading rooms – one of the more convenient is the Biblioteca Bartomeu March Servera (see p.93).

Markets Palma's big Rastrillo (flea market) is held every Saturday morning,
8am–2pm, on Avgda Gabriel Alomar i Villalonga, between Plaça Porta d'es
Camp and c/Manacor. There's a fresh fruit and vegetable market on Plaça
Navegació, just west of Avgda Argentina (Mon–Sat 7am–2pm); and a daily
flower market on Passeig de la Rambla.

Pharmacies Central pharmacies include Farmacia Castañer, Plaça Rei Joan
Carles I 3; Farmacia Llobera, Plaça Santa Eulalia 1; and Farmacia A Nadal,
Plaça Cort 1. A full list of pharmacies is in the Yellow Pages under *farmàcies*
(Castilian *farmacias*).

Post office The old central *correu*, at c/Constitució 5, was being refurbished
at the time of writing. In the meantime, its services were transferred to the post
office at Passeig d'es Born 15 (Mon–Fri 8.30am–8.30pm, Sat 9.30am–2pm).

Shopping Palma has a healthy range of specialist shops, listed in the tourist
office's comprehensive *Artesanía* leaflet. The ritziest **clothes** stores are concentrated on and around Avgda Jaume III and the adjoining Plaça Joan Carles
I. For **souvenirs**, head to La Concha, c/Jaume II 19, which stocks brightly-
coloured Spanish fans, olive-wood trinkets, garish Spanish plates, model
cherubs, mini-gigantones (carnival figures) and *siurells* – tiny, white clay
whistles flecked with red and green paint and shaped to depict a figure, an ani-

Listings

mal or a scene (a man sitting on a donkey, for instance) – cheap and cheerful gifts which have been given as tokens of friendship in Mallorca for hundreds of years. **Glass-making** is a traditional island craft (see p.199) and Vidrias Gordiola, c/Victoria 2 (Mon–Fri 10am–1.45pm & 4.30–8pm, Sat 10am–1.45pm; ☎971 711 541) features a fine range of clear and tinted glassware, from bowls, vases and lanterns through to some wonderfully intricate chandeliers. Old-fashioned La Casa del Olivo, on c/Pescateria Vella, a tiny alley off c/Jaume II (Mon–Fri 9.30am–1.30pm & 4.30–8pm, Sat 9.30am–1.30pm) is an Aladdin's cave of **olive-wood carvings**, with everything from spoons, bread boards and salad bowls to more eccentric-looking items. **Artificial pearls** are made at Manacor (see p.206) by Majorica, who have dozens of official agents in Palma as well as their own outlet at Avgda Jaume III 11 ☎971 725 268.

Taxis Taxi ranks can be found outside major hotels. Alternatively, telephone Taxi Palma Radio (☎971 401 414) or Radio Taxi (☎971 755 440).

Trains The tourist office has train timetable details or you can phone direct: the Palma to Inca line is on ☎971 752 245; Palma to Sóller on ☎971 752 051.

Travel agencies There are dozens of travel agencies in Palma, listed in full in the Yellow Pages under *agències de viatges* (Castilian, *agencias de viajes*). Two helpful downtown choices are Viajes Iberia, Passeig d'es Born 14 ☎971 726 743, and Mallorca Tours, Sant Miquel 50 ☎971 722 606.

Around Palma

Arched around the sheltered waters of the **Badia de Palma** are the package tourist resorts that have made Mallorca synonymous with the cheap and tacky. In recent years the Balearic government have done their best to improve matters – greening resorts, restricting high-rise construction and redirecting traffic away from the coast – but their inherited problems remain. In the 1960s and 1970s, the bay experienced a building boom of almost unimaginable proportions as miles of pristine shoreline sprouted concrete and glass hotel towers, overwhelming the area's farms and fishing villages. There were few planning controls, if any, and the legacy is the mammoth sprawl of development that now extends, almost without interruption, from **S'Arenal** in the east to **Magaluf** in the west – with Palma roughly in the middle. To make matters worse, it is also debatable as to whether the recent move away from high-rise construction is well-conceived. The new villa complexes that are now the fashion gobble up the land at an alarming rate and multiply traffic. Furthermore, although the new villas are rarely more than three storeys high and built in a sort of pan-Mediterranean style – some with Neoclassical features, others more reminiscent of Spanish design – they end up looking terribly, remorselessly suburban. As a consequence, although the thirty-kilometre-long stretch of coast between S'Arenal and Magaluf is divided into a score or more resorts, it's often impossible to pick out where one ends and the next begins. That said, most of the resorts have evolved their own identities, either in terms of the nationalities they attract, the income group they appeal to, or the age range they cater for.

East of Palma lies **S'Arenal**, mainly geared up for German tourists and focused on the youth scene, with dozens of pounding bars and clubs open right through the night. S'Arenal also fringes one of Mallorca's best **beaches**, the **Platja de Palma**, which stretches from S'Arenal round to **Ca'n Pastilla**, but although the beach is superb, the flat shoreline behind it accommodates an unprepossessing, seemingly endless strip of restaurants, bars and souvenir shops.

West of Palma, the coast bubbles up into the low, rocky hills and sharp coves that prefigure the mountains further west. The sandy beaches here are far smaller – and some are actually artificial – but the terrain makes the tourist development seem less oppressive. **Cala Major**, the first stop, was once the playground of the jetset. It's hit grittier times, but some of the grand old buildings have survived and the **Fundació Pilar i Joan Miró**, which exhibits a fine selection of Miró's work in what was once his home and studio, makes a fascinating detour. The neighbouring resort of **Illetes** is a good deal more polished, boasting comfortable hotels and attractive cove beaches, while, moving west again, **Portals Nous** has an affluent and exclusive air born of its swanky marina. Next comes British-dominated **Palma Nova**, a major package holiday destination popular with all ages, adjoining youthful, very British **Magaluf**, where modern high-rise hotels and thumping nightlife back a substantial sandy beach. South of Magaluf there's a real surprise, for here at last is a small portion of the coast that's not been developed – a pine-studded peninsula sheltering the charming cove beach of **Portals Vells**. West of Magaluf the coastal highway leaves the Badia de Palma for dreary **Santa Ponça** before pushing onto **Peguera**, a large, sprawling resort with attractive sandy beaches and a relaxed family atmosphere. Next door – and much more endearing – is tiny **Cala Fornells**, where pretty villas thread along the coastal hills and a pair of first-rate hotels overlook a wooded cove (and concrete-slab beaches). From here, it's another short hop to the good-looking bay that holds **Camp de Mar**, which is currently in the throes of a massive expansion.

Camp de Mar is the last major development within Palma's orbit. Further west, the scenery assumes a prettier, hillier aspect as you approach Andratx (covered in Chapter 2).

Practicalities

Although these resorts boast hundreds of **hotels**, *hostals* and apartment buildings, nearly all are block-booked by the package tourist industry from May or June through to September or October, with frugal pickings for the independent traveller. We've selected some of the more interesting and enjoyable package hotels, as well as picking out several relatively inexpensive places where there's a reasonable chance of finding a vacancy independently in high season. Two smallish resorts on this coast where the tourist development is not too oppressive are Illetes and Cala Fornells; the former has its own sandy beaches, though they are small, while the latter is within easy reach of the fine sandy beaches of Peguera. The bathing is particularly good at both. Out of season, many places simply close down,

but at those which remain open, it's well worth haggling over th
price.

We haven't highlighted resort **nightlife** at all, since the livelies
discos and clubs are, as a general rule, concentrated in the tackie
spots. This coast also has hundreds of **restaurants** and cafés, but th
choice is not as diverse as you might expect, and for the most par
standards are not very high: the vast majority of them serve eithe
low-price pizzas and pastas or a sort of pan-European tourist menu

Transport

With Palma's Plaça Espanya as the hub, public **transport** along th
coast is fast and efficient. **EMT** bus #15 travels the old coastal roa
east through Ca'n Pastilla to S'Arenal; bus #21 heads west as far a
Palma Nova; and bus #3 runs through Cala Major to Illetes. In addi
tion, the **Catalina Marqués** bus company operates the "Playaso
routes, with frequent buses from Plaça Espanya, Plaça Rei Joa
Carles I and other Palma city centre points west to Magaluf, Sant
Ponça, Peguera and Camp de Mar.

*For frequen-
cies and
journey times,
see p.118.*

Driving is straightforward: the *autopista* shoots along the coas
from S'Arenal right round to Palma Nova and then slices across
narrow peninsula to reach Santa Ponça and Peguera. Alternatively
you can take the old coastal road (numbered the C719 west o
Palma), which meanders through most of the resorts at a snail'
pace.

East of Palma

The *autopista* rushes **east** out of Palma with tourist resorts on on
side and the **airport** on the other. The flatlands backing onto th
coast were once prime agricultural land, pastoral days recalled b
the ruined windmills – built to pump water out of the marshy topso
– that lie scattered over the landscape. The alternative route, alon
the old coastal road, is a bit more interesting and a lot slower; tak
the turning off the *autopista* just beyond the city walls, signposte
to Ca'n Pastilla. The old road tracks through the gritty suburbs o
Portixol and Es Molinar en route to **CALA GAMBA**, an unassumin
little place with a pleasant horseshoe-shaped harbour. Close by
CA'N PASTILLA is the first substantial tourist resort on this part o
the coast, its fifty-odd hotels and apartment buildings set in a roug
rectangle of land pushed tight against the seashore. The place i
short on charm and certainly too close to the airport for sonic com
fort, but it does herald the start of the fine Platja de Palma beach.

Sometimes, Les Meravelles and S'Arenal

The **Platja de Palma**, the four-kilometre stretch of sandy beach tha
defines the three coterminous (and indistinguishable) resorts o
SOMETIMES, LES MERAVELLES and **S'ARENAL**, is crowded with
serious sun-seekers, a sweating throng of bronzed and oiled bodie

slowly roasting in the heat. The beach is also a busy pick-up point, the spot for a touch of verbal foreplay before the night-time bingeing begins. It is, as they say, fine if you like that sort of thing – though older visitors look rather marooned. A wide and pleasant walkway lined with palm trees runs behind the beach and this, in turn, is edged by a long sequence of bars, restaurants and souvenir shops. A toy-town tourist "train" shuttles up and down the walkway, but there's so little to distinguish one part of the beach from another that it's easy to become disoriented. To maintain your bearings, keep an eye out for the series of smart, stainless-steel beach bars, each numbered and labelled, in Castilian, "*balneario*", strung along the shore: Balneario no. 15 is by the Ca'n Pastilla marina, while no. 1 is near S'Arenal harbour.

Singling out any part of this massive complex is a pretty pointless exercise, but the area around S'Arenal harbour does at least have a concentration of **facilities**. There's car rental, currency exchange, boat trips and nightclubs, and you can eat well at the lively terrace bar of the harbourside *Club Nàutico*, where the paella is delicious. S'Arenal also boasts **Aquacity** (May–Oct daily 10am–5pm; Oct closed Sat; 2400ptas/€14.42; ☎971 440 000), a huge leisure complex of swimming pools, water flumes and kiddies' playgrounds, in between the *autopista* and the east edge of the resort, about 15km east of Palma.

There are similar water parks at Magaluf (see p.115) and Port d'Alcúdia (see p.191).

Accommodation

All three resorts extend a few blocks inland to encompass dozens of **places to stay**. The cheapest accommodation is provided by the **youth hostel**, the *Playa de Palma*, at c/Costa Brava 13 in Sometimes (☎971 260 892; ①; dorm beds 1500ptas/€9.02). To get there, take EMT bus #15 from Palma's Plaça Reina or Plaça Espanya (takes 25min), and ask to be put off at the giant *Hotel Iberostar Royal Cristina* on the main road. The hostel is a couple of hundred metres further along the road on the left, and is only a couple of minutes' walk from Balneario no. 9. It's fairly clean but has only 65 beds, so advance reservations are strongly recommended. It should be open all year, but sometimes closes for a month or two in the winter.

At the other end of the market, the four-star *hotel Iberostar Royal Cristina*, on Arenas de Bilbao (☎971 492 550, fax 971 490 003; ⑥), offers luxury rooms and apartments, although it doesn't overlook the beach. Another mid-range option is the three-star *Royal Cupido*, a bright, modern, 200-room hotel which backs onto the beach a couple of minutes' walk west of the *Royal Cristina* at c/Marbella 32 (☎971 264 300, fax 971 265 510; ⑥).

West to Cala Major

Crowded **CALA MAJOR** snakes along a hilly stretch of coastline a kilometre or two **west** of Palma's ferry port. Overlooking the main street (which comprises a section of the C719 coast road), occasional *Modernista* mansions and the luxurious *Nixe Hotel* are reminders of halcyon days when the resort was a byword for elegance. The king of Spain still runs a palace here – the Palacio de Marivent, on the main street close to the *autopista* at the east end of the resort.

The Fundació Pilar i Joan Miró

Opposite the Palacio de Marivent, a turning signposted to Gènova leads up the hill for 500m to the complex where the painter Joan Miró lived and worked for much of the 1950s, 1960s and 1970s, now dubbed the **Fundació Pilar i Joan Miró**, c/Joan de Saridakis 29 (Tues–Sat 10am–7pm, Sun 10am–3pm; mid-Sept to mid-May Tues–Sat closes 6pm; 700ptas/€4.21).

*EMT bus #4
passes the
Fundació
hourly on its
way between
Palma's Plaça
Reina and
Gènova.*

Initially – from 1920 – the young Miró was involved with the Surrealists in Paris and contributed to all their major exhibitions: his wild squiggles, supercharged with bright colours, prompted André Breton, the leading theorist of the movement, to describe Miró as "the most Surrealist of us all". In the 1930s he adopted a simpler style, abandoning the decorative complexity of his earlier work for a more minimalist use of symbols, though the highly coloured forms remained. Miró returned to Barcelona, the city of his birth, in 1940, where he continued to work in the Surrealistic tradition, though as an avowed opponent of Franco his position was uneasy. In 1957 he moved to Mallorca, its relative isolation offering a degree of safety. His wife and mother were both Mallorcan, which must have influenced his decision, as did the chance to work in his own purpose-built studio with its view of the coast. Even from the relative isolation of Franco's Spain he remained an influential figure, prepared to experiment with all kinds of media, right up until his death in Cala Major in 1983.

The expansive hillside premises of the Fundació include Miró's old **studio**, an unassuming affair with views over the bay that has been left pretty much as it was at the time of his death. It's worth a quick gander for a flavour of how the man worked – tackling a dozen or so canvases at the same time – but unfortunately you're only allowed to peer through the windows.

Opposite are the angular lines of the bright-white art gallery, the **Edificio Estrella**, which displays a rotating and representative sample of the artist's work drawn from a prodigious supply: Miró was nothing if not productive. The Fundació holds 134 paintings, 300 engravings and 105 drawings, as well as sculptures, gouaches and preliminary sketches – more than six thousand works in all. There are no guarantees as to what will be on display, but you're likely to see a decent selection of his paintings, the familiar dream-like squiggles and half-recognizable shapes that are intended to conjure up the unconscious, with free play often given to erotic associations. The gallery also stores a comprehensive collection of Miró documents and occasionally hosts exhibitions.

Illetes

At well-heeled **ILLETES**, just along the coast from Cala Major and 7km west of Palma, a ribbon of restaurants, hotels and apartment buildings bestrides the steep hills that rise high above the rocky shoreline. There's precious little space left, but at least the generally low-rise buildings are of manageable proportions. A string of tiny cove beaches punctuates the coast, the most attractive being the pine-shaded **Platja Cala Comtesa**, at the southern end of the resort, alongside a restricted military zone.

Illetes is sometimes written Illetas.

The long main street, Passeig d'Illetes, runs past several good hotels. The most enjoyable is the *Bon Sol*, about halfway along (☎971 402 111, fax 971 402 559; ⑧), which tumbles down the cliffs to the seashore and its own artificial beach. A family-run concern, the hotel has all the conveniences you could want and the better rooms have fine views out over the bay. Its clientele is staid and steady, befitting the antique-crammed interior. Another good choice is the *Gran Hotel Albatros*, located near the north end of Passeig d'Illetes (☎971 402 211, fax 971 402 154; ⑦); rooms have balconies and air conditioning and there's a swimming pool and private access to the sea. There are similar facilities at the luxurious, five-star *Hotel Melià de Mar* (☎971 402 511, fax 971 405 852; ⑨), which overlooks the seashore close to the *Bon Sol*, while equally spacious lodging is to be found a couple of minutes' walk south along the coast at the attractive *Hotel-residencia Illetas* (☎971 402 411, fax 971 401 808; ⑨). Most visitors eat in their hotels, but there's a smattering of smart **cafés** on the main drag, including *Es Parral* towards the south end of the resort (☎971 701 127), which serves Mallorcan cuisine.

Bendinat and Portals Nous

The C719 avoids Illetes but cuts through the peripheries of **BENDINAT**, a couple of kilometres further along the coast. On the south side of the road, the resort's leafy streets meander down to the seashore, lined by the villas of the well-to-do. It's a pretty spot and tucked away on a quiet, rocky cove is the charming *Hotel Bendinat*, c/Rossegada (☎971 675 725, fax 971 677 276; ⑨; May–Oct), dating from the 1950s and built in the traditional *hacienda* style, with a beautiful arcaded terrace overlooking the sea. You can stay either in the main building, where most of the bedrooms have balconies, or in one of the trim, whitewashed bungalows that dot the gardens.

On its west side, Bendinat merges with the larger **PORTALS NOUS**, another ritzy settlement where polished mansions fill out the green and hilly terrain abutting the coast. There's a tiny beach too, set beneath the cliffs and reached via a flight of steps at the foot c c/Passatge del Mar. In contrast to the studied elegance of the sid streets, the resort's main drag (also the C719) is disappointing drab, though it does lead to the glitzy marina, one of Mallorca's mo exclusive, where the boats look more like ocean liners than pleasur yachts. Close by, **Marineland** is one of the tackiest but most popula attractions on the island, with shark tanks and a tropical fish aquar um, as well as exploitative dolphin, sealion and parrot shows (dail April–Sept 9.30am–6pm; Jan–March & Oct to mid-No 9.30am–5pm; 2100ptas/€12.62). Kids love the place; adults mostl suffer in silence.

Portals Nous has a number of three-star **hotels**, but, with much c the shoreline occupied by affluent private villas and apartment they're restricted to the side streets, well away from the sea. Pick c the bunch is the comfortable *Fabiola*, c/Torrent 19 (☎971 675 82£ fax 971 677 006; ⑨), set in the middle of the wealthiest part of tow and a short walk from both the marina and the beach. Of the rows c **restaurants** and bars down at the marina, a particular recommenda tion is *Binnacle* (☎971 676 977), a smart and fairly formal restau rant which specializes in seafood.

Palma Nova and Calvià

Old Mallorca hands claim that **PALMA NOVA**, 4km west of Portal Nous, was once a beauty spot, and certainly its wide and shallow bay with good beaches among a string of bumpy headlands, still has it moments. But for the most part, the bay has been engulfed by broad, congested sweep of hotels and tourist facilities. With th development comes a vigorous **nightlife** and a plethora of accorr modation options on or near the seashore – though, as elsewhere most are block-booked by tour operators throughout the season Amongst the resort's many **hotels**, recommendable places includ the three-star *Playa Trópico*, a well-maintained and good-lookinç modern establishment at Passeig de la Mar 38, just off the seafron (☎971 680 512, fax 971 682 613; ⑨; June–Oct). Other option include the *Hotel Playa Comodoro*, Passeig Cala Blanca 9 (☎97 682 061; ⑦; April–Oct), a standard-issue tower with balconied dou ble rooms looking out over the bay; and the comparable, thougl slightly more luxurious, four-star *Hotel Delfín Playa* (☎971 68(100, fax 971 680 112; ⑦), which faces the beach at the centre of th resort from behind Passeig de la Mar. The giant *Hotel Sol Mirlos* i a five-minute walk from the beach on c/Pinzones (☎971 681 900 fax 971 681 912; ⑦; Jan–Oct), as is its identical neighbour *Hotel So Tordos* (☎971 680 250, fax 971 681 912; ⑦; April–Oct).

Some 6km north of Palma Nova, tucked away in the hills behin the coast, is the tiny town of **CALVIÀ**, the region's administrativ centre – hence the lavish and oversized town hall, paid for by th profits of the tourist industry. The parish church of **Sant Joa**

Baptista (daily 10am–1pm) dominates the town, its greying stone dating from 1245, though the Gothic subtleties mostly disappeared during a nineteenth-century refurbishment that left a crude bas-relief carving of the Garden of Gethsemane above the main door. There are pleasant views across the surrounding countryside from the church, and the adjacent square holds a series of modern murals. Opposite the square, *Bar Rosita* serves *tapas*, coffee and cakes, and, just down the hill, the excellent *Méson Ca'n Torrat* (☎971 670 682; closed Tues) specializes in roast legs of lamb and suckling pig. EMT bus #20 runs from Palma through Palma Nova to Calvià four times daily.

Around Palma

From Calvià, it's a short drive west to Capdellà and the Serra de Tramuntana, which are covered in Chapter 2.

Magaluf and around

Torrenova, on the chunky headland at the far end of Palma Nova, is a cramped and untidy development that slides into **MAGALUF**, whose high-rise towers march across the next bay down the coast. For years a bargain-basement package holiday destination, Magaluf has finally lost patience with its youthful British visitors. In 1996 the local authorities won a court order allowing them to demolish twenty downmarket hotels in an attempt to end – or at least control – the annual binge of "violence, drunkenness and open-air sex" that, they argued, now characterized the resort. The high-rise hotels were duly dynamited and an extensive clean-up programme has subsequently freshened up the resort's appearance. However, short of demolishing the whole lot, there's not too much anyone can do with the deadening concrete of the modern town centre – and the demolished blocks will anyway be replaced, albeit by more upmarket hotels. Whether these draconian measures will change tourist behaviour remains to be seen, but it doesn't help that the resort's British visitors still seem determined to create, or at least patronize, a bizarre caricature of their homeland: it's all here, from beans-on-toast with Marmite to pubs such as *Tom Brown's Chicken & Steak Inn* and the *Benny Hill Party Pub*.

Stuck on the western edge of Magaluf, **Aquapark** (daily: June–Sept 10am–6pm; May & Oct 10am–5pm; 2150ptas/€12.92; ☎971 130 811) is a recently renovated giant-sized water park with swimming pools, water chutes and flumes. Some claim that it beats S'Arenal's Aquacity. In fact, there isn't much in it, though perhaps it's worth noting that Magaluf's version tends to attract more Brits than S'Arenal's. Both are immensely popular and draw kids in their hundreds. Across the road from Aquapark is a second **theme park** where the main event is a replica Wild West town that must rank as one of the most incongruous sights in Spain. The park was originally called Dorado, but it's in the process of being reinvented. At the time of writing, its hoarding carried the slogan "Western Park: Crazy Wet West".

There are similar water parks at S'Arenal (see p.111) and Port d'Alcúdia (see p.191).

In the unlikely event that you want to find a room in Magaluf, you can get a free map giving the location of all the resort's hotels at the

seasonal **tourist office**, on the square one block back from the beach
at Avinguda Pere Vaquer Ramis 1 (June–Aug Mon–Fri 9am–1pm &
3–5pm; ☎971 131 126).

South to Portals Vells

Things pick up beyond Magaluf: the eastern reaches of the pine-clad
peninsula that extends south of the resort have been barely touched
by the developers. In consequence, however, there aren't any **buses**
beyond Magaluf, so you'll have to drive, walk or cycle.

The clearly signposted road south to Portal Vells begins on the
west side of Magaluf where the *autopista* merges into the C719.
After about 1.5km, the road cuts past the Aquapark theme park and
then keeps straight at a fork where the road to Santa Ponça curves
off to the right. South of the fork, the road narrows into a country
lane, passing a golf course before heading off into the woods. After
about 4km, a steep turning on the left leads down 1km to **Cala Mago**
(still signposted in Castilian as Playa El Mago), where a rocky little
headland with a shattered guard house has lovely beaches to either
side. Park and walk down to whichever cove takes your fancy: the
nudist beach on the right with its smart café-restaurant, or the
delightful pine-shaded strand on the left with its beach bar, tiny port
and sprinkling of villas. Both provide sunbeds and showers.

Continuing a further 600m past the Cala Mago turning, a second
side road cuts for a kilometre down to the cove beach of **PORTALS
VELLS**. Despite a bar-restaurant and a handful of villas, it remains a
pleasant, pine-scented spot of glistening sand, rocky cliffs and clear
blue water, especially appealing early in the morning before it gets
crowded. Clearly visible from the beach are the **caves** of the headland on the south side of the cove. A footpath leads to the most interesting, an old cave church where the holy-water stoup and altar have
been cut out of the solid rock – the work of shipwrecked Genoese
seamen, according to local legend.

Beyond the Portals Vells turning, the road continues south for
1.5km as far as a broken-down barbed-wire fence at the start of a
military zone. You can't drive any further and you're not supposed to
walk beyond the fence either, but some people do, braving the no-
entry signs to scramble through the pine woods and out along the
headland for about 1.5km to reach the solitary **Cap de Cala Figuera**
lighthouse.

Santa Ponça and around

West of Magaluf, the C719 trims the outskirts of **SANTA PONÇA**,
perhaps the least endearing of all the resorts on this stretch of coast.
Mostly a product of the 1980s, this sprawling, still-expanding conurbation has abandoned the concrete high-rises of yesteryear for a
pseudo-vernacular architecture that's littered the hills with scores of
tedious villas. That said, the aesthetic gloom is at least partly lifted

by the setting – with rolling hills flanking a broad bay – and the substantial sandy beach offers safe bathing.

Peguera and Cala Fornells

Sprawling **PEGUERA**, about 6km north of Santa Ponça, is strung out along a lengthy, partly pedestrianized main street – the Avinguda de Peguera – immediately behind several generous sandy beaches. There's nothing remarkable about the place, but it does have an easy-going air and is a favourite with families and older visitors alike. It also possesses a baffling one-way system, which it is best to avoid. The C719 loops right round Peguera and the easiest approach, if you're just after the beach, is from the west. Head into the resort along the main street and park anywhere you can before you reach the pedestrianized part of the Avinguda de Peguera; it's the pedestrianization which sends you weaving through the resort's side streets.

The two signed turnings that lead to the neighbouring (and much prettier) resort of **CALA FORNELLS** are also reached along the main street on the west side of Peguera. The first turning is on the edge of Peguera, the second is at the Casa Pepe supermarket. Take the second turning and the road climbs up to a string of chic, *pueblo*-style houses that perch on the sea cliffs and trail round to the tiny centre of the resort, where a wooded cove is set around a minuscule beach and concreted sunbathing slabs. Although Cala Fornells tends to be overcrowded during the daytime, at night the tranquillity returns, and it makes a good base for a holiday. You can also stroll out into the surrounding woods along a wide, dirt track which runs up behind the hotels, cutting across the pine-scented hills towards the stony cove beach of **Caló d'es Monjo**, 1.5km to the west.

Cala Fornells has two fetching **hotels**, both behind the beach at the end of the access roads: the sprucely modern, four-star *Coronado* (☎971 686 800, fax 971 687 457; ⑨; Jan–Oct), where all 140 bedrooms have sea views and balconies; and the more sympathetic, green-shuttered and white-painted *Cala Fornells* (☎971 686 950, fax 971 687 525; ⑦; Feb–Oct). If your wallet won't stretch to either of these, you might consider staying in Peguera, where there are plenty of bargain-basement *hostals* in the characterless side streets sloping up from the seafront. Peguera's seasonal **tourist office** at the east end of the resort, Avinguda de Peguera 76 (Mon–Sat 9am–1pm & 3–5pm; ☎971 687 083), issues comprehensive accommodation lists as well as local maps giving the location of all the resort's hotels.

For **food**, Peguera has dozens of bright, inexpensive cafés and restaurants, from pizza joints through to seafood places. The best place in town is *La Gran Tortuga* (☎971 686 023; closed Mon), which overlooks the seashore on the road from the Casa Pepe supermarket to Cala Fornells. It serves superb seafood, has a terrace bar and even boasts its own swimming pool. A three-course evening meal will set you back about 5000ptas/€30.05, but you can enjoy its excellent lunches for much less.

Camp de Mar

Tucked away among the hills 3km west of Peguera, **CAMP DE MAR** has an expansive beach and fine bathing, though the scene is marred by the presence of two thumping great **hotels** dropped right on the seashore – the *Hotel Playa* (☎971 235 025, fax 971 208 775; ⑤; April–Oct), a British favourite, and the smarter, four-star *Club Camp de Mar* (☎971 235 200, fax 971 235 110; ⑦; Feb–Oct), which caters mainly for Germans. Both are modern high-rises equipped with spacious, balconied bedrooms. The resort is also in the middle of a massive expansion with building work in progress and brand new villa complexes now trailing back from the beach in an all-too-familiar semi-suburban sprawl. All the same, the beach is an amiable spot to soak up the sun and it's hard to resist the eccentric café stuck out in the bay and approached via a rickety walkway on stilts – or try the *Bar La Siesta*, overlooking the beach, for romantic sunsets and wonderful paellas.

A minor road twists west from Camp de Mar over wooded hills to Port d'Andratx – see p.157.

Travel details

Local buses

EMT buses from **Palma** to: the airport (#17; every 15min 6am–9.30pm & every 30min 9.30pm–1.30am; 25min); Cala Major (#3; every 10min; 15min); Gènova (#4; hourly; 30min); Illetes (#3; every 10min; 20min); Palma Nova (#21; every 30min; 30min); Portals Nous (#21; every 30min; 25min); S'Arenal (#15; every 10min; 30min).

Catalina Marqués buses (the "Playasol" routes) from **Palma** (Plaça Espanya and Plaça Joan Carles I) to: Andratx (hourly; 45min); Camp de Mar (hourly; 40min); Magaluf (May–Oct 16 daily; Nov–April 11 daily; 25min); Palma Nova (May–Oct 16 daily; Nov–April 11 daily; 20min); Peguera (May–Oct hourly; Nov–April Mon–Fri 12 daily, Sat & Sun 6 daily; 35min); Port d'Andratx (hourly; 45min).

Island-wide buses

Palma to: Alaró (2–3 daily; 25min); Alcúdia (May–Oct Mon–Sat hourly, 5 on Sun; Nov–April Mon–Sat 5 daily, 3 on Sun; 1hr); Andratx (hourly; 45min); Artà (Mon–Sat 4 daily, 1 on Sun; 1hr 25min); Banyalbufar (1 daily; 35min); Cala d'Or (May–Oct Mon–Sat hourly, 2 on Sun; Nov–April 2–4 daily; 1hr 10min); Cala Figuera (May–Oct Mon–Sat 1 daily; 1hr 20min); Cala Millor (Mon–Sat 7–9 daily, 2 on Sun; 1hr 15min); Cala Rajada (Mon–Sat 4 daily, 1–2 on Sun; 1hr 30min); Camp de Mar (hourly; 40min); Ca'n Picafort (2–5 daily; 1hr); Colònia de Sant Jordi (May–Oct Mon–Sat 8 daily, 2 on Sun; Nov–April Mon–Sat 4 daily, 2 on Sun; 1hr); Coves del Drac (May–Oct Mon–Sat 4 daily, 1 on Sun; Nov–April 1 daily; 1hr); Covetes (for Es Trenc beach; May–Oct 1 daily; 1hr); Deià (5 daily; 45min); Esporles (Mon–Sat 7 daily, 2 on Sun; 20min); Estellencs (1 daily; 45min); Felanitx (3–4 daily; 50min); Inca (Mon–Fri 9 daily, 4 on Sat, 2 on Sun; 30min); La Granja (1 daily; 25min); Lluc (1–2 daily; 1hr); Manacor (Mon–Sat 7 daily, 3 on Sun; 45min); Montuiri (2–3 daily; 40min); Muro (2–4 daily; 50min); Petra (2–3 daily; 45min); Platja de Formentor (May–Oct Mon–Sat 1 daily; 1hr 15min); Pollença (3–5 daily; 1hr); Port d'Alcúdia (May–Oct Mon–Sat hourly, 5 on Sun; Nov–April Mon–Sat 5 daily, 3 on Sun; 1hr 5min); Port d'Andratx (hourly; 45min); Port de Pollença (3–5 daily; 1hr 10min); Port de Sóller (via the tunnel: Mon–Fri 5 daily, 2 on Sat, no Sun service; 35min; via Valldemossa: 5 daily; 55min); Porto Colom (1–3 daily; 1hr 10min); Porto Cristo (Mon–Sat 7 daily, 3 on Sun; 1hr 10min); Santanyí (May–Oct Mon–Sat hourly, 2 on Sun; Nov–April 2–4 daily; 1hr 10min); Sineu (2 daily; 1hr); Sóller (via the tunnel: Mon–Fri 5 daily, 2 on Sat, no Sun service; 30min; via Valldemossa: 5 daily; 50min); Valldemossa (5 daily; 30min).

Peguera to: Andratx (May–Oct Mon–Sat 7 daily, 3 on Sun; Nov–April 1 daily; 10min); Estellencs (Mon–Sat 1 daily; 1hr); Port d'Andratx (May–Oct Mon–Sat 8 daily, 3 on Sun; Nov–April 1 daily; 10min); Sant Elm (May–Oct Mon–Sat 7 daily, 3 on Sun; Nov–April 1 daily; 20min); Valldemossa (Mon–Sat 1 daily; 1hr 10min).

Trains

Palma to: Binissalem (hourly; 30min); Inca (hourly; 40min); Sóller (5 daily; 1hr 15min).

Chapter 2

Southwestern Mallorca

Mallorca is at its scenic best in the gnarled ridge of the **Serra de Tramuntana**, the imposing mountain range which stretches the length of the island's western shore, its rearing peaks and plunging seacliffs intermittently intercepted by valleys of olive and citrus groves. Midway along and cramped by the mountains is **Sóller**, an antiquated merchants' town that serves as a charming introduction to the region, especially when it's reached on the scenic narrow-gauge train line from Palma. From Sóller, it's a short hop down to the coast to **Port de Sóller**, a popular resort on a deep and expansive bay. This geographical arrangement – the town located a few kilometres inland from its eponymous port – is repeated across Mallorca, a reminder of more troubled days when marauding corsairs obliged the islanders to live away from the coast. The mountain valleys in the vicinity of Sóller shelter the bucolic stone-built villages of **Fornalutx**, **Orient** and **Alaró**, which is itself close to **Binissalem**, one of the most diverting little towns of the central plain, Es Pla. Also within easy reach of Sóller, set beside the main C711 Sóller–Palma road, are two eminently appealing gardens – the splendid oasis-like **Jardins d'Alfàbia** and the terraces of **Raixa**.

The section of the Serra de Tramuntana extending northeast from Sóller to the Cap de Formentor is covered in Chapter 3.

The central plain, Es Pla, is covered in depth in Chapter 4.

Southwest of Sóller, the principal coastal road, the **C710**, threads up through the mountains to reach the beguiling village of **Deià**, tucked at the base of formidable cliffs and famous as the former home of Robert Graves. Beyond lies the magnificent Carthusian monastery of **Valldemossa**, whose echoing cloisters temporarily accommodated George Sand and Frédéric Chopin, and the gracious *hacienda* of **La Granja**, another compelling stop. Continuing southwest, the C710 wriggles high above the shoreline, slipping through a sequence of mountain hamlets, of which **Banyalbufar** and **Estellencs** are the most picturesque, their tightly terraced fields tumbling down the coastal cliffs. A few kilometres further and you leave the coast behind, drifting inland out of the mountains and into the foothills that precede the market town of **Andratx**. Beyond, on Mallorca's southwestern tip, lie the safe waters of **Port d'Andratx**, a medium-sized resort draped around a handsome inlet, its villas

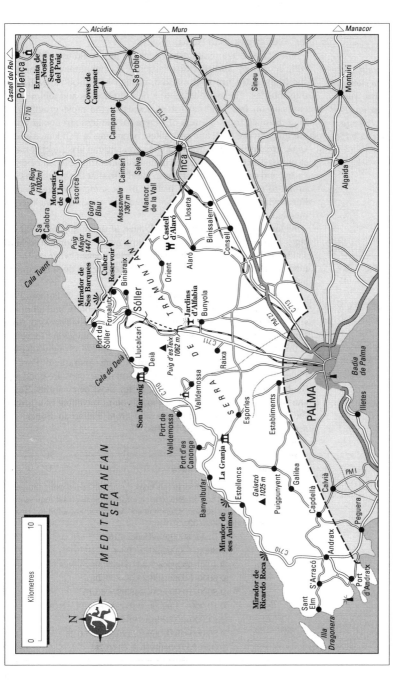

announcing the start of the intense tourist development that eats up the coast eastwards to Palma.

Accounts of two more day hikes, from Lluc and Port de Pollença, are on p.168 and p.182.

The Serra de Tramuntana provides the best walking on Mallorca, with scores of **hiking trails** latticing the mountains. Generally speaking, paths are well marked, though apt to be clogged with thornbushes. There are trails to suit all aptitudes and all levels of enthusiasm, from the easiest of strolls to the most gruelling of long-distance treks. Details of several of the less strenuous walks are given in the text, and two hikes, beginning in Valldemossa and Deià, are described in depth. Spring and autumn are the best times to embark on the longer trails; in mid-summer the heat can be enervating and water is scarce. Bear in mind also that the mountains are prone to mists, though they usually lift at some point in the day. For obvious safety reasons, lone mountain walking is not recommended.

As far as **beaches** are concerned, most of the region's coastal villages have a tiny, shingly strip – nothing more. The longest strip of sand is at Port de Sóller, but this is no great shakes, whereas Deià's modest strand has a wild and wonderful setting, as does its equivalent at Estellencs.

With regards to **accommodation**, Port d'Andratx, Sóller and Port de Sóller have the widest range of *hostals* and hotels, and all of the villages in this region have at least a couple of places. That said, from June to early September, sometimes beyond, vacancies are extremely thin on the ground and advance reservations are strongly advised. To compensate, distances are small – from Andratx to Port de Pollença via the C710 is only about 130km – the roads are good and the **bus** network is perfectly adequate for most destinations. **Taxis** can work out a reasonable deal too, if you're travelling in a group: the fare for the forty-kilometre trip from Palma to Sóller, for instance, is about 5100ptas/€30.65.

Accommodation price codes

All the accommodation prices in this book have been coded using the categories below, which correspond to each establishment's **least expensive double room** in high season, excluding special offers. For a full explanation of these codes, see p.39.

① Under 3000ptas/Under €18.03
② 3000–4000ptas/ €18.03–€24.04
③ 4000–6000ptas/€24.04–€36.06
④ 6000–8000ptas/€36.06–€48.08
⑤ 8000–10,000ptas/€48.08–€60.10
⑥ 10,000–14,000ptas/€60.10–€84.14
⑦ 14,000–20,000ptas/€84.14–€120.20
⑧ 20,000–25,000ptas/€120.20–€150.25
⑨ Over 25,000ptas/Over €150.25

Sóller and around

At the end of the train line from Palma lies **Sóller**, one of the most laid-back and enjoyable towns on Mallorca – an ideal and fairly inexpensive base for exploring the surrounding mountains. Most visitors, though, stick religiously to the coast, taking the rumbling tram down to the popular and amenable seaside resort of **Port de Sóller**. There are much nicer bathing spots not far away – especially Cala Deià – but the port does offer good restaurants and a cluster of low-price hotels. However, the best of this region lies inland. To the northeast, Sóller's mellow mansions fade seamlessly into the orchards and farmland that precede the charming hamlets of **Biniaraix** and **Fornalutx**, both within in easy walking distance of town. Further afield, on the landward side of the Serra de Tramuntana, lie the verdant gardens of the **Jardins d'Alfàbia** and the hamlet of **Orient**, on the road to the remote ruins of the **Castell d'Alaró**. Beyond the castle are the attractive little towns of **Alaró** and **Binissalem**, the centre of Mallorca's wine industry.

Transport

The quickest route from Palma to Sóller is along the **C711** road, which tunnels straight through the mountains. The twenty-kilometre journey takes about thirty minutes and it costs 525ptas/€3.16 per car to use the three-kilometre **tunnel**. You can avoid the tunnel by driving along a serpentine road over the mountains, though this adds about 6km to the trip.

The train from Palma to Sóller

The 28-kilometre **train** journey from Palma to Sóller is a delight, dipping and cutting through the mountains and fertile valleys of the Serra de Tramuntana. The line was completed in 1911 on the profits of the orange and lemon trade: the railway was built to transport the fruit to Palma, at a time when it took a full day to make the trip by road. The rolling stock is tremendously atmospheric too, with narrow carriages – the gauge is only 914mm – which look like they've come out of an Agatha Christie novel.

First the train has to clear the scratchy suburbs of Palma, but within about fifteen minutes it's running across pancake-flat farmland with an impenetrable-looking line of steep peaks dead ahead. After clunking through the outskirts of Bunyola, the train threads upwards to spend five minutes tunnelling through the mountains, where the noisy engine and dimly lit carriages give the feel of a rollercoaster ride. Beyond, out in the bright mountain air, are the steep valleys and craggy thousand-metre peaks at the heart of the Serra de Tramuntana, and everywhere there are almond groves, which are vivid with blossom in January and February.

There are five departures daily from Palma station throughout the year (sometimes six from Sóller), the whole ride taking just under an hour and a quarter. An ordinary one-way ticket costs 380ptas/€2.28, twice that for a return. There's also a mid-morning Turist train, whose only distinction is a brief photo-stop in the mountains at the Mirador Pujol d'En Banja; a one-way ticket on this costs 735ptas/€4.42, a return 1115ptas/€6.70.

There's a fast and frequent direct **bus** service from Palma to Sóller and Port de Sóller via the tunnel; other buses are routed via Valldemossa and Deià. More intermittent services run along the main coastal road, the C710, from Andratx to Valldemossa and on to Sóller and Port de Sóller.

Trains from Palma to Sóller link with ramshackle old **trams** that clunk down to the coast at Port de Sóller, 5km away. The trams, ex-San Francisco rolling stock dating from the 1930s, depart every half-hour or hour daily from 7am to 9pm; the fifteen-minute journey costs 115ptas/€0.69 one-way. A second train line runs from Palma to Inca via Binissalem and Lloseta. This is not a particularly scenic trip and the trains are modern and functional, but from Monday to Friday the service is fast and frequent, with trains leaving every hour or half-hour between 6am and 9pm. At the weekend, however, there are just two trains a day from Palma, one from Inca. The one-way fare from Palma to Inca is a mere 255ptas/€1.53.

Sóller

Rather than any specific sight, it's the general flavour of **SÓLLER** that appeals, the town's narrow, sloping lanes cramped by eighteenth- and

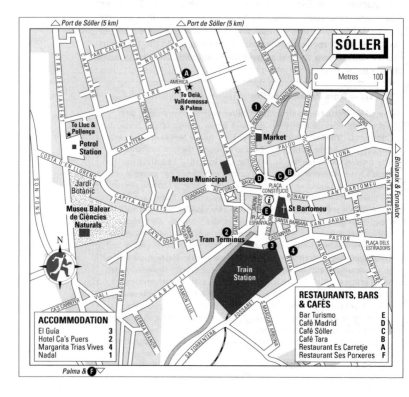

nineteenth-century stone houses whose fancy grilles and big wooden doors once hid the region's rich fruit merchants. A couple of minor museums fill out a wander through the town, and the picturesque country villages of **Biniaraix** and **Fornalutx** are in walking distance.

Arrival and information

Buses from Lluc and Pollença drop passengers beside the Campsa petrol station on the main Sóller–Palma road to the west of the town centre. From here, it's a five-minute stroll into the centre: walk south from the petrol station and take the first left down Costa d'en Llorenç, at the end of which turn right onto c/Capità Angelets and keep going east. Buses from Palma, Valldemossa and Deià arrive beside Plaça Amèrica, from where it's about five minutes' walk south to Plaça Constitució.

The buses heading both east and west along the coast from Sóller are often full. To make sure of a seat, you should board at Port de Sóller, where these services originate.

The **tourist office** is in the town hall next to the church on Plaça Constitució (Mon–Fri 9.30am–1.30pm; ☎971 630 200, *www.soller-net.com*). It has leaflets detailing local accommodation, provides maps of the town and its environs and issues a quick synopsis of local hikes prepared by "Catherine", a local expat who also offers a wide range of well-planned and informative **guided walks** into the surrounding mountains. These last for between four-and-a-half and six hours, cost between 1700ptas/€10.22 and 3600ptas/€21.64 per person, and take place three to six times weekly throughout much of the year. Most of the hikes require a reasonable degree of fitness and the price usually covers minibus travel to the trailhead, but not food or drink. Reservations, a minimum of 24 hours ahead, are essential on ☎971 633 373 (mobile ☎609 620 226). You can, of course, do the hikes yourself, in which case you'll need an IGN **hiking map**; the newspaper shop directly across the square from the tourist office usually has a limited supply – but you shouldn't count on it.

Accommodation

Although Sóller's **accommodation** options are very limited, there's actually more chance of finding a vacant room here during the high season than there is down at the port.

Hotel Ca's Puers, c/Isabel II 39 ☎971 638 004, fax 971 630 429 (*www.caspuers.com*). Plush hotel occupying a handsome old stone house about 300m from the main square. Has just six rooms, each of which is tastefully decorated in immaculate style. Closed Nov, early Dec & Jan. ⑧.

Hotel El Guía, c/Castanyer 2 ☎ & fax 971 630 227. Easily the best place in town, a lovely, old-fashioned one-star hotel approached across a pretty little courtyard. Bygones litter the foyer, which leads to pleasantly furnished and attractive rooms. To get there, walk down the steps from the train station platform and turn right. April–Oct. ④.

Casa de Huéspedes Margarita Trías Vives, c/Reial 3 ☎971 634 214. Pleasant rooms in an attractive old terraced house close to the train station. Stay at the back (away from the road) if you're a light sleeper. April–Oct. ③.

Hostal-residencia Nadal, c/Romaguera 27 ☎ & fax 971 631 180. Simple, central two-star, with 26 rooms both with and without showers, in a neatly decorated and well-kept house about five minutes' walk north of Plaça Constitució. Open all year. ③.

The Town

All streets lead to the main square, **Plaça Constitució**, an informal, pint-sized affair of crowded cafés and grouchy mopeds just down the hill from the train station. The square is dominated by the hulking mass of the church of **St Bartomeu** (Mon–Thurs 10.30am–1pm & 2.45–5.15pm, Fri & Sat 10.30am–1pm). The most appealing features of this crude but somehow rather fetching neo-Gothic remodelling of the medieval original are the enormous and precisely carved rose windows stuck high in the main façade and the decorative excess of the enormous and apparently pointless balustrade. Inside, the cavernous nave is suitably dark and gloomy, the penitential home of a string of gaudy Baroque altarpieces.

A couple of minutes' walk northwest at c/Sa Mar 13, the **Museu Municipal** (Mon–Fri 10am–6pm, Sat 11am–1pm; 100ptas/€0.60) comprises a rather half-hearted sequence of period rooms in a renovated merchant's mansion. It's hardly unmissable, but the antique kitchen, with its majolica plates and old pots and pans, is mildly diverting, and the chapel-shrine showcases some interesting votive offerings.

Retracing your steps to the south end of c/Sa Mar, either turn left along c/Bauçà, walk straight across Plaça Constitució and keep going down c/Sa Lluna for the three-kilometre stroll to the pretty village of Biniaraix (see opposite); or alternatively turn right down c/Rectoria for the five-minute walk west to the **Museu Balear de Ciències Naturals** (Balearic Museum of Natural Sciences; Tues–Sat 10am–8pm, Sun 10.30am–1.30pm; Oct–March Tues–Sat closes 5.30pm; 300ptas/€1.80). This museum occupies an old merchant's dwelling stuck beside the main Palma–Sóller road, although the interior has been stripped out to accommodate a series of modest displays. Temporary exhibitions occupy the top two floors and usually feature Balearic geology and fossils. The permanent collection is exhibited on the ground floor and is devoted to the leading botanists of yesteryear including Archduke Ludwig Salvator. The labelling is in Catalan, but English leaflets are available at the ticket desk, which also issues a free English-language brochure identifying and illustrating many species of local flora. This is a necessary introduction to the neat and trim **Jardí Botànic** (same hours), which rolls down the hillside in front of the house. The garden is divided into thirteen small areas, six of which (M1–M6) are dedicated to Balearic species, with shade-loving plants, for instance, in M4, mountain plants in M5, and dune and sea-cliff species in M2.

For more on Archduke Salvator, see p.143.

Eating and drinking

Sóller's **café-bars** provide an abundance of low-cost snacks and light meals during the day and early evening. The **restaurant** scene is more limited, and although there are a couple of decent spots, you're better heading off to the restaurants down at the port.

Bar Turismo, Avgda d'es Born s/n. By the tram lines just up from Plaça Constitució, this convivial little bar is an amenable spot to nurse a drink.

Café Madrid, c/Bauzá 2. A popular no-frills café-bar just off Plaça Constitució, with sandwiches and *tapas* starting at 400ptas/€2.40.

Café Soller, Plaça Constitució 14. With modern art displayed on the walls, this is one a cheerful cafés on the main square. Fresh *ensaimadas* as well as tasty *tapas* (500ptas/€3.01) and *racions* (900ptas/€5.41). A good bet for breakfast.

Café Tara, c/Sa Lluna 5. A straightforward café just off Plaça Constitució serving shoppers with delicious pastries during the day, and concentrating in the evening on pizzas (averaging 700ptas/€4.21). Usually closes around 6 or 7pm.

Restaurant El Guía, c/Castanyer 2 ☎971 630 227. In the hotel of the same name, this is a real treat. A little formal for some, but the prices are very reasonable, with a delicious *menú del día* for around 2500ptas/€15.03. Closed Mon; plus limited opening hours Nov–March.

Restaurant Es Carrete, c/Cetre s/n ☎971 633 996. Great neighbourhood spot at Plaça Amèrica done up in rustic style. You can get a meal of chicken for as little as 900ptas/€5.41, but the swordfish is more of a treat even if it does cost twice as much.

Restaurant Ses Porxeres, Carretera Sóller s/n ☎971 613 762. Something of an island institution, this rustic-style restaurant located alongside the Jardins d'Alfàbia at the south end of the C711 Sóller tunnel is well-known for its game, prepared in the traditional Catalan manner. Other dishes are very Catalan too – for a main course reckon on about 2000ptas/€12.02. You should always book a table, but note that Sundays can be booked up weeks in advance.

The Ses Porxeres *is south of town beside the Jardins d'Alfàbia – see p.131.*

East of Sóller: Biniaraix and Fornalutx

Following c/Sa Lluna east from Sóller's main square, it takes about half-an-hour to stroll to the village of **BINIARAIX**, passing orchards and farmland latticed with ancient irrigation channels and dry-stone walls. The village, nestled in the foothills of the Serra de Tramuntana, is tiny – just a cluster of handsome old stone houses surrounding a dilapidated church and the smallest of central squares – but it is extraordinarily pretty and is also the starting point for one of Mallorca's busiest **hiking** routes, commonly called the **Cornadors Circuit**. This comprises a thirteen-kilometre trail which takes about six hours to negotiate, weaving a circuitous course through the mountains to finish up back in Sóller. To get to the trailhead, walk uphill from the square along c/Sant Josep and, after about 200m, you'll reach a spring and cattle trough. A sign here offers a choice of hiking routes: left for the Camí del Marroig, right for the more interesting **Camí d'es Barranc**, the first, and most diverting, part of the Cornadors Circuit.

The Camí d'es Barranc follows an old cobbled track – originally built for pilgrims on their way to Lluc – which ascends the **Barranc de Biniaraix**, a beautiful gorge of terraced citrus groves set in the shadow of the mountains. After about an hour and a half's walking you'll reach the head of the ravine, where a large barn sporting paint-

Traffic on c/Sa Lluna is one-way into Sóller

A local landowner has been restricting access to hikers on the Cornadors Circuit beyond the Barranc de Biniaraix. Check with the Sóller tourist office in advance before you set out to hike the whole circuit.

ed signs on its walls is the obvious landmark. Beyond this point the going gets appreciably tougher and the route more difficult to work out, so you'll need to have a hiking map with you. Otherwise, you'll have to return the way you came.

Fornalutx

FORNALUTX, a couple of kilometres east of Biniaraix along a narrow, signposted country lane, is touted as the most attractive village on Mallorca, and it certainly has a superb location. Orange and lemon groves scent the valley as it tapers up towards the settlement, whose honey-coloured stone houses huddle against a mountainous backdrop. Matching its setting, the quaint centre of Fornalutx fans out from the minuscule main square, its narrow cobbled streets stepped to facilitate mule traffic, though nowadays you're more likely to be hit by a Mercedes than obstructed by a mule: foreigners love the place and own about half of the village's three hundred houses. This sizeable expatriate community sustains one excellent **restaurant**, the *Bella Vista* (☎971 631 590), just down from the main, square on the road back towards Sóller. Enjoying fabulous views over the valley, it offers seafood and traditional Mallorcan cuisine, with full meals costing around 2500ptas/€15.03. It's fine just to have a drink here too, or you can head off to the main square, where there are a couple of small cafés.

*A taxi from
Fornalutx to
Sóller costs
1700ptas/€10.
22. If you don't
spot one hang-
ing around,
call ☎971 630
571.*

As for **accommodation**, the village boasts the charming, one-star *Hostal Fornalutx*, c/Alba 22 (☎971 631 997; ⑥), which occupies an attractively furnished and spotlessly clean old stone house with a terraced garden overlooking the orchards behind. Reservations are esssential here and at the neighbouring – and very similar – *Ca'n Reus*, c/Alba 26 (☎ & fax 971 631 174; ⑦), though the decor at the latter is a tad more self-conscious, a chic rendition of the rustic. To get to c/Alba, walk down the main street from the square (as for the *Bella Vista*) and take the first left just beyond the conspicuous railings – a minute's stroll.

Port de Sóller

PORT DE SÓLLER is one of the most popular spots on the west coast, and its handsome horseshoe-shaped bay, ringed by forested mountains, must be the most photographed place on the island after the package resorts around Palma. However, the high jinks of the Badia de Palma are about the last thing imaginable down here – for, grafted onto the old fishing port and naval base, is a low-key resort geared up for families. There's no point in staying just for the swimming, since, although the water is warm and calm, it's often surprisingly murky (courtesy of the yachts at anchor). The two diminutive sandy beaches are also not much to boast about: one is near the boat dock and overlooked on all sides by the road, hotels and restaurants, while the other, the **Platja d'en Repic** on the southern side of the bay, offers a little more seclusion, but not much. Nevertheless, Port de Sóller does have

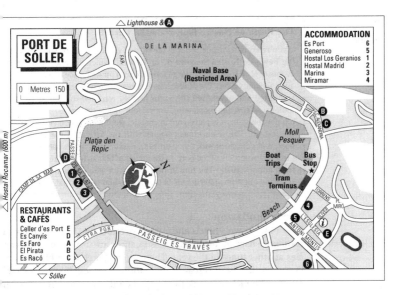

PORT DE
SÓLLER

ACCOMMODATION

Es Port	6
Generoso	5
Hostal Los Geranios	1
Hostal Madrid	2
Marina	3
Miramar	4

DE LA MARINA

Naval Base
(Restricted Area)

Platja den
Repic

Moll
Pesquer

Boat
Trips

Bus
Stop

Tram
Terminus

Beach

**RESTAURANTS
& CAFÉS**

Celler d'es Port	E
Es Canyis	D
Es Faro	A
El Pirata	B
Es Racó	C

0   Metres   150

△ Lighthouse & **A**

CAMP DE SA MAR

PASSEIG ES TRAVÉS

CTRA PORT

▽ Sóller

some merits, especially its selection of excellent seafood restaurants and the enjoyable hour-long hike west to the **lighthouse** (*far*), which guards the cliffs of Cap Gros above the entrance to its inlet. From here, the views out over the wild and rocky coast and back across the harbour are truly magnificent, especially at sunset. Directions to the lighthouse couldn't be easier as there's a tarmac road all the way: from the tram terminus, walk round the southern side of the bay past Platja d'en Repic and keep going, following the signs.

The coastal walk from Deià to Port de Sóller, described on p.142, emerges from the mountains behind the Platja d'en Repic.

Arrival and information

Trams from Sóller shadow the main road and clank to a stop beside the jetties, bang in the centre of town. From here, it's a couple of minutes' walk east to the **tourist office**, located beside the church on c/Canonge Oliver (March–Oct Mon–Fri 10am–1pm & 3–6.30pm; March–Sept also Sat 10am–1pm; March–June also Sun 10am–1pm; ☎971 633 042). They carry a reasonable range of local information, including restaurant and accommodation lists, maps and boat-trip details.

Bike rental is available from Vivas, back towards Platja d'en Repic at Passeig Es Través 14 (☎971 630 088). In summer, **boats** leave the dock by the tram terminus for day excursions along the coast – northeast to Cala Tuent (April–Oct 1 weekly; 2000ptas/€12.02) and Sa Calobra (3 daily; 2000ptas/€12.02), and southwest to Sa Foradada (1 weekly; 2000ptas/€12.02). Cala Tuent (see p.163) is the most diverting of the destinations, though each trip is a good way of seeing a chunk of coast. You pay for the round-trip, but you don't, of course, have to come back.

The Festa de Nostra Senyora de la Victòria

If you're around Port de Sóller in the second week of May, be sure to catch the **Festa de Nostra Senyora de la Victòria**, which commemorates the events of May 1561 when a large force of Arab pirates came to a sticky end after sacking Sóller. The Mallorcans had been taken by surprise, but they ambushed and massacred the Arabs as they returned to their ships and took grisly revenge by planting the raiders' heads on stakes. The story – bar decapitations – is played out in chaotic, alcoholic fashion every year at the festival. The re-enactment begins with the arrival of the pirates by boat, and continues with fancy-dress Christians and Arabs battling it out through the streets of the port, to the sound of blanks being fired in the air from antique rifles. The tourist office can give you a rough idea of the schedule of events, plus details of the dances and parties that follow.

Accommodation

Most of the town's hotels and *hostals* overlook the bay and although **rooms** are hard to find in high season, there are usually lots of vacancies at other times of the year. There are no hotel tower blocks here but rather a ring of three- to four-storey blocks dating back to the 1960s. The pick overlook the Platja d'en Repic, a narrow wedge of sand about 1.5km round the bay from the tram terminus.

Hotel Es Port, c/Antoni Montis s/n ☎971 631 650, fax 971 631 662. This three-star hotel at the back of the port, a few minutes' walk from the waterfront, boasts lovely gardens, a swimming pool and a charming reception area set inside a renovated manor house. The guest rooms are, however, far less endearing, occupying a sprawling modern extension. ④.

Hotel Generoso, c/Marina 4 ☎971 631 450, fax 971 632 200. This routine modern block near the tram terminus has a hundred frugal rooms. ⑤.

Hostal Los Geranios, Passeig de Sa Platja s/n ☎971 631 440, fax 971 63 651. Straightforward two-star seafront hotel overlooking the Platja d'en Repic with a hundred rooms on four floors. ④.

Hostal-residencia Madrid, Passeig de Sa Platja s/n ☎971 631 812. Well-kept 1970s two-star beside the Platja d'en Repic. Most of the rooms have bayside balconies. Feb to mid-Nov. ⑤.

Hotel Marina, Passeig de Sa Platja s/n ☎971 631 461, fax 971 634 182 Pleasant two-star hotel overlooking the Platja d'en Repic. The rooms are kitted out in brisk, modern style and most have bayside balconies. Feb to mid-Nov. ⑥.

Hotel Miramar, c/Marina 12 ☎971 631 350, fax 971 632 671. A standard-issue modern block overlooking the bay from near the tram terminus, with just thirty frugal rooms. ③.

Eating and drinking

Port de Sóller heaves with **cafés** and **restaurants**, but standards are very variable: some serve up mediocre food with the package tourist in mind, others are more authentically *Mallorquín* – or at least Spanish. The majority are dotted along the bayshore, with a cluster of better restaurants on c/Santa Caterina d'Alexandria, a short side street that cuts up from the waterfront close to the naval base. As for bars, there are one or two tourist spots, but you're better off drinking where you eat.

Cafeteria Es Faro, Cap Gros ☎971 633 752. Few restaurants can boast a finer location, perched high up on the cliffs at the entrance to the harbour. The views from the outside terrace are nothing short of spectacular. During the day, the *Es Faro* offers coffees, light meals and an excellent *menú del día*; at night it's à la carte – and the seafood is delicious. Reservations recommended; reasonable prices.

Celler d'es Port, c/Antoni Montis 17A ☎971 630 654. Port de Sóller may swim with tourists, but there's room for the locals too, and many of them gather here at this unassuming neighbourhood café-bar where the food is inexpensive and the emphasis is on traditional Mallorcan dishes. Closed Wed.

Restaurant El Pirata, c/Santa Caterina d'Alexandria 7 ☎971 631 497. The flashy piratical decor is a little over the top, but the food – especially the seafood – is first-rate.

Restaurant Es Racó, c/Santa Caterina d'Alexandria 6 ☎971 633 639. Cosy, family-run restaurant with an extensive menu featuring all the Spanish favourites; try the sardines. For a main course, reckon on 1800ptas/€10.82.

Restaurant Es Canyís, Passeig de Sa Platja s/n ☎971 631 406. Bright and cheerful, with angular modern decor, this bistro-style restaurant offers a good range of Spanish dishes from its bayshore premises behind the Platja d'en Repic. The snails are a house special. Main courses average 1500–2000ptas/ €9.02–€12.02.

The Jardins d'Alfàbia and Raixa

Heading south from Sóller, the main road to Palma tunnels through the Serra de Tramuntana – though you can, as a scenic alternative, hairpin up and over the mountains instead. On this second, longer route the road threads its way past the **Coll de Sóller**, a rocky pass with a car park and lookout point offering splendid views out over the coast.

Whichever route you choose, be sure to stop by the **Jardins d'Alfàbia** (Mon–Fri 9.30am–6.30pm, Sat 9.30am–1pm; Sept–May Mon–Fri closes 5.30pm; 700ptas/€4.21). These lush and beautiful terraced gardens surround a genteel *hacienda* close to the southern entrance to the tunnel. Shortly after the Reconquest, Jaume I granted the estate of Alfàbia to a prominent Moor by the name of Benhabet. Seeing which way the historical wind was blowing, Benhabet, as governor of Pollença, had given his support to Jaume, provisioning the Catalan army during the invasion. There was no way Jaume I could leave his Moorish ally in charge of Pollença (and anyway it was already pledged to a Catalan noble), but he was able to reward him with this generous portion of land. Benhabet planned his new estate in the Moorish manner, channelling water from the surrounding mountains to irrigate the fields and fashion oasis-like gardens. Generations of island gentry added to the estate without marring Benhabet's original design, thus creating the homogenous ensemble that survives today.

From the roadside, you follow a stately avenue of plane trees towards the house, but, before you reach the gatehouse, you're directed up a flight of stone steps and into the **gardens**. Here, a footpath

Beside the Jardins d'Alfàbia is the outstanding Restaurant Ses Porxeres – see p.127.

leads past ivy-covered stone walls, gurgling watercourses and bright ly coloured flowers cascading over narrow terraces. Trellises of jas mine and wisteria create patterns of light and shade, while palm and fruit trees jostle upwards, allowing only the occasional glimpse of the surrounding citrus groves. At the end of the path, the gardens' high light is a verdant jungle of palm trees, bamboo and bullrushes tan gling a tiny pool. It's an enchanting spot, especially on a hot summer's day, and an outdoor **bar** sells big glasses of freshly squeezed orange juice, a snip at 250ptas/€1.50. A few paces away is the **house**, a rather mundane, veranda'd *hacienda* whose handful of rooms house an eccentric mix of antiques and curios. Pride of place goes to a superb fourteenth-century **oak chair** adorned with delightful bas relief scenes honouring Mallorca's royals. The uncrowned Jaume IV ordered the chair, though he never had a chance to sit on it: after the Battle of Llucmajor in 1349, in which the Aragonese killed his father Jaume III, he was captured and spent the rest of his days in exile.

*For more on
Jaume IV, see
p.242.*

At the front of the house, the cobbled **courtyard** is shaded by a giant plane tree and surrounded by good-looking, rustic outbuildings Beyond lies the **gatehouse**, an imposing structure sheltering a fine coffered ceiling of Mudéjar design, with an inscription praising Allah

Raixa

Pushing on south along the C711 from the Jardins d'Alfàbia, it's about 5km to the short gravel lane that leads west to **Raixa**, the one-time country estate of the eighteenth-century antiquarian Cardinal Antonic Despuig. The Cardinal carved terraced **gardens** out of the hill beside his country home and then proceeded to decorate them with Neoclassical statues, water fountains and even bits of old masonry recovered from medieval buildings in Palma – all in the fashionable Italian style of his day. Despuig saw himself as a leading light of the Enlightenment, but underneath the cultured cassock was a medieval piety: he died in Italy and on his deathbed he left instructions for his heart to be cut out and buried close to the body of Mallorca's favourite saint, Catalina Thomàs (see p.146). Today, the manor house is out of bounds and Despuig's terraced gardens (Wed–Sun 11am–7pm 500ptas/€3.01) in need of repair, but it's still a lovely secluded spot and you can climb up through the gardens to reach the belvedere which offers extensive views out across the surrounding countryside

*Cardinal
Despuig left
his collection
of classical
sculpture to
the city of
Palma – see
p.99.*

The small purple roadsign to Raixa is easy to miss: travelling south from Sóller, if you reach the traffic island at the junction of the C711 and the PM114/PM203, you've come too far. Double back and the Raixa turning is about 500m to the north.

Orient and around

In between Alfàbia and Raixa, a country road (the PM201 and then the PM210) forks east off the C711 to loop past the plane trees and sun bleached walls of the unassuming market town of **BUNYOLA**, before snaking across the forested foothills of the Serra de Tramuntana. It's a beautiful drive (the tarmac's in good condition too, though some of the bends are nerve-jangling), and after about 13km you'll come to ORI-ENT. This remote hamlet of ancient houses is scattered along the eastern side of the lovely Vall d'Orient, with hills rising all around olive and almond groves. There's even somewhere to **stay** in the village, the simple, tiny *Hostal-residencia Muntanya*, c/Bordoy 6 (☎971 615 373; ⑤), although this is as nothing compared to the romantic *Hotel L'Hermitage* (☎971 180 303, fax 971 180 411, *info@hermitage-hotel.com*; Feb to early Nov; ⑨), a luxuriously renovated medieval manor house roughly 1km east of Orient on the PM210. The hotel gardens are lovely, the scenery gorgeous and the **restaurant**, with its mammoth antique olive press, excellent, even if the decor is a little twee. Advance reservations are pretty much essential and, if you're paying this sort of money, try to get one of the four rooms in the old manor house, rather than one of the sixteen in the modern annexe.

The Castell d'Alaró

Beyond the *Hotel L'Hermitage*, the PM210 sticks to the ridge overlooking the narrow valley of the Torrent d'en Paragon for around 3km, before veering south to slip between a pair of molar-like hills whose bare rocky flanks tower above the surrounding forest and scrub. The more westerly of the two sports the sparse ruins of the **Castell d'Alaró**, originally a Moorish stronghold but rebuilt by Jaume I. Visible for miles around, the castle looks impregnable on its lofty perch, and it certainly impeded the Aragonese invasion of 1285: when an Aragonese messenger suggested terms for surrender, the garrison's two commanders responded by calling the Aragonese king Alfonso III "fish-face", punning on his name in Catalan (*anfos* means "perch"). When the castle finally fell, Alfonso had the two roasted alive. Goodness knows what he'd have done if they'd called him something really rude.

Access to the castle is from the south: coming from Orient, watch for the signposted right turn just beyond the "Kilometre 18" stone marker. The first 3km of this narrow side road are well-surfaced, but the last 1.3km is gravel and dirt, with a tight series of hairpins negotiating a very steep hillside – especially hazardous after rain. The road emerges at a car park and an old ramshackle farmstead, whose barn now holds the **restaurant** *Es Verger* (☎971 510 711). It's tempting to linger here: the views down over the plain are sumptuous and the food delicious, particularly the house speciality, oven-baked lamb. From the restaurant, you can also spy the ruins of the castle above, about an hour's walk away along a clearly marked track. The trail leads to the castle's stone gateway, beyond which lies an expansive wooded plateau accommodating the fragmentary ruins of the fortress, plus the tiny pilgrims' church of **Mare de Déu del Refugi**. There's a simple restaurant and bar up here too, serving traditional Mallorcan food: the *pa amb oli* is a snip at 500ptas/€3.01.

Alaró

Back on the PM210, it's about 1.5km south from the castle turn-off to the town of **ALARÓ**, a sleepy little place of old stone houses fanning out from an attractive main square, **Plaça Vila**. A long and elegant arcaded gallery flanks one side of the square, and a second is shadowed by the **church**, a fortress-like, medieval affair whose honey-coloured sandstone is embellished with Baroque details. The square also has a couple of first-rate **restaurants**, where local families gather on the weekend. There's not much to divide the two, but the *Traffic*, at no. 8 (☎971 879 117; closed Tues & Wed lunch), is perhaps the better, its Mallorcan specialities – notably its casseroles – served up in a pleasantly renovated old mansion with a wood beamed ceiling and a high stone arch. Less specifically *Mallorquín* is the *Restaurant Gaia*, just off the main square at c/Petit 11 (April–Oct Mon–Sat 7.30–11.30pm; ☎971 518 119), which features an inventive international menu with, for instance, quiche and artichokes in a cheese sauce for 1900ptas/€11.42.

Should you want to **stay**, there is a *hostal* here, the two-star *Ca'n Tiu*, whose eleven modest rooms are located above the *Restaurant Gaia* at c/Petit 11 (☎ & fax 971 510 974; ④). The street is quite busy, so you might prefer to ask for a room at the back.

Binissalem and Lloseta

Just south of Alaró, you leave the foothills of the Serra de Tramuntana behind for the central plain of Mallorca, **Es Pla**. The northern peripheries of the plain hold **BINISSALEM**, an appealing country town that has long been the centre of the island's wine industry. Binissalem looks dull and ugly from the main C713 Palma–Alcúdia road, so most people zip straight through without stopping, but the tatty semi-industrial sprawl that straddles the main road camouflages an antique town centre, whose narrow streets contain a proud ensemble of old stone mansions dating from the seventeenth and eighteenth centuries. The Romans settled here and so did the Moors – Binissalem could be derived from the Arabic "Bani Salaam", meaning Sons of Peace – but the town's commercial heyday began in the sixteenth century, boosted by its vineyards and stone quarries.

See p.50 for more about Mallorcan wine.

The old town zeroes in on its main square, the **Plaça Església**, a pretty, stone-flagged piazza lined with benches where local old timers shoot the breeze in the shade of the plane trees. The north side of the square is dominated by the **Església Nostra Senyora de Robines**, the clumpy, medieval nave of which is attached to a soaring neo-Gothic bell tower added in 1908. Inside, the single-vaulted nave is dark and gloomy, its most distinctive features being its glitzy Baroque altarpiece and the grooved stonework that graces the ceilings of the transepts and the apse. This grooved stonework pops up all over town, representing the cockle-shell emblem of **St James the Greater**, one of the apostles. James witnessed the Transfiguration and the capture of Jesus in the Garden of Gethsemane and was the first of the apostles to be martyred, at the hands of Herod in 44 AD, but, despite his early demise, Spanish legend insists that he visited Spain and preached here. The same stories assert that James's body was brought from Jerusalem to Spain and buried at Santiago de Compostela in the far northwest of Spain, and although these tales verge on the ridiculous, they made St James one of Spain's most venerated saints. An especially good time to visit Binissalem is in the third week of July, during the week-long **festivities** that precede the saint's feast day on July 25.

Another good festival is the Festa d'es Vermar – see p.136.

Strolling southwest from the Plaça Església, along c/Concepció, it's a short distance to the **Ajuntament** (Town Hall), and a few minutes more to **Can Sabater**, c/Bonaire 25, one of the town's most distinguished patrician mansions. This was once the home of the writer Llorenç Villalonga (1897–1980), whose most successful novel was *The Dolls' Room*, an ambiguous portrait of Mallorca's nineteenth-century landed gentry in moral decline. In his honour, the house has been turned into the **Casa Museu Llorenç Villalonga** (Mon–Sat 10am–2pm; also Tues & Thurs 4–8pm; free), with detailed Catalan explanations of his life and times as well as his library and study. The house is typical of its type, and is adorned with elegant stone arches and has high-ceilinged rooms redolent of oligarchic comfort. It also has its own chapel: the island's richer families usually had their own live-in priests.

If you double back along c/Bonaire and take a right turn along c/Sant Vicenç de Paul just before you reach the Ajuntament, you'll soon reach **c/Pere Estruch**, a cobbled street flanked by the town's most complete sequence of old stone houses, adorned by a medley of wooden shutters and wrought-iron balconies.

Practicalities

Buses pull in beside the C713 road at the foot of c/Bonaire, a five- to ten-minute walk from the Plaça Església. Binissalem is also on the Palma–Inca **train** line, and regular trains from both directions stop at the station on the northern edge of the town centre; a five- or ten-minute walk from the station, straight down c/S'Estació and right at the end along c/Porteta, brings you to Passeig d'es Born beside the church on Plaça Església. Binissalem has no tourist office as such, but there are free town **maps** and brochures in the foyer of the Ajuntament, close to the church on c/Concepció – just help yourself.

Binissalem boasts one of Mallorca's finest **hotels**, *Scotts*, right in the centre of town at Plaça Església 12 (☎971 870 100, fax 971 870 267, *www.scottshotel.com*; ⑨). The house was originally owned by an almond grower, and has been immaculately restored, its sweeping stone arches and high ceilings enclosing three suites decorated in elegant, broadly nineteenth-century style. At the back, the old stone outbuildings surround a leafy courtyard and contain more recent rooms, each decorated in crisp modern style. Breakfast is served on

Binissalem

a sunny terrace at the back of the hotel, and there's a swimming pool. The hotel has nineteen rooms in all, and prices are firmly (and justifiably) in the luxury category, starting at about 28,000ptas/€168.28 for a double room. The owner, an American, is familiar with every nook and cranny of the island; his first novel, *The Bloody Bokhara* (see p.264), was published in 2000.

Scotts offers light suppers three evenings a week (advance reservations required) and there's also a cosy, polished **restaurant** in the town centre – *El Suizo*, c/Pou Bo 20 (☎971 870 076), where they present an imaginative international menu featuring local ingredients. It's about five minutes' walk from Plaça Església: walk south down c/Bonaire, turn right along c/Reg, left down c/Llorenç Moya and it's on the right at the fork. On Plaça Església itself is the inexpensive locals' hangout *Café Plaça*, where they serve up tasty *tapas* in spartan surroundings.

If you can't be in Binissalem for the July festivities around the day of St James (see p.134), try to aim for the delightful **Festa d'es Vermar** (Festival of the Grape Harvest) in the third week of September, when the cordoned-off streets are lined with trestle tables weighed down with all sorts of local wines and foods, proudly presented by their makers.

Lloseta

The old shoemaking town of **LLOSETA**, about 4km east of Binissalem, drapes over a steep little hill, its pleasant central square, the **Plaça Espanya**, decorated by a medieval church surmounted by the most petite of bell towers. Otherwise, Lloseta is really rather humdrum, but it is home to the Palau Aiamans, the grand eighteenth-century, L-shaped mansion of the local bigwig, located next to the church on the main square. The house has recently been converted into a luxury **hotel**, the *Ca's Comte* (☎971 873 077, fax 971 519 192, *www.cascomte.com*; ⑨), whose modernist interior – all stone arches, glass tables and marble floors – contains just eight splendid rooms.

Plaça Espanya is a ten-minute walk north up c/Mestre Antoni Vidal from the Lloseta **train station**, just up the line from Binissalem in the Inca direction. The *Ca's Comte* has a **restaurant**, but you may be better off heading for *Restaurant Ca'n Carrossa*, c/Guillem Santandreu 38 (☎971 514 023; closed Sun), where they serve outstanding Mallorcan dishes at reasonable prices. This family-run place is about 200m west of Plaça Espanya's southern edge.

The southwest coast

The southwesterly reaches of the Serra de Tramuntana rise out of the flatlands around Palma, with the range's forested foothills and sheltered valleys soon giving way to the craggy, wooded mountains that crimp most of the **southwest coast**. Several fast roads link Palma with the coast – the prettiest runs to Valldemossa – and a delightful network of country roads patterns the foothills, but the key sights (and the best scenery) are most readily reached along the main coastal road, the **C710**.

The south-west coast

From Sóller, the C710 skirts the broad and wooded slopes of the Puig d'es Teix to reach **Deià**, an ancient mountain village which perches precariously high above the seashore, clinging to the fame brought by associations with the writer Robert Graves. The next 20km of coastline boasts three of Mallorca's star attractions, allied to some of its finest coastal scenery: **Son Marroig**, the well-appointed mansion of the Mallorca-loving archduke, Ludwig Salvator; the hill-top monastery of **Valldemossa**, complete with its echoing cloisters and choice examples of modern art; and the old grandee's mansion and estate of **La Granja**. This captivating trio is hard to beat, although the tiered hamlets that decorate the coast further down the road are also instantly beguiling. Of these, both **Banyalbufar** and **Estellencs** occupy fine sites and are well worth at least a fleeting visit. Alternatively, you can travel inland from La Granja, climbing the slopes of the leafy foothills and rambling through secluded valleys of almond, olive and carob trees to reach the charming village of **Galilea**. Both the Galilea route and the C710 coast road emerge from the Serra de Tramuntana at **Andratx**, a crossroads town with easy access to the tiny port of **Sant Elm** and the more commercialized harbour-cum-resort of **Port d'Andratx** in the far southwest.

There are fine walks connecting Valldemossa with Deià (see p.150) and Deià with Port de Sóller (see p.142).

Beach lovers have meagre pickings in this part of the island. There's a good sandy beach with safe swimming at Sant Elm, but further up the coast, shingle strips will have to suffice. The most impressive of these is **Cala Deià**, set in the shadow of the mountains at the end of a narrow ravine. **Accommodation** can be hard to find, too. Each of the destinations mentioned above, with the exception of Galilea, has at least a couple of places to stay, but you're strongly advised to book well ahead for any stays between June and September or even October. Deià, Banyalbufar and Port d'Andratx have a cluster of hotels and *hostals*, and so represent the best bets for a last-minute vacancy, with Sant Elm the fourth favourite.

Transport

A **bus** service runs regularly from Palma to Valldemossa, Son Marroig and Deià, continuing on to Sóller and Port de Sóller. There are also fast and frequent buses from Palma to Andratx and Port d'Andratx. Along the C710 coast road between Andratx and Valldemossa, however, you're limited to a four-times-a-week bus service which originates in Peguera (see p.117).

For frequencies and journey times, see p.159.

Distances between destinations are short, so **taxis** can work out a reasonable proposition if you're in a group: the fare for the twenty-kilometre trip from Port de Sóller to Valldemossa, for example, is about 4000ptas/€24.04, or Palma to Deià 4700ptas/€28.25.

Deià

DEIÀ, 10km west of Sóller, is beautiful. The mighty Puig d'es Teix
(1062m) meets the coast here, and, although the mountain's lower
slopes are now gentrified by the villas of the well-to-do, it retains a
formidable, almost mysterious presence, especially in the shadows of

There's a basic
plan of Deià
on p.141.

a moonlit night. Deià's main street, c/Arxiduc Lluís Salvador, doubles
as the coastal highway, skirting the base of the Teix and showing off
most of the village's hotels and restaurants. **Buses** between Palma,
Valldemossa and Port de Sóller scoot through Deià five times daily in
each direction (Nov–March reduced service on Sun). There's no
tourist office, but the village's hotels and *hostals* will gladly provide
local advice on walks and weather. They'll also fix you up with a **taxi**,
or you can call Sóller's Autotaxis ☎971 630 571.

At times, Deià's main street is too congested to be much fun, but
the tiny heart of the village, tumbling over a high and narrow ridge
on the seaward side of the road, can still retain a surprising tranquillity. Labyrinthine alleys of old peasant houses curl up to a pretty
country **church**, in the precincts of which is buried **Robert Graves**,
the village's most famous resident – his headstone marked simply
"Robert Graves: Poeta, E.P.D" (*En Paz Descanse*, "Rest In Peace").
From the graveyard, there are memorable views out over the coast
and of the Teix, with banks of carefully terraced fields tumbling
down from the mountain towards the sea. The church itself is a modest little affair, decked out with Baroque altar pieces, and one of its
outbuildings holds a tiny museum, the **Museu Parroquial** (donation
100ptas/€0.60), where there's a folksy assortment of religious bric-
a-brac and, on the stairs, a photo of Graves in his Deià study.

Graves put the village on the international map (see box), and
nowadays Deià is the haunt of long-term expatriates, mostly ex-hip-
pies and artists living on ample trust funds, judging from the kind of
monthly rents that are charged here. These inhabitants congregate at

Directions to
Cala Deià are
given in the
first part of
the "Coastal
Walk" route to
Port de Sóller
– see p.142.

the **Cala Deià**, the nearest thing the village has to a beach – some
200m of shingle at the back of a handsome rocky cove of jagged
cliffs, boulders and white-crested surf. It's a great place for a swim,
the water clean, deep and cool, and there's a ramshackle beach bar.
Most of the time, the cove is quiet and peaceful, but parties of day-
trippers do sometimes stir things up. It takes about twenty minutes
to walk from the village to the *cala*, a delightful stroll down a wooded ravine. To drive there, head north along the main road out of Deià
and watch for the sign about 600m beyond the *Restaurant El Olivo*.

Accommodation

Deià boasts two of the most luxurious **hotels** on the island as well as
a handful of delightful, less expensive places. There's a reasonable
chance of finding a room on spec at any time of the year, but you're
really much better off making a reservation at least a day or two in
advance.

Robert Graves in Deià

The English poet, novelist and classical scholar **Robert Graves** (1895–1985) had two spells of living in Deià, the first in the 1930s, and the second from the end of World War II until his death. During his earlier stay, he shared a house at the edge of the village with **Laura Riding**, an American poet and dabbler in the mystical. Riding had arrived in England in 1926 and, after she became Graves's secretary and collaborator, the two of them began an affair – unknown to either of their spouses. The tumultuous course of their relationship created sufficient furore for them to decide to leave England, choosing to settle in Mallorca on the advice of Gertrude Stein in 1930. The fuss was not simply a matter of morality – many of their friends were indifferent to adultery – but more to do with the self-styled "**Holy Circle**" they had founded, a cabalistic and intensely self-preoccupied literary-mystic group. The last straw came when Riding, in her attempt to control the group, jumped out of a window exclaiming "Goodbye, chaps", and the besotted Graves leapt after her. No wonder his mate T.E. Lawrence ('of Arabia') wrote of "madhouse minds" and of Graves "drowning in a quagmire".

The two both recovered, but the dottiness continued once they'd moved to Deià, with Graves acting as doting servant to Riding, whom he reinvented as a sort of all-knowing matriarch and muse. Simultaneously, Graves thumped away at his prose: he had already produced *Goodbye to All That* (1929), his bleak and painful memoirs of army service in the World War I trenches, but now came his other best-remembered books, **I, Claudius** (1934) and its sequel **Claudius the God** (1935), historical novels detailing the life and times of the Roman emperor. Nonetheless, to Graves these "pot-boilers", as he styled them, were secondary to his poetry, and indeed his verse works of this period, usually carefully crafted love poems of melancholic tenderness in praise of Riding, were well received by the critics.

At the onset of the Spanish Civil War, Graves and Riding left Mallorca, not out of sympathy for the Republicans – Graves was far too reactionary for that – but to keep contact with friends and family. During their exile Graves was ditched by Riding, and he subsequently took up with a mutual friend, **Beryl Hodge**. After Graves had returned to Deià in 1946, he worked on *The White Goddess*, a controversial study of prehistoric and classical myth that argued the existence of an all-pervasive, primordial religion based on the worship of a poet-goddess. Hodge joined him in the midst of his labours (the book was published in 1948), and in 1950 they were married in Palma. They didn't live happily ever after. Graves had a predilection for young women, claiming the need for female muses to inspire his poetic vision; his wife outwardly accepted this waywardness, but without much enthusiasm. Meanwhile, although Graves's novels became increasingly well-known and profitable, his poetry, with its preoccupation with romantic love, fell out of fashion, and his last anthology, *Poems 1965–1968*, was widely criticized by the literary establishment.

Nevertheless, Graves's international reputation as a writer attracted a steady stream of visitors to Deià from the ranks of the literati, with the occasional film-star dropping by to add to the self-regarding stew. By the middle of the 1970s, however, just as an acclaimed BBC TV production of *I, Claudius* was bringing his books to a wider public in his native country, Graves had begun to lose his mind, and ended his days in sad senility.

Fonda Villa Verde, c/Ramón Llull 19 ☎971 639 037, fax 971 639 485. This lovely little pension perches on the side of a hill in the antique centre of the village, between the main road and the church. The rooms are immaculate and there's a charming shaded terrace overlooking Puig d'es Teix. March–Nov. ⑤.

Hostal Miramar, c/Ca'n Oliver s/n ☎ & fax 971 639 084. A pleasant one-star *hostal* up above – and signposted from – the C710 about halfway through the village, with just nine frugal rooms both with and without private shower. April–Oct. ④.

Hotel Costa d'Or, 2km east along the C710 coast road at the hamlet of Llucalcari ☎971 639 025, fax 971 639 347. This splendid one-star hotel occupies a simply wonderful setting, overlooking an undeveloped slice of coast and surrounded by pine groves and olive terraces. There's a shaded terrace bar and a splendid outdoor swimming pool. The rooms vary, although all are spotlessly clean: there are some doubles in two buildings at the back of the complex, while the more expensive rooms look directly over the sea. April–Oct. ⑤.

Hotel Es Moli, Carretera Deià s/n ☎971 639 000, fax 971 639 333. Four-star luxury in a grand, lavishly refurbished old mansion overlooking the C710 at the west end of the village, surrounded by lovely gardens and equipped with a swimming pool. There are ninety air-conditioned bedrooms here, each kitted out in dapper, modern style; most have balconies with sea views. This is undoubtedly one of Mallorca's best hotels. Mid-April to Oct. ⑨.

S'Hotel d'es Puig, c/Es Puig 4 ☎971 639 409, fax 971 639 210, *puig@futur-net.es*. A smart and tastefully furnished hotel with eight bedrooms in an elegantly converted, four-storey old stone house located in the old centre of the village, between the C710 and the church. March to mid-Nov. ⑦.

Hotel-residencia La Residencia, c/Arxiduc Lluís Salvador s/n ☎971 639 011, fax 971 639 370, *laresidencia@atlas-iap.es*. Deià's second luxury hotel is also sited in a gracious old mansion – on the main drag at the east end of the village, opposite the old centre – but its furnishings and fittings are more self-conscious than the rival *Es Moli*. The hotel's clean, modern lines are superimposed on rooms with an antique appearance boasting big wooden bedsteads, timbered ceilings and the like. ⑨.

Eating and drinking

As for eating and drinking in Deià, you're spoiled for choice. Dotted along the main street c/Arxiduc Lluís Salvador are several smart and polished **restaurants** plus a number of more modest **café-bars**, ideal for nursing a drink and, especially in the off-season, checking out the expat scene.

Bar-restaurant Deià, c/Arxiduc Lluís Salvador s/n. Light meals and snacks with a pan-European slant. In an attractive setting at the west end of the village, with an outdoor terrace overlooking a steep ravine.

Café La Fábrica, c/Arxiduc Lluís Salvador s/n. An unpretentious café-bar at the west end of the village, offering reasonably priced *tapas*, *bocadillos* and the traditional *pa amb oli* (bread rubbed with olive oil). Limited opening hours in winter.

Café Las Palmeras, c/Arxiduc Lluís Salvador s/n. Amenable café on the main road about halfway into the village with a shaded terrace much frequented by chess-playing expats. The food is mediocre, with Italian standbys from around 800ptas/€4.81.

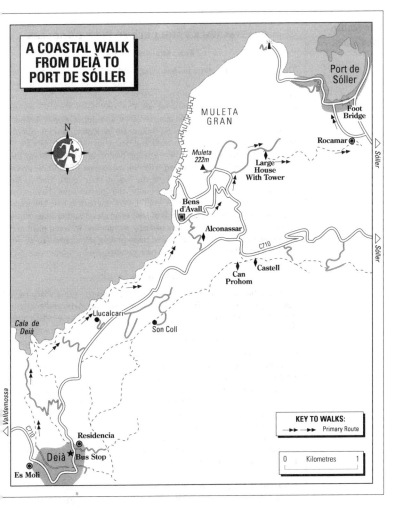

A COASTAL WALK FROM DEIÀ TO PORT DE SÓLLER

MULETA GRAN

Port de Sóller

Foot Bridge

Rocamar

Muleta 222m

Large House With Tower

Bens d'Avall

Alconassar

C710

Castell

Can Prohom

Llucalcari

Son Coll

Cala de Deià

Residencia

Deià ★ Bus Stop

Es Moli

KEY TO WALKS:
▶▶ ── ▶▶ Primary Route

0 ── Kilometres ── 1

Restaurant Es Racó d'es Teix, c/Vinya Vella 6 ☎971 639 501. Delightful little restaurant in an old stone house with an exquisite shaded terrace, located a steep 300m or so above the main road, about halfway into the village – watch for the sign. The seafood is good and so are the Mallorcan dishes, with prices a deal lower than you'll find down on the main drag. Closed Tues.

Restaurant Jaime, c/Arxiduc Lluís Salvador s/n ☎971 639 029. First-rate restaurant on the main drag about halfway into the village which specializes in traditional Mallorcan cuisine, with dishes from around 1800ptas/€10.82.

Restaurant El Olivo, c/Arxiduc Lluís Salvador s/n ☎971 639 011. If your wallet is stuffed with cash, try this chi-chi restaurant located in a former mill that is now part of *Hotel La Residencia*. Gourmets recommend the place – and the broadly Medditerranean menu is widely regarded as top-notch.

A COASTAL WALK FROM DEIÀ TO PORT DE SÓLLER

12KM; 4HR–4HR 30MIN

This delightful **walk** starts in Deià village and ends at the *Rocamar* hotel in Port de Sóller. There's a fairly regular bus service between the two places which makes the round trip relatively straightforward, but be sure to confirm bus times before you set out. The coast north of Deià is dotted with pine trees and abandoned olive terraces, and slopes steeply down to the sea from the high massif of Sa Galera. On such steep terrain, run-off water plays havoc with terrace walls and paths, so although this walk is mainly easy, care is needed where erosion has occurred. All the way the **views** are superlative, beginning with the panorama of the blue-green waters of Cala Deià. The views from the bus on your return journey are equally outstanding: notice especially the picturesque hamlet of **Llucalcari**, which cannot be seen from the coastal path below. The walking route, which sometimes drops almost to sea-level and at other times rises to avoid difficult ground, is partially waymarked with red paint and cairns, although a certain amount of route-finding is required. There are stiles at all the boundary fences the path crosses.

THE ROUTE

From the **bus stop** in Deià, walk in the Palma direction to a sharp right bend in the main road. Turn right down the shallow steps and continue downhill, past the Archeological Museum-cum-Historical Research Centre. After a few minutes take a right fork, where the road is marked with a "no through way" sign. Where the lane ends, follow the signposted footpath which continues in the same direction. About 150m further, the footpath is marked by a green painted wooden arrow. After about five minutes, turn right (north) by a white "Cala" sign painted on a stone. Some 200m further on, the path joins a surfaced road, veering slightly to the left before reaching, after about 500m, tiny **Cala Deià**, with its cluster of small boats and a beach bar serving meals in summer.

The **coastal path** begins up a flight of steps some 50m before the road ends. There is another flight of steps closer to the beach, but this just leads to a public toilet (the key for which is kept at the beach bar). After ascending the steps of the coastal path, ignore a left branch after about five minutes, but only a couple of minutes later follow the line of red painted stones left where the stepped path swings right. The path immediately turns right along a terrace, crosses a low wall and then turns sharp left downhill beside the wall. One minute later it turns right again and leads to an attrac-

Restaurant Sa Dorada, c/Arxiduc Lluís Salvador s/n ☎971 639 481. One of the best places in town for fish, with main courses from around 1800ptas/ €10.82. Located about halfway into the village on the main road.

Son Marroig

South from Deià, the C710 snakes through the mountains for 3km to reach **Son Marroig**, an imposing L-shaped mansion perched high above the seashore (and just below the road). The house dates from late medieval times, but was refashioned in the nineteenth century to

tive headland among pine trees, overlooking the sea and the white rocks of Cala Deià.

Continue straight on along the path to the north, passing a **mirador** (viewpoint) with a private path descending to it from an unseen house above. Below the *mirador*, steps descend to a rocky inlet. Go halfway down these, then turn off right and ascend the earth path waymarked with red paint spots. Later, after crossing two stiles, there are notices saying "**No picnic**" next to a large circular table with surrounding seats – a useful landmark. Here the path forks left downhill, leading to another stile and, a few minutes later, passes below a stone enclosure and then past the left edge of a wall where the ground rises steeply inland. After the wall follow the direction of the red paint marks leading uphill to a headland with a few almond trees growing in bare red earth.

Round the corner beyond the headland there's an eroded gully, its edge protected with a wire fence. The path becomes less clear hereabouts. Go inland past a **white house**. Ascend to a terrace, which contours round the hillside to a two- or three-metre gap in the gully fence. At this point the stream which created the gully has been culverted. At the end of this terrace follow the lower path to reach the next stile and another terrace, quite low down near the sea. Next, go uphill by a **fallen tree**, cross a headland among boulders and heather, and then go fairly steeply upwards through terraces of olive trees. This part of the route is well marked and leads in about fifteen minutes to a path which contours left above a steep cliff to reach another stile.

The path then descends into and out of a stream bed and goes over a stile into a lane. Turn left, and when the lane ends find the continuation of the footpath on the right. Five minutes later this reaches a **concrete road** near some houses. Follow it uphill and, after a few minutes of steep walking, cross another stream bed (usually dry) by means of the metal pegs in the enclosing dry-stone walls – an awkward manoeuvre which requires two free hands. Turn right along the wide road by the *Bens d'Avall* **restaurant** (closed in winter), and follow the road uphill for 1.5km to reach the Muleta road junction. Turn left, then right, heading along a track towards a **large farmhouse with a square tower**.

The most direct route to **Port de Sóller** is to turn right and go through the gate towards the house with tower, following a path to the right between the buildings. Continue through a gate to the mule track, which leads down to the *Rocamar* hotel. Below the *Rocamar*, turn left for the Platja d'en Repic, Port de Sóller's largest beach, or right for the trams on the main road to Sóller.

The account of Port de Sóller starts on p.128.

become the favourite residence of the Habsburg archduke **Ludwig Salvator** (1847–1915). Dynastically insignificant but extremely rich, the Austrian noble was a man in search of a hobby – and he found it in Mallorca. He first visited the island at the age of 19, fell head-over-heels in love with the place, and returned to buy this chunk of the west coast. Once in residence, Ludwig immersed himself in all things *Mallorquín*, learning the dialect and chronicling the island's topography, archeology, history and folklore in astounding detail. He churned out no fewer than seven volumes on the Balearics and, per-

haps more importantly, played a leading role as a proto-environmen-
talist, conserving the coastline of his estates and, amongst many projects, paying for a team of geologists to chart the Coves del Drac (see
p.218).

The Son Marroig estate (Mon–Sat 9.30am–2pm & 3–5pm
350ptas/€2.10) comprises the house, its gardens and the headland
below. The **house** boasts a handful of period rooms, whose antique
furnishings and fittings are enlivened by an eclectic sample of
Hispano-Arabic pottery. On display too are some of the archduke's
manuscripts and pen drawings, as well as several interesting pho-
tographs of him. It won't be long, however, before you're out in the
garden, whose terraces are graced by a Neoclassical belvedere of
Tuscan Carrara marble. The views out along the jagged, forested
coast are gorgeous.

Down below the garden is a slender promontory, known as **Sa
Foradada**, "the rock pierced by a hole", where the archduke used to
park his yacht. The hole in question is a strange circular affair, sited
high up in the rock face at the end of the promontory. It takes about
forty minutes to **walk** the 3km down to the tip of land, a largely
straightforward excursion to a delightfully secluded and scenic spot.
A sign on the gate at the beginning of the path (up the hill and to the
left of the house) insists you need to get permission at Son Marroig
before setting out – but this is just to make sure you pay the admission fee. There should be few problems with direction-finding on the
walk: about 100m beyond the gate, keep right at the fork in the
track, and as you approach the end of the promontory, think carefully before deciding to attempt the precarious climb beyond the old
jetties. On your return, you can slake your thirst at the **café-bar** *Son
Marroig* overlooking the coast from beside the car park near the
house.

Valldemossa and around

South of Son Marroig, the C710 stays high above the coast, twisting
through what was once the archducal estate en route to the intriguing ancient hill-town of **VALLDEMOSSA**. The town may at first
appear disappointing if you're coming from Deià, as the C710 cuts
first through the drab western outskirts. The best approach is from
the **south**, where, with the mountains closing in, the 15km road from
Palma squeezes through a narrow, wooded defile before entering a
lovely valley, whose tiered and terraced fields ascend to the town, a
sloping jumble of rusticated houses and monastic buildings back-
clothed by the mountains.

The origins of Valldemossa date to the early fourteenth century,
when the asthmatic **King Sancho** built a royal palace here in the hills
where the air was easier to breathe. Later, in 1399, the palace was
gifted to Carthusian monks from Tarragona, who converted and
extended the original buildings into a **monastery**, which is now

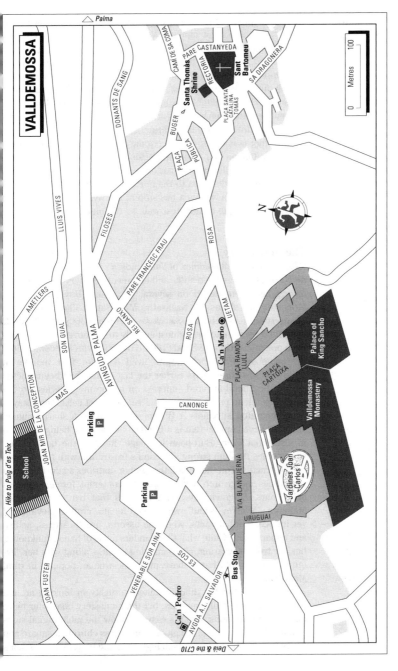

VALLDEMOSSA

△ Palma

Santa Thomàs Shrine

Sant Bartomeu

CAMÍ SA COMA

PARE CASTANYEDA

RECTORIA

PLAÇA SANTA CATALINA TOMAS

SA DRAGONERA

DONANTS DE SANG

BUGER

PLAÇA PÚBLICA

LLUIS VIVES

FILOSES

ROSA

N

AMETLERS

SON GUAL

PARE FRANCESC FRAU

REI SANXO

AVINGUDA PALMA

ROSA

UETAM

Ca'n Mario ◉

PLAÇA RAMON LLULL

Palace of King Sancho

MAS

JOAN MIR DE LA CONCEPTION

CANONGE

PLAÇA CARTOIXA

Valldemossa Monastery

Parking P

Parking P

VIA BLANQUERNA

Jardines Joan Carlos

School

Hike to Puig d'es Teix △

JOAN FUSTER

VENERABLE SOR AINA

ES COS

URUGUAI

Bus Stop ♦

Ca'n Pedro ◻

AVGDA A.L. SALVADOR

Deià & the C710 ▽

0   Metres   100

Mallorca's most visited building after Palma cathedral. Besides the monastery, there's not much to Valldemossa. The narrow cobbled lanes of the oldest part of town tumble prettily down the hillside beneath the monastery, but it only takes a few minutes to explore them and there are only two specific sights: the imposing bulk of the church of **Sant Bartomeu** and – round the back along a narrow alley, c/Rectoria 5 – the humble birthplace of **Santa Catalina Thomàs**, a sixteenth-century nun revered for her piety, the interior of which has been turned into a glitzy little shrine.

Valldemossa is a stop for the regular **buses** between Palma, Deià and Sóller and, on four days a week, for the single bus from Peguera, Andratx and Estellencs. Orientation is easy: a modern bypass skirts the centre of Valldemossa to the north; there are several car parks along this road, as well as a bus stop at the west end of town from where it's a couple of minutes' walk to the monastery. There's no tourist office.

The monastery

Most of the present complex of Valldemossa's **Real Cartuja de Jesús de Nazaret** is of seventeenth- and eighteenth-century construction, having been remodelled on several occasions (Royal Carthusian Monastery of Jesus of Nazareth; Mon–Sat 9.30am–6pm, Sun 10am–1pm; Nov–Feb Mon–Sat closes 4.30pm; 1300ptas/€7.81). It owes its present notoriety almost entirely to the novelist and republican polemicist **George Sand** (1804–76), who, with her companion, the composer **Frédéric Chopin**, lived here for four months in 1838–39. Just three years earlier the last monks had been evicted during the liberal-inspired suppression of the monasteries, so the pair were able to rent a commodious set of vacant cells. Their stay is commemorated in Sand's *A Winter in Majorca*, a sharp-tongued and sharp-eyed epistle that is a big deal hereabouts, being available in just about every European language. Reading the book today, what comes through strongly is Sand's frustration with the ossified social structures on the island, though her diatribes against reaction sometimes merge into a mean-spirited contempt for her Spanish neighbours. Ungraciously, Sand explains that her nickname for Mallorca, "Monkey Island", was coined for its "crafty, thieving and yet innocent" inhabitants, who, she asserts, are "heartless, selfish and impertinent". Quite what the islanders made of Sand is unknown, but her trouser-wearing, cigar-smoking image – along with her "living in sin" – could hardly have made the woman popular in rural Mallorca.

The monastery sometimes closes for lunch (1 or 1.30pm to 3pm).

See p.256 for a more edifying extract from Sand's book.

There's an obvious, though limited curiosity in looking around Sand and Chopin's old quarters, but the monastery boasts far more interesting diversions, and it's easy to follow the multilingual signs around. A visit begins in the gloomy, aisle-less **church**, a square and heavy construction with a kitsch high altar and barrel vaulting that's

distinguished by its late Baroque ceiling paintings and fanciful bishop's throne, though the lines of the nave are spoiled by the clumsy
wooden stalls of the choir. Beyond the church lie the shadowy **cloisters**, where the first port of call is the **pharmacy**, which survived the
expulsion of the monks to serve the town's medicinal needs well into
the twentieth century. Its shelves are crammed with a host of beautifully decorated majolica jars, antique glass receptacles and painted
wood boxes, each carefully inscribed with the name of a potion or
drug.

The nearby **prior's cell** is, despite its name, a comfortable suite of
bright, sizeable rooms, enhanced by access to a private garden with
splendid views down the valley. The cell, and the adjoining library,
dining and audience rooms, are graced by a wide assortment of religious *objets d'art*. These include a handsome assortment of majolica and tin-glazed tiles and, displayed in the library, two fine but unat-
tributed medieval triptychs: the *Adoration of the Magi*, a charmingly naive painting in the Flemish style, and an intricate three-panel
marble sculpture celebrating the marriage of Pedro II of Aragón.
This degree of luxury – the other cells are of similar proportions –
was clearly not what the ascetic St Bruno had in mind when he founded the Carthusian order in the eleventh century. Nevertheless, it's
hard to blame the monks at Valldemossa for lightening what must
have been a very heavy burden of privations. Bruno's rigorous
regime, inspired by his years as a hermit, had his monks in almost
continuous isolation, gathering together only for certain church services and to eat in the refectory on Sundays. At other times, lay
brothers fed the monks through hatches along the cloister corridors,
though this was hardly an onerous task: three days a week the monks
had only bread and water, and they never ate meat. The diet and the
mountain air, however, seemed to suit them: the longevity of the
Valldemossa monks was proverbial.

Along the corridor, **Cell no. 2** exhibits miscellaneous curios relat-
ing to Chopin and Sand, from portraits and a lock of hair to musical
scores and letters (it was in this cell that the composer wrote his
"Raindrop" Prelude). There's more of the same next door in **Cell
no. 4**, plus Chopin's favourite piano which, after three months of
unbelievable complications, only arrived just three weeks before the
couple left for Paris. Considering the hype, these incidental memen-
tos are something of an anticlimax. Neither do things improve much
in the ground-floor galleries of the adjacent **Museu Municipal**, which
feature local landscape painters and take a stab at tracing the dili-
gent endeavours of Archduke Ludwig Salvator. But don't give up: the
upstairs section of the museum, entitled the Museu Municipal Art
Contemporani, has a small but outstanding collection of **modern art**,
including work by Miró, Picasso, Francis Bacon and sketches by
Henry Moore. There's also a substantial sample of the work of the
Spanish modernist Juli Ramís (1909–1990), from geometric abstrac-

*There's an
account on
p.142 of
Archduke
Salvator's
estate at Son
Marroig.*

tions through to forceful, expressionistic paintings like *The Blue
Lady* (*Dama Blava*).

Back beside the prior's cell, be sure to take the doorway which
leads outside the cloisters to the **Palace of King Sancho**. It's not the
original medieval palace – that disappeared long ago – but this fortified mansion is the oldest part of the complex and its imposing walls,
mostly dating from the sixteenth century, accommodate a string of
handsome period rooms cluttered with faded paintings and other
curios. There's also an eccentric wooden drawbridge linking two
rooms above the original entrance situated on the far side of the
building, away from the cloisters. The "palace" was used as a political prison for much of its history, its most celebrated internee being
the liberal reformer Gaspar de Jovellanos, a victim of the royal
favourite Manuel de Godoy, who had him locked up here from 1801
to 1802. Nowadays, the palace has regular displays of folk dancing
and there are hourly free **piano concerts** of Chopin's music.

Practicalities

Accommodation in Valldemossa itself is limited to the *Ca'n Mario*,
c/Uetam 8 (☎971 612 122, fax 971 616 029; ④), an attractive little
hostal where an elegant, antique-cluttered foyer leads to comfortably
old-fashioned rooms. It's situated just a minute's walk from the
monastery – from the pedestrianized area between the cloisters and
the palace, go down the slope and take the first turning on the right –
and is a popular spot, so reservations are pretty much essential. The
only other option nearby, off the C710 just over 2km west of town, is
the solitary *Hotel Residencia Vistamar* (☎971 612 300, fax 971
612 583; ⑨), an opulently converted eighteenth-century *finca* whose
gardens and swimming pool abut a deep, green gully that plunges
down towards the sea. It's a fancy place to stay, and the rooms are
decorated in traditional style with dark wood and bright fabrics.

The centre of Valldemossa is packed with **restaurants and cafés**.
Many of them are geared up for day-trippers and offer fairly dire fast
food at inflated prices, but there's a handful of quality places
amongst the dross. *Ca'n Mario*, c/Uetam 8 (☎971 612 122), is a
pocket-sized family-run restaurant on the upper floor of
Valldemossa's one and only *hostal* (see above), serving traditional
Mallorcan food. *Ca'n Pedro*, Avgda Arxiduc Lluís Salvador s/n
(☎971 612 170; closed Sun eve), is a large and traditional café-
restaurant with a large and traditional menu; the food isn't exactly
memorable, but it does just fine and prices are very reasonable. It
can, though, get packed out with tourists. *Ca'n Costa* (☎971 616
134; closed Tues) is a popular restaurant occupying a *finca* about
2km north of town on the Deià road; the decor is over the top – old
farm equipment and other rusticated touches – but the shaded terrace is lovely, and the Mallorcan cuisine is excellent and affordable,
with main courses from around 1500ptas/€9.02.

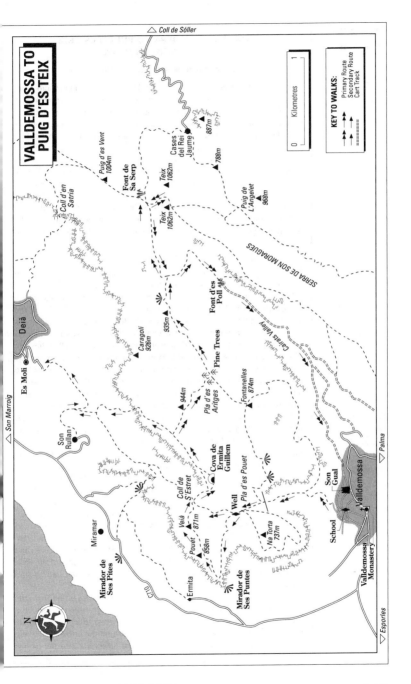

VALLDEMOSSA TO PUIG D'ES TEIX

△ Coll de Sóller

Puig d'es Vent
1004m

Cases
del Rei
Jaume

Font de
Sa Serp

887m

Teix
1062m

788m

Teix
1062m

Puig de
L'Angelet
968m

Coll d'en
Satria

SERRA DE SON MORAGUES

935m

Font d'es
Poll

Carragoli
926m

Pine Trees

Carrats Valley

△ Son Marroig

Es Moli

Deià

944m

Pla d'es
Aritges

Fontanelles
874m

Son
Rullan

Cova de
Ermita
Guillem

Coll de
S'Estret

Well

Pla d'es Pouet

Son
Gual

Valldemossa

Miramar

Veià
871m

Pouet

858m

Na Torta
737m

School

Mirador de
Ses Pites

Ermita

Mirador de
Ses Puntes

Valldemossa
Monastery

N

▽ Palma

▽ Esporles

KEY TO WALKS:
Primary Route
Secondary Route
Cart Track

Kilometres
0   1

FROM VALLDEMOSSA TO PUIG D'ES TEIX
BY THE ARCHDUKE'S PATH

12.5KM; 674M OF ASCENT; 4HR 30MIN–5HR

The terrain between Valldemossa and Deià is mountainous and wild, abounding in steep cliffs and rocky summits; the lower slopes are wooded but the tops are almost devoid of vegetation, with numerous dramatic viewpoints, many of them overlooking the sea. The land is rough but, as elsewhere in Mallorca, the mountains are criss-crossed by footpaths first made by charcoal burners, olive growers and hunters. These paths can be stony, but this area was also subject to the attentions of the nineteenth-century Austrian archduke **Ludwig Salvator** (see p.142), who had some wonderful paths constructed so that he could ride around on horseback admiring the scenery. Today, walkers can still benefit from the archduke's efforts because his estate was acquired in 1967 by ICONA, Mallorca's organization for nature conservation. This circular walk – which can be lengthened or shortened to suit – is a classic, showing the best of the area.

THE ROUTE

From Valldemossa's bypass near the monastery, proceed along c/Venerable Sor Aina past the small car park and take the first right – c/Joan Miró – up to the school. Climb the steps at the left-hand side of the school, then turn right and almost immediately left. Go to the end of the street, turn right, descend slightly, then turn left up a wide path that leads into the woods, entered by a stile over a gate. The stony path rises moderately steeply in numerous bends to reach an opening in the wall at the edge of the wooded plain, the **Pla d'es Pouet**; a shortcut near the top is way-marked, but it makes little difference which way you go. From the wall, go straight on across the level ground to reach an old **well** (now polluted) in a large clearing with a rotten fallen tree. This well is a vital reference point in a confusing area and it is essential to take your bearings carefully.

*An extra
45min loop
lets you take
in Veià – see
opposite.*

For the main walk be careful to take the path bearing slightly right, northeast at first and then north, which leads easily up to the **Coll de S'Estret de Son Gallard**. On the col is a barrier of brushwood set up by hunters who still practise the traditional *caza a coll* method, which you can observe: birds are lured into flying along artificial tunnels created by cutting passages through the trees, then captured in nets. From the nearby V-shaped stone seats, the path continues uphill to the right. **Cova de Ermita Guillem**, an interesting hermit's cave that offers excellent shelter if you are unlucky with the weather, can be visited to the south of the main path – look for a branch path on the right, which leads to the enclosure in front of the cave. The cave looks well cared for and contains icons and candles. To rejoin the uphill main path, retrace your steps for about 100m and then branch sharply off to the right. The most spectacular part of the walk begins here: it's a wide and easy walkway on the edge of cliffs with a simply breathtaking view.

As you approach the Caragolí peak, a path branching off left towards the cliffs offers the possibility of an adventurous **descent to Deià** by a thrilling, but precarious cliff path. If you're tempted to try this, find the start by making for the largest of the holm oaks on the horizon, growing out of a pothole. A path from this holm oak descends into the woods below, where you should look out for a large *sitja* (charcoal-worker's shelter), with two stone shelters and a stone bread oven; turn right here, join another track and turn left. Reaching a gate, double-back along terraces to a *caseta* (field-house), from where a path leads down to the *Es Moli* hotel in Deià.

*From Deià, you
can follow a
coastal trail to
Port de Sóller –
see p.142.*

From the main path, you can spy Port de Sóller down on the coast and the mountains Major, Teix and Galatzó rising high above the seashore. Then the path climbs southeast to 944m before descending gently over a sloping, arid plain, the **Pla d'es Aritges** (*aritge* is smilax, a plant with vicious backward-curving thorns). A path junction at an isolated group of pine trees offers a shortcut back to Valldemossa **via Fontanelles**. To continue on the main route, take the left fork northeast, which brings you over a 935-metre top and, shortly after, to a viewpoint overlooking Deià. After this the path swings southeast and begins to descend to the Teix path junction.

A metre-high conical cairn marks the Teix path junction. Here, branch left (northeast) on a path that scrambles up a little gully and then proceed over a wall positioned at right angles to the edge of a cliff. Stone steps take you to the top of the wall and an iron ladder down the far side. From here, it's an easy walk to the **Pla de Sa Serp**, a plain where there is a spring, the **Font de Sa Serp**. A well-used path leads up to the col between the two tops and on to the main west summit of Teix (1062m), where the views are especially good to the northeast, looking over the Sóller valley to Mitx Dia, the western summit of Puig Major, with the tops of Cornadors, L'Ofre and the Alfàbia ridge forming a stunning skyline. Return to the Teix path junction by the same route (avoid the difficult-to-follow route southwest from Teix towards Sa Bussa) and turn left to follow the main track down the **Cairats valley**. First you'll come to an old "snowhouse" (a deep hole used for storing ice in winter), then a mountain hut and below that a spring and picnic site, the **Font d'es Poll** (Well of the Poplar). The wide track beyond is rather stony but you'll have no trouble finding the route. On the way down the valley you'll see reconstructions of a *sitja*, a charcoal-worker's shelter, signposted and labelled. Keep on the main track down the Cairats valley, going over a wall via stone steps to the left of a locked gate. Ignore two branches to the left and then join a road which leads past a number of large new houses down to an old house with a square tower, **Son Gual**, from where there's a splendid view over the old part of Valldemossa.

EXTENSION OF THE WALK TO
MIRADOR DE SES PUNTES AND VEIÀ

1.5KM; 116M OF ASCENT; 45MIN

From the well in the clearing on the Pla d'es Pouet, take the path which leads northwest at first, before zigzagging uphill and swinging west. Fork left shortly after passing an old bread oven to reach the **Mirador de Ses Puntes**. From this superb viewpoint, return to the fork and take the left branch, which rises through the trees to the top of **Pouet** (858m) and, after a little dip, **Veià** (871m). For much of the way the path is the wide bridleway built by the archduke and from it you can look down on Sa Foradada, a rocky headland near his old house, Son Marroig. From the ruined shelter on Veià the path descends to the Coll de S'Estret de Son Gallard, where you rejoin the main path a little up from the well.

Port de Valldemossa

The closest spot to Valldemossa for a swim is **PORT DE
VALLDEMOSSA**, a hamlet set in the shadow of the mountains at the
mouth of a narrow, craggy cove. There's no public transport, but the
drive down to the hamlet, once Valldemossa's gateway to the outside
world, is stimulating: head west out of Valldemossa along the C710
and, after about 1.5km, turn right at the sign and follow the twisty
side road for 6km through the mountains. Port de Valldemossa's
beach is small and shingly, and prone to be battered by the surf, but
the scenery is stunning and the village sports a handful of **restaurants**. Pick of the bunch is the busy *Es Port* (☎971 616 194), which
has a well-deserved reputation for its superb seafood, with main
courses from around 2000ptas/€12.02.

La Granja and around

Nestling in a tranquil wooded and terraced valley some 10km southwest from Valldemossa is the *hacienda* of **La Granja** (daily:
April–Oct 10am–7pm, Nov–March 10am–6pm; 1200ptas/€7.21). To
get there, follow the C710 for about 8.5km from Valldemossa and
take the signposted left turn; the once-daily Palma–Estellencs **bus**
stops by the entrance. The house and its grounds make for a popular
package-tourist trip, but, despite the many visitors, the estate main-
tains a languorous air of old patrician comfort. There's hardly anything new or modern on view, but this doesn't seem contrived. La
Granja was occupied until very recently by the Fortuny family, who
took possession in the mid-fifteenth century; after about the 1920s,
it seems that modernization simply never crossed their minds.

From the entrance in front of the main forecourt, signs direct you
up round the back of the house, past an incidental collection of well-
weathered farming tackle and on into the tiny formal **gardens**. Next
door, a small patio leads to the main **house**, a ramshackle sequence
of apartments strewn with domestic clutter – everything from chil-
drens' games and mannequins, through old costumes, musical
instruments and a cabinet of fans, to a fully equipped antique
kitchen. There's also a delightful little theatre, where plays were
once performed for the household in a manner common amongst
Europe's nineteenth-century rural landowners. Likewise, the dining
room, with its faded paintings and heavy drapes, has a real touch of
country elegance, as does the graceful first-floor loggia. Look out
also for the finely crafted, green-tinted Mallorcan chandeliers and
the beautiful majolica tile-panels that embellish several walls.

*For an
account of
Mallorcan
olive-oil pro-
duction, see
pp.258–261.*

Tagged onto the house, a series of **workrooms** recall the days
when La Granja was a profitable and almost entirely self-sufficient
concern. A wine press, almond and olive-oil mills prepared the
estate's produce for export, whilst plumbers, carpenters, cobblers,
weavers and sail makers all kept pace with domestic requirements
from their specialized workshops. The Fortunys were one of

Mallorca's more enlightened landowning families, and employees were well fed by the kitchen staff, who made cheeses, bread and preserves by hand. The main kitchen is in one of the **cellars**, where you'll also find a grain store and a "torture chamber", an entirely inappropriate recent addition. Moving on, you'll soon reach the family **chapel**, a diminutive affair with kitsch silver-winged angels, and then the expansive **forecourt**, shaded by plane trees and surrounded by antiquated workshops where costumed "artisans" practise traditional crafts such as wood-turning and candle-making. This part of the visit is a bit bogus, but good fun all the same – and the homemade pastries and doughnuts (*bunyols*) are lip-smacking. Your visit may also coincide with a mildly diverting display of Mallorcan **folk dancing** (summer Wed & Fri 3–5pm).

Esporles

On the road southeast from La Granja towards Palma, it's a couple of kilometres to **ESPORLES**, an amiable, leafy little town whose elongated main street follows the line of an ancient stone watercourse. This is Mallorca away from the tourist zone and although there's no special reason to stop, it's an attractive place to overnight. The town's one and only place to **stay** is the one-star *Hostal Central* (☎971 610 202; ③), an unassuming *hostal* in an appealing old stone house just off the main drag by the church at Plaça Espanya 8. Esporles has somewhere good to **eat** too, the *Restaurant s'Escudella* (☎971 610 700), where the oven-roasted lamb is a treat; it's located a few metres from the church, across the street at c/Sant Pere 4.

Galilea and around

Heading southwest from La Granja, a narrow and difficult country road heads up a V-shaped valley before snaking through the foothills of the Serra de Tramuntana. After 10km you come to **PUIGPUNYENT**, a workaday farmers' village marginally enhanced by a seventeenth-century church with a squat bell tower.

Continuing southwest, the road threads for another 4km along a benign valley of citrus groves and olive trees on its way to **GALILEA**, an engaging scattering of whitewashed farmsteads built in sight of a stolid hilltop church. There's a rusty old café-bar beside the church, but the best place to soak up the bucolic atmosphere is at the *Restaurant-Bar Galilea* (☎971 614 329; closed Wed), below the church and beside the through road. The views from the terrace are gorgeous and the Mallorcan **food** is both delicious and cheap, with filling snacks from just 700ptas/€4.21.

Southwest of Galilea, the road wriggles its way through to the unremarkable settlement of **CAPDELLÀ**, before squeezing through the mountains – the most beautiful, and nerve-jangling, part of the drive – for a further 9km to enter Andratx from the east.

Andratx is covered on p.155.

Banyalbufar and around

Back on the C710, just beyond the turning for La Granja, a narrow
side road forks down to the coast at **PORT D'ES CANONGE**. The
five-kilometre journey down through thickly forested hills is splendid, but the settlement itself is disappointing, a scrawny, modern
urbanització flanking a shingle beach.

You'd do far better to stay on the main coast road for a further
6km, enjoying spectacular views on the way to the attractive village
of **BANYALBUFAR**, whose terraced fields cling gingerly to the
coastal cliffs. The land here has been cultivated since Moorish times,
with a spring above the village providing a water supply that's still
channelled down the hillside along slender watercourses into open
storage cisterns (which are the unlikely-looking home for a few
carp). The village itself is bisected by its main street, the C710,
which is flanked by whitewashed houses and narrow cobbled lanes.
The cute main square perches above the C710, overlooked by a
chunky parish church dating from the fifteenth century.

Banyalbufar is a fine place to unwind and there's a rough and
rocky **beach** fifteen minutes' walk away down the hill – ask locally for
directions since the lanes that lead there are difficult to find. The village has three places **to stay**. The *Hotel Mar y Vent*, on the main
street towards the east end of the village (☎971 618 000, fax 971
618 201; Feb–Nov; ⑦), has an enticing exterior but its rooms are
spartan – although most have balconies with views of the sea, and
there's a rooftop swimming pool too. However, there's probably
more chance of a vacancy at the rather more agreeable *Hostal
Baronia*, at the west end of the main drag (☎ & fax 971 618 146;
April–Oct; ④), an old-fashioned, laid-back sort of place with an outside pool and forty plain but perfectly adequate balconied bedrooms.
At both these places, the guest rooms are in modern extensions at
the back which have been attached to much older houses at the front.
The third choice of accommodation is the *Hotel Sa Coma* (☎971
618 034; Feb–Oct; ⑤), an unappealing concrete lump below the main
street.

Banyalbufar has a fair selection of **cafés** and **restaurants** strung
along the main street. The *Café Bellavista* (closed Sun) serves salads, omelettes and light meals and has a seaview terrace, as does the
best restaurant hereabouts, the *Son Tomas*, towards the west end of
the village (☎971 618 149; closed Tues), where the steaks are great
and the delicious "fish of the day" costs around 2200ptas/€13.22.

Estellencs

About 1km southwest of Banyalbufar stands perhaps the most
impressive of the lookout points that dot the coastal road, the
Mirador de Ses Ànimes, a sixteenth-century watchtower built as a
sentinel against pirate attack and now providing stunning views

along the coast. **ESTELLENCS**, 6km further on, is similar to
Banyalbufar, with steep coastal cliffs and tight terraced fields,
though if anything it's even prettier. There's almost no sign of tourist
development in the village, its narrow, winding alleys adorned with
old stone houses and a trim, largely eighteenth-century parish
church – peep inside for a look at the exquisite pinewood reredos. A
steep, but driveable, two-kilometre lane leads down from the village,
past olive and orange orchards, to **Cala Estellencs**, a rocky, surf-buf-
feted cove that shelters a shingly beach and a summertime bar.

Estellencs has one **hotel**, the routinely modern, two-star *Maristel*,
with great views down over the coast (☎971 618 529, fax 971 618
511; Jan–Oct; ⑥). Amongst a handful of **cafés**, the low-price
Cafeteria Estallenchs, opposite the hotel, sells substantial and tasty
snacks. The best **restaurant** is the *Montimar* (☎971 618 576), sited
in a graceful old mansion across from the church, which serves
splendid traditional meals, including rabbit dishes for
1700ptas/€10.22. Its principal rival is the adjacent *Son Llarg*
(☎971 618 564), also in a fine old house and specializing in traditional Mallorcan cuisine.

Andratx and around

Heading southwest from Estellencs, the C710 threads along the lit-
toral for 6km before slipping through a tunnel and – immediately
beyond – passing the stone stairway up to the **Mirador de Ricardo
Roca**. At 400m above the sea, this lookout point offers some fine
coastal views, and you can wet your whistle at the *Es Grau* restaurant next door.

Beyond the mirador, the C710 makes a few final flourishes before
turning inland, worming up and over forested foothills on its way to
ANDRATX, a small and unassuming town 19km southwest of
Estellencs and just 23km west of Palma. The main event here is the
Wednesday morning **market**, a tourist favourite, but otherwise there's
not much to detain you, though the old houses and cobbled streets of
the upper town form a harmonious ochre ensemble. The upper town
culminates in the fortress-like walls of the thirteenth-century church of
Santa Maria, built high and strong to deter raiding pirates, its
balustraded precincts offering panoramic views down to the coast.

Sant Elm

From Andratx, a handsome country road heads west through the
coastal hills to the low-key resort of Sant Elm (sometimes signposted in Castilian as San Telmo). After 3km you'll stumble across the
hillside hamlet of **S'ARRACÓ**, then enter a pretty, orchard-covered
landscape, which buckles up into wooded hills and dipping valleys as
it nears the seashore.

SANT ELM is little more than one main street draped along the
shore, with a sandy beach at one end and a harbour at the other.

There are plans to expand the resort, but at present it's a quiet spo
where there's a reasonable chance of a **room** in high season, either
at the conspicuous *Hotel Aquamarín* (☎971 239 105, fax 971 239
125; May–Oct; ④), a spectacularly unsuccessful concrete edifice
built in the style of an old watchtower and equipped with spartan
rooms; or, preferably, at the *Hostal Dragonera* (☎971 239 086, fax
971 239 013; ⑤), a simple modern building with clean and neat
rooms, the best of which have balconies with sea views.

For such a small place, there's a surprisingly wide choice of **cafés
and restaurants** dotted along the main street. The seafront *Bar
restaurant Flexas* serves delicious snacks and meals at low prices,
while the set meal at the *Hostal Dragonera* costs a very reasonable
1800ptas/€10.82. The harbourside *Restaurant Na Caragola*
(☎971 109 299) has a charming terrace and sea views, as well as a
wide-ranging menu – from pizzas to paella with main courses any
where between 600ptas/€3.61 and 2000ptas/€12.02.

There is a regular **bus** service to Sant Elm from Andratx and
Peguera during the summer (May–Oct), and a reasonable service the
rest of the year. Buses pull in beside the *Hotel Aquamarín* at the
south end of the main drag. There are also **boats** running between
Sant Elm and Port d'Andratx (March–Oct 1 daily; 800ptas/€4.81
return); call ☎971 757 065 (mobile ☎639 617 545) for timetable
details.

Illa Dragonera

From Sant Elm's minuscule harbour, **boats** take a few minutes to
shuttle across to the austere offshore islet of **Illa Dragonera**. This
uninhabited chunk of rock, some 4km long and 700m wide, lies at an
oblique angle to the coast, with an imposing ridge of seacliffs dominating its northwestern shore. Behind the ridge, a rough track travels
the length of the island, linking a pair of craggy capes and their light
houses. Most people visit for the scenic solitude, but the island is also
good for **birdlife**: ospreys, shags, gulls and other seabirds are plenti-
ful and there may be chance sightings of several species of raptor.

*For more on
Mallorca's
birdlife, see
p.251.*

There are two ways of getting to the island. A passenger **ferry** rat-
tles across from Sant Elm, dropping passengers about halfway up the
east shore at a tiny cove-harbour (May–Sept Tues–Thurs, Sat & Sun
5 daily; 1600ptas/€9.62; rest of year Mon–Sat 4 daily
1200ptas/€7.21). You should make arrangements for your return
trip, which is included in the fare, on the outward journey. For further details, call ☎971 470 449 (mobile ☎639 617 545). If, however, you're lukewarm about tramping the island, you may prefer to
take a two-hour **cruise**, which allows half an hour on Dragonera and
spends the rest of the time nosing along the local coastline
(May–Sept Mon & Fri 2 daily; 1600ptas/€9.62). Reservations are a
good idea, though not essential. For sailing times, ask at the harbour
or call ☎971 757 065 (mobile ☎639 617 545).

Port d'Andratx

The picturesque port and fishing harbour of **PORT D'ANDRATX**, 6km southwest of Andratx, has been transformed by low-rise shopping complexes and apartment blocks. However, it's not quite a classic case of overdevelopment: there's still no denying the prettiness of the setting, with the port standing at the head of a long and slender inlet that's flanked by wooded hills. The heart of the **old town**, which slopes up from the south side of the bay, hints at former virtues in its cramped network of ancient lanes. Sunsets show the place to best advantage, casting long shadows up the bay, and it's then that the old town's gaggle of harbourside restaurants crowd with holidaymakers and expatriates, a well-heeled crew, occasionally irritated by raucous teenagers.

The nearest sandy beach is east over the hills at Camp de Mar – see p.118.

Arrival and information

Port d'Andratx may be rather sedate, but it's still an enjoyable place to spend a night or two, especially as it possesses several outstanding seafood restaurants, and it's easy to reach. There are regular **buses** from Andratx, Camp de Mar and Palma, and these pull in at the back of the bay, a brief walk from both the old town (on the left as you face the sea) and the big, modern marina (on the right). In addition, from March to October **boat trips** arrive here once daily from Sant Elm (800ptas/€4.81) and Peguera (2200ptas/€13.22); for timetable details, call ☎971 757 065 (mobile ☎639 617 545) or ask at the **tourist office**, which is just up from the harbourfront in the old

The account of Peguera is on p.117.

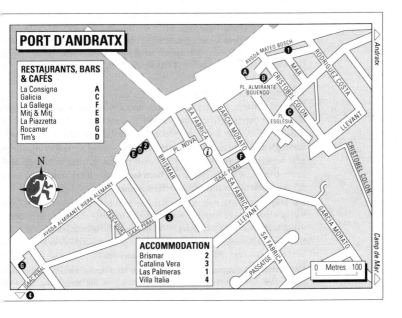

The south-west coast

part of town (hours vary, but usually include Mon–Fri 11.30am–2.30pm; ☎971 671 764). Apart from having boat trip details, they also issue useful leaflets detailing half-day and day-long hikes in the surrounding hills. There's a **taxi** rank about halfway along the old town harbourfront, or you can call Radio Taxi Andratx on ☎971 136 398; the fare to Camp de Mar is about 950ptas/€5.71, to Sant Elm 1800ptas/€10.82.

Accommodation

Even in the height of the season, there's a good chance of finding a vacant **room** in Port d'Andratx, but you're much safer making a reservation ahead. The options are, however, limited to a couple of inexpensive *hostals* and two hotels, one a bargain, the other full-blown luxury. All are located on or near the old town's harbourfront.

Hostal Las Palmeras, Avgda Mateo Bosch 12 ☎971 672 078. There are sixteen bare and cheerless rooms at this two-star *hostal* situated near the east end of the old town's harbourfront. Open all year. ③.

Hostal-residencia Catalina Vera, c/Isaac Peral 63 ☎971 671 918. This appealing establishment occupies a neatly shuttered and whitewashed building in a quiet location, flanked by a small orchard one block up from the harbourfront, and has seventeen frugal but neat rooms, some with showers, some without. April–Oct. ④.

Hotel Brismar, c/Almirante Riera Alemany 6 ☎971 671 600, fax 971 671 183. A pleasant, old-fashioned two-star place with fifty spotless, en suite rooms, the pick of which have port-facing balconies (though avoid these if you're a light sleeper – there's a bar next door). Open all year. ⑤.

Hotel Villa Italia, Camí Sant Carles s/n ☎971 674 011, fax 971 673 350. An opulent, 1920s twin-towered mansion set behind a steeply terraced garden with luxuries such as a rooftop swimming pool, as well as gorgeous views out over the bay. It's located a five-minute stroll west of the old part of town along Camí Sant Carles, an extension of c/Isaac Peral. ⑨.

Eating and drinking

The old town is packed with **cafés** and **restaurants**, which line up along the harbourfront and crowd the more central portions of c/Isaac Peral, one block up the hill. Generally speaking, standards are high and a local feature is the seafood – good almost everywhere and superb at the town's two Galician places. Eating is the big deal here, but there are a couple of **bars** too, lively little spots that hum till the early hours throughout the summer.

Bar Mitj & Mitj, c/Almirante Riera Alemany 8. This is the flashiest bar in town with a wide range of sounds – house through to jazz – and imaginative decor which takes in contemporary art installations on the outside balcony.

Bar Tim's, c/Almirante Riera Alemany 10. More subdued than the *Mitj & Mitj* next door, this cosy, little bar caters to an older crowd.

Cafeteria La Consigna, Avgda Mateo Bosch 26. Popular and enjoyably modern coffee house-cum-patisserie about a third of the way along the harbourfront with great cakes, croissants and coffees.

Pizzeria La Piazzetta, Plaça Almirante Oquendo 2 ☎971 672 700. Popular pizzeria on a pleasant pedestrianized square just off – and about one-third of the way along – the harbourfront, serving tasty pizzas and pastas from 800ptas/€4.81 as well as a range of reasonably priced seafood dishes.

Restaurant Galicia, c/Isaac Peral 37 ☎971 672 705. Highly recommended Galician place serving mouthwatering seafood without the pretensions of some of its rivals down on the harbourfront. Has simple, traditional decor and very reasonable prices.

Restaurant La Gallega, c/Isaac Peral 52 ☎971 671 338. Excellent, bistro-style Galician restaurant specializing in seafood, with main courses from 1900ptas/€11.42.

Restaurant Rocamar, c/Almirante Riera Alemany 29 ☎971 671 261. A well-established restaurant at the west end of the harbourfront offering delicious seafood; also has a lovely waterside terrace.

Travel details

Buses

Alaró to: Palma (2–3 daily; 25min).

Andratx to: Camp de Mar (May–Oct hourly; Nov–April every 2hr; 10min); Palma (hourly; 45min); Peguera (May–Oct Mon–Sat 7 daily, 3 on Sun; Nov–April 1 daily; 10min); Port d'Andratx (May–Oct hourly; Nov–April every 2hr; 10min); Sant Elm (May–Oct Mon–Sat 7 daily, 3 on Sun; Nov–April 1 daily; 10min); Valldemossa (Mon–Sat 1 daily; 1hr).

Deià to: Palma (5 daily; 45min); Port de Sóller (5 daily; 25min); Sóller (5 daily; 20min); Valldemossa (5 daily; 15min).

Port d'Andratx to: Andratx (May–Oct hourly; Nov–April every 2hr; 10min); Camp de Mar (May–Oct hourly; Nov–April every 2hr; 20min); Palma (hourly; 45min); Peguera (May–Oct Mon–Sat 8 daily, 3 on Sun; Nov–April 1 daily; 10min).

Port de Sóller to: Deià (5 daily; 25min); Palma (via the tunnel: Mon–Fri 5 daily, 2 on Sat, no Sun service; 35min; via Valldemossa: 5 daily; 55min); Sóller (7 daily; 5min); Valldemossa (5 daily; 30min).

Sant Elm to: Andratx (May–Oct Mon–Sat 7 daily, 3 on Sun; Nov–April 1 daily; 10min); Peguera (May–Oct Mon–Sat 7 daily, 3 on Sun; Nov–April 1 daily; 20min).

Sóller to: Deià (5 daily; 20min); Palma (via the tunnel: Mon–Fri 5 daily, 2 on Sat, no Sun service; 30min; via Valldemossa: 5 daily; 50min); Port de Sóller (7 daily; 5min); Valldemossa (5 daily; 30min).

Valldemossa to: Andratx (Mon–Sat 1 daily; 1hr); Banyalbufar (Mon–Sat 1 daily; 30min); Deià (5 daily; 15min); Estellencs (Mon–Sat 1 daily; 45min); Palma (5 daily; 30min); Peguera (Mon–Sat 1 daily; 1hr 10min); Port de Sóller (5 daily; 35min); Sóller (5 daily; 30min).

Trains

Binissalem to: Inca (hourly; 10min); Lloseta (hourly; 5min); Palma (hourly; 30min).

Lloseta to: Binissalem (hourly; 5min); Inca (hourly; 5min); Palma (hourly; 35min).

Sóller to: Palma (5 daily; 1hr 15min).

Chapter 3

Northern Mallorca

The section of the Serra de Tramuntana extending southwest from Sóller to Andratx is covered in Chapter 2.

Northern Mallorca's greatest draw is the magnificent **Serra de Tramuntana** mountain range, which runs along the island's extravagantly beautiful western shore and reaches a precipitous climax in the rearing peaks to the northeast of Sóller. The peaks are so severe that they force the main coastal road, the C710, inland and permit only the most occasional access to the sea. A rare exception is the extraordinary side road that snakes down to both overcrowded **Sa Calobra** and the attractive beach at **Cala Tuent**, but it's the well-appointed monastery of **Lluc** that remains the big draw here – for religious islanders, who venerate an effigy of the Virgin known as La Moreneta, and tourists alike. Pushing on along the coast, the C710 emerges from the mountains to slip past the ancient town of **Pollença**, whose tangle of stone houses cluster a fine, cypress-lined Way of the Cross. Pollença is one of Mallorca's most appealing towns and it's also within easy reach of both the comely coastal resort of **Cala Sant Vicenç** and the wild rockiness of the **Península de Formentor**, the northernmost bony spur of the Serra de Tramuntana. The peninsula shelters the northern shore of the Badia de Pollenca, which is home to the laid-back and low-key resort of **Port de Pollença**, whilst the next bay down holds the more upbeat and flashy **Port d'Alcúdia**. Close by, the old, walled town of **Alcúdia** has a clutch of modest historical sights and pocket-sized **Muro** has a splendid main square. The **Parc Natural de S'Albufera** takes the prize as the best birdwatching wetland on Mallorca.

Accounts of two more day hikes, from Valldemossa and Deià, are on p.150 and p.142.

The Serra de Tramuntana is fine hiking country with **hiking trails** patterning the mountains. Suggestions for several comparatively easy walks are given in the text and we have also described in detail two outstanding day-long hikes, starting at Pollença and at Lluc. Northern Mallorca also boasts fine **beaches**, from the long golden strands that stretch round the bays of Pollença and Alcúdia to the more discreet charms of the cove beaches at Cala Sant Vicenç.

As regards **accommodation**, the resorts of Northern Mallorca – primarily Port de Pollença, Port d'Alcúdia and Cala Sant Vicenç – muster a veritable phalanx of hotels and *hostals*, but this is predom-

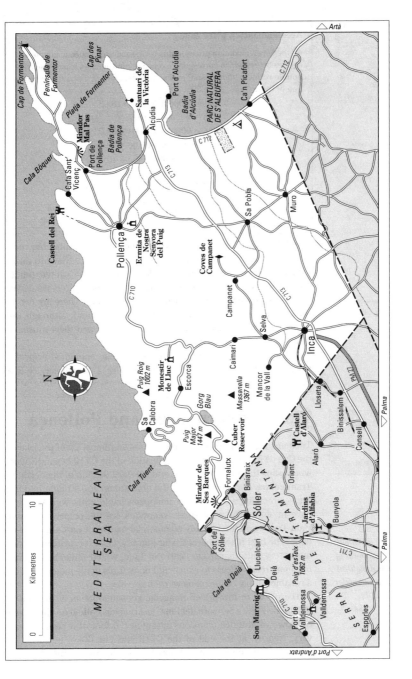

inantly package territory and from June to early September, and
sometimes beyond, independent travellers are well advised to make
advance reservations. In the shoulder season and in winter, things
are much easier (and cheaper), though many places do close down.
It is also worth considering staying at a **monastery**. There are two in
this region, at Lluc and just outside Pollença, and, although the
rooms at both are frugal, they are inexpensive and there's usually
space at any time of the year.

Getting around by public transport is easy enough – even the
smaller places have a reasonable **bus** service – though service is a
mite patchy on Sundays and in the winter.

The northern coast and Pollença

The most interesting approach to the northernmost tip of the island,
the Cap de Formentor, is the continuation of the **C710** beyond Sóller,
which slips through the highest and harshest section of the Serra de
Tramuntana. For the most part, the mountains drop straight into the
sea – precipitous and largely unapproachable cliffs with barely a
cove in sight. The accessible exceptions are the comely beach at
Cala Tuent and the horribly commercial hamlet of **Sa Calobra** next
door. The best place to break your journey, however, is inland at the
monastery and pilgrimage centre of **Lluc**, which offers a diverting
museum, ready access to excellent hiking trails in the mountains and
a reliable supply of inexpensive rooms.

*See p.123 for
an account of
the delightful
town of Sóller
and its
environs.*

There's more low-priced monastic accommodation at the hilltop
Ermita de Nostra Senyora del Puig, just outside **Pollença**, a beguiling
old town of grandee mansions sitting at the foot of a beautiful calvary. Nearby, at the end of the C710 and just 60km northeast of
Sóller, is **Port de Pollença**, a low-key, medium-sized resort with a

long sandy beach which drapes around the Badia de Pollença. The resort is a popular summertime retreat for the inhabitants of Palma, abounds in places to stay, and is within easy striking distance of the dramatic seacliffs of the **Península de Formentor** on the northernmost tip of the island.

The northern coast and Pollença

Transport

There are several **bus** services, including year-round long-distance services linking Palma with Lluc, Pollença and Port de Pollença. In addition, from May to October there's a once-daily weekday bus from Palma to Formentor. However, perhaps the most useful bus runs along the C710 from Port de Sóller, stopping at Sóller, Lluc, Pollença, Port de Pollença, Alcúdia and Port d'Alcúdia. This operates from May to October twice daily (not on Sundays). It is extremely popular – so popular, in fact, that would-be passengers often can't get on. To increase your chances of finding a place for a journey east along the coast, try to board at Port de Sóller rather than waiting at the second stop, Sóller.

For frequencies and journey times, see p.194.

Cala Tuent, Sa Calobra and Escorca

Heading northeast from Sóller, the C710 zigzags up into the mountains. After about 5km the C710 passes the steep byroad that leads down to the beautiful hamlet of Fornalutx (see p.127). Then there's a last lingering look over the coast from the **Mirador de Ses Barques**, before the road snakes inland, tunnelling through the western flanks of **Puig Major**, the island's highest mountain at 1447m. Beyond the tunnel is the **Gorg Blau** (Blue Gorge), a bare and bleak ravine that was a well-known beauty spot until a hydroelectric scheme filled it with a trio of puddle-like reservoirs. The second of the three is the **Embalse de Cúber** (Cúber Reservoir), an unappetizing expanse of water redeemed by its birdlife. The reservoir forms a natural amphitheatre in the mountains and attracts birds, notably several different types of raptor, in numbers. For a better look follow the easy footpath which circumnavigates the reservoir; it takes a couple of hours to complete. To the immediate north rear the craggy flanks of Puig Major, but the dramatic trail which twists up to the summit from the military base beside the main road remains off-limits because of its radar station. This makes **Puig de Massanella** (1367m), which looms over the gorge to the east, the highest mountain that can be climbed on Mallorca.

Puig de Massanella is best ascended from Lluc – see p.168.

Cala Tuent

At the far end of the Gorg Blau the road tunnels into the mountains, to emerge just short of a left turn leading to Cala Tuent and Sa Calobra. This turnoff makes for an exhilarating, ear-popping detour to the seashore, the well-surfaced road hairpinning its way down the mountain slopes so severely that at one point it actually turns 270 degrees to run under itself.

About 10km down this road, there's a fork: head left over the hills for the four-kilometre journey to the **Ermita de Sant Llorenç**, a tiny medieval church perched high above the coast, and **CALA TUENT**, where a smattering of villas cling to the northern slopes of Puig Major as it tumbles down to the seashore. Ancient orchards temper the harshness of the mountain, and the gravel and sand beach is one of the quietest on the north coast. It's a lovely spot to while away a few hours and, provided you stay well inshore, the swimming is safe. There's nowhere to stay, but an excellent **café-restaurant** sits on the far side of the cove – the *Es Vergeret*, where lunch is the finest meal of the day, a wide range of fish and meat dishes from 1900ptas/€11.42, best devoured at the terrace bar in sight of the sea.

Sa Calobra

Heading right at the fork, it's just 2km more to **SA CALOBRA**, a modern resort occupying a pint-sized cove in the shadow of the mountains. There's nothing wrong with the setting, but the place is an overvisited disaster. Almost every island operator deposits a busload of tourists here every day in summer and the crush is quite unbearable – as is the overpriced and overcooked food at the local cafés. The reason why so many people come here is to visit the impressive box canyon at the mouth of the **Torrent de Pareis** (River of the Twins). It takes about ten minutes to follow the partly tunnelled walkway round the coast from the resort to the mouth of the canyon. Here, with sheer cliffs rising on every side, the milky-green river trickles down to the narrow bank of shingle that bars its final approach to the sea – though the scene is transformed after heavy rainfall, when the river crashes down into the canyon and out into the sea.

Escorca

Back on the C710 road, about 4km northeast of the Cala Tuent and Sa Calobra turnoff and 26km northeast of Sóller, is **ESCORCA**, a poorly defined scattering of houses that is the starting point for the **descent of the Torrent de Pareis**, a famous, though very testing route, which requires rock-climbing skills, wetsuits and ropes. The river drops from here to Sa Calobra through a formidable, seven-kilometre-long limestone gorge, which takes about six hours to negotiate. The descent is not practicable in winter, spring, or after rainfall, when the river may be waist-high and the rocks dangerously slippery. A small sign formerly marked the start of the trail, across the road from the conspicuous *Restaurant Escorca*; unfortunately, the old sign has been taken down and although a new one is promised, it hasn't turned up yet.

The Monestir de Lluc

Tucked away in a remote valley about 35km northeast of Sóller, the austere, high-sided dormitories and orange-flecked roof tiles of the

Península de Formentor

Olive trees

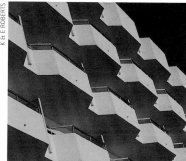
Holiday apartments, Cala Millor

Cap de Formentor

Cala Mondragó

Ermita de Nostra Senyora de Bonany, Petra

Watch-tower

Deià

Cala San Vicenç

Torrent de Pareis

Castell de Santueri

Monestir de Nostra Senyora de Lluc (Monastery of Our Lady of Lluc) stand out against the greens and greys of the surrounding mountains. It's a magnificent setting for what has been Mallorca's most important place of pilgrimage since the middle of the thirteenth century. The religious significance of the place, however, goes back much further: the valley's prehistoric animistic inhabitants deified the local holm-oak woods, and the **Romans** picked up on the theme, naming the place from *lucus*, the Latin for "sacred forest". After the reconquest, however, the **monks** who settled here were keen both to join a purely Christian etymology and to enhance their reputation. They invented the story of a shepherd boy named Lluc (Luke) stumbling across a tiny, brightly painted statue in the woods. Frightened by his discovery, the lad collared the nearest monk, and when the pair returned heavenly music filled their ears, bright lights dazzled their eyes, and celestial voices declared the statue an authentically heaven-sent image of the Virgin.

Buses to Lluc, which is situated 700m off the C710, stop in the car park right outside the monastery. In addition to the bus which runs from Port de Sóller and Sóller to Pollença (May–Oct only), there are also services to Lluc at least once a day from Palma via Inca; it leaves Palma at or around 9am or 10am, and heads back from Lluc at 5pm or 6pm.

The monastery complex

Lluc's present monastic complex (daily: April–Sept 10am–6.30pm; Oct–March 10am–5.30pm; free) is an imposing and formal-looking affair mostly dating from the eighteenth and early nineteenth centuries that is now home to this much-venerated statue. At the centre of the complex is the main shrine and architectural highlight, the **Basílica de la Mare de Déu de Lluc**, graced by an elegant Baroque facade. To reach it, pass through the monastery's stately double-doored entrance and keep straight on to the second – and final – courtyard, where a dreary statue of Bishop Campins, who overhauled Lluc in the early part of the last century, does the basilica's good looks a disservice. Dark and gaudily decorated, the church is dominated by heavy jasper columns, the stolidness of which is partly relieved by a dome over the crossing. On either side of the nave, stone steps extend the aisles round the back of the Baroque high altar to a small chapel. This is the holy of holies, built to display the statue of the Virgin, which has been commonly known as **La Moreneta** ("the Dark-Skinned One") ever since the original paint-work peeled off in the fifteenth century to reveal brown stone underneath. Just 61cm high, the Virgin looks innocuous, her face tweaked by a hint of a smile and haloed by a jewel-encrusted gold crown. In her left arm she cradles a bumptious baby Jesus, who holds the "Book of Life" open to reveal the letters alpha and omega. Every day, during the 11am mass, the **Escolania de Lluc**, a boys' choir founded in the early sixteenth century with the stipulation that it must b "composed of natives of Mallorca, of pure blood, sound in gramma and song", performs in the basilica. They're nicknamed *Los Blauets* "The Blues", for the colour of their cassocks.

Just inside and to the right of the basilica's main entrance, a sma door leads into a covered passage, site of the monastery's informa tion desk and a stairway, which climbs up one floor to the enjoyabl **Museu de Lluc** (daily: April–Sept 10am–5.30pm, Oct–Marc 10am–1.30pm & 2.30–5.30pm; 300ptas/€1.80). After a modest sec tion devoted to archeological finds from the Talayotic and Roma periods come cabinets of intricate old vestments, exquisite gold an silver sacred vessels, medieval religious paintings, and an intriguin assortment of votive offerings – folkloric bits and bobs brought her to honour La Moreneta. The museum also boasts an extensive co lection of **majolica** (see box), glazed earthenware mostly shaped int two-handled drug jars and show dishes or plates, of which some tw or three hundred are on display. The designs vary in sophisticatio from broad and bold dashes of colour to carefully painted naturalis tic designs, but the colours remain fairly constant, restricted by th available technology to iron red, copper green, cobalt blue, mar ganese purple and antimony yellow. The last, disappointing sectio of the museum displays the paintings and drawings of the early twer tieth-century artist **José Coll Bardolet**.

The Camí dels Misteris del Rosari

Back outside the monastery's double-doored entrance, walk a fev metres to the west and you'll soon spot the large, rough-hewn co umn at the start of the **Camí dels Misteris del Rosari** (Way of th Mysteries of the Rosary), a broad pilgrims' footpath that winds it way up the rocky hillside directly behind the monastery. Dating fror

---

Majolica

In the fifteenth century, there was a vigorous trade in decorative pottery from Spain to Italy via Mallorca. The Italians coined the term "**majolica**" to describe this imported Spanish pottery after the medieval name for the island through which it was traded, but thereafter the name came to be applied to all tin-glazed pottery. The process of making majolica began with the mixing and cleaning of clay, after which it was fired and retrieved at the biscuit (earthenware) stage. The biscuit was then cooled and dipped in a liquid glaze that contained tin and water. The water in the glaze was absorbed, leaving a dry surface ready for decoration. After painting, the pottery was returned to the kiln for a final firing, which fused the glaze and fixed the painting. Additional glazings and firings added extra lustre. Initially, majolica was dominated by greens and purples, but technological advances added blue, yellow and ochre in the fifteenth century. Majolica of one sort or another was produced in Mallorca up until the early twentieth century.

THE GUIDE: CHAPTER

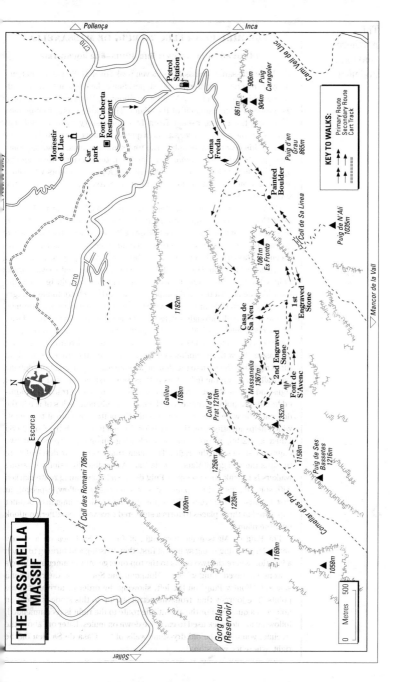

THE MASSANELLA MASSIF

KEY TO WALKS:
- → Primary Route
- → Secondary Route
- ===== Cart Track

△ Pollença

△ Inca

Petrol Station

Font Cuberta Restaurant

Monestir de Lluc

Car park

Camí Vell de Lluc

C710

861m

906m
Puig Caragoler

904m

Coma Freda

Puig d'en Grau 865m

Painted Boulder

Coll de Sa Línea

Puig de N'Ali 1035m

1061m
Es Fronto

1182m

Casa de Sa Neu

1st Engraved Stone

Massanella 1367m

2nd Engraved Stone

Font de S'Avenc

1352m

Mancor de la Vall

C710

Galileu 1186m

Coll d'es Prat 1210m

•1158m

Puig de Ses Bassetes 1216m

Escorca

N

Coll des Romani 706m

1258m

1239m

1009m

Comellar d'es Prat

1169m

1058m

Gorg Blau (Reservoir)

△ Sóller

0   500
Metres

NORTHERN MALLORCA

167

THE HIKE FROM LLUC TO PUIG DE MASSANELLA

14KM; 887M OF ASCENT; 5HR 30MIN–6HR ROUND-TRIP.

The large **Massanella massif** has eleven peaks over 1000m and is defended by many crags and steep rocky slopes. Since the construction of a military establishment put Puig Major out of bounds, Massanella has become the best-loved high summit of the island. There are several well-defined paths and the classic **ascent from Lluc monastery**, with magnificent views, uses the best of these. Although quite strenuous, the route is not difficult and is deservedly popular. The top is all bare rock, although some small plants grow where moisture lingers in the crevices. Keep an eye open for black vultures, and for the friendly Alpine accentors who often appear on the summit or down by **Font de S'Avenc**, the spring on the southern flank.

From the front of the monastery, walk up through the car park to the **Font Cuberta restaurant**, turning left behind it to follow the road up to join the C710 at a junction on the Coll de Sa Batalla. Turn towards Inca and go past the petrol station, where walkers arriving by car may park. The ascent of Massanella from here takes about two and a quarter hours.

Cross the bridge and turn right through the iron gates onto a wide track. Follow the track for 250m past a spring and water trough. Ignoring the Camí Vell de Lluc, a restored footpath to Caimari which continues straight on, swing sharp right uphill following the red painted waymarks. Continue on the wide track through a gate into the area of the Coma Freda farm, whose owner charges 500ptas/€3.01 at this gate. Pause when you come to a wide opening into a field to look at the impressive **Es Fronto**, a high spur of Massanella with precipitous cliffs. At this point the track to the farm turns right and the path to the Puig de Massanella goes straight on, outside the wall enclosing the field. This path is well used and marked with paint signs and cairns. Rising through the woods, it joins a wide track by a **painted boulder**, a point of reference which you should note as it's of use in the descent. The wide track actually reaches the bottom of a dip at this point, which helps identify it on the way back. Turn left to reach the **Coll de Sa Linea** at 822m, where there is a clearing among the trees and two engraved stones on the right. The main track begins to descend here towards the village of Mancor de la Vall. A possible diversion for strong walkers is to make the ascent of **Puig de N'Ali** by a winding route marked with some cairns and red paint signs; it's not easy to follow, especially at first because of the trees. The top is unusual, with an immense boulder supported in three places to form a sheltered cave with a southern outlook over the plain.

For Puig de Massanella, turn right at Coll de Sa Linea up a clearly defined path rising in big swings at first, then twisting and turning to reach a junction where the two paths to the top diverge. At the junction, there's a **stone** engraved "Puig y Font" (Mountain and Spring) on the right-hand side and "Font y Puig" on the left, showing the order of arrival at these points. The journey time from the petrol station to this stone is about an hour and a quarter. For the ascent, the route to the right is recommended, following an old track used to carry ice down on mules. Later on, above the treeline, you'll see the old dry-stone walls of the **Casa de Sa Neu** on the right, where ice was stored.

After the path almost levels out, it meanders through boulders and clumps of carritx grass in a shallow valley. The southerly path coming up from Font de S'Avenc (which is described below as part of the descent) passes a second engraved stone, and joins the northerly path about 100m or 200m northeast of this second stone.

Beyond here, head towards the dip between the highest peak of **Massanella** (1367m) and the secondary peak to the southwest (1352m), then veer right to the main peak. This is where you're most likely to see a black vulture. Be careful how you go as there's a pothole some 20m deep not a stone's throw from the summit. On a good day the view from the top encompasses almost the entire island, from the Formentor headland in the northeast to the Bay of Palma. To the north, vertical cliffs plunge 150m to the **Coll d'es Prat** (1210m), above which lies the northern section of the Massanella massif. Puig Major is readily identified by the radar domes on the summit and the splendid cliffs below.

THE DESCENT

To descend, retrace your steps to where the southerly path joins. This southerly path offers an awkward descent over sharp cornered limestone boulders lying at all angles, with deep crevices in between. If you wish to use it, turn right to the second engraved stone, on the edge of a sloping shelf below the summit. An obvious rocky staircase leads down to a spring, the **Font de S'Avenc**, outside which is a red earth platform conspicuous in the grey rocky landscape. Steps lead down to an upper cave where a table and benches have been cut out of the rock, and a further set of steps leads down to a lower chamber with two basins of water (you need a torch to see inside the lower cave). The flies that infest this cavern make it an unlikely picnic spot, but it offers shelter from lightning and rain.

The path from the spring contours to the east at first, splitting briefly into two; take either branch. The route is marked, but pay careful attention to where you're going as there are many goat paths and natural ledges to lead walkers astray. Follow the marked path back into the trees and on to reach the first engraved stone, which signals the junction with the old mule track used on the ascent. Now it's a question of retracing your steps, turning left at the Coll de Sa Linea and right at the painted boulder, before passing through Coma Freda farm again.

ALTERNATIVE ASCENT VIA COLL D'ES PRAT

WITH DESCENT AS ABOVE; 16KM; 1022M OF ASCENT; 6HR–6HR 30MIN ROUND-TRIP.

An alternative and longer ascent can be made by following the old track from Coma Freda up the valley on the north side of Massanella to the high **Coll d'es Prat** (1210m), then descending the **Comellar d'es Prat** valley for about 1km, until a way is found up to the 1158-metre col between Puig de Ses Bassetes (1216m) and Massanella by a short easy scramble. From this col, the direct ascent of the southwest ridge to a secondary peak of Massanella (1352m) is for rock-climbers only, but a walkers' route is found by a rising traverse, east at first, then looking out for the cairns which show the way up the steep and rocky ground. These cairns are difficult to see in the grey rocky wilderness and a descent by this route is not recommended.

1913, the solemn granite stations marking the way are of two types simple stone pediments and, more intriguingly, rough trilobat columns of Gaudí-like design, each surmounted by a chunky crown and cross. The prettiest part of the walk is round the back of the hil where the path slips through the cool, green woods with rock over hangs on one side and views out over the bowl-shaped Albarca valle on the other. It takes about ten minutes to reach the crucifix at th top of the hill, and afterwards it's possible to stroll or drive down int the Albarca valley by following the country road that begins to th left of the monastery's main entrance. The valley is shadowed b **Puig Roig** (1002m), but there is nowhere in particular to aim for an the road fizzles out long before you reach the coast. For a longe **hike** into the mountains, see p.168.

Practicalities

Accommodation at the monastery is highly organized, with simple self-contained apartment-cells. In summer phone ahead if you war to be sure of space, but at other times simply book at the monastery information office on arrival (☎971 871 525, fax 971 517 09 *info@lluc.net*). Double rooms cost 4400ptas/€26.44 per night, bu the price drops to 3900ptas/€23.44 for stays of three days and more A room for four people costs 5000ptas/€30.05 for one night. Singl rooms cost about eighty percent of the double-room price.

For **food**, there are several cafés and restaurants beside the ca park, but far preferable is the monks' former dining room, a grandl restored old hall of wooden beams and wide stone arches. The foo is traditional Spanish, with main courses from 1500ptas/€9.02; th meat dishes are much better than the fish. An interesting alternativ is *Restaurant Es Guix* (☎971 517 092), a curious and solitary li tle place with its own spring-fed pool hidden away in a wooded ravin about 3km from the monastery. The restaurant has a traditional rus tic look – it was founded in 1970 – and its meat dishes are ofte praised. To get there, take the Inca turning off the C710 near th monastery and watch for the sign.

Pollença and around

Founded in the thirteenth century, the tranquil little town of POL LENÇA nestles among a trio of hillocks 20km northeast of Lluc where the Serra de Tramuntana fades into coastal flatland. Followin, standard Mallorcan practice, the town was established a few kilome tres from the seashore to militate against sudden pirate attack, wit its harbour, **Port de Pollença** (see p.177), left as an unprotected out post. For once the stratagem worked. Unlike most of Mallorca's ol towns, Pollença successfully repelled a string of piratical onslaught the last and most threatening of which was in 1550, when the noto rious Turkish corsair Dragut came within a hair's breadth of victor In the festival of **Mare de Déu dels Àngels** on August 2, the towns

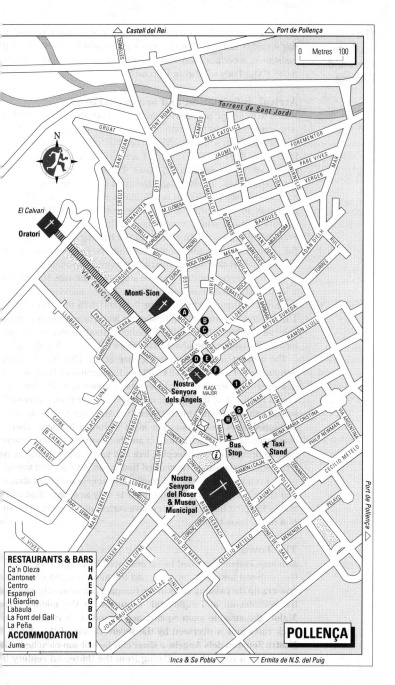

POLLENÇA

Castell del Rei △   △ Port de Pollença

0   Metres   100

Torrent de Sant Jordi

El Calvari
Oratori

Monti-Sion

Nostra Senyora dels Angels

PLAÇA MAJOR

Nostra Senyora del Roser & Museu Municipal

Bus Stop ★

★ Taxi Stand

Port de Pollença △

Inca & Sa Pobla ▽   ▽ Ermita de N.S. del Puig

RESTAURANTS & BARS

Ca'n Oleza	**H**
Cantonet	**A**
Centro	**E**
Espanyol	**F**
Il Giardino	**G**
Labaula	**B**
La Font del Gall	**C**
La Peña	**D**

ACCOMMODATION

Juma	**1**

people celebrate their escape with enthusiastic street battles, th
day's events named after the warning shouted by the hero of th
resistance, a certain Joan Más: "Mare de Déu dels Àngels, assisti
mos!" ("Our Lady of Angels, help us!").

Arrival, information and accommodation

Buses to Pollença, primarily from Palma, Port de Pollença and Llu
stop immediately to the south of Plaça Major, at the foot of c/Anto
Maura. The town's **tourist office** (Tues–Sat 9am–1pm & 5–8pm, Su
9am–1pm; ☎971 865 467) is just across the street, in front of th
church of Nostra Senyora del Roser. Pollença's tiny centre is be
explored on foot, but outlying attractions such as the resort of Cal
Sant Vicenç (see p.175) can be affordably reached by **taxi**. There's
taxi rank in the centre at the corner of Avinguda Pollentia ar
c/Reina Maria Cristina, or you can call Radio Taxi Pollença ☎97
866 396. If you're **driving** in, avoid the baffling one-way streets (
the old part of town and enter town from the south, turning off th
main Inca–Port de Pollença road along Avinguda Pollentia.

There's only one central place **to stay** – the first-rate *Hotel Jum*
a smart and tasteful conversion of an old stone merchant's house i
the heart of things at Plaça Major 9 (☎971 535 002, fax 971 53
155, *www.hoteljuma.com*; ⑦; March–Oct). The rooms are comfor
able, air-conditioned and tidily furnished in modern style; those ove
looking the square cost about 1200ptas/€7.21 more than the other

The nearest alternative lodgings are at the *Ermita de Nostr*
Senyora del Puig ☎971 184 132, on the summit of Puig de Mar
just over 2km south of town (see the account opposite for dire
tions). Here, ten of the original monks' cells have been renovated
provide simple rooms for between two and four guests apiece
1000ptas/€6.01 per person per night including bedding. There
also space for thirty on the floor of another room, but in this case yo
have to bring your own sleeping bag and you don't save any mone
– the price is the same. Be warned that it can get cold and windy
night, even in the summer. All guests have access to shared showe
and there's a refectory, but the food is only average. Most of th
guests sleeping in the dormitory have turned up on spec: to be sur
of a room, book ahead.

The Town

Although Pollença avoided being destroyed by Dragut, not much (
the medieval town has survived, and the austere stone houses tha
now cramp the twisting lanes of the compact centre mostly date fro
the seventeenth and eighteenth centuries. In the middle, **Plaç**
Major, the amiable main square, accommodates a cluster of laj
back cafés and is overseen by the severe facade of the church (
Nostra Senyora dels Àngels, a sheer cliff-face of sun-bleached ston
pierced by a rose window. Dating from the thirteenth century b

extensively remodelled in the Baroque style five centuries later, the church's gloomy interior has a mildly diverting sequence of ceiling and wall paintings, as well as a whopping, tiered and towered high altarpiece. The original church was built for the Knights Templar, a rich and secretive organization founded as a military order in support of the Crusades, but suppressed by the pope in 1312 following trumped-up charges of heresy, sorcery and bestiality. The Templars' Pollença possessions – as those elsewhere – passed to the Hospitallers of St John, a rival knightly order who struggled on until 1802 when the Spanish king appropriated all they owned.

The northern coast and Pollença

Plaça Major is the site of a lively fruit and veg market on most Sunday mornings.

Close by, along c/Antoni Maura – and behind a tiny square housing an antique water wheel, a stumpy watchtower and the tourist office – stands the deconsecrated church of **Nostra Senyora del Roser** (July–Sept Tues–Sat 10am–1pm & 5.30–8.30pm, Sun 10am–1pm; rest of year Tues–Sun 11am–1pm; free). The entrance is flanked by a curious piece of modern sculpture, chiselled in the shape of a bookcase. Inside, the church hosts contemporary art exhibitions, but these struggle to compete with the gaudiness of the church – from the barrel-vaulted ceiling through to the flamboyant Baroque high altar. In the adjoining Claustre Santo Domingo (cloisters) is the **Museu Municipal** (same hours; 250ptas/€1.50), which contains a modest collection of contemporary paintings, including past and present winners of the town's annual art competition, the Certamen Internacional d'Arts Plàstiques. Here also is a ragbag of local archeological finds, a curious assortment of folkloric and ecclesiastical bric-à-brac, plus several good examples of Mallorcan Gothic art. Amongst the latter, look out for the work of Francesc Comes (1379–1415), whose dexterity in catching the subtle texture of skin is reminiscent of his Flemish contemporaries.

There are works by Comes and other Mallorcan Gothic painters on display in Palma – see pp.82, 83 & 87.

Pollença's pride and joy is its **Via Crucis** (Way of the Cross), a long, steep and beautiful stone stairway, graced by ancient cypress trees which ascends **El Calvari** (Calvary hill) to the north of the town centre. At the top, a much-revered thirteenth-century statue of **Mare de Déu del Peu de la Creu** (Mother of God at the Foot of the Cross) is lodged in a simple, courtyarded **oratori** (chapel), whose whitewashed walls sport some of the worst religious paintings imaginable. However, the views out over coast and town are sumptuous. On Good Friday, a figure of Jesus is slowly carried by torchlight down from the *oratori* to the church of Nostra Senyora dels Àngels, in the **Davallament** (Lowering), one of the most moving religious celebrations on the island.

The Ermita de Nostra Senyora del Puig

There are further magnificent views from the **Ermita de Nostra Senyora del Puig**, a rambling, mostly eighteenth-century monastery perched on top of the Puig de Maria, a 320-metre-high hump facing the south end of town. The monastic complex, with its fortified walls, courtyard, chapel, refectory and cells, has had a chequered history, alternately abandoned and restored by both monks and nuns. The Benedictines now own the place, but the monks are gone and today a custodian supplements the order's income by renting out cells to tourists (see p.172). There is nothing specific to see, but the setting is extraordinarily serene and beautiful, with the mellow honey-coloured walls of the monastery surrounded by ancient carob and olive trees, a million miles from the tourist resorts visible far below.

It takes just over an hour to walk to the monastery from the centre of Pollença

To get to the monastery, take the signposted turning off the main Pollença–Inca road just south of town; head up this steep lane until it fizzles out after 1.5km, to be replaced by a cobbled footpath which winds up to the monastery's entrance. It's possible to drive to the top of the lane, but unless you've got nerves of steel for the ascent, you're better off parking elsewhere. Note that there have been reports of cars left at the foot of the lane overnight being vandalized; although this is unusual, you might prefer to park in town instead.

Eating and drinking

Pollença does very well for **restaurants**, supported by the villa owners who gather here every evening from the surrounding countryside. The **bar** scene is less convincing, but there are several reasonably lively spots in the vicinity of Plaça Major, with one or two occupying the converted basements of old mansions. All these bars serve food of some description, mostly inexpensive *tapas*.

Bar Centro, c/Temple 3. Atmospheric little bar of rudimentary appearance just up from the main square. Retreat here if the nearby *Café Espanyol* (see below) gets too much.

Bar Hotel Juma, Plaça Major 9. Good range of tasty *tapas* sold in the brisk, modern bar of Pollença's one and only hotel. Rapid-fire service and reasonable prices – a standard portion costs about 350ptas/€2.10. The outside terrace overlooking the main square is especially enticing.

Bar La Peña, c/Temple 2. Traditional neighbourhood café-bar with a wide range of delicious *tapas* from 250ptas/€1.50, and *racions* from 450ptas/€2.71. Has long been one of the best places in town for an inexpensive meal.

Bar Labaula, c/Horta 18. One of Pollença's more fashionable haunts, occupying an imaginatively renovated basement of an antique stone mansion.

Café Espanyol, on Plaça Major. The liveliest, noisiest spot in town. A good old-fashioned place with dog-eared decor plus a baffling (and, later on in the day, baffled) mixture of locals and tourists.

Restaurant Ca'n Olesa, Plaça Major 12 ☎971 532 908. Good central location and low prices, but the pastas and pizzas that feature on the menu are hardly distinctive. Stick instead to the *cocina mallorquina* dishes.

Restaurant Cantonet, c/Monti-Sion 20 ☎971 530 429. This fashionable restaurant just north of Plaça Major offers top-notch international cuisine from a limited menu – à la carte, or a fixed menu at about 2500ptas/€15.03. In the summer, you can eat out on the terrace of the large church a few metres away. Closed Tues.

Restaurant Il Giardino, Plaça Major 11 ☎971 534 302. One the best restaurants in town, this smart bistro-style place offers a superb range of French-Italian dishes from about 2000ptas/€12.02, all prepared with great flair.

Restaurant La Font del Gall, c/Monti-Sion 4 ☎971 530 396. Chic little spot just off the Plaça Major with an international, French-inspired menu. It's a justifiably popular spot, where you should allow 4000ptas/€24.04 for a full meal including wine.

The Castell del Rei

The battered ruins of the medieval **Castell del Rei** (Castle of the King) are glued to a remote and inhospitable crag, which rears high above the sea about 7km north of Pollença. This remote fastness was founded by the Moors and strengthened by Jaume I to guard the northerly approaches to Pollença against pirate attack. In this regard, however, it was something of a failure: the pirates simply ignored it, preferring to land at nearby Cala Sant Vicenç instead. More successfully, it held out for months against the Aragonese invasion of 1285 and was the last fortress to surrender to Pedro of Aragón, the supplanter of the Mallorcan king Jaume III, in 1343. Subsequently, the castle was used as a watchtower, finally being abandoned in 1715.

It takes about two hours to **walk** there from Pollença, an undemanding hike along a country lane, and then a forest footpath leading through the pretty Ternelles valley. On the northern edge of Pollença, a turning signposted to Ternelles leads off the C710, twisting north past attractively renovated old *fincas* and olive and citrus groves. After 1.6km, you'll reach a guarded gate set in the narrow defile at the entrance to the Ternelles valley. If you're driving, you have to park here. An easy-to-follow, rough and dusty track leads to another set of gates, beyond which the path starts to rise, climbing through oak woods to a stretch of mixed woodland dominated by pines. Further on, the trees thin out and the castle ruins can be spied in the distance. About 100m after the start of a fenced-off area on the right-hand side, fork left off the main track – which continues down to the shingly beach at **Cala Castell** – for the climb up to the ruins.

The problem, however, is getting in: the castle is on a vast private estate, whose owner allows visitors only limited access. Globespan (see p.179) or the tourist office in Port de Pollença are the best places to ask for information about current opening times.

The sign to Ternelles on the C710 is small and faded and easy to miss; the turning is about 800m west of the junction where the roads to Port de Pollença and to Inca meet the C710.

Cala Sant Vicenç

One of Mallorca's more agreeable resorts, **CALA SANT VICENÇ**, 6km northeast of Pollença, boasts an attractive, solitary setting, its medley of well-heeled villas and modern hotels gambolling over and around a wooded ravine just behind a pair of pint-sized sandy **beaches**. The fly in the aesthetic ointment is the overpowering *Hotel Don Pedro*, insensitively located on the minuscule headland separating the beaches, but the resort is still a delightful spot for a swim – the

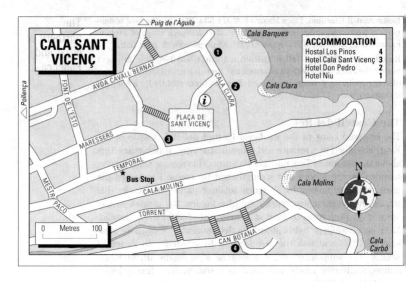

CALA SANT VICENÇ

△ Puig de l'Àguila

Cala Barques

Cala Clara

PLAÇA DE SANT VICENÇ

★ Bus Stop

Cala Molins

Cala Carbó

N

AVDA CAVALL BERNAT

CALA CLARA

FONT DEL ESTIU

MARESSERS

TEMPORAL

CALA MOLINS

MESTRE PACO

TORRENT

CAN BOTANA

△ Pollença

Pollença

0   Metres   100

water is crystal clear and the beach is sheltered from the wind. In addition, you can **hike** out onto the wild and wind-licked seashore that extends to either side of the resort. One tempting option is the moderately strenuous hoof north up the adjoining headland to the top of **Puig de l'Àguila** (206m), from where there are grand views over the surrounding coast and back over the resort. This 6km hike takes around three hours; the first part uses a rough stone road, the second follows a well-defined path which leads to the base of Puig de l'Àguila – but you'll still need a proper IGN map to find your way.

Buses from Lluc and Pollença stop in town on Avinguda Temporal, from where it's a short walk northeast to the **tourist office** on Plaça Sant Vicenç (June–Sept Mon–Fri 9am–2pm, Sat 9.30am–12.30pm; ☎971 533 264): head along Avinguda Temporal towards the seashore, turn left down c/Cala Clara and then left again. This is package territory, so vacant **rooms** are extremely thin on the ground in summer. That said, you might try the *Hotel Niu*, a comfortably old-fashioned low-rise next to the beach (☎971 530 100, fax 971 531 220; ⑦), or the more secluded two-star *Hostal Los Pinos* at c/Can Botana s/n on the southern edge of the resort (☎971 531 210; ④; May–Oct), which has twenty spick-and-span rooms and its own pool. Cala Sant Vicenç's smartest hotel is the four-star *Cala Sant Vicenç*, located in the centre of the resort away from the beach off Avinguda Temporal at Maressers 2 (☎971 530 250, fax 971 532 084; ⑨; Feb–Nov); it's a tasteful spot with all mod cons and just forty guest rooms.

The resort has a good supply of **cafés** and **restaurants**, beginning with the pizzeria operated by – and adjacent to – the *Hotel Cala Sant Vicenç*. Arguably the best restaurant is the *Cavall Bernat* ☎971

530 250, which offers an international menu that includes traditional Mallorcan dishes.

Port de Pollença

Things are much busier over at **PORT DE POLLENÇA**, but it's still all pleasantly low-key. With the mountains as a shimmering backcloth, this family-oriented resort arches through the flatlands behind the Badia de Pollença, a deeply indented bay whose sheltered waters are ideal for swimming. The **beach** is the focus of attention, a narrow, elongated sliver of sand that's easily long enough to accommodate the crowds, though as a general rule you'll have more space the further south (towards Alcúdia) you walk. A rash of apartment buildings and hotels blights the edge of town, and the noisy main road to Alcúdia cuts through the centre, but there are no high-rises to speak of and the resort is dotted with attractive whitewashed and stone-trimmed villas. All together it's quite delightful, especially to the north of the marina, where a portion of the old beachside road – along **Passeig Anglada Camarasa** – has been pedestrianized.

Arrival, information and accommodation

Buses to Port de Pollença from, amongst many places, Pollença, Palma, Alcúdia, Port d'Alcúdia and Port de Sóller stop by the marina right in the town centre. A couple of minutes' walk away is the **tourist office**, just up behind the seafront at c/Joan XXIII 46 (June–Sept Mon–Fri 9am–1.30pm & 4–7pm, Sat 9am–1pm; Oct–May Mon–Fri 8am–3.30pm, Sat 9am–1pm; ☎971 865 467), which has loads of local information and accommodation lists.

Port de Pollença has around a dozen **hotels** and not quite as many **hostals**. Needless to say, most of the rooms are block-booked by the tour operators, but there's a fairly good chance of finding a vacancy in the places listed below, especially in the shoulder season.

Hostal Bahía, Passeig Voramar 31 ☎971 866 562, fax 971 865 630. In a lovely location, a few minutes' walk north of the marina along the seashore, this pleasant, unassuming one-star *hostal* offers thirty rooms in one of the port's older villas. April–Oct. ⑤.

Hostal-residencia Borrás, Plaça Miquel Capllonch 16 ☎971 866 447, fax 971 865 093. Agreeable two-star *hostal*. Most of the rooms are comfortably spacious and you can eat breakfast in the pretty little courtyard. Overlooks the old town's tiny main square, a couple of minutes' walk from the beach. April–Sept. ④.

Hotel Capri, Passeig Anglada Camarasa 69 ☎971 866 601, fax 971 866 461. Standard-issue modern hotel just north of the marina with thirty pleasant rooms. Overlooks the beach, where it's flanked by the pedestrianized walkway – the prettiest part of town. May–Oct. ⑥.

Hotel Daina, c/Atilio Boveri 2 ☎971 866 250, fax 971 866 145. Straightforward block hotel with three stars and sixty rooms. The public areas are decorated in brisk modern style and the rooms are somewhat bleak – they come equipped with some ponderous neo-baronial furniture – but everything is in order. May–Nov. ⑦.

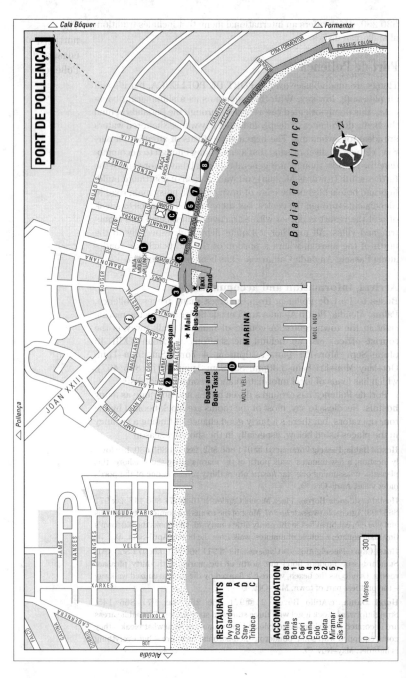

PORT DE POLLENÇA

△ Cala Bóquer   △ Formentor

△ Pollença

△ Alcúdia

Badia de Pollença

MARINA

★ Taxi Stand

★ Main Bus Stop

★ Boats and Boat-Taxis

RESTAURANTS

Ivy Garden	B
Pozo	A
Stay	D
Tribeca	C

ACCOMMODATION

Bahia	8
Borrás	1
Capri	6
Daina	4
Eolo	3
Goleta	2
Miramar	5
Sis Pins	7

0   Metres   300

Hostal-residencia Eolo, Plaça Enginyer Gabriel Roca 2 ☎971 866 550, fax 971 866 301. Straightforward, middle-sized *hostal* metres from the marina. Rooms are somewhat spartan, but perfectly OK. A hikers' favourite. Open all year. ⑤.

Hostal-residencia La Goleta, Passeig Saralegui 118 ☎971 865 902, fax 971 866 002. No fuss, two-star *hostal* with sixteen rooms in an attractive five-storey building on the traffic-heavy seafront south of the marina. The front rooms have balconies, but suffer from the noise from below. Mid-March to Oct. ⑤.

Hotel Miramar, Passeig Anglada Camarasa 39 ☎971 866 400, fax 971 864 075. Attractive three-star hotel in an elegant building – all iron grilles and stone lintels. Every room has its own balcony, but try to get a room at the front with a sea view, or you might be plonked at the back looking out over Carretera Formentor. April–Oct. ⑦.

Hotel-residencia Sis Pins, Passeig Anglada Camarasa 77 ☎971 867 050, fax 971 534 013. This medium-sized three-star hotel occupies a handsome white-washed and balconied villa on the waterfront. Very comfortable. April–Oct. ⑦.

In and around town

The flatlands edging the Badia de Pollença and stretching inland as far as Pollença and along the bay to Alcúdia make for easy, scenic cycling. **Mountain bikes** can be rented from March, c/Joan XXIII 89 (Mon–Sat 9am–1pm & 3–8pm, Sun 9am–12.30pm; ☎971 864 784), as can **mopeds** and **motorcycles**. Mountain bikes cost in the region of 1200ptas/€7.21 for one day, 2200ptas/€13.22 for two days, 3200ptas/€19.23 for three days, or 6500ptas/€39.07 for a week. Ordinary bicycles work out at about half the price. **Car rental** companies include La Parra, c/Joan XXIII 20 ☎971 866 721, and Avis, along the street at no. 80 ☎971 865 394.

The walking holiday specialists **Globespan** have an office on the waterfront at Passeig Saralegui 114 (☎971 864 711; after 7pm, mobile ☎678 453 117; *globespan@atlas-iap.es*), where you can pay to join one of their day-long **guided walks**. These are graded according to difficulty, with the easier rambles (the majority) costing anywhere between 1600ptas/€9.62 and 3500ptas/€21.04 per person; the more difficult hikes cost between 3000ptas/€18.03 and 4000ptas/€24.04. Transport is included, but you need to take your own food and water. Staff will provide all the details and you should book a minimum of 24 hours beforehand.

For a change of scene, **water taxis** shuttle between the marina and the Platja de Formentor, one of Mallorca's most attractive beaches (April–Oct 5–7 daily; 30min; 900ptas/€5.41 each way). **Boat trips** cruise the bay (June to mid-Oct Mon–Sat 1 daily; 2hr 30min; 2000ptas/€12.02), or work their way along to Cap de Formentor (same times and price). There's also the option of making a delightful three-kilometre **hike** across the neck of the Península de Formentor to **Cala Bóquer** (see box on p.182).

*For more on
the Platja de
Formentor and
Cap de
Formentor, see
p.180.*

Eating and drinking

Port de Pollença heaves with **restaurants**. Many offer run-of-the-mill tourist fodder and there's a plethora of pizza places, but others serve the freshest of seafood and skilfully blend Catalan and Castilian cuisines. As a general rule, competition keeps **prices** down to readily affordable levels, with around 1500ptas/€9.02 or 2000ptas/€12.02 covering a main course at all but the ritziest establishments.

Pizzeria Eolo, Plaça Enginyer Gabriel Roca 2 ☎971 865 749. There's nothing gourmet about this place, but the pizzas are tasty, filling and inexpensive. Beneath the *hostal* of the same name.

Restaurant El Pozo, c/Joan XXIII 25 ☎971 866 777. Less expensive than its seafront rivals, this informal, laid-back café-bar-cum-restaurant offers a good range of local dishes and is strong on seafood. A couple of minutes' walk from the marina.

Restaurant Ivy Garden, c/Llevant 14 ☎971 866 271. This outstanding restaurant, arguably the best in town, features an inventive modern menu at reasonable prices. Dishes change, but recent examples have included fillet of salmon with pesto and lemon dressing for 1800ptas/€10.82, and duck with ginger sauce for 2200ptas/€13.22.

Restaurant Stay, on the Moll Vell jetty ☎971 864 013. This long-established restaurant, with its crisp modern decor and attentive service, is renowned for the quality of its seafood – though the main courses tend to the minimal. Prices are above average, but nothing too excessive and well worth it for the romantic seashore setting. It's a very popular spot, so reservations are pretty much essential.

Restaurant Tribeca, Carretera Formentor 43 ☎971 866 423. Small and intimate bistro-style restaurant with an imaginative modern menu – anything from crepes to lamb couscous. Smart but competitively priced, with dishes averaging about 1800ptas/€10.82. Centrally located at the junction with c/Llevant.

The Península de Formentor

Heading northeast out of Port de Pollença, the road clears the military zone at the far end of the resort before weaving up into the hills at the start of the twenty-kilometre-long **Península de Formentor**, the final spur of the Serra de Tramuntana. At first, the road (which suffers a surfeit of tourists from mid-morning to mid-afternoon) travels inland, out of sight of the true grandeur of the scenery, but after about 4km the **Mirador de Mal Pas** rectifies matters with a string of lookout points perched on the edge of plunging, north-facing seacliffs. There are further stunning views, in this case over the south shore, from the **Talaia d'Albercutx** watchtower viewpoint, but you'll have to be prepared to tackle the rough side road that climbs the ridge opposite the Mirador de Mal Pas.

The Platja de Formentor

It's a couple of kilometres along the main road from the Mirador de Mal Pas to a roadside car park (600ptas/€3.61), from where a ten-minute walk through the woods leads to the **Platja de Formentor**, a ne-clad beach of golden sand in a pretty cove. It's a beautiful spot, ith views over to the mountains on the far side of the bay, though it an get a little crowded. From May to October, you can get here from alma and Port de Pollença on a once-daily **bus** service (not on Sun), r there's also a twice-daily bus year-round from Alcúdia and Port 'Alcúdia (not on Sun). The best way to arrive is by **water taxi** from ollença (April–Oct 5–7 daily; 30min; 900ptas/€5.41 each way).

At the far end of the beach, and with its own access road from near e car park, stands the **Hotel Formentor** (☎971 899 100, fax 971

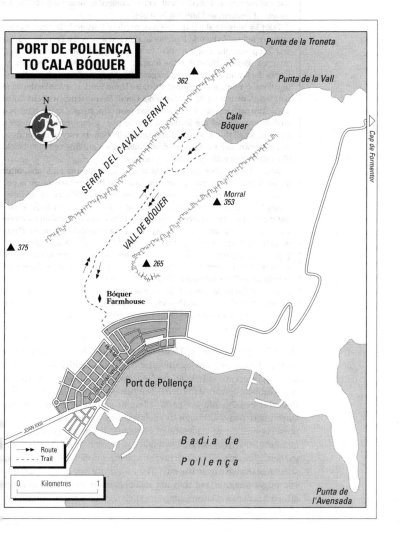

A VALLEY WALK FROM
PORT DE POLLENÇA TO CALA BÓQUER

6KM; 101M OF ASCENT; 1HR 30MIN.

The walk through the sheltered **Vall de Bóquer** is an attractive, easy stroll over gently undulating ground, coast-to-coast across the neck of the Península de Formentor. Return is by the same route, about 3km each way. The walk is popular with family groups, being suitable for most ages and abilities – though the last leg down to the beach can be overgrown and difficult for young children – and is also favoured by ornithologists for the variety of resident and migrant **bird life**.

Start by walking along the seafront north of Port de Pollença's marina and turn left up **Avinguda Bocchoris**. Proceed across the Formentor road and keep straight along a wide footpath fringed with pine trees and tamarisk. Beyond the end of the footpath is an untidy area whose tarmac marks the layout of a proposed housing development. Ahead, at a sign saying "Predio Bóquer Propriedad Privada Camin Particular," take the wide path north with the ridge of Serra del Cavall Bernat straight ahead. After 150m the path swings to the northeast past olive trees. On the right is a striking example of the lentisk or mastic tree, a dark evergreen with a resinous smell that grows to three metres. Its flowers vary in colour from red to brown and are succeeded by fruits, which are first red then black. The other trees with long pods are carobs.

About 75m further on, the path veers left at the car park and, after about 250m, passes through an iron gate. The **Bóquer farmhouse** is just ahead on the right, while on the left, opposite the farmhouse, is an interesting but neglected **terraced garden** shaped like a ship with its prow facing out to sea – the terraces were watered from stone irrigation channels fed from holding tanks, all now dry. There's a splendid view of the Badia de Pollença from here and, at the far end of the garden, some fine examples of the *Agave americana*, a succulent whose flower spikes reach heights of three metres. On the farmhouse side of the path there's an equally impressive two-metre-high opuntia cactus.

Beyond the farmhouse, the path turns round to the right, heading north through a small iron gate, then ascends steadily for about 500m, passing between large rocks. Niches in the rocks are occupied by clumps of dwarf

865 155; ⑨). Opened in 1930, this wonderful hotel – arguably the island's best – lies low against the forested hillside, its *hacienda* style architecture enhanced by Neoclassical and Art Deco features and exquisite terraced gardens. The place was once the haunt of the rich and fashionable – Charlie Chaplin and Scott Fitzgerald both stayed here – and although its socialite days are long gone, the hotel preserves an air of understated elegance. It has every facility, and dinner is served on an outside terrace perfumed by the flowers of the gardens; breakfast is taken on the splendid upper-floor loggia with spectacular views over the bay. The rooms are not quite as grand as you might imagine, but they are still charming. Stay here if you can afford it; there's a surprisingly good chance of a vacant room, even in high summer.

an palms, and you will probably see the blue rock thrushes that inhabit the
area. Here and further along the walk, you may also spot wheatears, black-
eared wheatears, black redstarts, rock sparrows and wryneck, as well as
buzzards, peregrines, kestrels, booted eagles, the occasional osprey,
Eleonora's falcons in spring and summer, stone chats and goldfinches.
Various warblers pass through this area on migration too, but the big
ornithological sight here is the **black vulture**, with a wingspan of around
two metres, which glides the air currents of the north coast. There's a fairly good chance of spotting one from the Vall de Bóquer, and if you're really lucky you'll get a close view, its large, black body contrasting with a
brownish head, beak and ruff.

Beyond the boulders the path descends, becoming less rocky, then
passes through a gap in a dry-stone wall before ascending gently for
about 150m – a scattering of pine trees 50m to the left offers a shady
spot for a picnic. This area has been heavily grazed by the valley's
semi-wild goats, leaving the vegetation sparse and scrubby. The most
noticeable plant is *Asphodelus microcarpus*, which grows up to two
metres high, bearing tall spikes of white flowers with a reddish brown
vein on each petal. Not even the goats like it. Other common shrubs are
the *Hypericum balearicum*, a St John's wort whose yellow flowers
are at their best in spring and early summer, and the narrow-leaved cistus and spurges, whose hemispherical bushes bear bright yellow
glands.

At the top of the next incline the path passes through another wall.
About 50m off to the right of the junction of wall and path, more or less
due south, is a 1.5m-high **tunnel**, inside which is a spring. Be careful, however, if you venture in, as it's popular with goats, who like the water and
shade. They'll sometimes panic and charge out if they see you coming.

To descend to the sea take the path which bears to the left and then runs
down alongside a dried-up watercourse amidst the cries of sea birds and
the whispering of the tall carritx grass. Patches of aromatic blue-flowered
rosemary line the path. The **beach** at the end of the walk at Cala Bóquer is
disappointing. It's predominantly shingle, with at most only a couple of
metres of sand, and can be dirty. Nevertheless, the *cala* offers good swimming in clean water.

To return to Port de Pollença, retrace your steps along the same route.

The Cap de Formentor

Beyond the turn-off for the hotel, the main peninsula road runs along
wooded ridge before tunnelling through Mont Fumat to emerge on
the rocky mass of **Cap de Formentor**. This tapered promontory of
peak sea-cliffs and scrub-covered hills offers magnificent views and
a fruitful area for **birdwatching**, especially from the silver-domed
lighthouse stuck on the windswept tip. The lighthouse itself is out of
bounds, but you can wander round its rocky environs, where the
sparse vegetation is a perfect habitat for lizards and small birds,
especially the deep-blue feathered rock thrush and the white-rumped
rock dove. From the lighthouse you can also view the steep, east-
ward-facing sea-cliffs which shelter colonies of nesting Eleonora's
falcons from April to October, whilst circling overhead there are

often ravens, martins and swifts. During the spring and summ
migrations, thousands of seabirds fly over the cape, Manx and Cory
shearwaters in particular. If you're ready for a snack before headir
back from the cape, pop into the **coffee bar** next to the lighthouse

The Badia d'Alcúdia

Moving south from Port de Pollença, it's just 10km round the bay
the compact old town of **Alcúdia**, whose main claims to fame are
imitation medieval walls and the battered remains of the old Roma
settlement of Pollentia. Within easy striking distance lies the meg
resort of **Port d'Alcúdia**, where glistening sky-rises sweep arour
the glorious sandy beach of the **Badia d'Alcúdia**. In summer t
place is probably best avoided – it's far too crowded to be much fi
– but the shoulder seasons are more relaxing when the beach is cor
paratively uncrowded. In the wintertime you'll barely see a soul, b
most of the hotels and many of the restaurants are closed.

Port d'Alcúdia's assorted hotels, villas and apartment blocl
stretch almost without interruption round the bay to the resort
Ca'n Picafort, 10km south. The developers drained the swamplar
that once extended behind this coastal strip years ago, but one sma
wetland has been protected as the **Parc Natural de S'Albufera**,
real birdwatchers' delight. Further behind the coast lies a tract of fe
tile farmland dotted with country towns, amongst which **Muro**, wi

---

From Palma direct to Alcúdia

Alcúdia is best seen in conjunction with a visit to Pollença and the Serra de
Tramuntana, covered in the first section of this chapter, but if you're in a
hurry to get there from Palma you could follow the more direct, far less
memorable route northeast from Palma across the island's central plain.

The fastest option is to take the **autopista** (the PM27) from Palma to
Inca, where it terminates, and then pick up the C713 for the last leg of the
journey. Alternatively, you could follow the C713 all the way from Palma,
passing through or skirting several small towns along the way. Amongst
these are **Binissalem** (see p.134) – well worth a visit – as well as **Lloseta**
(see p.136) and **Sa Pobla** (see p.194), both of which are of passing interest, though the scenery hereabouts is a tad dull.

The autopista merges with the C713 on the western outskirts of the central plain's largest settlement, **Inca**, an ugly industrial place that's best
avoided unless you're a devotee of leather goods (which are available at
several factory shops beside the main road as it swings around the edge of
the town). East of Inca the C713 pushes on to the coast through a more
attractive landscape – arable land liberally scattered with broken-down
windmills.

There is an excellent **bus** service from Palma to Alcúdia and Port
d'Alcúdia, and you can also travel by **train** from Palma through Binissalem
and Lloseta to the terminus at Inca, from where buses connect to the north
coast.

---

s imposing church and old grandee mansions, is easily the most
iverting.

Accommodation is concentrated in Port d'Alcúdia, but in the sum-
nertime it's nearly all reserved for package tourists. Possible alter-
atives include both of Mallorca's official **campgrounds**, which bor-
er the Badia d'Alcúdia. One, the *Sun Club Picafort*, lies on the edge
f Ca'n Picafort, the other – the *Club San Pedro* – is located further
outh outside Colònia de Sant Pere (see p.209). The former is much
he better of the two, though in both cases advance reservations are
rongly advised.

Transport connections, particularly from May to October, are very
ood. Frequent **buses** link Port de Pollença, Pollença, Alcúdia, Port
'Alcúdia and Ca'n Picafort. There are also regular services to
lcúdia and its port from Palma, and reasonable summertime con-
ections from Port de Sóller and Sóller as well.

lcúdia and around

o pull in the day-trippers, pint-sized **ALCÚDIA** wears its history on
s sleeve. The crenellated wall that encircles much of the town cen-
'e is mostly a modern imitation of the medieval original, and,
lthough the sixteenth- to eighteenth-century houses behind it are
enuine enough, the whole place is overly spick and span. In fact, lit-
e can be seen today which reflects the town's true historical impor-
ance. Situated on a neck of land separating two large, sheltered
ays, the site's strategic value was first recognized by the
hoenicians, who settled here in around 700 BC and used the place
s a staging-post for sea trade between northwest Africa and Spain.
. few Phoenician trinkets have been unearthed here – most notably
xamples of their delicate, coloured glass jewellery – but their town
isappeared when the Romans built their island capital, **Pollentia**,
n top of the earlier settlement. In 426, the place was destroyed by
he Vandals and lay neglected until the Moors built a fortress in about
00, naming it Al Kudia (On the Hill). After the Reconquest, Alcúdia
rospered as a major trading centre for the western Mediterranean,
 role it performed well into the nineteenth century, when the town
lipped into a long and gentle decline – until tourism refloated its
conomy.

he Town

only takes an hour or so to walk around the antique lanes of
lcúdia's compact centre and explore the town walls and their forti-
ed gates. This pleasant stroll can be extended by a visit to six spe-
ific sights, which combine to make an enjoyable whole, although
one of them is compelling in itself.

Beginning at the old town's eastern entrance, on Plaça Carles V,
alk through the gateway and keep to the main drag – here c/Moll –
nd you'll soon reach the slender Plaça Constitució, lined with pave-

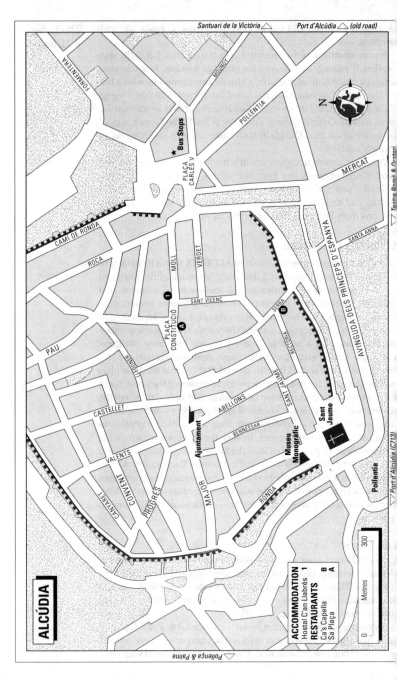

ALCÚDIA

Santuari de la Victòria △ **Port d'Alcúdia** △ (old road)

N

Bus Stops ★

PLAÇA CARLÉS V

POLLENTIA
MOUROY
TORMENTERA

MERCAT

SANTA ANNA

CAMI DE RONDA
ROCA
MOLL
VERDET
SANT VICENÇ
PLAÇA CONSTITUCIO
SERRA
RECTORIA
AVINGUDA DELS PRINCEPS D'ESPANYA

PAU

CASTELLET

SANT JAUME

ABELLONS

Ajuntament
BENNESSAR

Museu Monogràfic

Sant Jaume

VALENTS

CANYARET
CONVENT
PROGRES
MAJOR
RONDA

△ Pollença & Palma

▽ Port d'Alcúdia (C713)

Pollentia

▽ Teatre Romà & Oratori

0   Metres   300

ACCOMMODATION
Hostal C'an Llabrés   1
RESTAURANTS
Ca's Capella   B
Sa Plaça   A

ent cafés. Just beyond, on c/Major, is Alcúdia's best-looking build-
g, the **Ajuntament** (Town Hall), a handsome, largely seventeenth-
ntury structure with an elegant stone balcony and overhanging
ves. From c/Major, take any of the several sidestreets that lead to
e southwest corner of the old town, where you'll find perhaps the
ost diverting of Alcúdia's sights, the **Museu Monogràfic**, c/Sant
ume 2 (April–Sept Tues–Fri 10am–1.30pm & 5–7pm, Sat & Sun
).30am–1pm; Oct–March Tues–Fri 10am–1.30pm & 3.30–5.30pm,
t & Sun 10.30am–1pm; 200ptas/€1.20). It's a small museum, just
e large room, but it is stuffed with a satisfying assortment of arche-
ogical bits and bobs, primarily Roman artefacts from Pollentia,
cluding amulets, miniature devotional objects and tiny oil-burning
mps. Across the street, dominating this portion of the old town, is
e heavyweight and heavily reworked Gothic church of **Sant Jaume**,
hich holds a modest religious museum (Tues–Fri 10am–1pm, Sun
)am–noon; 100ptas/€0.60). Close by, on the other side of the ring
ad just beyond the church, lie the broken pillars and mashed-up
alls that comprise the meagre remains of Roman **Pollentia** (site
en same times as Museu Monogràfic; 300ptas/€1.80). Nearly all
e stone has been looted by the townsfolk over the centuries, so it's
) longer possible to discern the layout of the former capital, which
disappointing.

*You can get a
joint ticket at
the Museu
Monogràfic or
the Pollentia
ruins, valid for
both sites, for
400ptas/€2.40.*

By contrast, the open-air remains of the Roman theatre – the
eatre **Romà** (open access; free) – are much more substantial.
ating from the first century BC, this is the smallest of the twenty
oman theatres to have survived in Spain. Nonetheless, despite its
odest proportions, the builders were able to stick to the standard
pe of layout with eight tiers of seats carved out of the rocky hillside,
vided by two gangways. Inevitably, the stage area, which was con-
ructed of earth and timber, has disappeared. It is a lovely spot, set
nidst fruit and olive trees, a ten-minute stroll to the south of the old
wn. The short, signed footpath to the Roman theatre begins on
Santa Anna, a pretty country lane lined by old stone walls that runs
uth from the ring road a couple of hundred metres east of the
mains of Pollentia.

About 500m north from the path to the Roman theatre, another
ort, clearly signposted footpath heads off c/Santa Anna, this one
ading to the **Oratori de Santa Anna**, a diminutive medieval chapel
erlooking the main C713 road between Alcúdia and Port d'Alcúdia.
you're driving to either of the footpaths, note that c/Santa Anna is
e-way into town. To reach c/Santa Anna by car, head east from the
ellentia ruins along the ring road, then take the old Port d'Alcúdia
ad and watch for the sign.

racticalities

ses halt beside the town walls on Plaça Carles V. Once you've
plored the town, there's no strong reason to hang around, but

*Alcúdia has no
tourist office.*

there is one (and only one) **place to stay**. This is the no-frills *Hostc
Ca'n Llabrés* (☎971 545 000; ④), with a handful of rooms above
café-bar right in the middle of town on Plaça Constitució.

There are several good places **to eat**, beginning with the smal
Restaurant Sa Plaça ☎971 546 278, also on Plaça Constitucic
where they offer traditional Mallorcan cuisine with main course
averaging around 1800ptas/€10.82. A less expensive choice is th
cosy café-bar of *Ca's Capella*, just east of the church of Sant Jaume
in an old stone building at the far end of c/Rectoria. It's nothing to
special, but the pizzas and salads are fine and it's a little off the bea
en track – which is useful, since Alcúdia heaves with day-trippers i
the summer.

The Santuari de la Victòria

A steep and rocky promontory pokes a wild finger out into the ocea
just beyond Alcúdia, its northern shore traversed by a narrow roa
which begins at the easternmost intersection on Alcúdia's ring roa
This promontory road slices past the suburban villas of **BONAIR**
before emerging into more scenic terrain, offering fine views of th
Badia de Pollença as it bumps over the steep, pine-clad ridges tha
fringe the coast. After 4.3km, the road slips past the barracks-lik
120-bed **youth hostel**, the *Albergue Juvenil d'Alcúdia* (☎ & fa
971 545 395; ①; March–Sept), where school parties predominat
and vacant beds are a rarity. There's precious little point in turnin
up here on the off-chance, and even reservations need to be mad
well in advance. There's no public transport.

About 1km further along the headland, a turning on the righ
climbs 500m up the wooded hillside to the **Santuari de la Victòri**
a fortress-like church built in the seventeenth century to hold an
protect a crude but much-venerated statue of the Virgin. It was a ne
essary precaution: this part of the coast was especially prone t
attack and, even with these defences, pirates still stole the statu
twice, though on both occasions the islanders eventually got it back
The church is reverentially gloomy inside, its most noteworthy fea
tures being its barrel vaulting and the extravagant Baroque alta
piece framing the statue. The adjacent **restaurant**, the *Mirador d
la Victòria* (reservations required; ☎971 547 173; closed Mon
occupies a magnificent location with sweeping sea views, which ca
be enjoyed from an expansive terrace. The food is first-rate to
guinea fowl and chicken are two specialities.

The Santuari is also the starting point for **hikes** further along th
promontory, whose severe peaks are dotted with ruined defensiv
installations, including a watchtower and an old gun emplacemen
The obvious draw is the 315-metre **Penya Roja** mountain, fro
whose summit there are more great views. The outward part of th
hike, leading up through woods and beneath steep cliffs, is quit
strenuous, ascending 160m in 2.5km, and takes about two hour

return is by the same route. It begins on the wide and clearly sign-posted dirt road that climbs up behind the Santuari, but the later sections are on trails that require an IGN (or similar) hiking map.

Port d'Alcúdia

PORT D'ALCÚDIA, 2km south of Alcúdia, is easily the biggest and busiest of the resorts on the north coast, its myriad restaurants and café-bars attracting crowds from a seemingly interminable string of high-rise hotels and apartment buildings. This is not, however, to equate this resort with some of its seamier rivals, for the tower blocks are relatively well distributed, the streets are neat and tidy and there's a prosperous and easygoing air, with families particularly well catered for. Predictably, the daytime focus is the **beach**, a superb arc of pine-studded golden sand which stretches south for 10km from the two purpose-built jetties of Port d'Alcúdia's combined marina, cruise boat and fishing harbour. About 500m east of the marina along the headland lies the **commercial port**, Mallorca's largest container terminal after Palma.

Arrival, information and accommodation

Port d'Alcúdia acts as northern Mallorca's summertime transport hub, with **bus** services to and from Palma, Port de Sóller, Artà, Cala Millor and Cala Rajada, as well as neighbouring towns and resorts. Most local and long-distance bus services travel the length of **Carretera d'Artà**, the main drag, which slices right through the resort, running broadly parallel to the bay. The main **tourist office**

Port d'Alcúdia has no bus station. Buses drop off at clearly signed stops along the main road, Carretera d'Artà.

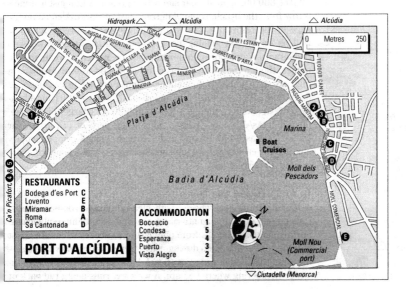

RESTAURANTS
Bodega d'es Port **C**
Lovento **E**
Miramar **B**
Roma **A**
Sa Cantonada **D**

ACCOMMODATION
Boccacio **1**
Condesa **5**
Esperanza **4**
Puerto **3**
Vista Alegre **2**

PORT D'ALCÚDIA

The Badia d'Alcúdia

(Easter–Oct Mon–Sat 9am–7pm; ☎971 892 615) is situated on Carretera d'Artà about 2km south round the bay from the marina. The office can supply all sorts of information, most usefully free maps marked with all the resort's hotels and apartments.

In season, vacant **rooms** are few and far between, but there's a vague chance of finding something amongst the low-priced *hostals* clustered behind the marina in the oldest and tattiest part of the resort. The least expensive rooms here – basic, no-frills affairs – are provided by the mundanely modern *Puerto*, c/Teodor Canet 29 (☎ & fax 971 545 447; ⑥; April–Oct), and the *Vista Alegre*, which at least has the advantage of being on the seafront and open year-round, Passeig Marítim 22 (☎971 547 347; ③).

In winter most of the hotels and *hostals* close down, but in the shoulder seasons it's sometimes possible to get a good deal at one of the plusher **hotels**. Places to try include the whopping 300-room, three-star *Boccacio*, near the tourist office at Avgda Pere Mas i Reus 3 (☎971 891 375, fax 971 891 987; ⑦; Feb–Oct), and the comparable, though more luxurious, five-star *Playa Esperanza*, about 4km south of the marina along the seashore (☎971 890 568, fax 971 890 938; ⑨; Feb to early Nov). Both have the full range of facilities, including swimming pools and sports facilities, but the *Esperanza* has the advantage of a beachside location, as does the *Hotel Condesa de la Bahía* (☎971 890 120, fax 971 890 049; ⑥), a huge L-shaped complex about 3km south of the marina, open year-round with every facility from bike rental to a children's playground.

There's also the possibility of **camping** at *Sun Club Picafort* (☎971 860 002), an all-year site with a great location just a stone's throw from the beach, some 9km southeast of Port d'Alcúdia on the edge of the resort of Ca'n Picafort. It has five hundred pitches, as well as its own swimming pool, tennis courts, supermarket and restaurant. Watersports equipment can be rented, as can mobile homes, though these usually need to be booked well in advance. In high season (mid-June to mid-Sept) tent-pitching prices begin at 321ptas/€1.93 for a small tent and rise to 750ptas/€4.51 for a family tent. In addition, there's a 3397ptas/€20.42 charge for the site, plus 550ptas/€3.31 per person, plus seven percent IVA tax. A car costs 750ptas/€4.51 extra, and there are small supplementary charges for electrical hook-ups and hot water. Off-season rates are around 25 percent less.

In and around the town

A tourist "**train**" (on wheels, with clearly marked roadside stops) runs up and down the length of the resort at hourly intervals, transporting sunbaked bodies from one part of the beach to another. Not that there's very much to distinguish anywhere from anywhere else – the palm-thatched *balnearios* (beach bars) are a great help in actually remembering where you are. A walkway runs along the back of

Ferries to Menorca

Iscomar (☎902 119 128) operates **car ferries** from Port d'Alcúdia to Ciutadella on Menorca once or twice daily. Journey time is three and a half hours, and the one-way passenger fare is 4400ptas/€26.44. Vehicles up to 4.5m in length cost an additional 7800ptas/ €46.88, but remember that local car rental firms do not allow their vehicles to leave Mallorca.

the beach, which is usually more crowded to the north. Just as crowded, and located a kilometre or so inland along Avinguda del Tucan, is the much-vaunted **Hidropark**, a gigantic pool complex with all sorts of flumes and chutes (May–Oct daily 10am–6pm; 2200ptas/€13.25).

There are similar water parks at S'Arenal (see p.111) and Magaluf (see p.115).

There's a superabundance of **car, moped and bike rental** companies strung out along Carretera d'Artà. Mountain bikes work out at about 1200ptas/€7.21 per day, or 3200ptas/€19.23 for three days; cars are 4200ptas/€25.24 and 9900ptas/€59.50 respectively. Summer **boat trips**, leaving from the marina, explore the rocky, mountainous coastline to the northeast of Port d'Alcúdia: the shorter excursion travels as far as the tip of the headland, the Cap des Pinar, without venturing into the Badia de Pollença (April–Oct 3 daily; 3hr; 1800ptas/€10.82); the longer version continues round this headland and across the bay to the Platja de Formentor (May–Oct 3 weekly; 4hr; 2200ptas/€13.22).

Eating and drinking

There are dozens of **cafés** and **restaurants** in Port d'Alcúdia, and although many of them are identikit pizzerias and tourist-style places serving mediocre versions of Spanish food, the scene is on the up with an ever-increasing number of distinctive – and distinguished – exceptions.

Pizzeria Roma Restaurant, Avgda Pere Mas i Reus s/n. This is one of the more authentically Italian of Port d'Alcúdia's many pizzerias, with a wide-ranging menu offering pizzas and pastas through to crepes (which are particularly good) and steaks. It's located just off Carretera d'Artà, across and just up the street from the main tourist office.

Restaurant Lovento, c/Gabriel Roca 33 ☎971 545 048. Just away from the main tourist zone, up along the waterfront near the commercial port, this smooth and polished spot offers superb seafood at affordable prices – try the monkfish.

Restaurant Miramar, Passeig Marítim 2 ☎971 545 293. Well-established seafront restaurant serving a fine range of seafood. Main courses average about 1800ptas/€10.82.

Bodega d'es Port, c/Gabriel Roca 1. A new place on the waterfront, in between the marina and the commercial port, that is decked out in an appealing version of traditional bodega style with wide windows, wooden chairs and a stone façade. It's a great place for a drink and you can graze on a first-rate selection of *tapas*.

Restaurant Sa Cantonada, c/Gabriel Roca 7 ☎971 548 771. Not so long ago, no one in their right mind would have offered *cocina mallorquina* – traditional Mallorcan cuisine – in a resort, but mercifully things are changing. This chic little spot, situated on the waterfront in between the marina and the commercial port and decorated in a crisp permutation on traditional bodega style, proves the point with outstanding food; main courses average a very reasonable 1500–2000ptas/€9.02–€12.02.

The Parc Natural de S'Albufera

Port d'Alcúdia lies at the beginning of an intensively developed tourist zone, which takes advantage of the great swath of pine-studded sandy beach which stretches around the Badia d'Alcúdia. Some lessons have been learnt from earlier developments – there are more recreational facilities and at least some of the coast has been left unscathed – but first impressions are primarily of concrete and glass. The beach and the sky-rises end on the outskirts of **CA'N PICAFORT**, once an important fishing port; its harbour-marina still preserves vestiges of its earlier function but today the town is an uninteresting suburban sprawl.

In this unpromising environment, the 2000-acre **Parc Natural de S'Albufera** (daily: April–Sept 9am–7pm; Oct–March 9am–5pm; free), a segment of pristine wetland on the west side of Ca'n Picafort, makes a wonderful change. Swampland once extended round much of the bay, but large-scale reclamation began in the nineteenth century, when a British company dug a network of channels and installed a steam engine to pump the water out. These endeavours were prompted by a desire to eradicate malaria – then the scourge of the local population – as much as by the need for more farmland. Further drainage schemes accompanied the frantic tourist boom of the 1960s, and only in the last decade has the Balearic government recognized the ecological importance of the wetland and organized a park to protect what little remains.

The **park entrance** is clearly signposted on the C712, about 6km southeast of Port d'Alcúdia's marina. From the entrance, a country lane leads just over 1km inland to the reception centre, **Sa Roca** (daily 9am–1pm & 2–7pm; Oct–March closes 5.30pm; free; ☎971 892 250). Here you can pick up a free map, a permit and a list of birds you might see. There's a small wildlife display here too and an adjacent building houses a second flora and fauna identity parade. Note that you can't drive down the country lane; the best bet is to **cycle** here or take a **bus** to the entrance and walk. (Buses from Port d'Alcúdia to Ca'n Picafort and points southeast stop close to the entrance.) If you do bring a vehicle you'll have to find a parking space near the entrance, either in the sidestreets or at the conspicuous *Hotel Parc Naturel*, where there's a dedicated parking area for S'Albufera visitors. The hotel is located a few metres east of – and opposite – the park entrance.

Footpaths and cycle trails head out from Sa Roca to explore the reedy, watery tract beyond. It's a superb habitat, where ten well-appointed hides allow excellent **birdwatching** – the best on the island. Over 200 different types of birds have been spotted, including resident wetland-loving birds from the crake, warbler and tern families; autumn and/or springtime migrants such as grebes, herons, cranes, plovers and godwits; and wintering egrets and sandpipers. Such rich pickings attract birds of prey in their scores, especially kestrels and harriers. The open ground edging the reed beds supports many different **wild flowers**, the most striking of which are the orchids that bloom during April and May.

The Badia d'Alcúdia

For more on Mallorca's birdlife, see p.251.

Muro and around

From the C712 on the west side of Ca'n Picafort, a gentle country road heads west across a pancake-flat, windmill-studded hinterland to reach the hilltop town of **MURO**, a sleepy little place dotted with big old town houses built by wealthy landowners. There's a big bash here on January 16 at the **Revetla de Sant Antoni Abat** (Eve of St Antony's Day), when locals gather round bonfires to drink and dance, tucking into specialities like sausages and eel pies (*espinagades*), made with eels from the nearby marshes of S'Albufera. Quite what St Antony – an Egyptian hermit who spent most of his long life in the desert resisting his urges – would have made of these high jinks it's hard to say. There again, he certainly wouldn't have been overwhelmed by temptation if he had stuck around Muro for the rest of the year.

St Antony (251–356) is known as the father of monasticism for founding the first ascetic Christian community.

The Town

Long distance **buses** from Palma as well as local services from Ca'n Picafort and Port d'Alcúdia pull in close to Muro's handsome main square, Plaça Constitució, an attractive open area flanked by old stone houses. The square is shadowed by the domineering church of **St Joan Baptista**, a real hotchpotch of architectural styles, its monumental Gothic lines uneasily modified by the sweeping sixteenth-century arcades above the aisles. A slender arch connects the church to the adjacent **belfry**, an imposing seven-storey construction partly designed as a watchtower; sometimes it's possible to go to the top, where the views out over the coast are superb – and sometimes it isn't. The church's cavernous interior holds a mighty vaulted roof and an immense altarpiece, a flashy extravaganza of columns, parapets and tiers in a folksy rendition of the Baroque.

From the main square, it's a couple of minutes' walk east to the **Museu Etnològic**, c/Major 15 (April–Sept Tues–Sat 10am–2pm & 5–8pm, Sun 10am–1pm; Oct–March Tues–Sat 10am–1pm & 4–6pm, Sun 10am–1pm; 300ptas/€1.80). This is surely one of the least visited museums on the island: the custodians seem positively amazed when a visitor shows up. It occupies a rambling old mansion and showcases a motley assortment of local bygones, from old agricultural implements, pottery and apothecary jars through to Mallorcan

bagpipes and traditional costumes. Amongst the agricultural equipment there's a broken-down example of a mule- or donkey-driven
water wheel, a *noria*. Introduced by the Moors, these were common
features of the Mallorcan landscape for hundreds of years, though
there are few of them left today. Among the pottery, look out for the
siurels, miniature green- and red-painted figurines created in a naive
style. Now debased as a mass-produced tourist trinket, they were
originally made as whistles – hence the spout with the hole – shaped
in the form of animals, humans and mythological or imaginary figures.

That's just about it for Muro, though on a hot summer's day you'll
be glad of a drink at one of the **cafés** around the main square. Best
of the bunch is *Los Arcos*, a neat modern little place with a good
range of inexpensive *tapas*; it's located at the back of a mini-square,
just off Plaça Constitució and across from the church.

Sa Pobla

From Muro, it's just 4km northwest to the dusty little agricultural
town of **SA POBLA**, whose straightforward gridiron of old streets is
at its prettiest in the main square – the Plaça Constitució – which is
the site of a busy Sunday morning **market**. Also of interest is **Can
Planes**, c/Antoni Maura 6 (Tues–Sat 10am–2pm & 4–8pm, Sun
10am–2pm; 300ptas/€1.80), a late nineteenth-century mansion
which has been turned into a cultural centre incorporating a contemporary art gallery and toy museum. The mansion is poorly signed
and can be hard to find – it's located at the north end of c/Antoni
Maura (which runs north–south across the west side of the town centre), close to its intersection with Carretera Inca, the main road to
Inca. The gallery's permanent collection features the work of
Mallorcan artists and foreign artists resident on the island since the
1970s and there is an ambitious programme of temporary exhibitions too. Upstairs, the toy museum boasts an intriguing assortment
of nineteenth- and early to mid-twentieth-century toys and games –
some four thousand exhibits in all, from miniature rocking horses
and carousels to baffling board games.

Travel details

Buses

Alcúdia to: Ca'n Picafort (May–Oct every 15min; Nov–April 11 daily; 30min);
Lluc (May–Oct Mon–Sat 2 daily; 1hr 10min); Palma (May–Oct Mon–Sat hourly,
5 on Sun; Nov–April Mon–Sat 5 daily, 3 on Sun; 1hr 5min); Platja de Formentor
(May–Oct Mon–Sat 2 daily; 35min); Pollença (May–Oct every 15min;
Nov–April 11 daily; 30min); Port d'Alcúdia (May–Oct every 15min; Nov–April
11 daily; 15min); Port de Pollença (May–Oct every 15min; Nov–April 11 daily;
20min); Port de Sóller (May–Oct Mon–Sat 2 daily; 2hr).

Cala Sant Vicenç to: Pollença (3–5 daily; 15min); Port de Pollença (3–5 daily; 20min).

Ca'n Picafort to: Alcúdia (May–Oct every 15min; Nov–April 11 daily; 30min); Lluc (May–Oct Mon–Sat 2 daily; 1hr 45min); Muro (2–3 daily; 10min); Palma (2–5 daily; 1hr); Pollença (May–Oct every 15min; Nov–April 11 daily; 30min); Platja de Formentor (May–Oct Mon–Sat 2 daily; 50min); Port d'Alcúdia (May–Oct every 15min; Nov–April 11 daily; 20min); Port de Pollença (May–Oct every 15min; Nov–April 11 daily; 1hr); Port de Sóller (May–Oct Mon–Sat 2 daily; 2hr 30min); Porto Cristo (May–Oct Mon–Sat 3 daily; 50min).

Lluc to: Alcúdia (May–Oct Mon–Sat 2 daily; 1hr 10min); Ca'n Picafort (May–Oct Mon–Sat 2 daily; 1hr 45min); Palma (1–2 daily; 1hr); Pollença (May–Oct Mon–Sat 2 daily; 50min); Port d'Alcúdia (May–Oct Mon–Sat 2 daily; 1hr 15min); Port de Pollença (May–Oct Mon–Sat 2 daily; 55min); Port de Sóller (May–Oct Mon–Sat 2 daily; 1hr 15min).

Muro to: Ca'n Picafort (2–3 daily; 10min); Palma (2–8 daily; 50min); Port d'Alcúdia (2–3 daily; 20min); Sa Pobla (2–8 daily; 10min).

Platja de Formentor to: Alcúdia (May–Oct Mon–Sat 2 daily; 35min); Palma (May–Oct Mon–Sat 1 daily; 1hr 15min); Port d'Alcúdia (May–Oct Mon–Sat 2 daily; 25min); Port de Pollença (May–Oct Mon–Sat 1 daily; 20min).

Pollença to: Alcúdia (May–Oct every 15min; Nov–April 11 daily; 30min); Cala Sant Vicenç (3–5 daily; 15min); Ca'n Picafort (May–Oct every 15min; Nov–April 11 daily; 30min); Lluc (May–Oct Mon–Sat 2 daily; 50min); Palma (3–5 daily; 1hr); Port d'Alcúdia (May–Oct every 15min; Nov–April 11 daily; 25min); Port de Pollença (6–16 daily; 10min); Port de Sóller (May–Oct Mon–Sat 2 daily; 1hr 45min).

Port d'Alcúdia to: Alcúdia (May–Oct every 15min; Nov–April 11 daily; 15min); Cala Rajada (May–Oct Mon–Sat 2 daily; 40min); Ca'n Picafort (May–Oct every 15min; Nov–April 11 daily; 20min); Lluc (May–Oct Mon–Sat 2 daily; 1hr 15min); Muro (2–3 daily; 20min); Palma (May–Oct Mon–Sat hourly, 5 on Sun; Nov–April Mon–Sat 5 daily, 3 on Sun; 1hr 10min); Platja de Formentor (May–Oct Mon–Sat 2 daily; 25min); Pollença (May–Oct every 15min; Nov–April 11 daily; 25min); Port de Pollença (May–Oct every 15min; Nov–April 11 daily; 20min); Port de Sóller (May–Oct Mon–Sat 2 daily; 2hr 5min); Porto Cristo (May–Oct Mon–Sat 3 daily; 1hr).

Port de Pollença to: Alcúdia (May–Oct every 15min; Nov–April 11 daily; 20min); Cala Sant Vicenç (3–5 daily; 20min); Ca'n Picafort (May–Oct every 15min; Nov–April 11 daily; 1hr); Lluc (May–Oct Mon–Sat 2 daily; 55min); Palma (3–5 daily; 1hr 10min); Platja de Formentor (May–Oct Mon–Sat 2 daily; 20min); Pollença (6–16 daily; 10min); Port d'Alcúdia (May–Oct every 15min; Nov–April 11 daily; 20min); Port de Sóller (May–Oct Mon–Sat 2 daily; 1hr 50min).

Port de Sóller to: Alcúdia (May–Oct Mon–Sat 2 daily; 2hr); Ca'n Picafort (May–Oct Mon–Sat 2 daily; 2hr 30min); Lluc (May–Oct Mon–Sat 2 daily; 1hr 15min); Palma (via the tunnel: Mon–Fri 5 daily, 2 on Sat, no Sun service; 35min; via Valldemossa: 5 daily; 55min); Pollença (May–Oct Mon–Sat 2 daily; 1hr 45min); Port d'Alcúdia (May–Oct Mon–Sat 2 daily; 2hr 5min); Port de Pollença (May–Oct Mon–Sat 2 daily; 1hr 50min).

Chapter 4

Eastern Mallorca

For most visitors, the hinterland of **eastern Mallorca** – largely comprising the fertile central plain **Es Pla**, bounded to the west by the mountainous Serra de Tramuntana and to the east by the Serres de Llevant, the hilly range that shadows the coast – is simply a monotonous interlude between airport and resort. However, this is a complete historical turn-around. Until the twentieth century, Es Pla largely defined Mallorca: the majority of the island's inhabitants lived here, it produced enough food to meet almost every domestic requirement, and Palma's gentry were reliant on Es Pla estates for their income. Mallorca's medieval kings constructed hilltop fortresses along the Serres de Llevant to defend "The Plain" from marauding pirates, leaving the eastern shoreline an unprotected area fit only for a smattering of insignificant fishing villages and tiny ports. And this situation persisted until the tourist boom stood everything on its head. From the 1960s onwards, the developers simply bypassed Es Pla to focus on the picturesque coves of the east coast, where they constructed a long string of brash resorts.

You'll find accounts of the northern Es Pla towns elsewhere – for Binissalem, see p.134; for Muro, see p.193.

The towns of Es Pla have largely chosen to ignore the tourist industry and, although things are beginning to change, even now very few put themselves out to attract visitors. There's hardly anywhere to stay, restaurants are thin on the ground and tourist offices are even rarer. As a consequence, visiting the region is mostly a matter of day-trips – and, arguably, none the worse for that. It's here that you can get the full flavour of an older, agricultural Mallorca, whose softly hued landscapes are patterned with olive orchards, chunky farmhouses and country towns of low, whitewashed houses huddled beneath outsized churches. Admittedly, there's precious little to distinguish one settlement from another, but there are exceptions, most notably **Sineu**, which has a particularly imposing parish church, and **Petra**, with its clutch of sights celebrating the life and times of the eighteenth-century Franciscan monk and explorer Junipero Serra. Other sights worth making a beeline for are the impressive monastery perched on the summit of **Puig Randa** and, in the Serres de Llevant, both the hilltop shrine at **Artà** and the delightful medieval

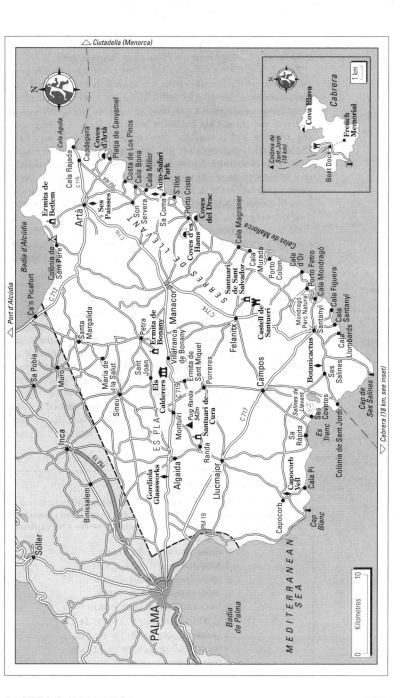

castle at **Capdepera**. All these destinations are readily accessible from the C715, which runs the 70km from Palma to Artà.

The ancient fishing villages of the **east coast** have mostly been swallowed up within mega-resorts, whose endless high rises and villa complexes blotch the land for miles. There are, however, a couple of enjoyable seaside towns which have avoided the worst excesses of concrete and glass: **Cala Rajada**, a lively holiday spot bordered by fine beaches and a beautiful pine-shrouded coastline, and **Cala Figuera**, which surrounds a lovely, steep-sided cove. Different again is tiny **Cala Mondragó**, for here development has been stalled and a slice of coast protected by the creation of a park – a welcome move, albeit rather late in the day. The east coast also boasts the cave systems of **Coves d'Artà** and **Coves del Drac**, justifiably famous for their extravagant stalactites and stalagmites.

On the **south coast**, the scenery changes again with hills and coves giving way to sparse flatlands, whose only star turn is the port-cum-resort of **Colònia de Sant Jordi,** from where boat trips leave for the scrubby remoteness of the fauna-rich island of **Cabrera**.

Practicalities

Given the difficulty of finding a room in the coastal package resorts and the general dearth of **accommodation** in the interior, advance reservations are a good idea – and pretty much essential in the height of the season. Bear in mind also that this region holds four of the six island **monasteries** offering rooms – and they usually have space. There are simple, inexpensive but characterful lodgings at the Santuari de Nostra Senyora de Cura, on Puig Randa near Algaida; the Ermita de Sant Salvador, outside Felanitx; and the Ermita de Nostra Senyora de Bonany, near Petra. The Ermita de Sant Miquel, near Montuïri, also offers rooms, and these are much smarter (and more expensive).

Accommodation price codes

All the accommodation prices in this book have been coded using the categories below, which correspond to each establishment's **least expensive double room** in high season, excluding special offers. For a full explanation of these codes, see p.39.

① Under 3000ptas/Under €18.03

② 3000–4000ptas/ €18.03–€24.04

③ 4000–6000ptas/€24.04–€36.06

④ 6000–8000ptas/€36.06–€48.08

⑤ 8000–10,000ptas/€48.08–€60.10

⑥ 10,000–14,000ptas/€60.10–€84.14

⑦ 14,000–20,000ptas/€84.14–€120.20

⑧ 20,000–25,000ptas/€120.20–€150.25

⑨ Over 25,000ptas/Over €150.25

Travelling by **bus** presents problems. Palma has direct links with almost every resort and town, but services between the towns of Es Pla are virtually non-existent, while those along the coast are patchy. Broadly speaking, you'll manage to get around most easily in the north between Cala Rajada, Artà and Cala Millor, and to the south between Cala d'Or, Cala Figuera and Colònia de Sant Jordi. Elsewhere, you'll be struggling without a car.

East from Palma to Artà

The C715, which whisks through the agricultural landscape due east from Palma, is lined with roadside tourist attractions. The most successful of these are the **Gordiola Glassworks**, which houses a superb museum, and **Els Calderers**, a big old country house which was once the focus of a prosperous estate but is now a museum illustrating *hacienda* life in the nineteenth century. The third choice, the pearl-making factory of **Perlas Majorica** at Manacor, lags some way behind. By far the most interesting detours from the highway are to the monastery surmounting **Puig Randa** and to **Sineu**, once the site of a royal palace and now the prettiest town on the plain. Neither should **Artà**, tucked away amongst the Serres de Llevant, be overlooked, not only for its delightful location, but also for its proximity to the fascinating Talayotic settlement of **Ses Paisses** and the laidback mini-resort of **Colònia de Sant Pere**.

Buses from Palma to Manacor and Artà are fast and frequent and there's also a reasonably regular service to Montuïri, Sineu and Petra. As for **accommodation**, both Artà and Sineu have one excellent hotel each, and there are monastery rooms on Puig Randa, at the Ermita de Sant Miquel near Montuïri and at the Ermita de Bonany near Petra.

The Gordiola Glassworks

Some 19km east of Palma along the C715 is the **Gordiola Glassworks** (Ca'n Gordiola; April–Oct Mon–Sat 9am–8pm, Sun 9am–1pm; Nov–March Mon–Sat 9am–1.30pm & 3–7pm, Sun 9am–1pm; free), which occupies a conspicuous castle-like building whose crenellated walls and clumsy loggias date from the 1960s. Don't be put off by its appearance, however, or by the herd of tourist coaches parked outside. For a start, you can watch highly skilled glassblowers in action, practising their precise art in a gloomy hall designed to resemble a medieval church and illuminated by glowing furnaces. Guides explain the techniques involved – the fusion of silica, soda and lime at a temperature of 1100°C – and you can hang around for as long as you like. Perhaps inevitably, this is all part of a public relations exercise intended to push you towards the adjacent **gift shops**. Here, amongst a massive assortment of glass and ceram-

A guidebook to
the museum
costs
950ptas/€5.71
from the gift
shop.

ic items, you'll find everything from the most abysmal tourist tat to works of great delicacy, notably green-tinted chandeliers of traditional Mallorcan design priced anywhere between 180,000ptas/ €1081.82 and 470,000ptas/€2824.76.

The gift shops are one thing, but the **museum**, tucked away on the top floor, is quite another. The owners of the glassworks, the Gordiola family, have been in business in Mallorca since the early eighteenth century, when the first of the line, Gordiola Rigal, arrived from the Spanish mainland. Since then, seven successive generations have accumulated an extraordinary collection of glassware: each of the museum's fifty-odd cabinets is devoted to a particular theme or country and each is labelled.

On display are the earliest Gordiola work, green-coloured jugs of a frothy consistency, where the shade and the trapped air bubbles were unwanted. Heated by wood and coal, the original hoop-shaped furnaces had windows through which works in progress could be rotated. With such limited technology, it was impossible to maintain a consistently high temperature, so the glass could neither be clarified nor cleared of its last air bubbles. Aware of these deficiencies, the next of the line, Bernardo Gordiola, spent years in Venice cultivating the leading glassmakers of the day, and the results of what he learnt can be seen in the same display case. He developed a style of Mallorcan-made jugs decorated with *laticinos*, glass strips wrapped round the object in the Venetian manner, and, in general, improved the quality of the glass. Amongst later Gordiola work, kitchen- and tableware predominate – bottles, vases, jugs and glasses – in a variety of shades, of which green remains the most distinctive. There's also a tendency to extrapolate functional designs into imaginative, ornamental pieces, ranging from hideous fish-shaped receptacles designed for someone's mantlepiece to the most poetic of vases.

Yet Gordiola glassware is just a fraction of the collection. Other cabinets feature pieces from every corner of the globe, beginning with finds from Classical Greece, the Nile and the Euphrates. There's also an exquisite sample of early Islamic glassware, Spanish and Chinese opalescents, and superb Venetian vases dating from the seventeenth and eighteenth centuries. More modern items includes goblets from Germany and Austria, devotional pieces from Poland, traditional Caithness crystal from Scotland, and a striking melange of Norwegian Art Nouveau glasswork. The museum also exhibits decorative items from cultures where glass was unknown – an eclectic ensemble of pre-Columbian pieces worked in clay, quartz and obsidian, along with the zoomorphic and anthropomorphic basalt figures characteristic of the Sahara.

Algaida and around

ALGAIDA, just off the main highway 2km east of the glassworks, is typical of the small agricultural towns that sprinkle Mallorca's central plain – low, whitewashed houses fanning out from an old Gothic-Baroque church. There's nothing remarkable about the place, but if you're travelling the C715 you'll need to pass through here to reach **Puig Randa**, the highest of a slim band of hills on the north side of Llucmajor. Beginning around 3km south of Algaida, the road to the 542-metre summit – a well-surfaced but serpentine affair, some 5km long – starts by climbing through the hamlet of **RANDA**, a pretty little place of old stone houses harbouring a comfortable three-star hotel-residencia, *Es Reco de Randa* (☎971 660 997, fax 971 662 558, *esreco@fehm.es*; ⑧). The hotel, with just fourteen rooms and an outdoor swimming pool, is usually booked up months in advance during the summer, but there's often a vacancy out of season. It also has a delightful terraced restaurant, where the specialities include roast lamb and suckling pig.

East from Palma to Artà

Llucmajor and the road to Cala Pi are described on p.231.

Puig Randa

The top of **Puig Randa** is flat enough to accommodate a substantial walled complex, the **Santuari de Nostra Senyora de Cura** ("Hermitage of Our Lady of Cura" – Cura is the name of the upper part of Puig Randa). Entry is through a seventeenth-century portal, but most of the buildings beyond are plain and modern, the work of the present incumbents, Franciscan monks who arrived in 1913 after the site had lain abandoned for decades. The scholar and missionary **Ramon Llull** founded the original hermitage in the thirteenth century, and it was here that he prepared his acolytes for their missions to Asia and Africa. Succeeding generations of Franciscans turned the site into a centre of religious learning, and the scholastic tradition was maintained by a grammar school, which finally fizzled out in 1826. The Llull connection makes the monastery an important place of pilgrimage, especially for the **Bendición de los Frutos** (Blessing of the Crops), held on the fourth Sunday after Easter.

For more on Ramon Llull, see p.91 & p.242.

Nothing remains of Llull's foundation. The oldest surviving building is the quaintly gabled **chapel**, parts of which date from the 1660s. Situated to the right of the entrance, the chapel has a familiar, domestic ambience inside, its narrow, truncated nave spanned by a barrel-vaulted roof. Next door, in the old school, there's a modest **museum** (donation requested) with a collection of ecclesiastical bric-à-brac and a few interesting old photos taken by the Franciscans before they rebuilt the place. It only takes a few minutes to look around and soon you'll be moving on to the nearby terrace **café**, which offers average food and superb views out across the island. There are a couple of other belvederes on the hilltop, plus an information office by the main entrance where you can get free maps and fix yourself up with a **room** in the guest quarters – a self-contained, modern block of basic bedrooms (advance bookings on ☎971 120 260; ①).

There are two other, less significant sanctuaries on the lower slopes of Puig Randa. Heading back down the hill, past the radio masts, it's a couple of kilometres to the easily missable sharp left turn for the **Santuari de Sant Honorat**, which comprises a tiny church and a few conventual buildings of medieval provenance. Back on the main summit road, a further 1.2km down the hill, is the more appealing third and final monastery, the **Santuari de Gràcia**, which is approached through a signposted gateway on the left and along a short asphalt road. Founded in the fifteenth century, the white-washed walls of this tiny sanctuary are tucked underneath a severe cliff face, which throngs with nesting birds. The simple barrel-vaulted church boasts some handsome majolica tiles, but it's the panoramic view of Es Pla's rolling farmland that holds the eye.

Montuïri and around

Travelling east of Algaida on the C715, you'll soon reach the giant-sized Munper leather shop and then the **Perlas Orquidea factory**, where artificial pearls are made up from glass globules, an industry for which Mallorca is internationally famous. The sales rooms are extensive and you can glimpse aspects of the production process, though the factory tours of the Perlas Majorica plant in Manacor are a tad more illuminating. Better still, leave the C715 and pop into **MONTUÏRI**, a gentle sweep of pastel-shaded stone houses on a low hill immediately north of the main road. In the heart of the town, it's worth taking a peek at the largely Gothic church of **Sant Bartomeu**, an imposing pile plonked next to the small main square that is the possessor of several fine Baroque retables.

*Manacor,
further east on
the main road,
is covered on
p.206.*

If you stay on the C715 east of Montuïri, the next place of interest is the fascinating old country house of Els Calderers (see p.205). However, there are a couple of options for detours off the road at this point. From Montuïri, you can follow a side road north to Sineu and Petra (see opposite), or alternatively you can take the country lane, signposted south off the C715 just east of Montuïri, up to the hilltop **Ermita de Sant Miquel** (☎971 646 314). From here, there are wide views over Es Pla, and the monastery has a café-restaurant and a handful of attractively refurbished monastic cells with shared bathrooms (⑥). There are more panoramic views nearby at another former monastery, the **Santuari de Monti-Sion** (☎971 647 185), which overlooks the unassuming country town of **PORRERES**, 12km southeast of Montuïri. Porreres built its wealth on wine, apricots and almonds, and the town once rivalled Palma, a heyday recalled by its whopping church. On the southwest edge of Porreres, a narrow country road snakes up to the monastery, threading through almond orchards and ultimately a light dusting of pine trees. From the monastery car park, a wide flight of steps leads to the deep arches of the main entrance, beyond which the central courtyard is flanked by an arcaded gallery and shadowed by a chapel, a cheerless affair dating from 1513. Until fairly recently, there was a school here and the old refectory now houses a simple bar-restaurant, whilst the surrounding monastic cells provide **group accommodation** – a minimum of 22 people at 1000ptas/€6.01 per night for a bunk bed (without linen) in one large room.

Sineu and Petra

SINEU, 12km north of Montuïri, is undoubtedly the most interesting of the ancient agricultural towns of Es Pla. Glued to a hill at the geographical centre of the island, the town had obvious strategic advantages for the independent kings of fourteenth-century Mallorca. Jaume II built a royal palace here; his asthmatic successor Sancho came to take the upland air; and the last of the dynasty, Jaume III, slept in Sineu the night before he was defeated and killed at the battle of Llucmajor by Pedro of Aragón. The new Aragonese monarchs had no need of the Sineu palace, which disappeared long ago, but former pretensions survive in the massive stone facade of **Nostra Senyora de los Angeles**, the grandest parish church on the island. Built in the thirteenth century, the church was extensively remodelled three hundred years later, but the majestic simplicity of the original Gothic design is still plain to see – though it's in a poor state of repair. At the side, a single-span arch connects with the colossal free-standing bell tower, and at the front, at the top of the steps, a big, modern and aggressive statue of a winged lion – the emblem of the town's patron, St Mark – stands guard, courtesy of Franco's cronies.

Beside the church is the unassuming main square, Sa Plaça, where you'll find the first of two excellent, traditional Mallorcan **bar-restaurants**, the *Celler Ca'n Font* (☎971 520 313), which serves hearty, inexpensive snacks from 700ptas/€4.21. The cavernous interior doubles as a wine vault, hence the enormous wooden barrels. A couple of minutes' walk away, the *Celler Es Crup*, c/Major 18 (☎971 520 187), has similar decor but a more welcoming atmosphere, and the food, if anything, is even better, with main courses at around 1000ptas/€6.01. Both places are at their busiest on Wednesdays, when the town fizzes with one of Mallorca's biggest fresh produce and livestock **markets**. Sineu also has (and this is something of a surprise) a classy **hotel**, the *Leon de Sineu*, c/Bous 129 (☎971 520 211, fax 971 855 058, *www.hotel-leon-sineu.com*; ⑦), set in a beautifully refurbished mansion five minutes' stroll from Sa Plaça: walk down the hill from the square, turn first right and keep going. The hotel's wood-beamed foyer is spacious and elegant and each of the bedrooms is tastefully furnished in an uncluttered antique style. At the back, the well-tended garden has an outdoor swimming pool and a terrace for breakfast-time; it's all quite delightful.

Petra and around

Nothing very exciting happens in **PETRA**, 11km east of Sineu, but it was the birthplace of **Junipero Serra**, the eighteenth-century

Franciscan friar who played an important role in the settlement of Spanish North America. Serra's missionary endeavours began in 1749 when he landed at Veracruz on the Gulf of Mexico. Despite a particularly unpleasant voyage, he and his band of monks promptly walked 500km to Mexico City, thereby completing the first of many mind-boggling treks. For eighteen years Serra thrashed around the remoter parts of Mexico until, entirely by chance, political machinations back in Europe saved him from obscurity. In 1768, Carlos III claimed the west coast of the North American continent for Spain and, to substantiate his claim, dispatched a small expeditionary force of soldiers and monks north. Serra happened to be in the right place at the right time, and was assigned to lead the priests. Even by Serra's standards, the walk from Mexico City to California was pretty daunting, but almost all the force survived to reach the Pacific Ocean somewhere near the present US–Mexico border in early 1769. Over the next decade, Serra and his small party of priests set about converting the Native Americans of coastal California to the Catholic faith, and established a string of nine missions along the Pacific coast, including San Diego and San Francisco. Pope John Paul II beatified Serra in 1988.

There's a statue of Serra at Palma's Basílica de Sant Francesc – see p.89.

Petra makes a reasonable hand of its connection with Serra. In the upper part of town, on c/Major, is the chunky church of **Sant Bernat**, beside which – down a narrow side street – lies a modest sequence of majolica panels honouring Serra's life and missionary work. This simple tribute is backed up by a self-effacing **museum** in a pleasant old house at the end of this same side street (Mon–Fri 9am–8pm; donation requested), with several rooms devoted to Serra's cult: the honours paid to him, the books written about him, and the paintings of him. Another room focuses on Serra's work in California, with photos and models of his foundations. Three doors up the street, at no. 6, is the humble whitewashed stone and brick **house** where he was born (same hours).

The museum and house are sometimes locked, but there are instructions posted outside explaining how to collect the key from the custodian.

Other than that, there's not too much reason to hang around – especially as Els Calderers (see opposite) is just 10km south – but Petra does have a good old-fashioned **café-restaurant**, *Es Celler*, c/Hospital 46 (☎971 561 056), where they serve quality Mallorcan dishes featuring rabbit, pigeon and pig.

Some 5km southwest of Petra is the hilltop **Ermita de Nostra Senyora de Bonany**, which offers extensive views over Es Pla. To get there, take the Felanitx road out of Petra and, on the edge of the village, watch for the sign. The monastery is at the end of a bumpy, four-kilometre country lane, and takes its name from events in 1609 when desperate locals gathered here at the chapel to pray for rain. Shortly afterwards, the drought broke and the ensuing harvest was a good one – hence *bon any* ("good year"). The prettiest feature of the complex is the **chapel**, which is approached along an avenue of cypress and palm trees and comes complete with a rose window, twin towers and a little cupola. The monastery's conspicuous stone cross was erected in honour of Junipero Serra, who left here bound for the Americas in 1749. It also has five simple double **rooms** (☎971 561 101; ②). There's hot water (in one bathroom) and cooking facilities, but you have to bring your own food and bedding.

Els Calderers

Els Calderers (daily: April–Sept 10am–6pm; Oct–March 10am–5pm; 1000ptas/€6.01) is a charming country house dating mostly from the eighteenth century that bears witness to the wealth and influence once enjoyed by the island's landed gentry. The house is tucked away at the end of a country lane 2km north of – and clearly signposted from – the C715 between Montuïri and Villafranca de Bonany. It was built for the Veri family as the focus of a large estate, which produced a mixed bag of agricultural produce. The main cash crop was originally grapes, though this changed in the 1870s when phylloxera, a greenfly-like aphid, destroyed Mallorca's (and most of Europe's) vineyards. The Veris switched to cereals, and at the beginning of the twentieth century were at the forefront of efforts to modernize Mallorcan agriculture, much to the consternation of some of their more stick-in-the-mud neighbours, and to the horror of a workforce used to more traditional methods.

Flanked by a pair of crumpled-looking lions, the entrance to the **house** leads to a sequence of handsome rooms surrounding a cool courtyard with a well. All are kitted out with antique furniture, *objets d'art* and family portraits, and each has a clearly defined function, from the dainty music room to the hunting room, with assorted stuffed animal heads, and the master's office, with big armchairs and a much-polished desk. You can also see the family's tiny chapel (like every landed family on the island, the Veris had a live-in priest) and there's more religious material upstairs in the assorted prints that line the walls. They're neither original nor of good quality, but they give the flavour of the mawkish piety that characterized the island's landed class in the late nineteenth century. Attached to, but separate from, the family house are the living quarters of the *amo* (farm manager), the barn and the farmworkers' kitchen and eating area. To complete your visit, take a stroll round the animal pens, though don't expect to see much farmyard activity in the heat of the day. The animals are breeds traditionally used on Mallorcan farms, though they're here to illustrate the past rather than to be of any practical use.

It takes an hour or so to wander round the house and the adjacent animal pens, more if you stop at the simple little **café**, where they serve traditional Mallorcan snacks – the *pa amb oli* (bread rubbed with olive oil) with ham and cheese is delicious.

Manacor

MANACOR declares its business long before you arrive: vast road-side hoardings promote its furniture and **artificial pearl** factories. On the strength of these, the city has risen to become the second urban centre of Mallorca, smaller than Palma but large enough to have sprawling suburbs on all sides. It's far from compelling, but Manacor does have an industrial independence distinctly lacking elsewhere.

To catch the passing tourist trade, Manacor also musters several modern attractions, situated beside the C715 on the west side of town. The first, the **Oliv-Art** olive wood shop and museum, is more shop than museum, churning out thousands of household ornaments – oversized ashtrays and the like – stained a sticky-looking brown. Sometimes these verge on the kitsch, but mostly they're just ugly. The life-size plastic dinosaurs outside don't make things any better.

A few doors down is the first of the town's several Perlas Majorica artificial pearl shops, but skip it in favour of the company's factory, 300m further east along the main road and well signposted as the **Pearl Centre** (Mon–Fri 9am–1pm & 3–7pm, Sat & Sun 10am–1pm; free). At this main complex, you can go on a **free factory tour**, a somewhat perfunctory cruise giving just a general insight into the manufacturing process. The core of the imitation pearl is a glass globule on to which are painted many layers of a glutinous liquid primarily composed of fish scales. The finished item – anywhere between soft yellow and metallic grey – is gently polished and then included within many different types of jewellery. Artificial pearls last longer than, and are virtually indistinguishable from, the real thing, but consequently they're expensive – as you'll discover at the end of the tour when you're shepherded into the adjacent showroom and **gift shop**.

If you decide to take a peek at Manacor's busy centre, then head for the lively **main square** and be sure to try the local speciality – spicy, black pork sausage (*sobrasada de cerdo negro*).

Artà and around

Beyond Manacor the C715 veers northeast to run parallel to the coast, with the flatlands soon left behind for the easy peaks of the **Serres de Llevant**. The top end of this mountain range bunches to fill out Mallorca's northeast corner, providing a dramatic backdrop to **ARTÀ**, an ancient hill town of sun-bleached roofs clustered beneath a castellated chapel-shrine. It's a delightful scene, though at close quarters the town is something of an anticlimax – the cobweb of cramped and twisted alleys doesn't quite match the setting.

Buses to Artà from several directions, including Palma, Cala Rajada and Ca'n Picafort, stop on the C715 at the edge of the town centre. From the bus stops, it's a couple of hundred metres west to the foot of the short main street, **c/Ciutat**. If you've driven here, finding somewhere handy to **park** can be a bit awkward: try along c/Ciutat and the adjoining main square, Plaça Conqueridor.

The ten-minute trek to the **Santuari de Sant Salvador**, the panoramic shrine at the top of Artà, is a must. It's almost impossible to get lost – just keep going upwards. Follow c/Ciutat as it slices across the edge of Plaça Conqueridor, and then head straight on up to **Plaça Espanya**, a leafy little piazza that is home to the town hall. Beyond, a short stroll through streets of gently decaying mansions brings you to the gargantuan parish church of Sant Salvator. From this unremarkable pile, steep stone steps and cypress trees lead up the Via Crucis (Way of the Cross) to the *santuari*, which, in its present form, dates from the early nineteenth century, though the hilltop has been a place of pilgrimage for much longer. The Catalan soldiers of the Reconquest demolished the Moorish fort that once stood here and replaced it with a shrine accommodating an image of the Virgin Mary which they had imported with them. This edifice was, in its turn, knocked down in 1820 in a superstitious attempt to stop the spread of an epidemic that was decimating the region's population. Built a few years later, the interior of the present chapel is hardly awe-inspiring – the paintings are mediocre and the curious seventeenth-century statue behind the high altar has Jesus smiling like an imbecile – but the views out over eastern Mallorca more than compensate.

There are several **café-restaurants** along c/Ciutat, the best being *Café Parisien*, at no. 18 (☎971 835 440), a trendy little place with an outside terrace, modernist decor and tasty *tapas* and salads at reasonable prices. The *Restaurant Ca'n Balaguer* (☎971 835 003), on the other side of the street at no. 19, is a more traditional place where the emphasis is on Mallorcan dishes. Artà has one first-rate **hotel**, the *Casal d'Artà*, which occupies an immaculately restored, three-storey grandee mansion overlooking Plaça Espanya at c/Rafael Blanes 19 (☎ & fax 971 829 163; ⑥).

Ses Paisses

About 1km south of Artà lie the substantial and elegiacally rustic remains of the Talayotic village of **Ses Paisses** (April–Sept daily 9am–1pm & 3–7pm; Oct–March Mon–Fri 9am–1pm & 2.30–5pm, Sat 9am–1pm; 200ptas/€1.20). To get there, walk to the bottom of c/Ciutat, turn left along the main through-road (the C715) and watch for the signposted and well-surfaced country lane on the right. A clearly discernible footpath explores every nook and cranny of the site, and its numbered markers are thoroughly explained in the English-language **guidebook** available at the entrance (300ptas/ €1.80).

For more on Talayotic culture, see p.237.

Tucked away in a grove of olive, carob and holm-oak trees, the prehistoric village is entered through a monolithic gateway, whose heavy-

weight jambs and lintel interrupt the Cyclopean walls that still encircle
the site. These outer remains date from the second phase of the
Talayotic culture (c.1000–800 BC), when the emphasis was on consol-
idation and defence; in places, the walls still stand at their original size,
around 3.5m high and 3m thick. Beside the gate, there's also a modern
plinth erected in honour of Miquel Llobera, a local writer who penned
romantic verses about the place. Beyond the gateway, the central **talayot** is from the first Talayotic phase (c.1300–1000 BC), its shattered
ruins flanked by the foundations of several rooms of later date and
uncertain purpose. Experts believe the horseshoe-shaped room was
used, at least towards the end of the Talayotic period, for cremations,
whilst the three rectangular rooms were probably living quarters. In the
rooms, archeologists discovered various items such as iron objects and
ceramics imported from elsewhere in the Mediterranean. Some of them
were perhaps brought back from the Punic Wars (264–146 BC) by mercenaries – the skills of Balearic stone slingers were highly prized by the
Carthaginians, and it's known that several hundred accompanied
Hannibal and his elephants over the Alps in 218 BC.

The Ermita de Betlem

Hidden away in the hills 10km northwest of Artà is the **Ermita de
Betlem**, a remote and minuscule hermitage founded in 1805. The
road to the *ermita* begins immediately to the west of Artà's Plaça
Espanya, but the start is poorly signed and tricky to find (new signs
are promised). The road's rough surface and snaking course also
make for a difficult drive, so it's far better to **walk**. The first portion
is an easy stroll up along the wooded valley of the Torrent d'es
Cocones, but then – after about 3km – the road squeezes through the
narrowest of defiles, with the hills rising steeply on either side.
Beyond, the road begins to climb into the foothills of the Serra de
Llevant (here classified as the **Massís d'Artà**) until, some 3km after
the defile, a signposted left turn signals the start of the strenuous
part of the journey. Here, the track wriggles for 4km up the steep
hillside before finally reaching the *ermita*.

*Reckon on five
or six hours
for the walk
from Artà to
the* ermita *and
back.*

The buildings, which date from the hermitage's foundation, are
unassuming – although, if you've come this far, you'll undoubtedly
want to peep into the tiny **church**, where the walls are decorated with
crude religious frescoes. The hermitage doesn't offer accommodation or food, just picnic tables, which does seem a bit cruel if you've
hiked all the way here, but the views over the Badia d'Alcúdia are
magnificent. The adventurous can head down to the bay to the east
of Colònia de Sant Pere, but this is a difficult hike and you need to be
properly equipped.

Colònia de Sant Pere

West of Artà the C712 weaves through the hills on its way to Ca'n
Picafort and Port d'Alcúdia. On the way, it passes the turning for

COLÒNIA DE SANT PERE, a downbeat resort and one-time fishing village nestling beside the Badia d'Alcúdia, with the stern escarpments of the Massís d'Artà for a backdrop. New villa complexes have sprouted along the foreshore, but mercifully the developers have pretty much left the village alone – not that there's much to the place. Founded in 1881, Colònia de Sant Pere is no more than a few blocks across, its plain, low-rise, modern buildings set behind a small sandy beach. It's all very low-key and laid-back, and this, along with the setting, is the place's charm.

East from Palma to Artà

For **accommodation**, Colònia de Sant Pere has just one convenient *hostal*, the agreeable *Rocamar*, c/Sant Mateu 9 (☎ & fax 971 589 312; ⑤), an unassuming whitewashed and blue-shuttered building right in the centre three blocks back from the sea, with a restaurant on the ground floor and eight simple rooms up above. About 1.5km east of the village is one of Mallorca's few **campsites**, *Club San Pedro* (☎971 589 023; June to mid-Sept), which occupies a bleak and unappetizing location overlooking the bay. It can hold five hundred campers, and has a swimming pool, bar, restaurant and sports facilities. Tent-pitching prices begin at 321ptas/€1.93 for a small tent and rise to 750ptas/€4.51 for a family tent. In addition, there's a 1500ptas/€9.02 charge for the site, plus 640ptas/€3.85 per person, plus seven percent IVA tax. A car costs 750ptas/€4.51 extra, and there are small supplementary charges for electrical hook-ups and hot water.

Details of the nearby Sun Club Picafort *campsite are on p.190.*

You can **eat** well at the cosy *Acuàrium* (☎971 589 106), a restaurant serving the freshest of fish and a tasty *menú del día* (800ptas/€4.81); it's on c/Sant Mateu, opposite the *Rocamar*. There are several seafront reataurants too, the pick being the *Blau Mari* (☎971 589 407; March–Oct), which specializes in seafood and paellas.

The east coast

Mallorca's **east coast**, stretching for about 60km from Cala Rajada all the way south to Cala Llombards, is fretted by narrow coves, the remnants of prehistoric river valleys created when the level of the Mediterranean was much lower. All of these inlets have accrued at least some tourist development, ranging from a mild scattering of second homes to intensive chains of tower blocks. An attractive minor road links the resorts, running, for the most part, a few kilometres inland along the edge of the **Serres de Llevant**, a slim band of grassy hills which rises to over 500m at its two extremities, south outside Felanitx and north around Artà. If you have your own transport, this coastal route enables you to pick and choose destinations with the greatest of ease, dodging the crassest examples of over-development – principally Cala Millor, Calas de Mallorca and Cala d'Or – altogether.

Amongst the larger resorts, boisterous **Cala Rajada** is easily the most enticing, and is also within easy reach of excellent sandy beaches and the lovely medieval fortress of **Capdepera**. For a quiet day on the beach, however, you'll have to head much further south to the relatively untouched beaches of **Cala Mondragó**, now protected within a park, and **Cala Llombards**. In between these is scenic **Cala Figuera**, a lively, medium-sized resort that possesses some fine restaurants and a top-notch diving centre. The east coast is also famous for its limestone cave systems, with the most impressive formations found at the **Coves d'Artà** in the north, and the **Coves del Drac** at Porto Cristo.

It would be lovely to work your way down the coast, stopping for a couple of nights here and there, but the problem is **accommodation**. In the height of the season, locating a vacant room in one of the more attractive resorts can be a real tribulation – if you do find somewhere reasonable, you'll probably want to stay put. An alternative is to select a less popular spot, such as workaday **Porto Cristo** or dishevelled **Porto Colom**, where there's far more chance of a bed. Naturally, things ease up in the shoulder season, but in winter many hotels and *hostals* close down.

To explore the east coast thoroughly you'll need your own **transport**. All the major resorts have regular bus links with Palma and, in summer, there are good connections to Port d'Alcúdia from Porto Cristo and points north, but services up and down the coast are generally inadequate.

Cala Rajada

Awash with cafés, bars and hotels, vibrant **CALA RAJADA** lies on the southerly side of a stubby headland in the northeast corner of Mallorca. The town centre, an unassuming patchwork of low-rise modern buildings, is hardly prepossessing, but it is neat and trim and all around is a wild and rocky coastline, backed by pine-clad hills and sheltering a series of delightful **beaches**.

Arrival, information and accommodation

Most **buses** stop in the town centre on c/Juan Sebastian Elcano. From here, it's a couple of minutes' walk southeast to the main square, **Plaça dels Pins**, where you'll find the **tourist office** (Mon–Fri 9.30am–1.30pm & 2.30–5.30pm, Sat 9.30am–1.30pm; March–Oct also Sun 10am–1.30pm; ☎971 563 033). The office can supply an excellent range of local information including restaurant lists, bus schedules, details of car and bicycle rental firms, and free town maps marked with all the accommodation. They also have a popular, though not very detailed, pamphlet on **hiking tours** for 500ptas/€3.01, and sell tickets for the Palau Joan March gardens (see p.213).

There are no buses on Sundays.

The town centre is easy to explore on foot, but for the outlying beaches you'll probably want a **local bus**. Among several summertime services from the bus stops along c/Castellet, a short distance

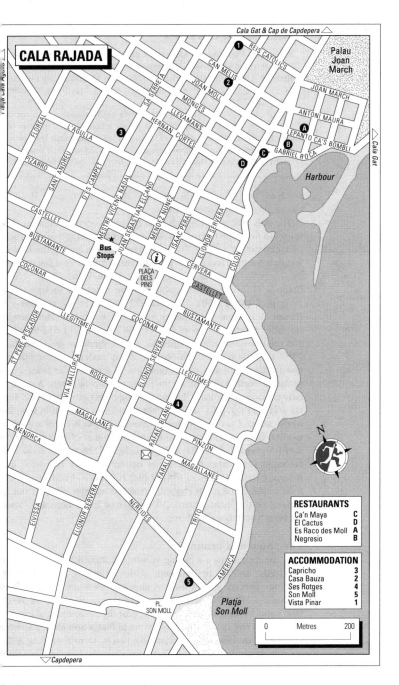

CALA RAJADA

Cala Gat & Cap de Capdepera △

Palau
Joan
March

Cala Gat △

Harbour

Bus
Stops

PLAÇA
DELS
PINS

Platja
Son Moll

Streets and places labelled on map:

Plaça Cala Agulla
Reis Catolics
Can Melis
Joan Moll
Monges
Llevamans
Hernan Cortes
Sa Serrera
Floral
L'Aguila
Pizarro
Sany Andreu
Des Campet
Mestre Vicenç Nadal
Juan Sebastian Elcano
Mendez Nuñez
Isaac Peral
Castellet
Bustamante
Coconar
St Pere Pescador
Llegitimes
Via Mallorca
Roges
Magallanes
Menorca
Eivissa
Elionor Servera
Rafael Blanes
Farallo
Nereides
Trito
America
Pinzon
Coconar
Cervera
Colon
Castellet
Gabriel Roca
Lepanto
Ca's Bombli
Antoni Maura
Joan March
Pl Son Moll

RESTAURANTS

Ca'n Maya	C
El Cactus	D
Es Raco des Moll	A
Negresio	B

ACCOMMODATION

Capricho	3
Casa Bauza	2
Ses Rotges	4
Son Moll	5
Vista Pinar	1

0   Metres   200

Boat trips from Cala Rajada

Boats leave Cala Rajada's harbour for regular summer excursions down
the east coast and back. Destinations include Porto Cristo (Feb–Oct
Mon–Sat 1 daily; 2200ptas/€13.22); Platja de Canyamel (April–Oct 3
daily; 1200ptas/€7.21); and the Coves d'Artà (April–Oct 3 daily;
1200ptas/€7.21).

A passenger-only **catamaran** service over to Ciutadella on Menorca is
operated by Cape Balear de Cruceros, whose offices are in the centre of
Cala Rajada at c/Pizarro 49 (☎971 818 517). The trip takes 1hr 15min
and there are one, two or three sailings a day, depending on the season. A
return ticket costs 8000ptas/€48.08, a one-way ticket 4000ptas/€24.04.

north of Plaça dels Pins, the most useful are to Cala Agulla, Platja de
Canyamel and the Coves d'Artà.

The only real problem with Cala Rajada is **accommodation**. The
town is a favourite German package resort and in high season you'll
be lucky to find a room. The best place to try is among the *hostals*
and hotels dotted around the pleasant residential streets just up from
the harbour. Reasonable bets here are the *Vista Pinar*, c/Reis
Catòlics 11, a large, comfortable two-star hotel with its own swimming pool (☎971 563 751, fax 971 565 721; ④); the one-star
Hostal Casa Bauza, c/Méndez Núñez 61, which has clean, simply
furnished rooms and a pool (☎971 563 844, fax 971 818 091; ③);
and the three-star *Hotel Capricho*, off c/L'Agulla at c/Sa Serreta 5
(☎971 563 500, fax 971 565 186; ⑦), a modern, air-conditioned
place with a pool and sports facilities. In the shoulder season, it's
probably worth trying one of the popular seafront hotels. A particularly good-value choice is the unassuming *Cala Gat* (☎971 563 166
fax 971 564 637; ⑥), which offers a secluded location in the pine
woods above Cala Gat. A more workaday option is the *Son Moll*, a
modern block overlooking the Platja Son Moll at c/Tritó 25 (☎971
563 100, fax 971 563 581; ⑥), with light and airy rooms, most with
balconies, and magnificent views out to sea. The three-star *Ses
Rotges*, c/Rafael Blanes 21 (☎971 563 108, fax 971 564 345; ⑥), is
a delightful place in an elegantly restored antique villa just out of
earshot of the main square. All the places listed here are closed
between November and March.

The town and around

Cala Rajada was once a fishing village, but there's little evidence of
this today, and the old **harbour**, at the far end of the main drag,
c/Elíonor Servera, is now used by pleasure boats and overlooked by
restaurants. From the harbour, walkways extend along the headland's south coast. To the southwest, past the busiest part of town, it
takes about five minutes to stroll round to **Platja Son Moll**, a slender
arc of sand overlooked by Goliath-like hotels. More rewarding is the
ten-minute stroll east to **Cala Gat**, a narrow cove beach tucked tight

ıp against the steep, wooded coastline. The beach is far from undis-
covered – there's a beach bar and at times it gets decidedly crowded
– but it's an attractive spot all the same.

Up above the footpath to Cala Gat you can glimpse some of the
modern sculptures that embellish the gardens of the **Palau Joan
March**, a lavish mansion built in 1916 for the eponymous tobacco
merchant, who was to become the richest man in Franco's Spain. The
entrance is on c/Joan March, a turning off c/Elíonor Servera just
beyond the harbour. The house isn't open to the public, but the gardens are – but opening times are at the discretion of the family.
Monday and Wednesday mornings are your best bet, but anyway you
can only arrange a visit through the town's tourist office
(500ptas/€3.01). This is a popular excursion, so it's advisable to
book ahead. Once you gain entrance, you'll find, amongst the pine
woods, a number of themed areas, including several contrasting terraces and an exquisite water garden with three separate pools
clogged by water lilies and shaded by orange and lemon trees. Over
forty sculptures decorate the gardens, mostly Spanish pieces but also
including a bronze by Rodin and examples of the work of three British
sculptors – Henry Moore, Barbara Hepworth and Anthony Caro.

Beyond the gardens, continuing east along c/Elíonor Servera, the
road twists steeply up through the pine woods to reach, after about
1 km, the bony headlands and lighthouse of the **Cap de Capdepera**,
Mallorca's most easterly point. The views out along the coast are a
treat.

On the northern side of Cala Rajada, c/L'Agulla crosses the
promontory to hit the north coast at **Platja Cala Agulla**. The
approach road, some 2km of tourist tackiness, is of little appeal, but
the beach, a vast curve of bright golden sand, is big enough to
accommodate hundreds of bronzing pectorals with plenty of space to
spare. The further you walk – and there are signed and shaded footpaths through the pine woods to assist you – the more isolation you'll
get.

Eating

The *Hotel Ses Rotges* (see opposite) boasts the best **restaurant** in
town, but it's pricey and there are scores of less expensive rivals.
Amongst many possibilities, which serve everything from sauerkraut
and sausages through to traditional Spanish cuisine, there are several good spots down at the harbour. Here you'll find tasty *tapas* at the
Es Racó des Moll, a fashionable little café-restaurant just a few
metres back from the harbour, as well as the waterfront *Pizzeria
Negresio*, a popular and cheerful cafeteria with low-price pizzas,
sandwiches, steaks and spaghetti. There's more inexpensive food at
El Cactus, a Mexican restaurant just up from the harbour at
c/Elíonor Servera 83 (☎971 564 609) and superb seafood at the
Ca'n Maya, close by at c/Elíonor Servera 80 (☎971 564 035).

Capdepera

Spied across the valley from the west or south, the crenellated walls
dominating **CAPDEPERA**, a tiny village 8km east of Artà and 3km
west of Cala Rajada, look too pristine to be true. Yet the triangular
fortifications are genuine enough, built in the fourteenth century by
the Mallorcan king Sancho to protect the coast from pirates. The village, snuggled below the walls, contains a pleasant medley of old
houses, its slender main square, Plaça de L'Orient, acting as a prelude to the steep steps up to the **Castell de Capdepera** (daily:
April–Oct 10am–8pm; Nov–March 10am–5pm; 200ptas/€1.20). The
steps are the most pleasant way to reach the castle, but you can also
follow the signs and drive up narrow c/Major. Flowering cactuses
give the fortress a special allure in late May and June, but it's a
beguiling place at any time, with over 400m of wall that is equipped
with a parapet walkway and shelters neat terraced gardens. At the
top of the fortress, **Nostra Senyora de la Esperança** (Our Lady of
Good Hope) is the quaintest of Gothic churches: its aisle-less, vaulted frame is furnished with outside steps leading up, behind the bell
gable, to a flat roof, from where the views are superb.

Run-of-the-mill **cafés** line up on Plaça de L'Orient – the best is
probably *L'Orient* – but Capdepera also has several excellent
restaurants. The pick is *La Fragua*, c/Es Pla d'en Coset 3 (☎971
565 050), an intimate, romantic spot where they serve delicious
Spanish meals. It's located just off Plaça de L'Orient, on the way up
towards the castle steps. There's nowhere to **stay** in Capdepera, but
it's easy enough to visit by bus from Artà, Cala Rajada, Cala Millor or
even Palma.

The Coves d'Artà

The succession of coves, caves and beaches notching the seashore
between Cala Rajada and Cala Millor begins promisingly with the
memorable **Coves d'Artà** (often signposted in Castilian as "Cuevas
de Artà"), reached along the first turning off the main coastal road
(the PM404) south of Capdepera. From May to October, **buses** run
two or three times a day (not on Sun) from Artà and Cala Rajada, or
you could elect for a **boat cruise** here from Cala Rajada (April–Oct 3
daily; 1200ptas/€7.21). **Tours** of the caves run every half-hour
(daily: July–Sept 10am–7pm; Oct–June 10am–5pm; 1200ptas/
€7.21) and the guides give a complete geological description in
tedious detail and in several languages including English as you wander the illuminated abyss. Allow about an hour for the visit – more if
there's a queue, as there sometimes is.

Visiting the caves for their scientific interest became fashionable
at the end of the nineteenth century amongst the rich and famous –
who included Jules Verne – and nowadays visits feature prominently
on package-tour itineraries. It wasn't, however, much of a treat to be

ere during the Reconquest, when a thousand Moorish refugees from ırtà were literally smoked out of the caves to be slaughtered by the ;atalan soldiers waiting outside.

The **entrance** to the caves is stunning, courtesy of a majestic stair-vay straight out of a horror movie which leads up to the yawning ıole, beckoning like the mouth of hell high in the cliffs above the ıay. This is the best of the numerous cave systems of eastern ʻlallorca, its sequence of cavernous chambers, studded with stalag- nites and stalactites, extending 450m into the rock face. Artificial ghting exaggerates the bizarre shapes of the caverns and their con-retions, especially in the **Hall of Flags**, where stalactites up to 50m ɔng hang in the shape of partly unfurled flags.

ˈlatja de Canyamel

ˈLATJA DE CANYAMEL is a recently developed cove resort, with mart modern villas draped around a pine-backed sandy beach in ight of a pair of rocky headlands. It's situated about 1km south of ɪe Coves d'Artà, though there is no connecting road: you have to eturn to the main coastal road, the PM404 running a few kilometres ⊓land, to make the journey. From May to October, local **buses** run ɾom Cala Rajada (Mon–Sat 3–4 daily) and Artà (Mon–Sat 2 daily) via ɪe Coves d'Artà, stopping in Platja de Canyamel outside the *Laguna ʃotel* (see below).

Don't confuse Platja de Canyamel with the tedious Costa de Canyamel urbanització immediately to the south.

Platja de Canyamel makes an agreeable spot for a few hours sun-ɪathing and there are a couple of good **restaurants** here too. In the entre, a short walk up from the beach, is the *Isabel*, where the eafood is fresh and well prepared, or you can sample traditional ʻlallorcan cuisine at the excellent *Porxada de Sa Torre* (☎971 841 ¦10; closed Mon & Nov–April), which occupies a tastefully convert-d old watchtower about 3km west of the beach along the access ɔad.

There are several **hotels** in Platja de Canyamel, but they are block-ɪooked by German tour operators and the only vague chance of a oom is at the *Laguna* (☎971 841 150, fax 971 841 049; May–Oct; Ɔ)), an attractive whitewashed hotel plonked right on the beach.

ʻala Millor and around

ʻontinuing south along the main coast road, you'll soon pass the ɪurning for the well-heeled villas of COSTA DE LOS PINOS, the ɪost northerly and prosperous portion of a gigantic resort conurba-ɪon centred on CALA BONA and CALA MILLOR. This is develop-ɪent gone quite mad, a swathe of apartment buildings, sky-rise ɪotels and villa-villages overwhelming the contours of the coast as ar as the eye can see. The only redeeming feature – and the reason or all this frantic construction in the first place – is the **beach**, a ɪagnificent two-kilometre stretch of sand fringed by what remains of the old pine woods. You can get plenty of information, including free maps, from the principal **tourist office** at Parc de la Mar 2, just behind the beach at the south end of Cala Millor (Mon–Fri 9am–1pm & 3–7pm, Sat 9am–1pm; ☎971 585 864).

To avoid this visual assault, stay on the main coastal road, which runs just inland from the resort, threading through the unappealing town of **SON SERVERA** before passing the **Auto-Safari Park**, 4km north of Porto Cristo, where a motley assortment of African animals roams open countryside (daily: April–Sept 9am–7pm; Oct–March 9am–5pm; 1700ptas/€10.22). Beyond, there are yet more acres of concrete and glass at **SA COMA** and **S'ILLOT**, though the main road, still set back from the coast, cuts a rustic route through vineyards and almond groves before reaching the multicoloured billboards which announce the cave systems of Porto Cristo.

Porto Cristo

Although **PORTO CRISTO** prospered in the early days of the tourist boom, sprouting a string of hotels and *hostals*, it's fared badly since mega-resorts such as Cala Millor and Cala d'Or were constructed nearby. Don't be deceived by the jam of tourist buses clogging the town's streets on their way to the nearby **caves** – few of their occupants will actually be staying here. Consequently, this is one of the very few places on the east coast where you're likely to find a room in July and August, and it's not too bad a spot to spend a night either, having benefited from a recent clean-up. The **beach**, a small sliver of sand, poor for sunbathing, cannot compete with the long flat strands of the new mega-resorts; it's tucked inside the harbour, a narrow V-shaped channel entered between a pair of rocky promontories that is one of the most sheltered ports on Mallorca's east coast.

Porto Cristo's origins are uncertain, but it was definitely in existence by the thirteenth century, serving as the fishing harbour and seaport of the inland town of Manacor. Nothing remains of the medieval settlement, however, and today the centre, which climbs the hill behind the harbour, consists of high-sided terraced buildings mostly dating from the late nineteenth and early twentieth centuries.

In August 1936, Porto Cristo was the site of a **Republican landing** to try to capture the island from the Falangists. The campaign was a fiasco: the Republicans disembarked over seven thousand men and quickly established a long and deep bridgehead, but their commanders, completely surprised by their initial success, quite literally didn't know what to do next. The Nationalists did: they counterattacked and, supported by the Italian air force, soon had the Republicans dashing back to the coast. Barcelona radio put on a brave face, announcing, "The heroic Catalan columns have returned from Mallorca after a magnificent action. Not a single man suffered from the effects of the embarkation."

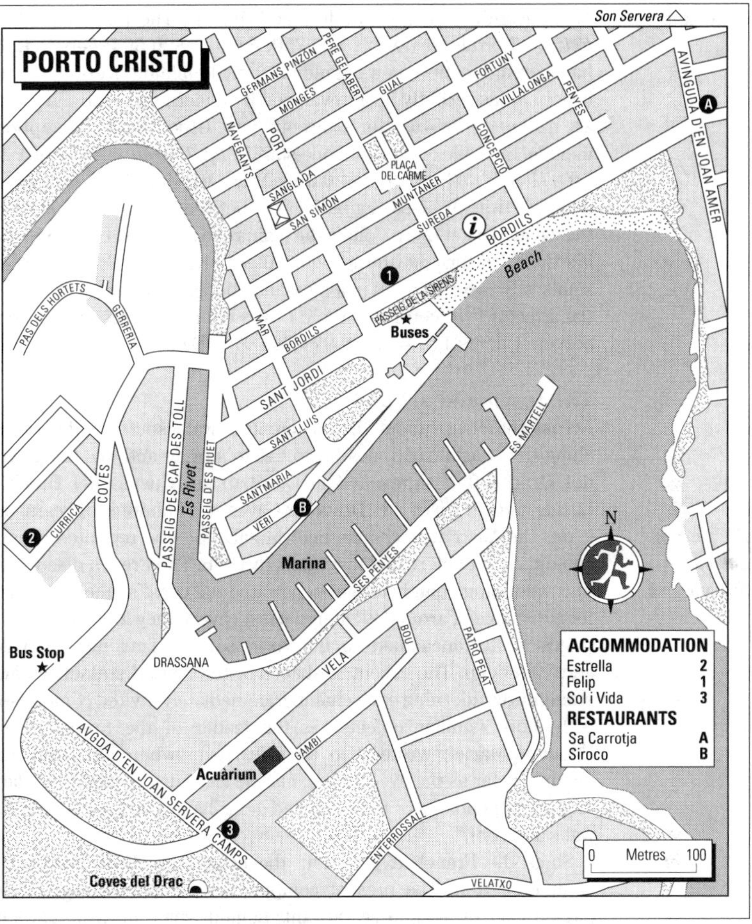
PORTO CRISTO
Son Servera
GERMANS PINZÓN
PERE GELABERT
MONGES
GUAL
FORTUNY
VILLALONGA
PENYES
AVINGUDA D'EN JOAN AMER
NAVEGANTS
PORT
PLAÇA DEL CARME
CONCEPCIÓ
SANGLADA
SAN SIMÓN
MUNTANER
SUREDA
BORDILS
Beach
PASSEIG DE LA SIRENS
Buses
PAS DELS HORTETS
GERRERIA
MAR
BORDILS
SANT JORDI
SANT LLUIS
ES MARTELL
PASSEIG DES CAP DES TOLL
Es Rivet
PASSEIG D'ES RIUET
SANTMARIA
VERI
COVES
CURRICA
Marina
SES PENYES
N
Bus Stop
DRASSANA
VELA
BOU
PATRÓ PELAT
ACCOMMODATION
Estrella 2
Felip 1
Sol i Vida 3
RESTAURANTS
Sa Carrotja A
Siroco B
AVGDA D'EN JOAN SERVERA CAMPS
GAMBI
Acuàrium
ENTERROSSALL
0 Metres 100
Coves del Drac
VELATXO

Arrival, information and accommodation

The main coastal road passes along Porto Cristo's seafront, and a sizeable number of long-distance **buses**, principally from Palma and Port d'Alcúdia, terminate in the centre beside the harbour and the beach. The **tourist office** is on the seafront directly behind the beach at c/Bordils 53A (Mon–Fri 8am–3pm; ☎971 558 328), and they provide useful maps of the town and neighbouring resorts. Beyond the beach, the harbour accommodates a large marina and then meets the oily-green Es Rivet river, which forms the town centre's southern perimeter.

For **accommodation**, Porto Cristo has half-a-dozen hotels and *hostals*. They are an undistinguished lot, but there is a good chance of a vacancy here even in July and August. The three-star *Hotel Felip*, c/Bordils 61 (☎971 820 750, fax 971 820 594; Feb–Oct; ⑦) has a great location, in a big old balconied building overlooking the beach. It has recently been revamped in modern style and the rooms are neat and trim – ask for a harbour view. Other less sightly options include the spick-and-span one-star *Hotel Estrella*, c/Curricà 16 (☎971 820 833, fax 971 820 892; May–Oct; ④), which occupies a plain postwar three-storey building in between the town centre and the caves. To get there, follow the main road south over the river and it's the third turning on the right. Alternatively, the *Sol i Vida* is a small, tidy two-star hotel in a pleasant wooded location on a residential street a few metres from the Coves del Drac caves, Avgda Joan Servera Camps 11 (☎ & fax 971 821 074; ④).

The town and around

Across the river, about fifteen minutes' walk south of the centre along the coastal road, lies Porto Cristo's pride and joy, the **Coves del Drac** (often signposted in Castilian as "Cuevas del Drach"). Locals had known of the "Dragon's Caves" for hundreds of years, but it was the Austrian archduke Ludwig Salvator who recruited French geologists to explore and map them in 1896. The French discovered four whopping chambers that penetrated the coast's limestone cliffs for a distance of around 2km. In the last cavern they found one of the largest subterranean lakes in the world, some 177m long, 40m wide and 30m deep. The eccentric shapes of the myriad **stalactites** and **stalagmites** adorning each chamber immediately invited comparison with more familiar objects. As the leader of the French team Edouard Martel, wrote, "On all sides, everywhere, in front and behind, as far as the eye can see, marble cascades, organ pipes, lace draperies, pendants of multi-faceted gems hang suspended from the walls and roof."

For more on Ludwig Salvator, see p.142.

Since the French exploration, the caves have been thoroughly commercialized. The present complex accommodates a giant **car park**, ticket office and **restaurant**, behind which lurk the gardens that lead to the flight of steps down to the caves. You may come to know each step well, as you can be forced to wait in line for ages especially at the weekend. **Guided tours** of the caves run every hour (daily: April–Oct 10am–5pm; Nov–March 10.30am–3.30pm; 1100ptas/€6.61).

Inside, the myriad concretions of calcium carbonate, formed by the dissolution of the soft limestone by rainwater, are shrewdly illuminated. Shunting you through the hour-long, multilingual tour, the guides invite you to gawp and gush at formations such as "the Buddha", "the Pagoda" and "the Snowy Mountain", and magnificent icicle-like stalactites, some of which are snowy white, others picking up hints of orange and red from the rocks they hang off. The *tour de force* is the larger of the two **subterranean lakes**, whose translucent waters flicker with reflected colours, the effects further enhanced by musicians drifting about in boats playing harmoniums (performances usually begin on the hour). At the end of the tour, most visitors leave on foot, but there's also the option of a brief boat ride across part of the lake. From the cave complex, it's a short walk across the car park to the well-stocked **Acuàrium** (daily: April–Oct 10.30am–5pm; Nov–March 11am–3pm; 800ptas/€4.81), where the glass tanks magnify such exotic horrors as electric eels, piranhas and stinging fish.

There's another cave system situated 2km west of Porto Cristo on the road to Manacor – though you'd hardly want to visit both. The **Coves d'es Hams** (or "Cuevas del Hams" in Castilian) follow the same format as their rival, with a sequence of somewhat smaller caverns lit to emphasize the beauty of the stalagmites and stalactites. Guided tours run about every half-hour (daily: April–Oct 10am–6pm; Nov–March 10.30am–5pm; 1500ptas/€9.02). As at the Coves del Drac, musicians play from boats on an underground lake (every 20min until 4.30pm).

Eating

With most of Porto Cristo's **restaurants and cafés** geared up for the passing tourist trade, getting a decent meal is none too easy. There are only a couple of places of any quality – *Sa Carrotja*, a low-key family-run restaurant at the first intersection north from the beach along c/Bordils at Avgda Joan Amer 45 (☎971 821 503); and the rather more polished *Siroco* (☎971 822 444), whose cosy terrace abuts the harbour a few metres south from the beach on c/Veri. Both are inexpensive.

South of Porto Cristo

The modern resorts disfiguring the pint-sized coves to the south of Porto Cristo reach their nadir at the **CALAS DE MALLORCA**, the collective name for a band of tourist settlements extending from Cala Magraner to Cala Murada. This part of the shoreline didn't have much charm in the first place – the coves are mostly scrawny and shadeless – and it's even less compelling now. Inland, however, the main coast road gives few hints of these scenic disasters as it wends its pastoral way past honey-coloured dry-stone walls and a smattering of ancient farmhouses in the lee of the Serres de Llevant.

Porto Colom

PORTO COLOM straggles round a long and irregular bay some 20km south of Porto Cristo. Originally a fishing village supplying the needs of the neighbouring town of Felanitx, the port boomed throughout most of the nineteenth century from the export trade in wine to France. The good times, however, came to an abrupt end when phylloxera wiped out the island's vines in the 1870s. The vil-

lagers returned to **fishing**, which still makes up a significant part of
the local economy: the boats they use, as well as some old boat
sheds, litter the kilometre-long **quay** on the southwest side of the
bay. The quayside, along with the modest settlement immediately
behind it, constitutes the heart of the present village and although
there's little to grab your attention, it's still an amiable, downbeat
spot. The oldest part of the village is about 300m from the west end
of the quay, round the back of the harbour, and comprises a small
parcel of pastel-shaded cottages shadowing a little square.
Elsewhere, the headlands overlooking the entrance to the bay house
a lighthouse and an unappetizing mix of villas and hotels, while over
the hill behind the village (about 1km to the south) is **Cala Marçal**, a
crowded, shadeless wedge of sand overlooked by the concrete flanks
of the eponymous hotel.

Buses, principally from Palma, arrive at the quayside. There's a
smattering of inexpensive and resolutely mundane **accommodation**,
including the *Hostal-residencia César*, c/Llaud s/n (☎971 825 302;
April–Oct; ③), and the equally undistinguished *Hostal Bahía Azul*,
Ronda Creuer Baleares 88 (☎971 825 280, fax 971 824 452; ④),
both situated amongst the scrubland at the far (east) end of the quay.
For something rather more comfortable, especially in the shoulder
season, try the three-star *Hotel Cala Marsal* (☎971 825 225, fax
971 825 250; April–Oct; ⑤) in Cala Marçal, a package-tour favourite
with sea-facing rooms and all the usual facilities from swimming
pools to tennis courts.

Porto Colom does rather better with its **restaurants**, the pick of
which are dotted along the quayside. The cream of the crop is the
Celler Sa Sínia (☎971 575 323; closed Mon) at the west end of the
quay, whose fish dishes are both reasonably priced and very tasty. At
the other end of the quay, just along Ronda Creuer Baleares, at no.
59, the smart *Ses Portadores* (☎971 825 271) is a good alternative;
it's a bit pricier, but the fish is just as fresh and there's a wider selection.

Felanitx and around

FELANITX, the main town hereabouts, is 13km inland from Porto
Colom. It's an industrious place, producing wine, ceramics and
pearls. Few would claim the town was beautiful, but it does have
more than a modicum of charm, its tangle of narrow streets lined by
handsome old houses that mostly date to the eighteenth and nineteenth centuries. The finest building is the church of **Sant Miquel**,
the honey-gold, Baroque facade of which gives an elegant air to the
largely modern main square, the **Plaça Constitució**. A plaque on the
church recalls the worst disaster to hit the town since the days of
pirate attack, when a wall collapsed killing over four hundred people
on their way from church. There are no other sights as such, but
strolling the old streets and alleys is an agreeable way to pass the odd

our and the best time to do it is on Sunday morning when the main square is given over to a lively fresh produce and craft **market**. In particular, look out for the capers produced locally and sold by size; the smallest are the most flavourful, either as *nonpareilles* (up to 7mm) or *surfines* (7–8mm).

Buses, which run to and from Palma and Porto Colom, stop by the main square. There is no tourist office and neither is there anywhere to **stay** – except the nearby Santuari de Sant Salvador (see below).

The east coast

Capers are tapèras *in Catalan, but you'll more often see the Castilian* alcaparras.

The Santuari de Sant Salvador

Within easy striking distance of Felanitx is one of the more scenic portions of the Serres de Llevant. The best approach is to head east along the road to Porto Colom for about 2km and take the signposted, four-kilometre tarmac byroad that wriggles up the mountain to the **Santuari de Sant Salvador**, recognizable from miles around by its conspicuous stone cross and enormous statue of Christ. Long an important place of pilgrimage, the monastery occupies a splendid position near the summit of the highest mountain in these parts, the 510-metre Puig Sant Salvador, with sumptuous views out over the east coast. The sanctuary was founded in the mid-fourteenth century, but the original buildings were razed by raiding pirates and most of today's complex is Baroque. The heavy gatehouse is its most conspicuous feature while, inside the compound, the eighteenth-century church shelters a much-venerated image of the Virgin Mary.

This was the last of Mallorca's monasteries to lose its monks – the last ones moved out in the early 1990s – and it now has fourteen spartan **guest rooms** housing between two and nine people (☎971 827 282). Ten of the rooms have shared bathrooms and cost 1200ptas/€7.21 per person; four are en suite and cost 1500ptas/€9.02 per person. There's hot water and a **café-restaurant** (it's best to call ahead to confirm opening hours) and bedding is provided. If you've got a car, you could make the sanctuary an unusual base for exploring the locality. It's certainly a very quiet place to stay.

The Castell de Santueri

The custodians at the Santuari de Sant Salvador should be able to point you towards the footpath to the **Castell de Santueri**, about 4km away across the hills to the south. The route is fairly easy to follow and the going isn't difficult, although it's still advisable to have a walking map and stout shoes. The path meanders through a pretty landscape of dry stone walls, flowering shrubs and copses of almond and carob trees, bringing you to the castle after about an hour and a half. Glued to a rocky hilltop, the battered ramparts date from the fourteenth century, though it was the Moors who built the first stronghold here. Getting inside the ruins is pot luck: sometimes you can, when a small entry fee is levied at the main gate, and sometimes you can't.

You can drive to the castle on a 5km country lane, signed off the Santanyí road about 2km south of Felanitx.

Cala d'Or and around

South along the coast from Porto Colom, the pretty little fishing villages that once studded the quiet coves as far as Porto Petro have been blasted by development. The interconnected resorts that now stand in their place are largely indistinguishable, a homogeneous strip of whitewashed, low-rise villas, hotels, restaurants and bars, all designed in a sort of *pueblo* style. Confusingly, this long string of resorts is now usually lumped together under the title **CALA D'OR**, though this name in fact refers to one particular cove which is one of the smallest. The "Cala d'Or" we refer to in this account is the original cove and not the whole development.

To be fair, the pseudo-Andalucian style of the new resorts blends well with the ritzy *haciendas* left by a previous generation of sunseekers, the latter largely concentrated on the humpy, pint-sized headland which separates Cala d'Or from its northerly neighbour **CALA GRAN**. These two fetching little coves, tucked between the cliffs and edged by narrow golden beaches, are the highlights of the area. The beaches are jam-packed throughout the season, but the swimming is perfect and the wooded coastline here is far preferable to the more concentrated development all around. Of equal appeal is the genteel and leafy headland on the south side of Cala d'Or, though this is a brief and flattering preamble to the massive marina and endless villas of **CALA LLONGA**.

Practicalities

Buses stop on Cala d'Or's crowded and charmless main drag, Avinguda Fernando Tarrago, two minutes' walk from the beach. Under various designations, this same street links the main cove resorts, from Cala Esmeralda in the north to Cala Llonga in the south – the whole distance about a twenty-minute walk. The area's **tourist office** is situated a few metres up from the Cala Llonga waterside (Mon–Fri 8.30am–2pm; May–Sept also Sat 8.30am–2pm; ☎971 657 463).

In the summertime, a tourist "train" on wheels, the mini tren, links Cala d'Or, Porto Petro and Cala Mondragó, stopping along the main street and beside all the beaches.

The tourist office provides free maps marked with all the hotels and *hostals*, though finding a place to **stay** is well-nigh impossible in the summer – a better bet is to try the *Nereida* at Porto Petro (see opposite). The most luxurious option – where you'll almost certainly need an advance reservation – is the four-star *Hotel Cala d'Or*, right above Cala d'Or's beach on Avinguda Bèlgica (☎971 657 249; April–Oct; ⑧). The hotel has seventy balconied bedrooms, each furnished in an attractive modern style with fine sea views, while the equally appealing public areas include a bar, restaurant and an outside swimming pool. Cala Gran also has a good upmarket hotel, the *Cala Gran* (☎971 657 100; April–Oct; ⑦), a bigger and brisker affair at the back of the beach, where the modern bedrooms have balconies and sea views, and there's every convenience including a swimming pool.

There are myriad **cafés and restaurants** around Cala d'Or and Cala Llonga, especially on the main street, Avinguda Fernando Tarrago. One that's worth hunting down is the popular *Ca'n Trompé*, close to the *Hotel Cala d'Or* at Avgda Bèlgica 12 (☎971 657 341; closed Dec–Feb), which serves delicious, though pricey, meals, with the emphasis on Mallorcan mainstays – the suckling pig is a real treat.

Porto Petro

Only recently swallowed into the Cala d'Or conurbation, **PORTO PETRO** rambles round a twin-pronged cove a couple of kilometres south of Cala Llonga. There's no beach here, so the development has been fairly restrained. The old fishing harbour has been turned into a marina, and villas dot the gentle wooded hillsides edging the coast, but it remains a quiet and tranquil spot – the only real activity is the promenade round the crystal-watered cove. The minuscule centre of the village perches on the headland above the marina, its cluster of whitewashed houses recalling the days before the tourists.

There's a reasonable chance of getting a **room** here at the two-star *Hostal Nereida* (☎971 657 223, fax 971 659 235; April–Oct; ⑨), a comfortable and neat little place with its own pool and rooftop sun terraces. The village has all the amenities to make for a good base: there's car and bike rental; daily **boat trips** around and about (see box); and regular *mini tren* connections up and down the coast to all the resorts between Cala d'Or and Cala Mondragó. There are also a couple of fine harbourside **restaurants**: the *Ca'n Martina* (☎971 657 517), at the head of the marina, boasts a paella to die for and a lovely outside terrace, whilst the nearby *Restaurant Porto Petro* (☎971 657 704) serves wonderful seafood from upper-floor premises overlooking the bay – try the sardines.

Boat cruises from Porto Petro

From May to October, there are once-weekly **boat cruises** from Porto Petro to Cabrera island (see p.230), currently on Tuesdays, departing at 9.30am and returning by 5pm. The cost is 4500ptas/€27.05 per person, and you should book ahead on ☎971 657 012.

The Mondragó Parc Natural and Cala Mondragó

It may be rather late in the day, but the Balearic government has recently stepped in to protect a small slice of the east coast by creating the **Mondragó Parc Natural**, whose diverse terrain covers almost 2000 acres of wetland, farmland, beach, pine and scrub about 3km south of Porto Petro. The park is in its infancy, so as yet the road signs are a bit confusing, but there are two car parks to aim for. Both are signposted from the C717 between Porto Petro and Santanyí.

The better target is the **Fonts de N'Alis** car park, located 100m from the tiny resort of Cala Mondragó (see below), while the other car park, **S'amarador**, is on the low-lying headland to the east of the cove. The park is a delightful area latticed with footpaths and country lanes, but the only maps that the Fonts de N'Alis **visitor centre** (☎971 181 022) currently issues are poor, although they do show the three hiking trails which have been marked out (more are planned). All three are easy loop trails, two of forty minutes, one of twenty. Until the visitor centre sorts itself out with proper hiking maps, the only reliable reference is the billboard map displayed outside.

CALA MONDRAGÓ, about 4km south of Porto Petro, is one of Mallorca's prettiest resorts. Before the creation of the park in 1990, there was some development here, but it's all very low key and barely disturbs the cove's beauty, with low, pine-clad cliffs framing a pair of sandy beaches beside crystal-clear waters. Predictably, the cove's "unspoilt" reputation and safe bathing acts as a magnet for sunlovers from miles around, but you can escape the crowds by **staying** the night (if there's space) at either of two beachside *hostals*. Choose from the *Hostal Playa Mondragó*, a straightforward, modern concrete block with forty plain but adequate rooms (☎ & fax 971 657 752; April–Oct; ④), or the rather more enticing *Hostal Condemar*, about 300m from the beach, where most of the rooms have balconies (☎ & fax 971 657 756; May–Oct; ④).

There are no **buses** to Cala Mondragó, but it is the terminus of the summertime *mini tren* which runs along the coast to and from Porto Petro and Cala d'Or.

Santanyí and around

The crossroads town of SANTANYÍ, 18km southwest of Porto Colom, was once an important medieval stronghold guarding the island's southeastern approaches. Corsairs ransacked the place on several occasions, but one of the old town gates, **Sa Porta**, has survived along with the occasional chunk of masonry extant from the old city walls. However, it's Santanyí's narrow alleys, squeezed between high-sided stone houses, that are the town's main appeal. Several pavement **cafés** edge the main square, but these should not detain you long, whether you're making the fast, fifty-kilometre journey west along the C717 to Palma or heading east to the coast.

Cala Figuera and Cala Santanyí

Travelling southeast from Santanyí, a 5km-long byroad cuts a pretty, rustic route through to CALA FIGUERA, whose antique harbour sits beside a fjord-like inlet below the steepest of coastal cliffs. Local fishermen still land their catches and mend their nets here, but nowadays it's to the accompaniment of scores of photo-snapping tourists. Up above, the pine-covered shoreline heaves with villas, hotels and *hostals*, although the absence of high-rise buildings means the development is never overbearing.

Cala Figuera is extremely popular, and there are precious few vacant **rooms** at its dozen or so establishments, even in the shoulder seasons. That said, if you do chance your arm the obvious place to start is on the steep pedestrianized ramp – c/Verge del Carmen – which leads up from the harbour. In this prime location, at no. 50, is the unassuming *Hostal Cala*, whose twenty rooms are stashed above a restaurant (☎971 645 018; April–Oct; ⑤). Close by at no. 58, the year-round *Hostal Ca'n Jordi* has just six simple bedrooms, also over a restaurant (☎ & fax 971 645 035; ③). Up the hill in the centre of the resort is another good choice, the two-star family-run *Hostal Ventura*, c/Pintor Bennareggi 17 (☎971 645 102; April–Oct; ③), which has a swimming pool and forty plain but perfectly adequate rooms.

Of Cala Figuera's many **restaurants**, the most distinguished are the seafood eateries lining c/Verge del Carmen. It's difficult to select – and hard to go wrong – but *La Marina* (☎971 645 052), *Ca'n Jordi* (☎971 645 035) and *Cala* (☎971 645 018) are all excellent and not too pricey. There are also several lively music **bars** and **discos** dotted along the main street. In terms of amenities, the resort has car and bike rental outlets, and, down by the harbour, a **diving school** (☎971 645 015) that rents out a wide range of sub-aqua gear to experienced divers, and arranges novice courses – three days of tuition for around 50,000ptas/€300.51.

What you won't get is a beach. The nearest is 4km west at **CALA SANTANYÍ**, a busy little resort with a medium-sized (and frequently crowded) beach at the end of a steep-sided, heavily wooded gulch. To get there, head back towards Santanyí for about 2km and follow the signs.

Cala Llombards

The next bay west from Cala Santanyí is little-developed **CALA LLOMBARDS**, a good-looking, pine-forested cove of gleaming sand, turquoise sea and sheer cliffs. There's a scrawny villa-village behind, not visible from the beach, a seasonal beach-bar and a dirt car park, but otherwise it's comparatively pristine – though litter louts do tend to spoil the place. Only rarely will you have the beach to yourself, but it is seldom crowded and makes a relaxing spot to while away a few hours.

There are no **buses** to Cala Llombards and even driving here can be a baffling experience on the narrow country roads that cover this part of the island. Your best bet is to take the road southwest from Santanyí towards Colònia de Sant Jordi and watch for the signed turning before you get to the roadside hamlet of **Es Llombards**; thereafter, Cala Lombards is 5km away – keep your eyes peeled for further signs. There's an alternative turnoff in Es Llombards itself.

The south coast

Mallorca's **south coast**, stretching from the island's most southerly point, Cap de Ses Salines, round to the rim of the Bay of Palma, has hardly been developed at all, but the reasons behind this lack of interest are pretty obvious when you come here. Most of the shoreline is unenticingly spartan, a long and low rocky shelf that meets the sea almost as an afterthought. There's barely a decent beach in sight. Behind is a flat, sparsely populated hinterland of little shade or variety. Villages are few and far between, and in places the land has an eerie sense of desolation – especially at the wind-buffeted **Cap de Ses Salines** – which some assert as its fascination.

A smattering of modern resorts gamely make the most of these disheartening surroundings. The best is undoubtedly **Colònia de Sant Jordi**, a curious amalgamation of plush tourist settlement and old seaport, which thoroughly deserves an overnight visit, not least because it offers boat trips to the remote islet of **Cabrera** and is near the wildlife-rich saltflats that back onto the region's longest beach, **Es Trenc**. Of the other resorts, **Cala Pi**, where a deep ravine frames a sandy beach, is the best-looking and although it doesn't offer much it is close to the substantial remains of prehistoric **Capocorb Vell**. East of Cala Pi things get much worse with the grim and untidy resorts of Valgornera, S'Estanyol and Sa Rapita, no more than clumps of mundane second homes decorating the treeless shoreline.

Planning an itinerary is straightforward. The best advice is to use as your baseline the **C717** road, which runs from Santanyí northwest to Ca'n Pastilla on the Bay of Palma, and branch off it as you wish. As ever, **accommodation** is at a premium. Throughout the season, your best chance by a long chalk is in Colònia de Sant Jordi, but from November to March nearly everything is closed and you'll almost certainly have to visit on a day trip. **Bus** services are adequate if you're heading somewhere specific from Palma, but are dreadful when you attempt to move between other resorts.

Cap de Ses Salines and Botanicactus

Heading southwest from Santanyí, a fast and easy country road drifts through a landscape of old dry stone walls, broken-down windmills, ochre-flecked farmhouses and straggling fields on its way towards Colònia de Sant Jordi. After about 4km, you pass through tiny **Es Llombards** and shortly afterwards reach the turning that leads the 10km down through coastal pine woods to the lighthouse on **Cap de Ses Salines**, a bleak, brush-covered headland which is Mallorca's most southerly point. The lighthouse itself is closed to the public, but there are fine views out to sea. Thekla larks and stone curlews are often to be seen on the cape, whilst gulls, terns and shearwaters glide about offshore, benefiting from the winds which, when they're up, can make the place intolerable.

Back on the road to Colònia de Sant Jordi, billboards welcome ou to **Botanicactus** (daily: April–Sept 9am–7pm; Oct–March am–5pm; 800ptas/€4.81), a huge botanical garden mostly devot- d to indigenous and imported species of cactus. A surprise here is he artificial lake, which encourages the growth of wetland plants – welcome splash in arid surroundings – but otherwise the place as all the atmosphere of a garden centre and is definitely miss- ble.

Colònia de Sant Jordi and around

bout 13km west of Santanyí is **COLÒNIA DE SANT JORDI**, whose /ide streets pattern a substantial and irregularly shaped headland. Buses, principally from Palma, stop at several central locations, ncluding the bus-stop at the north end of the old harbour, but the own is confusing, at least at first, and you'll need to get your bear- ngs. During the season, a toytown mini-train shuttles around town very hour or two, and there's a central **taxi** stand (☎908 142 187) t the c/Gabriel Roca and c/Pescadors intersection.

The main approach road is the **Avinguda Marqués del Palmer**, t the end of which – roughly in the middle of the headland – lies he principal square, the unremarkable **Plaça Constitució**. From ere, c/Sa Solta and then Avinguda Primavera lead west. At the nd of the avenue, the sprawling *Hotel Marqués del Palmer* sits ght against the **Platja d'Estanys**, whose gleaming sands curve ound a dune-edged cove. On the left (south) of Avinguda 'rimavera is the surprisingly pleasant main tourist zone, the dom- neering lines of its flashy hotels broken by low-rise villas and andscaped side streets. On the right (north) are the **Salines de** 'Avall, saltpans which once provided the town with its principal ource of income.

East from Plaça Constitució along c/Major, and then left (north) own c/Gabriel Roca, is the old **harbour**, the most diverting part of own. Framed by an attractive, early twentieth-century ensemble of alconied houses, the port makes the most of a handsome, horse- hoe-shaped bay. There's nothing special to look at, but it's a relax- ng spot with a handful of restaurants, fishing smacks, a marina and pocket-sized beach, the **Platja Es Port**. Furthermore, a footpath eads – in about five minutes – round the bay from this beach north nto the slender, low-lying headland that accommodates the much nore extensive sands of the **Platja d'es Dolç**.

The **tourist office** is on the upper floor of the town hall at c/Doctor Barraquer 5 (Mon–Fri 9am–1pm & 5–7.30pm, Sat 9am–1pm; ☎971 56 073). To get there, follow c/Gabriel Roca south from the harbour nd take the first road on the right. Staff issue free town maps and ave information about local **bike rental** shops (cycling in the flat- ands around the resort is a popular and enjoyable pastime), as well s details of local accommodation.

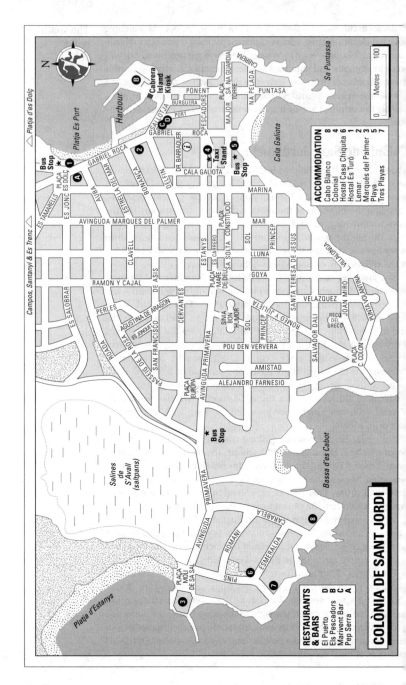

COLÒNIA DE SANT JORDI

ACCOMMODATION

Cabo Blanco	8
Colonial	4
Hostal Casa Chiquita	6
Hostal Es Turó	1
Lemar	2
Marqués del Palmer	3
Playa	5
Tres Playas	7

RESTAURANTS & BARS

El Puerto	D
Es Pescadors	B
Marivent Bar	C
Pep Serra	A

Accommodation

In the budget range of **accommodation**, there's a handful of hotels and *hostals* beside and behind the harbour – and these are your best chance if you're looking for a last-minute room in season. In addition, there is a selection of glossy modern hotels in the resort area at the west end of Avinguda Primavera, all glistening towers of air-conditioned, balconied bedrooms offering panoramas of the sea.

Hotel Cabo Blanco, c/Carabela 2 ☎971 655 075, fax 971 656 318. A polished three-star hotel located at the west end of Avinguda Primavera with pools and attractive gardens, plus a great seashore location. One of the better package-tour hotels. April–Oct. ⑤.

Hostal Casa Chiquita, c/Esmeralda 14 ☎971 655 121, fax 971 655 431. This smart and well-tended *hostal* occupies a rambling, pueblo-style modern villa in the tourist zone at the west end of Avinguda Primavera. It has a good-looking garden, with lots of exotic cactuses, and 18 smartly decorated ensuite guest rooms. March to early Nov. ⑧.

Hostal Colonial, c/Gabriel Roca 9 ☎971 656 182, fax 971 655 278. Eight spartan rooms in a basic one-star *hostal*, the cheapest place in town. March–Oct. ③.

Hostal Es Turó, c/Ingeniero Roca 38 ☎971 655 057. Unassuming one-star *hostal* in a solid three-storey building plonked right on the Es Port beach. Rooftop bathing and eighteen guest rooms – the rooms at the back look out over the beach. May–Oct. ④.

Hotel Lemar, c/Bonança 1 ☎971 655 178, fax 971 655 162. A whitewashed and balconied old building right in the centre of things, with ninety two-star rooms overlooking the harbour. Ask for one at the front. Mid-April to Oct. ⑦.

Hotel Marqués del Palmer, Avgda Primavera s/n ☎971 655 100, fax 971 656 369. Not quite as new and glitzy as some of its neighbours, but still a good-quality, comfortable, three-star hotel. Right on the beach at the west end of Avinguda Primavera. May–Oct. ⑤.

Hostal Playa, c/Major 25 ☎ & fax 971 655 256. About five minutes' walk from the harbour, this cosy and well-cared-for little *hostal* has folksy bygones in its public areas and eight spotless ensuite rooms. Breakfast is served on a pretty patio terrace with views along the seashore. Open all year. ⑤.

Eating

There's a cluster of first-rate **restaurants** beside the harbour, a pleasant low-key ensemble of places that attracts tourists for evening relaxation. Things get busy from around 8pm.

El Puerto, Sa Llotja s/n. This popular harbourfront spot divides into two: a café-bar offering bargain-basement pizzas and spaghetti, and a restaurant specializing in seafood (around 1600ptas/€9.62 for a main course).

Marivent Bar, Sa Llotja s/n. The best place in town for *tapas* – from around 600ptas/€3.61 – and a drink.

Els Pescadors, c/Sant Joan 58 ☎971 656 604. Superb seafood at an atmospheric little restaurant beside the fishing jetty. Fairly expensive – with main courses from around 2000ptas/€13.22 – but well worth it.

Pep Serra, c/Gabriel Roca 87 ☎971 655 399. An excellent, easygoing, family-run restaurant with a seashore terrace that serves a local delicacy – perch, caught off Cabrera island.

Es Trenc

One of Colònia de Sant Jordi's attractions is its proximity to **Es Trenc**, a 4km strip of sandy beach that extends as far as the eye can see. It's neither unknown, nor unspoilt, but the crowds are easily absorbed and the development only scratches away at the edges. To get there, head north from Colònia de Sant Jordi and, about 1km out of town, turn left towards Campos; then, some 2.8km along this road, take the signed left turn and follow the country lanes leading across the salt flats to the car park at the east end of the beach – a total distance of around 7km. This end of the beach is far more appealing than the other, which is splotched by the tatty holiday hamlet of **Ses Covetes**.

The saltpans backing onto the beach – the **Salines de Llevant** – and the surrounding farmland and scrubland support a wide variety of **birdlife**. Resident birds such as marsh harriers, kestrels, spotted crakes, fan-tailed warblers and hoopoes make a visit enjoyable at any time of year, but the best time to come is in the spring when hundreds of migrants arrive from Africa. Commonly seen in the springtime are avocets, little ringed plovers, little egrets, common sandpipers, little stints, black-tailed godwits, collared pratincoles and black terns. Several **footpaths** lead from Es Trenc beach into the saltpans, but it's not a good area to explore on foot: the scenery is boring, it's smelly and for much of the year insects are a menace. It's much better to drive round (or maybe cycle), using the maze-like network of narrow country lanes that traverse the saltpans and stopping anywhere that looks promising.

The island of Cabrera

*There are also
once-weekly
summer cruises to Cabrera
from Porto
Petro – see
p.223.*

Cabrera ("Goat Island") is a bumpy, scrub-covered chunk lying 18km offshore. Bare, almost entirely uninhabited, and no more than 7km wide and 5km long, it is still easily the largest of a clustered archipelago. The only significant hint of Cabrera's eventful past is the protective **castle** above its supremely sheltered harbour. Pliny claimed the island to have been the birthplace of Hannibal; medieval pirates hunkered down on it to plan future raids; and, during the Napoleonic Wars, the Spanish stuck nine thousand French prisoners of war out here and forgot about them (during their three-year captivity, two-thirds of them died from hunger and disease). More recently, the island was colonized by Franco's armed forces and now that they've departed, the island has been designated a national park.

A tiny kiosk beside Colònia de Sant Jordi harbour (April–Sept daily 8am–1pm & 5–9pm) has information on, and takes reservations for, **boat trips** to the island (April–Oct daily; 8hr; 5000ptas/€30.05; ☎971 649 034). There is nowhere to eat on Cabrera, so you should either take your own food or shell out 900ptas/€5.41 extra for food provided by the boat company – and drinks are extra too.

The day-trip starts with a fifty-minute voyage to the island followed by a speedy circumnavigation, weather permitting. On the final stretch, the boat nudges round a hostile-looking headland to enter the harbour, **Es Port** – a narrow finger of calm water edged by hills and equipped with a tiny jetty. From here, it's a stiff hoof up the path to the ruins of the fourteenth-century **castle** perched high above on Cabrera's west coast. The views from the fortress back to Mallorca are magnificent, and all sorts of **birds** can be viewed gliding round the sea-cliffs, including Manx and Cory's shearwaters and the rare Audouin's gulls, as well as peregrine falcons and shags. It is, however, the blue-underbellied **Lilfords wall lizard** that really takes the naturalists' biscuit: after you've completed the walk to the castle and back (which takes about twenty minutes each way), take time to have a drink down by the jetty, where you can tempt the Lilfords lizards out from the scrub with pieces of fruit.

The south coast

You can also visit **Cabrera Museum** (free), with displays that trace the history of the island and that are illustrated by a ragbag of archeological finds recovered from the island and its surrounding waters. The museum is housed in an attractively converted old wine cellar about ten minutes' walk from the jetty. The cellar was actually never used for its original purpose, since its construction coincided with the phylloxera louse epidemic that destroyed the island's vineyards in the 1870s. One further sight is the sombre **memorial** to the dead French prisoners of war, a short distance west of the museum.

On the return journey, the boat bobs across the bay to visit the **Cova Blava** (Blue Grotto), and heads right into the cave through the fifty-metre-wide entrance and on into the yawning chamber beyond. The grotto reaches a height of 160m and is suffused by bluish light, from which it gets its name; you can swim in it too.

Parts of Cabrera are unsafe to explore, as there's still a real danger from unexploded armaments left here by the military. Check with the park staff before you wander off into the interior.

Campos, Llucmajor and around

The unassuming town of **CAMPOS**, 13km northwest of Santanyí and 12km north of Colònia de Sant Jordi, hardly fires the imagination, though the fine facade of the immaculately restored Renaissance town hall and the chunky sixteenth-century church opposite both merit a look. Much more importantly, Campos boasts what many consider to be the best **patisserie** on the island – Pastisserie Pomar, in the main square at Plaça 20 (☎971 650 606).

LLUCMAJOR, the next settlement to the west, has little to detain you, despite its medieval origins as a market town and its long association with the island's shoemakers. It was here, just outside the old city walls, that Jaume III, the last of the independent kings of Mallorca, was defeated and killed by Pedro IV of Aragon.

Llucmajor is at the head of the byroad which leads south to Cap Blanc and Cala Pi. About 13km along this road lies **Capocorb Vell** (often signposted in Castilian as "Capicorp Vey"; Mon–Wed & Fri–Sun 10am–5pm; 250ptas/€1.50), whose extensive remains date

Llucmajor is 9km south of Puig Randa (see p.201) and 12km east of S'Arenal (see p.110).

from around 1000 BC. Surrounded by arid scrubland and enclosed within a modern dry-stone wall, this prehistoric village incorporates the battered ruins of five *talayots* and 28 dwellings. A footpath weaves round the haphazard remains, but most of what you see is not very inspiring and gives little idea of how the village was arranged. The most impressive features are the Cyclopean walls, which reach a height of four metres in places. To make more sense of what you see, pick up the free English leaflet at the entrance.

A short distance further south, just beyond the village of **CAPOC-ORB**, there's a choice of routes: straight on for **Cap Blanc**, a desultory cape with a lighthouse, or left for the four-kilometre trip to **CALA PI**. Spreading over a bleak headland, this resort is the remote setting for the glitzy *Club Cala Pi*, a self-contained resort complex that's a favourite with French tourists. In the cove there's a lovely **beach**, a tiny finger of sand wedged between high, pine-studded cliffs and fringed by ramshackle fishing huts. You won't find anywhere to **stay** on spec, but you can refresh your palate at the *Miguel* restaurant, where the grilled fish is very tasty, or snack at the **bar** next door.

Travel details

Buses

Artà to: Cala Rajada (Mon–Sat 6–8 daily, 1–2 on Sun; 10min); Ca'n Picafort (May–Oct Mon–Sat 2 daily; 45min); Coves d'Artà (May–Oct Mon–Sat 2–4 daily; 10min); Palma (Mon–Sat 4 daily, 1 on Sun; 1hr 25min); Platja de Canyamel (May–Oct Mon–Sat 2 daily; 15min); Port d'Alcúdia (May–Oct Mon–Sat 3 daily; 30min).

Cala d'Or to: Cala Rajada (May–Oct 5 daily; 20min); Coves del Drac (May–Oct Mon–Sat 6 daily; 20min); Palma (May–Oct Mon–Sat hourly, 2 on Sun; Nov–April 2–4 daily; 1hr 10min); Santanyí (May–Oct Mon–Sat hourly, 2 on Sun; Nov–April 2–4 daily; 1hr 10min).

Cala Figuera to: Cala Santanyí (May–Oct Mon–Sat 1 daily; 5min); Palma (May–Oct Mon–Sat 1 daily; 1hr 20min); Santanyí (Mon–Sat 2 daily; 15min).

Cala Millor to: Cala Rajada (May–Oct Mon–Sat 12 daily, 2 on Sun; Nov–April Mon–Sat 2 daily; 25min); Coves del Drac (May–Oct Mon–Sat 6 daily, 1 on Sun; 25min); Palma (Mon–Sat 7–8 daily, 2 on Sun; 1hr 15min); Port d'Alcúdia (May–Oct Mon–Sat 3 daily; 1hr).

Cala Pi to: Palma (May–Oct Mon–Sat 1 daily; 45min).

Cala Rajada to: Artà (Mon–Sat 6–8 daily, 1–2 on Sun; 10min); Cala Agulla (May–Oct Mon–Sat 4 daily; 5min); Cala de Sa Font (May–Oct Mon–Sat 4 daily; 10min); Cala Millor (May–Oct Mon–Sat 12 daily, 2 on Sun; Nov–April Mon–Sat 2 daily; 25min); Cala d'Or (May–Oct 5 daily; 20min); Ca'n Picafort (May–Oct Mon–Sat 4 daily; 35min); Capdepera (Mon–Sat 6–8 daily, 1–2 on Sun; 5min); Coves d'Artà (May–Oct Mon–Sat 4 daily; 25min); Palma (Mon–Sat 4 daily, 1–2 on Sun; 1hr 30min); Platja de Canyamel (May–Oct Mon–Sat 4 daily; 20min); Port d'Alcúdia (May–Oct Mon–Sat 2 daily; 45min).

Capdepera to: Cala Rajada (Mon–Sat 6–8 daily, 1–2 on Sun; 5min); Palma
Mon–Sat 4 daily, 1–2 on Sun; 1hr 30min).

Colònia de Sant Jordi to: Palma (May–Oct Mon–Sat 8 daily, 2 on Sun;
Nov–April Mon–Sat 4 daily, 2 on Sun; 1hr); Santanyí (2–4 daily; 25min).

Coves d'Artà to: Artà (May–Oct Mon–Sat 2–4 daily; 10min); Cala d'Or
(May–Oct Mon–Sat 6 daily; 20min); Cala Rajada (May–Oct Mon–Sat 2–4 daily;
5min).

Coves del Drac to: Cala Rajada (May–Oct Mon–Sat 6 daily, 1 on Sun; 25min);
Palma (May–Oct Mon–Sat 4 daily, 1 on Sun; Nov–April 1 daily; 1hr).

Felanitx to: Palma (3–4 daily; 50min); Porto Colom (1–3 daily; 15min).

Manacor to: Palma (Mon–Sat 7 daily, 3 on Sun; 45min); Porto Cristo (Mon–Sat
7 daily, 2–3 on Sun; 25min).

Montuïri to: Petra (2–3 daily; 10min); Palma (2–3 daily; 40min).

Palma to: Algaida (3–5 daily; 20min); Artà (Mon–Sat 4 daily, 1 on Sun; 1hr
25min); Cala d'Or (May–Oct Mon–Sat hourly, 2 on Sun; Nov–April 2–4 daily;
1hr 10min); Cala Figuera (May–Oct Mon–Sat 1 daily; 1hr 20min); Cala Millor
(Mon–Sat 7–8 daily, 2 on Sun; 1hr 15min); Cala Pi (May–Oct Mon–Sat 1 daily;
15min); Cala Rajada (Mon–Sat 4 daily, 1–2 on Sun; 1hr 30min); Calas de
Mallorca (May–Oct Mon–Sat 2 daily; 1hr); Colònia de Sant Jordi (May–Oct
Mon–Sat 8 daily, Sun 2 daily; Nov–April Mon–Sat 4 daily, 2 on Sun; 1hr); Coves
del Drac (May–Oct Mon–Sat 4 daily, 1 on Sun; Nov–April 1 daily; 1hr); Covetes
(for Es Trenc beach; May–Oct 1 daily; 1hr); Felanitx (3–4 daily; 50min);
Manacor (Mon–Sat 7 daily, 3 on Sun; 45min); Montuïri (2–3 daily; 40min);
Muro (2–4 daily; 50min); Petra (2–3 daily; 45min); Porto Colom (1–3 daily;
1hr 10min); Porto Cristo (Mon–Sat 7 daily, 3 on Sun; 1hr 10min); Porto Petro
(May–Oct 2 daily; 1hr 10min); Santanyí (May–Oct Mon–Sat hourly, 2 on Sun;
Nov–April 2–4 daily; 1hr 10min); Sineu (2 daily; 1hr).

Petra to: Montuïri (2–3 daily; 10min); Palma (2–3 daily; 45min).

Porto Colom to: Palma (1–3 daily; 1hr).

Porto Cristo to: Ca'n Picafort (May–Oct Mon–Sat 3 daily; 1hr); Palma via
Manacor (Mon–Sat 7 daily, 3 on Sun; 1hr 10min); Port d'Alcúdia (May–Oct
Mon–Sat 3 daily; 1hr).

Santanyí to: Cala Santanyí (May–Oct Mon–Sat 1 daily; 10min); Palma
(May–Oct Mon–Sat hourly, 2 on Sun; Nov–April 2–4 daily; 1hr 10min).

The Contexts

The historical framework

Earliest peoples

The earliest inhabitants of the Balearics seem to have reached the islands from the Iberian peninsula, and carbon-dating of remains indicates that human occupation was well established by 4000 BC. The discovery of pottery, flints and animal horns fashioned into tools suggests that these early people were **Neolithic pastoralists**, who supplemented their food supplies by hunting, particularly the *Myotragus balearicus*, a species of mountain goat now extinct. Hundreds of these animals' skulls have been discovered and several are exhibited in the islands' larger museums. The frequency of these finds has encouraged some experts to assert that the *Myotragus* was domesticated, the principal evidence being the remains of what might be crude corrals found on the coast near Valldemossa; this assertion is, however, strongly contested.

Why, or how, these Neolithic peoples moved to the Balearic Islands is unknown. Indeed, the first landfall may have been accidental, made by early seafarers travelling along the shores of the Mediterranean – part of the wave of migration that is known to have taken place in the Neolithic period. Many of the oldest archeological finds have been discovered in natural **caves**, where it seems likely that these early settlers first sought shelter and protection. Later, cave complexes were dug out of the soft limestone that occurs on the islands, comprising living quarters, usually circular and sometimes with a domed ceiling, as well as longer, straighter funerary chambers. These complexes represent the flourishing of what is commonly called the **Balearic Cave Culture**.

The Balearic cave dwellers soon came into regular contact with other cultures; the Mediterranean, with its relatively calm and tide-free waters, has always acted as a conduit of civilization. The discovery of Beaker ware at Deià indicates one of the earliest of these outside influences. The **Beaker People**, whose artefacts have been found right across Western Europe, are named after their practice of burying their dead with pottery beakers. They had knowledge of the use of bronze, an alloy of copper and tin, and they exported their bronze-working skills to the Balearics in around 1400 BC. This technological revolution marked the end of the cave culture and the beginning of the Talayotic period.

The Talayotic period

The megalithic remains of the **Talayotic period**, which extended almost to the Christian era, are strewn all over Mallorca and Menorca – though, surprisingly, there's no evidence of them on Ibiza. The structure that gives its name to the period is the **talayot** (from *atalaya*, Arabic for "watchtower"), a cone-shaped tower with a circular base, between five and ten metres in height, built without mortar or cement. There are literally dozens of ruined *talayots* on Mallorca and the detail of their original design varies from site to site: some are solid, others contain one or more chambers. Most are found in settlements, but there are solitary examples too. This diversity has helped to generate considerable debate about their original purpose, with scholars suggesting variously that they were built for defence, as dwellings for chieftains, as burial sites or as storehouses. The mystery of the *talayots* is compounded by their unusualness. The only Mediterranean structures they resemble are the Nuragh towers found on Sardinia. A Sardinian connection would support the view that this phase in the Balearics' development resulted from contact with other cultures, though Sardinia is but one of several options, with Egypt, Crete and Greece also touted as possible influences. Whatever the truth, it is clear that by 1000 BC a relatively sophisticated, largely pastoral society had developed on Mallorca, with at least some of the islanders occupying the walled settlements that still dot the interior. One example is at **Capocorb Vell** (see p231) south of Llucmajor, where you can still inspect four *talayots* and the remains of up to thirty houses. Another is at **Ses Paisses** (see p.207), a settlement of comparable proportions outside Artà. Like other Mallorcan and Menorcan settlements of the period – Talayotic culture reached its apogee on Menorca – Capocorb Vell and Ses Paisses were occupied well into the Roman period.

Phoenicians, Greeks and Carthaginians

Fearful of attack from the sea, Mallorca's Talayotic peoples built their walled settlements a few kilometres inland. This pattern was, however, modified during the first millennium BC, when the Balearics became a staging post for the **Phoenicians**, maritime traders from the eastern Mediterranean whose long voyages reached as far as Cornwall in southwest England. According to the Roman historian Pliny, the Phoenicians established a large settlement at Sanisera on Menorca's north coast and archeologists have also discovered Phoenician artefacts at **Alcúdia** on Mallorca (see p.185). In general, however, very few Phoenician remains have been found on the Balearics – just a handful of bronze items, jewellery and pieces of coloured glass.

The Phoenicians were displaced by **Greeks** from around 800 BC, as several city-states explored the western Mediterranean in search of trade and potential colonies. Like the Phoenicians, the Greeks appear to have used the Balearics primarily as a staging post, for no Greek buildings have survived on either Mallorca or Menorca. The absence of metal apparently made the islands unsuitable for long-term colonization, and the belligerence of the native population may have played a part too: the Greeks coined the islands' name, the "Balearics", which they derived from *ballein*, meaning "to throw from a sling". The islanders were adept at this form of warfare, and many early visitors were repelled with showers of polished sling-stones. (Some historians dispute this theory, claiming rather that

the name comes from the Baleri tribe of Sardinia.)

The Greeks were also discouraged from colonization by the growth of the **Carthaginian** empire across the western Mediterranean. The Phoenicians had established Carthage, on the North African coast, under the leadership of princess Elissa, better known as Dido, the tragic hero of Virgil's *Aeneid*. According to the Greek historian Diodorus Siculus, the Carthaginians began to colonize the Balearics in the early seventh century BC, and the islands were firmly under their control by the beginning of the third century BC, if not earlier. Little is known of the Carthaginian occupation except that they established several new settlements. It is also claimed that the famous Carthaginian general, Hannibal, was born on Cabrera island off Mallorca, though Ibiza and Malta claim this honour too.

In the third century BC, the expansion of the Carthaginian empire across the Mediterranean and up into the Iberian Peninsula triggered two **Punic Wars** with Rome. In both of these wars the Balearics proved extremely valuable, first as stepping stones from the North African coast to the European mainland and second as a source of mercenaries. Balearic slingers were highly valued and accompanied Hannibal and his elephants across the Alps in the Second Punic War, when (for reasons that remain obscure) the islanders refused gold and demanded payment in wine and women instead. After Hannibal's defeat by the Romans at the battle of Zama in 202 BC, Carthaginian power began to wane and they withdrew from Mallorca and Menorca, although they continued to have some influence over Ibiza for at least another seventy years.

Romans, Vandals and Byzantines

As the Carthaginians retreated so the **Romans** advanced, incorporating Ibiza within their empire after the final victory over Carthage in 146 BC. On Mallorca and Menorca, the islanders took advantage of the prolonged military chaos to profit from piracy, until finally, in 123 BC, the Romans, led by the consul Quintus Metellus, restored maritime order by occupying both islands. These victories earned Metellus the title "Balearico" from the Roman senate and two of the islands were given new names, Balearis Major (Mallorca) and Balearis Minor (Menorca).

For the next five hundred years all of the Balearics Islands were part of the **Roman Empire.**

mongst many developments, Roman colonists
introduced viticulture, turning the Balearics into a
ine-exporting area, and initiated olive-oil pro-
uction from newly planted groves. As was their
ustom, the Romans consolidated their control of
e islands by building roads and establishing
wns: on Mallorca they founded Pollentia
Icúdia) in the north and Palmaria on the south
past, near the site of modern Palma. Initially, the
alearics were part of the Roman province of
arraconensis (Tarragona), but in 404 AD the
lands became a province in their own right with
e name Balearica.

By this time, however, the Roman Empire was
in decline, its defences unable to resist the west-
ward-moving tribes of central Asia. One of these
bes, the **Vandals**, swept across the Balearics in
round 425 AD, thereby ending Roman rule. So
oroughgoing was the destruction they wrought
at very few signs of the Romans have survived
the only significant remains are those of
ollentia at Alcúdia (see p.185).

The Vandals had been Christianized long
efore they reached the Mediterranean, but they
vere followers of the **Arian** sect. This interpreta-
on of Christianity, founded by Arius, an
exandrian priest, insisted that Christ the Son
nd God the Father were two distinct figures, not
lements of the Trinity. To orthodox Christians,
iis seemed dangerously close to the pagan
elief in a multiplicity of gods and, by the end of
e fourth century AD, Arianism had been forcibly
xtirpated within the Roman Empire. However,
e sect continued to flourish amongst the
ermanic peoples of the Rhine, including the
andals, who, armed with their "heretical" beliefs,
ad no religious truck with their new Balearic
ubjects, persecuting them and destroying their
hurches. As a consequence, Christian remains
om this period have all but vanished.

In 533 the Vandals were defeated in North
frica by the Byzantine general, Count Belisarius
vho was the subject of a novel by one of
Iallorca's adopted sons, Robert Graves). This
rought the Balearics under **Byzantine** rule and,
r a time, restored prosperity and stability.
owever, the islands were too far removed from
onstantinople to be of much imperial impor-
ince and, when the empire was threatened
om the east at the end of the seventh century,
iey were abandoned in all but name.

The Moors

As the influence of Byzantium receded, so Islam
moved in from the south and east to fill the vac-
uum. In 707–8 the **Moors** of North Africa conducted an extended raid against Mallorca,
destroying its entire fleet and carrying away
slaves and booty. By 716 the Balearics' position
had become even more vulnerable with the
completion of the Moorish conquest of Spain. In
798 the Balearics were again sacked by the
Moors – who were still more interested in plun-
der than settlement – and in desperation the
islanders appealed for help to **Charlemagne**, the
Frankish Holy Roman Emperor. As emperor,
Charlemagne was the military leader of Western
Christendom (the pope was the spiritual leader),
so the appeal signified the final severance of the
Balearics' links with Byzantium and the East.

Charlemagne's attempt to protect the islands
from the Moors met with some success, but the
respite was only temporary. By the middle of the
ninth century, the Christian position had deteriorated so badly that the Balearics were compelled
to enter a non-aggression pact with the Moors,
and, to add to the islanders' woes, the Balearics
suffered a full-scale **Viking** raid in 859. Finally, at
the beginning of the tenth century, the **Emir of
Cordoba** conquered both Menorca and Mallorca.
Moorish rule lasted over three hundred years,
though internal political divisions among the
Muslims meant that the islands experienced several different regimes. In the early eleventh century, the emirate of Córdoba collapsed and control passed to the Wali (governor) of Denia, on
the Spanish mainland. This administration
allowed the Christians – who were known as
Mozarabs – to practise their faith, and the
islands prospered from their position at the heart
of the trade routes between North Africa and
Islamic Spain.

In 1085 the Balearics became an independent
emirate with a new dynasty of *walis*, from
Amortadha in North Africa. They pursued a more
aggressive foreign and domestic policy, raiding
the towns of the mainland and persecuting their
Christian citizens. These actions blighted trade
and thereby enraged the emergent city-states of
Italy at a time when Christendom was fired by
crusading zeal. Anticipating retaliation, the
Amortadhas fortified Palma, which was known at
this time as Medina Mayurka, and several mountain strongholds. The Christian attack came in

1114 when a grand Italian fleet – led by the ships of Pisa and supported by the pope as a mini-crusade – landed an army of 70,000 Catalan and Italian soldiers on Ibiza. The island was soon captured, but Mallorca, the crusaders' next target, proved a much more difficult proposition. Medina Mayurka's coastal defences proved impregnable, so the Christians assaulted the landward defences instead, the concentric lines of the fortifications forcing them into a long series of bloody engagements. When the city finally fell, the invaders took a bitter revenge, slaughtering most of the surviving Muslim population. However, despite their victory, the Christians had neither the will nor the resources to consolidate their position and, loading their vessels with freed slaves and loot, they returned home.

It took the Moors just two years to re-establish themselves on the islands, this time under the leadership of the **Almoravids**, a North African Berber tribe who had previously controlled southern Spain. The Almoravids proved to be tolerant and progressive rulers, and the Balearics prospered under them: agriculture improved, particularly through the development of irrigation, and trade expanded as commercial agreements were struck with the Italian cities of Genoa and Pisa. The Pisans – Crusaders earlier in the century – defied a papal ban on trade with Muslims to finalize the deal; consciences could, it seems, be flexible even in the "devout" Middle Ages when access to the precious goods of the east (silks, carpets and spices) was the prize.

Jaume I and the Reconquest

In 1203 the Almoravids were supplanted by the **Almohad** dynasty, who forcibly converted the islands' Christian population to Islam and started raiding the mainland. This was an extraordinary miscalculation, as the kingdoms of Aragón and Catalunya had recently been united, thereby strengthening the Christian position in this part of Spain. The unification was a major step in the changing balance of power: with their forces combined, the Christians were able to launch the **Reconquista**, which was eventually to drive the Moors from the entire peninsula. Part of the Christian jigsaw was the Balearics and, in 1228, the Emir of Mallorca imprudently antagonized the young **King Jaume I** of Aragón and Catalunya by seizing a couple of his ships. The king's advisers,

with their eyes firmly fixed on the islands' wealth, determined to capitalize on the offence. They organized the first Balearic publicity evening, a feast at which the king was presented with a multitude of Mallorcan delicacies and Catalan sailors told of the islands' prosperity. And so, insulted by the emir and persuaded by his nobility, Jaume I committed himself to a full-scale invasion.

Jaume's expedition of 150 ships, 16,000 men and 1500 horses set sail for Mallorca in September 1229. The king had originally planned to land at Pollença, in the northeast, but adverse weather conditions forced the fleet further south and it eventually anchored off Sant Elm. The following day, the Catalans defeated the Moorish forces sent to oppose the landing and Jaume promptly pushed east, laying siege to Medina Mayurka. It took three months to breach the walls, but on December 31 the city finally fell and Jaume was hailed as "**El Conqueridor**".

The cost of launching an invasion on this scale placed an enormous strain on the resources of a medieval monarch. With this in mind, Jaume subcontracted the capture of Ibiza, entering into an agreement, in 1231, with the Crown Prince of Portugal, Don Pedro, and the Count of Roussillon. In return for the capture of the island, the count and the prince were to be allowed to divide Ibiza between themselves, provided they acknowledged the suzerainty of Jaume. This project initially faltered, but was revived with the addition of the Archbishop of Tarragona. The three allies captured Ibiza in 1235 and divided the spoils, although Don Pedro waived his rights and his share passed to Jaume.

In the meantime, Jaume had acquired the overlordship of Menorca. Unable to afford another full-scale invasion, the king devised a cunning ruse. In 1232 he returned to Mallorca with just three galleys, which he dispatched to Menorca carrying envoys, while he camped out in the mountains above Capdepera on Mallorca. As night fell and his envoys negotiated with the enemy, Jaume ordered the lighting of as many bonfires as possible to illuminate the sky and give the impression of a vast army. The stratagem worked and the next day, mindful of the bloodbath following the invasion of Mallorca, the Menorcan Moors capitulated. According to the king's own account, they informed his envoys that "they gave great thanks to God and to me for the message I had sent them for they knew ell they could not long defend themselves against me". The terms of submission were generous: the Moors handed over Ciutadella, their principal settlement, and a number of other strongpoints, but Jaume acknowledged the Muslims as his subjects and appointed one of their leaders as his *rais* (governor).

The retention of Moorish government in Menorca, albeit under the suzerainty of the king, was in marked contrast to events on Mallorca. Here, the land was divided into eight blocs, with four passing to the king and the rest to his most trusted followers, who leased their holdings in the feudal fashion, granting land to tenants in turn for military service. In 1230 Jaume consolidated his position by issuing the **Carta de Població** (People's Charter), guaranteeing equality before the law, an extremely progressive precept for the period. Furthermore, Mallorca was exempted from taxation to encourage Catalan immigration, and special rights were given to Jews resident on the island, a measure designed to stimulate trade. Twenty years later, Jaume also initiated a distinctive form of government for Mallorca, with a governing body of six **jurats** (adjudicators) – one from the nobility, two knights, two merchants and one peasant. At the end of each year the *jurats* elected their successors. This form of government remained in place until the sixteenth century.

From a modern perspective, the downside of the Reconquest of Mallorca was the wholesale demolition of almost all Moorish buildings, with mosques systematically replaced by churches (at a later date the same policy was followed on Menorca). The main compensation is the architectural magnificence of **Palma Cathedral** (see p78), which was consecrated in 1269. Shortly afterwards, Jaume I died at Valencia. In his will he divided his kingdom between his two sons: Pedro received Catalunya, Aragón and Valencia, whilst **Jaume II** was bequeathed Montpellier, Roussillon and the Balearics. Jaume II was crowned in Mallorca on September 12, 1276.

The Kingdom of Mallorca

Jaume I's division of his kingdom infuriated Pedro, as Mallorca stood astride the shipping route between Barcelona and Sicily, where his wife was queen. He forced his brother to become his vassal, but in response Jaume II secretly schemed with the French. Predictably enough, Pedro soon discovered his brother's treachery and promptly set about planning a full-blooded invasion. However, Pedro died before the assault could begin and it was left to his son, **Alfonso III**, to carry out his father's plans. Late in 1285, Alfonso's army captured Palma without too much trouble, which was just as well for its inhabitants: wherever Alfonso met with resistance – as he did later in the campaign at the castle of Alaró – he extracted a brutal revenge. Indeed, even by the standards of thirteenth-century Spain, Alfonso was considered excessively violent and for his atrocities the pope excommunicated him – but not for long.

With Mallorca secured and Jaume deposed, Alfonso turned his attention to Menorca where he suspected the loyalty of the Moorish governor: the *rais* was allegedly in conspiratorial contact with the Moors of North Africa. Alfonso's army landed on Menorca in January 1287 and decisively defeated the Moors just outside Maó. The king's treatment of the vanquished islanders was savage: those Muslims who were unable to buy their freedom were enslaved, and those who couldn't work as slaves – the old, the sick and the very young – were taken to sea and thrown overboard. Alfonso rewarded the nobles who had accompanied him with grants of land and brought in hundreds of Catalan settlers. The capital, Medina Minurka, was renamed Ciutadella, and the island's mosques were converted to Christian usage, before being demolished and replaced.

Alfonso's violent career was cut short by his death in 1291 at the age of 25. His successor was his brother, Jaume, also the king of Sicily. A more temperate man, Jaume conducted negotiations through the papacy that eventually led, in 1298, to the restoration of the partition envisaged by Jaume I: he himself presided over Catalunya, Aragón and Valencia, while his exiled uncle, **Jaume II**, ruled as king of Mallorca and Menorca. Restored to the crown, Jaume II devoted a great deal of time to improving the commerce and administration of the Balearics. To stimulate trade, he established a weekly market in Palma, reissued the currency in gold and silver, and founded eleven towns in inland Mallorca, including Manacor, Felanitx, Llucmajor and Binissalem.

Jaume II attended to God as well as Mammon, and this period saw the building of many churches and monasteries. The king patronized the Mallorcan poet, scholar and Franciscan friar,

Ramon Llull (see pp.91 & 201), providing him with the finance to establish a monastic school near Valldemossa. Jaume also established new settlements on Menorca – most notably Alaior – and divided that island into seven parishes, ordering the construction of churches for each of them.

On his death in 1311, Jaume was succeeded by his asthmatic son, **Sancho**, who spent most of his time in his palace at Valldemossa, where the mountain air was to his liking. Nonetheless, he did his job well, continuing the successful economic policies of his father and strengthening his fleet to protect his territories from North African pirates. Mallorca boomed. The island had long served as the entrepôt between North Africa and Europe, its warehouses crammed with iron, figs, salt, oil and slaves, but in the early fourteenth century its industries flourished too, primarily shipbuilding and textiles. In 1325, the traveller Ramón Muntaner praised Palma as an "honoured city of greater wealth than any with the most businesslike inhabitants... of any city in the world." He may have been exaggerating, but not by much, and Palma's merchants were certainly inventive: spotting a gap in the market they went into crossbow-making and by 1380 they were exporting them by the boat-load.

Internationally, Sancho worked hard to avoid entanglement in the growing antagonism between Aragón and France, but Mallorca's future still looked decidedly shaky when he died without issue in 1324. Theoretically, the island should have passed to Aragón, but the local

nobility moved fast to crown Sancho's ten-year-old nephew as **Jaume III**. Hoping to forestall Aragonese hostility, they then had him betrothed to the king of Aragón's five-year-old daughter, though in the long term this marriage did the new king little good. After he came of age, Jaume III's relations with his brother-in-law, Pedro IV of Aragón, quickly deteriorated, and Pedro successfully invaded the Balearics in response to an alleged plot against him. Jaume fled to his mainland possessions and sold Montpellier to the French to raise money for an invasion. He landed on Mallorca in 1349, but was no match for Pedro and was defeated and killed on the outskirts of Llucmajor. His son, the uncrowned **Jaume IV**, was also captured and although he eventually escaped, he was never able to drum up sufficient support to threaten the Aragonese.

Unification with Spain

For a diversity of reasons the **unification** of the Balearics with Aragón – and their subsequent incorporation within Spain – proved a disaster. In particular, the mainland connection meant that the islands' nobility soon gravitated towards the Aragonese court, regarding their local estates as little more than sources of income to sustain their expensive lifestyles. More fundamentally, general economic trends moved firmly against the islands. After the fall of Constantinople to the Turks in 1453, the lucrative overland trade routes from the eastern Mediterranean to the Far East were blocked and, just as bad, it was the

---

THE JEWS IN MALLORCAN HISTORY

In 1391, crowds marched on Palma to object to heavy Aragonese taxation and absentee landlords; failing to find satisfaction, they instead vented their spleen on the city's **Jews**, massacring three hundred of them. Mallorca's large Jewish community, concentrated in Palma and Inca, had long played a crucial part in maintaining the island's money supply and supporting trade with North Africa, but they were treated in that strangely contradictory manner which was common across much of medieval Europe, alternately courted and discriminated against. They were, for instance, expected to live in their own ghettos and wear a distinctive type of dress, but were allowed (unlike their Christian neighbours) to divorce and re-marry. Predictably, they were often blamed for things over which they had no control, from famine to plague, and were intermittently subjected to pogroms like this one in 1395 and again in 1435 (see p.97). They were also subject to the attentions of the **Holy Office of the Inquisition**, who set up shop in Palma in 1484 determined to impose orthodoxy on all of the island's citizenry. The Inquisitors bore down on the Jews, most of whom either left or chose the course of least resistance and converted to Christianity, though a small percentage were burnt to death. As late as the 1970s, the descendants of these converts still formed a distinct group of Palma gold- and silversmiths.

---

ortuguese who discovered the way around the
pe of Good Hope to the Indies. In 1479,
ernando V of Aragón married Isabella I of
astile, thereby uniting the two largest kingdoms
Spain, but yet again this was bad news for the
anders. The union brought mainland preoccu-
ations and a centralized bureaucracy, which
ndered the islands a provincial backwater –
en more so when, following Columbus's reach-
g the Americas in 1492, the focus of European
ade moved from the Mediterranean to the
lantic seaboard almost at a stroke. The last
ommercial straw was the royal decree that for-
ade Catalunya and the Balearics from trading
ith the New World. By the start of the sixteenth
entury, the Balearics were starved of foreign cur-
ncy, and the islands' merchants had begun to
ave, signalling a period of long-term economic
ecline.

ixteenth-century decline

'allorca's political and economic difficulties
estabilized its social structures. As scapegoats,
e Jews focused some of the swirling antago-
isms that perturbed sixteenth-century Mallorca,
ut there were many other signs of discontent.
he aristocracy was divided into warring factions,
e country districts were set against the towns,
nd perhaps most destabilizing of all were high
xes and an unreliable grain supply. This turbu-
nce coalesced in an **armed uprising** of peas-
nts and artisans in 1521. Organized in a
ermania, or armed brotherhood, the insurrec-
onists seized control of Palma, whose nobles
eat a hasty retreat to either the safety of Palma's
astell de Bellver or the Alcúdia citadel; those
ho didn't move fast enough were slaughtered
the streets. The rebels soon captured the
ellver, and polished off the blue-bloods who
ad sought protection there, but Alcúdia held out
ntil relieved. It was a long wait: only in 1523 did
e forces of authority return under the command
f **Emperor Charles V**, king of Spain, Habsburg
oly Roman Emperor and the grandson of
ernando and Isabella. Charles negotiated gener-
us terms for the surrender of Palma, but once in
ossession of the city, promptly broke the agree-
ent and ordered the execution of five hundred
f the rebels, who were duly hung, drawn and
uartered.

Mallorca witnessed other sixteenth-century
orrors with the renewal of large-scale **maritime**
raids from North Africa. This upsurge of piratical
activity was partly stimulated by the final expulsion of the Moors from Spain in 1492, and partly by the emergence of the Ottoman Turks as a
Mediterranean superpower. Muslim raiders ransacked Pollença (1531 and 1550), Alcúdia (1551),
Valldemossa (1552), Andratx (1553) and Sóller
(1561), whilst the Ottoman admiral Khair ed-Din,
better known as **Barbarossa**, ravaged Menorca's
Maó in 1535. Muslim incursions continued until
the seventeenth century, but declined in frequency and intensity after a combined Italian
and Spanish force destroyed the Turkish fleet at
Lepanto in 1571.

Seventeenth- and eighteenth-century stagnation

Mallorca's woes continued throughout the seventeenth century. Trade remained stagnant and
the population declined, a sorry state of affairs
that was exacerbated by continued internal tensions. Palma, in particular, was plagued by
vendettas between its aristocratic families, with
the Canavall and Canavant factions regularly
involved in street battles and assassination,
whilst the (often absentee) landowners failed to
invest in their estates. By the 1630s the population problem had become so critical that Philip IV
exempted the islands from the levies that raised
men for Spain's armies – though this gain was
offset by the loss of 15,000 Mallorcans to **plague**
in 1652.

A new development was the regular appearance of **British** vessels in the Mediterranean, a
corollary of Britain's increasing share of the
region's seaborne trade and the Royal Navy's
commitment to protect its merchantmen from
Algerian pirates. The British didn't have much use
for Mallorca, and largely ignored it, but they were
impressed by Maó's splendid harbour. The interminable **War of the Spanish Succession**
(1701–14), fought over the vacant Spanish
throne, gave them the opportunity to seize control. The British captured Menorca in 1708 and
only relinquished their claim to the island in
favour of Spain in 1802, after three periods of
occupation. The war also affected Mallorca inso-
far as the islanders picked the wrong side. Most
of Spain favoured the French candidate, Philip of
Anjou, but Catalunya and Mallorca preferred the
Austrian Habsburg Charles III, who was supported by Britain and the Netherlands. Philip won,

and promptly stripped the island of its title of kingdom and removed many of its historic rights.

Mallorca was left pretty much untouched by the European conflicts that rippled around it during the early eighteenth century, but the island did not prosper. Instead, it turned in on itself, becoming a caste- and priest-ridden backwater preoccupied with its own internal feuds. By the 1740s, however, this reactionary introspection was ruffled by more progressive elements, who, influenced by the **Enlightenment**, brought liberal and rationalist ideas into island society. Conservatives and liberals came into prolonged conflict over Ramón Llull – the former keen to have him beatified, the latter eager to denigrate his complex mysticism. The traditionalists won, but the violent bitterness of the dispute combined with its length (1749–77) polarized the middle class and left Mallorcan society unstable. This failure to create a political discourse between rival factions mirrored developments in the rest of Spain, and both here and on the mainland instability was to define the nineteenth century. One other major change to be noted was Madrid's edict pronouncing Castilian as the official language of the Balearics in place of the local dialect of Catalan.

The nineteenth century

Mallorca struggled throughout most of the nineteenth century. The island was a neglected and extremely poor outpost, subject to droughts, famines and epidemics of cholera, bubonic plague and yellow fever. Consequently, the islanders were preoccupied with the art of survival rather than politics, and generally stayed out of the Carlist wars between the liberals and the conservatives which so bitterly divided the Spanish mainland. Many islanders emigrated, some to Algeria after it was acquired by the French in 1830, others to Florida and California. The leading political figure of the period was the historian **Josep Quadrodo**, who led the reactionary Catholic Union, which bombarded Madrid with petitions and greeted every conservative success with enthusiastic demonstrations.

Matters began to improve towards the end of the nineteenth century, when agriculture, particularly almond cultivation, boomed. Modern services, like gas and electricity, began to be installed and a regular steam packet link was established between Mallorca and the mainland.

Around this time too, a revival of **Catalan culture** led by the middle class of Barcelona, stirred the Mallorcan bourgeoisie. In Palma, Catalunyan novelists and poets were lauded, Catalan political groupings were formed, and the town was adorned with a series of magnificent *Modernist* buildings.

The Spanish Civil War

During the **Spanish Civil War** (1936–39), Mallorca and Menorca supported opposing sides. General Goded made Mallorca an important base for the Fascists, but when General Bosch attempted to do the same on Menorca, his NCOs and men mutinied and, with the support of the civilian population, declared their support for the Republic. In the event – apart from a few bombing raids and an attempted Republican landing at Porto Cristo (see p.216) – the Balearics saw very little actual fighting. Nevertheless, the Menorcans were dangerously exposed towards the end of the war, when they were marooned as the last Republican stronghold. A peaceful conclusion was reached largely through the intervention of the British, who brokered the surrender of the island aboard *HMS Devonshire*. Franco's troops occupied Menorca in April 1939 and the *Devonshire* left with 450 Menorcan refugees.

Modern Mallorca

Since 1945 the most significant development has been the emergence of **mass tourism** as the principal economic activity, though Mallorca's charms had been discovered by the rich and famous long before. Frédéric Chopin and George Sand spent the winter of 1838–39 at Valldemossa (see p.144), and Edward VII and the German Kaiser regularly cruised the Balearics before World War I. The high-water mark of this elitist tourist trade was reached in the 1930s when the Argentinian poet Adan Diehl opened the *Hotel Formentor* (see p.181). Diehl advertised the hotel in lights on the Eiffel Tower and attracted guests such as Edward VIII, the Aga Khan and Winston Churchill. From such small and privileged beginnings, the Balearics' tourist industry mushroomed at an extraordinary rate after World War II. In 1950, Mallorca had just one hundred registered hotels and boarding houses; by 1972 the total had risen to over 1500.

The prodigious pace of development accelerated after the death of Franco in 1975, thereby further strengthening the local economy. One twist, however, was the relative price of real estate: traditionally, Mallorcan landowners with coastal estates had given their younger children the poorer agricultural land near the seashore, but it was this land the developers wanted – and were prepared to pay fortunes for. Inevitably, this disrupted many a household, but the repercussions were hardly extreme as the island's economy continued to grow at an extraordinary rate. Indeed, the archipelago now has one of the highest per capita incomes in Spain, four times that of Extremadura for instance, and well above the EU average. The Balearics also benefited from the political restructuring of Spain following the death of Franco. In 1978, the Spanish parliament, the Cortes, passed a new **constitution**, which reorganized the country on a more federal basis and allowed for the establishment of regional Autonomous Communities. In practice, the demarcation of responsibilities between central and regional governments has proved problematic, leading to interminable wrangling, not least because the Socialists, who were in power from 1983 to 1996, waivered in their commitment to decentralization. Nonetheless, the Balearics, constituted as the **Comunidad Autónoma de las Islas Baleares** in 1983, have used their new-found independence to assert the primacy of their native Catalan language – now the main language of education – and to exercise a tighter local control of their economy.

From 1996 to 2000, this trend towards **decentralization** continued under a Conservative government which was only able to secure a majority in the Cortes with the support of several regionally based nationalist parties, including Basque, Catalan and Balearic groupings. Consequently, these regional groups were in a more powerful position than their numbers would otherwise justify, and were able to keep the momentum of decentralization going despite the innate centralist tendencies of Madrid

Conservatives. In particular, most government expenditure came under the control of the regions and the Balearic administration used these resources to upgrade a string of holiday resorts and modernize much of the archipelago's infrastructure. In part, this reflected a particular concern with Ibiza and Mallorca's somewhat tacky image and was accompanied by the imposition of stricter building controls, a number of environmental schemes and the spending of millions of pesetas on refurbishing the older, historical parts of Palma.

The Conservative-led Balearic administration also made moves to curb tourist development, but in this they failed to keep pace with public sentiment – as exemplified by a string of large-scale demonstrations during 1998 and 1999. The demonstrations focused on four primary and inter-related concerns: the spiralling cost of real estate, foreign ownership of land (some twenty percent of Mallorca is now in foreign hands), untrammelled development and loutish behaviour in the cheaper resorts. This failure to keep abreast of popular feeling resulted in the defeat of the Conservatives in the 1999 **regional elections** and their replacement by an unwieldy alliance of regionalists, socialists and greens committed to halting further tourist development in its tracks. As one of its spokesmen expressed it: "We need to dignify the tourist sector, not promote it as the cheapest in Europe with the idea that you can come here and do whatever you like." Faced with an annual influx of around **thirteen million** holidaymakers, few islanders would disagree, but only time will tell whether the new administration can achieve their objectives. National events are not moving in their favour. In March 2000, the Conservatives won a second **general election**, but this time their leader, the dour **José María Aznar**, gained an overall majority in the Cortes and the role of the regionalists will inevitably be diminished. It is hard to predict quite how this will play, but it seems likely that the centre will attempt to claw back some control.

A chronology of Spanish history

C11th–5th BC	Phoenicians, Greeks and Celts invade Spain and intermingle with the native (Iberian) population.
C3rd BC	Carthaginians conquer southeast Spain, incorporating the region within their Mediterranean empire.
C3rd–2nd BC	Carthage and Rome wrestle for control of the Iberian Peninsula in the three Punic Wars. Rome wins all three and their final act is the destruction of Carthage (in present-day Tunisia) in 146 BC.
C2nd BC	Spain becomes part of the Roman Empire, its administrative capital established at Córdoba in 151 BC. The region's mines and granaries bring unprecedented prosperity, and roads, bridges and aqueducts are built to network the peninsula.
C1st AD	Christianity makes rapid progress across Roman Spain.
264–76	Barbarian tribes, the Franks and the Suevi, ravage the peninsula.
414	The Visigoths reach Spain and become the dominant military force, with their capital at Toledo.
711	Islamic Moors (Arabs and Berbers from North Africa) invade and conquer the Visigoths' kingdom in a whirlwind campaign that lasts just seven years. However a Christian victory at the battle of Covadonga (722) halts the Moorish advance and leads to the creation of the kingdom of the Asturias – a Christian toehold on the northwest corner of the Iberian peninsula.
756	Abd ar-Rahman I proclaims the Emirate of Córdoba, confirming Moorish control over almost all of Spain.
778	The Holy Roman Emperor Charlemagne invades Spain from France, but is defeated. In the dash back across the Pyrenees, the Christian rearguard – led by Roland – is hacked to pieces at Roncesvalles, inspiring the epic poem the *Chanson de Roland*. Charlemagne's subsequent endeavours meet with more success and undermine Moorish control of Navarra and Catalunya.
C9th	The Christian kingdoms of Catalunya and Navarra are founded.
C10th–early 11th	The Emirate of Córdoba flourishes, its capital becoming the most prosperous and civilized city in Europe. Abd ar-Rahman III breaks with Baghdad to declare himself caliph of an independent western Islamic empire.
C11th	The caliphate disintegrates into squabbling *taifas*, or petty fiefdoms. A local chieftain, El Cid, leads Christian forces against the Moors of Valencia, but his victories have no lasting effect. Independent Catalunya expands.

1037	Fernando I unites the kingdoms of Castile and León-Asturias.
1162	Alfonso II unites the kingdoms of Aragón and Catalunya.
C13th	The pace of the Christian Reconquest accelerates after the kings of Navarra, Castile and Aragón combine to defeat the Muslims at the crucial battle of Las Navas de Tolosa in 1212. Subsequent Christian victories include the capture of Mallorca (1229), Córdoba (1236), Valencia (1238) and Seville (1248). The reconquered territories are mostly distributed amongst the Christian nobility in great estates, the *latifundia*. Men from the ranks also receive land, forming a lower, larger land-owning class, the *hidalgos*.
1479	Castile and Aragón, the two pre-eminent Christian kingdoms, are united under Isabella I and Fernando V, the so-called Catholic Monarchs (*Los Reyes Católicos*). Spain subsequently emerges as a single political entity, with the Inquisition acting as a unifying force. The Inquisitors concentrate their attention on the Jews, expelling around 400,000 from Spain for refusing Christian baptism.
1492	The fall of Granada, the last Moorish kingdom. Columbus reaches the Americas.
1494	At the Treaty of Tordesillas, under the approving eye of the pope, Spain and Portugal divide the New World between them. Portugal gets Brazil and Spain takes the rest of modern-day Latin America.
1516–56	On the death of Fernando, his grandson Carlos I succeeds to the Spanish throne. Three years later Carlos also becomes Holy Roman Emperor – as Charles V – adding Germany, Austria and the Low Countries to his kingdom. Throughout his reign, he wages almost incessant war against his many enemies, principally the French, the Protestants and the Muslims of North Africa. He funds his campaigns with the gold and silver bullion that is pouring into Spain from the New World, where Spanish adventurers have conquered, colonized and exploited a vast new empire.
1519	Cortés lands in Mexico, seizing its capital two years later.
1532	Pizarro "discovers" Peru, capturing Cuzco the next year.
1539	Hernando de Soto stakes out Florida.
1541	Pedro de Valdivia founds Santiago, Chile.
1555	Charles V finally accepts he is unable to suppress the German Reformation and agrees to a compromise peace with the Protestants at the Treaty of Augsburg.
1556	Charles V abdicates. His son, Felipe II (Philip II), becomes king of Spain and its colonies, Naples, Milan and the Low Countries. His brother, Ferdinand I, becomes Holy Roman Emperor, ruling Germany and Austria. An ardent and autocratic Catholic, Felipe continues the militaristic policy of his father, but concentrates his efforts against the Protestants.
1567	The Protestants of the Low Countries rise against Felipe II, beginning a protracted conflict that will drain Spanish resources and exhaust the Low Countries.

| 1571 | Spain wins control of the Mediterranean after defeating the Turkish fleet at Lepanto. |

1581 — Spain annexes Portugal.

1588 — The English defeat Felipe II's Armada, eliminating Spain as a major sea power.

1598 — Felipe II dies. His legacy is an enormous but bankrupt empire: Spain's great wealth, so ruthlessly extracted from its colonies, has been squandered in over seventy years of continuous warfare.

C17th — The decline. Spain's international credibility is undermined by the loss of Portugal (1640) and the Netherlands (1648), emphasizing her military degeneration. Domestically, the poverty and suffering of the mass of the population – as compared with the opulence of the royal court – fuels regional discontent and insurrection. Cervantes publishes *Don Quixote* in 1605.

1701–14 — Europe's nation states slug it out in the War of the Spanish Succession. The Bourbon (French) claimant – as opposed to that of the Holy Roman Emperor – wins out to become Felipe V. The British pick up Gibraltar and Menorca. As Spain declines, so it moves into the French sphere of influence.

1804 — Napoleon crowned Emperor of France. Spain assists him in his war against England.

1805 — The British navy, under Nelson, destroys the Franco-Spanish fleet at Battle of Trafalgar.

1808 — Napoleon arrests the Spanish king and replaces him with his brother, Joseph. This starts the War of Independence (otherwise known as the Peninsular War) in which the Spaniards fight the French army of occupation with the help of their new-found allies, the British.

1811 onwards — The South American colonies take advantage of the situation to assert their independence, detaching themselves from Spain one by one.

1815 — The end of the Napoleonic Wars.

C19th — Further Spanish decline. The nineteenth century is dominated by the struggle between the forces of monarchist reaction and those of liberal constitutional reform. There are three bitter Carlist wars, named after one of the claimants to the throne. The progressives finally triumph in the 1870s, but the new government's authority is brittle and Spanish society remains deeply divided. Elsewhere, Puerto Rico, the Philippines and Cuba shake off Spanish control with the help of the US. Spain's American empire is at an end.

1900–31 — Liberals and conservatives fail to reach a secure constitutional consensus, keeping the country on a knife edge. Working-class political movements – of anarchist, Marxist and socialist inclination – grow in strength and stir industrial and political discontent. Spain stays neutral in World War I, but the success of the Russian Bolsheviks terrifies King Alfonso XIII and the bourgeoisie, who support the right-wing military coup engineered by General Primo de Rivera in 1923. Rivera dies in 1930 and the king abdicates in 1931 when anti-monarchist parties win the municipal elections.

1932–36   The new Republican government introduces radical left-of-centre reforms, but separatists (in Catalunya, Galicia and the Basque country), revolutionaries and rightists undermine its authority. Spain polarizes to the political left and right. Chaos and confusion prevail.

1936–39   The Spanish Civil War. General Francisco Franco leads a right-wing military rebellion against the Republican government. His Nationalists receive substantial support from Hitler and Mussolini. The Republicans get sporadic help from the Soviet Union and attract thousands of volunteers, organized in the International Brigades. The Civil War is vicious and bloody, ending in 1939 with a Fascist victory. Franco becomes head of state and bloody reprisals follow. Pope Pius XII congratulates the dictator on his "Catholic victory".

1939–75   Franco establishes a one-party state, backed up by stringent censorship and a vigorous secret police. By staying neutral during World War II, he survives the fall of Nazi Germany. In 1969, Franco nominates the grandson of Alfonso XIII, Juan Carlos, as his successor, but retains his vice-like grip on the country until his death in 1975.

1976–82   Juan Carlos recognizes the need for political reform and helps steer the country towards a parliamentary system. He reinforces his democratic credentials by opposing the attempted coup of 1981, when Colonel Tejero leads a group of Guardia Civil officers loyal to Franco's memory in the storming of the Cortes (parliament). The coup fails.

1982–96   In 1982, Felipe González's Socialist Workers' Party – the PSOE – is elected to office with the votes of nearly ten million Spaniards. It's an electoral landslide and the PSOE, buoyed up by the optimism of the times, promises change and progress. But González finds it hard to deliver and loses the enthusiasm of the left, his electoral power base. The left feels that González has followed a semi-monetarist policy, putting economic efficiency above social policies and rating the control of inflation as more urgent than the reduction of unemployment. Nevertheless, Spain's economy grows dramatically, the country becomes a respected member of the EU, and the PSOE attempts to deal with Spain's deep-seated separatist tendencies by permitting a large degree of regional autonomy. No effort is made to hunt down Franco's thugs – part of an accommodation between left and right designed to stop Spain from degenerating into a cycle of political revenge.

1996–2000   At the 1996 general election, the Conservative Popular Party led by José Aznar becomes the largest party in the Cortes, but does not get an overall majority. Aznar enlists the support of Catalan and Basque nationalist deputies to form an administration. The price is more powers to the regions. In government, Aznar moves his right-wing party to the political centre, mixing gestures to the unemployed (Spain's unemployment rate is the highest in the EU) and substantial investment in the country's infrastructure with privatization (of the national airline, Iberia, for one) and cuts in income tax. His measures are sufficiently well received for Aznar to win a second general election in March 2000 – and this time the Conservatives have an overall majority in the Cortes.

Flora and fauna

Despite its reputation as a hopelessly over-developed package-holiday destination, Mallorca has much to offer birders and botanists alike. Separated from the Iberian Peninsula some fifty million years ago, the Balearic archipelago has evolved (at least in part) its own distinctive flora and fauna, with further variations between Mallorca and the other islands. Among Mallorca's wildlife, it's the raptors inhabiting the mountains of the north-west – particularly the black vulture – which attract much of the attention, but there are other pleasures too, especially the migratory birds which gather on the island's saltpans and marshes in April and May and from mid-September to early October. The islands are also justifiably famous for their fabulous range of wild flowers and flowering shrubs.

Some of the island's most important habitats have, however, been threatened by the developers. This has spawned an influential conservation group, **GOB** (Grup Balear d'Ornitologia i Defensa de la Naturalesa), which has recently launched several successful campaigns. It helped save the S'Albufera wetlands from further development, played a leading role in the black vulture re-establishment programme, and successfully lobbied to increase the penalties for shooting protected birds. GOB has offices in Palma at c/Can Verí 1 ☎ 971 721 105.

The account below of Mallorca's flora and fauna serves as a general introduction, and includes mention of several important birding sites, cross-referenced to the descriptions given throughout the book. For more specialist information, some recommended **field guides** are listed on p.265.

Habitats

The Balearic Islands are a continuation of the Andalucian mountains of the Iberian Peninsula, from which they are separated by a submarine trench never less than 80km wide and up to 1500m deep. Mallorca, the largest of the islands, comprises three distinct geographical areas with two ranges of predominantly limestone hills falling either side of a central plain, **Es Pla**. Mallorca's northwest coast is dominated by the **Serra de Tramuntana**, a slim, ninety-kilometre-long range of wooded hills and rocky peaks, fringed by tiny coves and precipitous seacliffs, that reaches its highest point at Puig Major (1447m). Also edged by steep seacliffs is the **Serres de Llevante**, a range of more modest hills that runs parallel to the island's east shore and rises to 509m at the Santuari de Sant Salvador.

Mallorca has a temperate Mediterranean climate, with winter frosts a rarity. The Serra de Tramuntana protects the rest of Mallorca from the prevailing winds that blow from the north and catches most of the rain.

Flora

The characteristic terrain of Mallorca up to around 700m is **garrigue**, partly forested open scrubland where the island's native trees – Aleppo pines, wild olives, holm oaks, carobs and dwarf palms – intermingle with imported species like ash, elm and poplar. Between 700m and 950m, *garrigue* is gradually replaced by **maquis**, a scrubland of rosemary, laurel, myrtle and broom interspersed with swaths of bracken. Higher still is a rocky terrain that can only support the sparsest of vegetation, such as an assortment of hardy grasses and low-growth rosemary.

Across much of the island, this indigenous vegetation has been destroyed by cultivation.

owever, the **Aleppo pine** and the evergreen **olm oak** – which traditionally supplied acorns r pigs, wood for charcoal and bark for tanning are still common, as is the **carob tree**, which refers the hottest and driest parts of the island. guably the archipelago's most handsome tree, e carob boasts leaves of varying greenness d conspicuous fruits – large pods which start reen, but ripen to black-brown. The **dwarf palm**, ith its sharp lance-like foliage, is concentrated round Pollença, Alcúdia and Andratx. The **wild live** is comparatively rare (and may not be digenous), but the cultivated variety, which oasts silver-grey foliage and can grow up to 0m in height, is endemic and has long been a ainstay of the local economy. There are also **range** and **lemon** orchards around Sóller and numerable **almond** trees, whose pink and hite blossom adorns much of Mallorca in late nuary and early February.

Mallorca has a superb variety of **flowering hrubs**. There are too many to list here in any etail, but look out for the deep blue flowers of e **rosemary**; the reddish bloom of the **lentisk** r mastic tree); the bright yellow **broom** which egins blossoming in March; the many types of **ee heather**; and the autumn-flowering **straw-erry tree**, found especially around Ca'n Picafort. **ockroses** are also widely distributed, the most ommon members of the group being the oring-flowering grey-leafed cistus, with its vel-ety leaves and pink flowers, and the narrow-afed cistus whose bloom is white.

In spring and autumn the fields, verges, woods nd cliffs of Mallorca brim with **wild flowers**. here are several hundred species and only in e depths of winter – from November to January are all of them dormant. Amongst well-known pecies there are marigolds, daisies, violets, yel-w primroses, gladioli, poppies, hyacinths, sever- kinds of cyclamen, the resinous St John's wort ith its crinkled deep green leaves and, abun-ant in the pine woods near the sea and the ountains, many types of orchid. Two common ountain plants are the pampas-like grass **mpelodesmus mauritanica**, giant clumps of hich cover the hillsides, and a local variety of e sarsaparilla, **smilax balearica**, which flourish- s in limestone crevices where its sharp thorns re something of a hazard for walkers. Other ommon and prominent plants are the giant-zed **agave** (century plant), an imported amaryl- d with huge spear-shaped, leathery leaves of

blue-grey coloration, which produces a massive flower spike every ten years (just before it dies). There's also the distinctive **asphodel**, whose tall spikes sport clusters of pink or white flowers from April to June. The asphodel grows on overgrazed or infertile land and its starch-rich tubers were once used by shoemakers to make glue. Another common sight is the **prickly pear**, traditionally grown behind peasants' houses as a windbreak and toilet wall. A versatile plant, the smell of the prickly pear deflects insects (hence its use round toilets) and its fruit is easy to make into pig food or jam.

Finally, many islanders maintain splendid **gardens** and here you'll see species that flourish throughout the Mediterranean, most famously bougainvilleas, oleanders, geraniums and hibiscus.

Birds

The diverse **birdlife** of Mallorca has attracted ornithologists for decades. The island boasts a whole batch of resident Mediterranean specialists and these are supplemented by migrating flocks of North European birds that descend on the island in their thousands during the spring and autumn.

The limestone **Serra de Tramuntana** mountains crimping the western coast are a haven for birds of prey. The massive black vulture is the real star here. This rare and impressive raptor, with its near three-metre wingspan, breeds in small numbers, but its size and residency means there's a reasonable chance of a sighting. The Puig Roig area (see p.170) is an excellent place to see this vulture, although note that during late spring and summer there are sometimes access restrictions to the bird's active sea-cliff nesting areas. The booted eagle is another mountain highlight and there is a supporting cast of ospreys, red kites, Eleonora's falcons, kestrels and peregrines. The **Embalse de Cuber** (Cuber Reservoir; see p.163), just west of Lluc on the C710, provides a natural amphitheatre from where up to ten species of birds of prey can be seen, including ospreys and red-footed falcons hunting over the water itself. The colourful rock thrush breeds in the quarry just west of the reservoir dam and on the nearby crags. The **sea cliffs** of the western coast are the breeding grounds of shearwaters, Mediterranean shag, storm petrels and Audouin's gulls. The most impressive seabird

SELECTED SPECIAL BIRDS OF MALLORCA

The list below describes many of Mallorca's most distinctive **birds**. We have given the
English name, followed in italics by the Latin, a useful cross-reference for those without a
British field guide; we've used a capital for genus (first) name only. The description aims
to capture the character of the bird and also indicates any habitat preference.

Fan-tailed warbler   *Cisticola juncidis*
Very common breeding resident. Typical small
brown bird, but with very distinctive "zit-zit-zit"
song, usually uttered in flight. Prefers wetland
areas.

Nightingale   *Luscinia megarhynchos*
Common breeding summer visitor. Rich-brown-
coloured robin-like bird with astonishingly rich,
vigorous and varied song. Prefers to sing from
small bushes, often deep inside and out of sight.

Wryneck   *Jynx torquilla*
Breeding resident. Medium-sized bird with a
complex pattern of brown, grey and lilac
plumage. A member of the woodpecker family.
Favours olive groves.

Hoopoe   *Upupa epops*
Common breeding resident. Pigeon-sized pinky-
brown bird with black head-crest. It is named
after its distinctive "upupu upupu" call. Its
wings sport a complex black and white barring,
creating a striking sight when in flight. Favours
open areas with some trees nearby for nesting.

Black vulture   *Aegypius monachus*
Breeding resident of the northern mountains.
Massive, dark, powerful and solitary raptor with
a wingspan approaching three metres. The most
distinctive of the island's birds. Probably fewer
than fifty remain.

Booted eagle   *Hieraaetus pennatus*
Resident breeder. A small and incredibly agile
eagle, similar in size to a buzzard. Prefers the
mountains, but happily hunts over scrub and
grasslands.

Eleonora's falcon   *Falco eleonorae*
Fairly common breeding summer visitor. One of
the specialities of the western Mediterranean.
Dark, slim, elegant falcon. Hunts small birds
and large insects with fantastic speed and agili-
ty. Often seen hunting insects near water.

Rock thrush   *Monticola saxatilis*
Breeding summer visitor. Beautifully coloured
rock- and quarry-loving thrush. Males have a

pale blue head and orangey-red breast and tail.
Females are a less distinctive brown and cream

Blue rock thrush   *Monticola solitariu*
Common breeding resident. Blue-coloured thrush
recalling a deep blue starling. Can be found in
any rugged, rocky areas at any time of year.

Firecrest   *Regulus ignicapillu*
Common breeding resident. The smallest bird
on the island. This tiny pale green bird is named
after its vivid orange and yellow crown.
Abundant in any woodland.

Crossbill   *Loxia curvirostra*
Abundant breeding resident. The vivid red male
and the lemon-green females of this bulky finch
have an unusual crossed bill and a distinctive
parrot-like appearance. The bill is adapted to
extract seeds from pine cones.

Marmora's warbler   *Sylvia sarda*
Common breeding resident. A small blue-ish
grey warbler with a long, often-upright tail and
distinctive red eye-ring. Prefers the bushy cover
of the coastal lowlands.

Purple gallinule   *Porphyrio porphyri*
Breeding resident at S'Albufera only. This purple
blue oddity was re-introduced to its marshland
habitat at S'Albufera in 1991. It is now well established there. Its incredibly long feet and swollen
red bill make this hen-like bird very distinctive.

Little egret   *Egretta garzette*
Breeding resident. Long-legged, elegant white-
wading bird. In summer has beautiful long white
plumes trailing from the back of its head.
Breeds at S'Albufera only. A wetland specialist,
though well adapted to treetop life.

Purple heron   *Ardea purpurea*
Breeding summer visitor. Large, slender heron
of reed beds. Male has beautiful purple and
rich-brown tones to its plumage. Despite its size
it can be rather elusive, hiding in the dense
cover of reeds.

Black-winged stilt   *Himantopus himantopus*
Common breeding resident. Incredibly long-
legged black-and-white wader. Its medium size

is somewhat extended by its long, straight, fine, red bill. Can appear anywhere there is mud, but particularly common on saltpans.

Kentish plover   *Charadrius alexandrinus*
Common breeding resident. Small, delicate wader of saltpans and marshes. Its pale brown upper body contrasts with its gleaming white head-collar and underparts.

Cetti's warbler   *Cettia cetti*
Very common breeding resident. This rather nondescript, chunky, wren-like warbler prefers dense thickets close to water. It possesses an astonishingly loud explosive song: "chet-chet-chet-chetchetchet".

Great reed warbler   *Acrocephalus arundinaceus*
Breeding summer visitor. This large, unstreaked, brown warbler can be found in significant numbers where there is reed and marsh vegetation. Its song is a loud and harsh mixture of unusual grating, croaking and creaking noises.

Scops owl   *Otus scops*
Common breeding resident. This tiny owl (only 20cm tall) is stubbornly nocturnal. However, you will know it's there because at night its plaintive "tyoo" note is repeated every few seconds monotonously for long periods. Groves, plantations, small clumps of trees, conifer woodland and even gardens can host this bird.

Greater flamingo   *Phoenicopterus ruber*
Winter/spring visitor in small numbers. The unmistakable silhouette of this leggy wader with roseate wings, bill and legs can be seen on any wetland in spring, but in winter the southern areas and S'Albufera are best.

Great white egret   *Egretta alba*
Winter visitor. This marshland specialist is really just a large version of the commoner Little Egret – an all-white, tall, elegant heron.

Audouin's gull   *Larus audouinii*
Resident breeder. This rare gull favours the rocky coastline. It's the size and light grey colour of a typical "seagull" but boasts a rather splendid red bill. Unfortunately it takes three years for birds to reach this adult plumage and prior to this they are much less distinctive.

Bee-eater   *Merops apiaster*
Common spring visitor, rare summer breeder.

A brightly coloured, medium-sized bird, with a slim body, long pointed wings and slightly de-curved bill. If the iridescent greens, orange, yellow and blue of this bird weren't distinctive enough, its bubbling "pruuk" call is almost as recognizable. It prefers open, relatively flat, rugged countryside.

Egyptian vulture   *Neophron percnopterus*
Rare migrant. Medium sized raptor with small rather pointed protruding head and feather-less face. Wings held flat when soaring.

Cattle egret   *Bubulcus ibis*
Mainly winter visitor. This small heron-like wader is a regular winter visitor to the larger Balearic marshes. In winter it is white, but is distinguished from the Little Egret by its stubby all-yellow bill and stockier gait.

Night heron   *Nycticorax nycticorax*
Small resident population, increasing in summer with migrants. Adults of this stocky, medium-sized heron are an attractive combination of black, grey and white. In contrast younger birds up to three years old are a rather nondescript brown with cream speckling. This water bird is most active at night or dawn and dusk. By day they roost in the tree canopy or large bushes.

Stone curlew   *Burhinus oedicnemus*
Resident breeder, more common in summer. Thick-set wader that prefers dry rolling countryside to mud. Has a large, yellow, almost reptilian eye. Largely dull brown with some darker streaking, but with relatively distinctive long yellow legs. When in flight, its strikingly black and white wings become apparent.

Cory's shearwater   *Calonectris diomedia*
Common breeder on offshore islands, but seen regularly all along the coast from March to August. Fairly large seabird. Like all the shearwaters, this bird flies close to the sea's surface with stiff outstretched wings. This pattern of flight as well as its size (nearly half a metre long with a wing span of more than a metre) are its most distinctive features as its plumage is rather boring. At sea it appears dark-backed and dirty white below. A close view should reveal some yellow on the bill and a white eye ring. Thousands breed on offshore islands across the Balearics and at sea they will often mix with the smaller pale brown Mediterranean shearwater.

colonies are on the **Illa Dragonera**, off Sant Elm (see p.156), which is home to all these birds as well as over 75 pairs of Eleonora's falcons. If the weather is too rough to get to the island, the seabirds may be viewed from **La Trapa**, a small headland nature reserve of pristine coastal *garrigue* that is owned and operated by GOB. The reserve is about an hour's walk north of Sant Elm, but the going is fairly tough. A similarly good spot for seabirds is **Cap de Formentor** (see p.183), at the other end of the west coast, and birds from here wander the bays of Pollença and Alcúdia.

Characteristic birds of the island's **scrubland** can also be found around the Cuber Reservoir, including a variety of warblers and small songbirds, such as nightingales, larks, pipits and colourful chats. Another area of rich scrubland is the **Bóquer Valley** (see p.182), near Pollença. Thoughtless development has harmed the olive groves and almond orchards at the base of the valley, but the Bóquer remains a migration hotspot, its pine avenues and denser wooded slopes hosting firecrests and crossbills among more familiar woodland birds like tits and woodpigeons. If you venture to the north end of the valley, you should be rewarded with the colourful delights of Marmora's warbler and the blue rock thrush. In spring, hundreds of bee-eaters can be heard and seen in and around the valley, as these stunning birds move through to breed elsewhere in the Mediterranean.

Wetlands are a magnet for birds in the arid climate of the Mediterranean. Mallorca boasts the most important birdwatching spot in the whole of the Balearics, in the marshes of the **Parc Natural de S'Albufera** (see p.192). Here, resident species are augmented by hundreds of migrating birds, which find fresh water after their long journey north or south. Amongst scores of species, the shorter grasses shelter moorhens, coots, crakes and the recently re-introduced purple gallinule, while the reeds hide healthy numbers of several species of herons, bitterns and egrets as well as occasional flamingos. A wide variety of small wading birds visit the marsh, including the distinctively long-legged black-winged stilt and the abundant Kentish plover. The open water is popular with ducks and in spring large numbers of terns may be seen. In winter the variety of duck species increases and kingfishers are common. This rich diversity of birdlife attracts birds of prey and this is as good a place as any to see ospreys and marsh harriers. In addition, over one

hundred Eleonora's falcons have been seen together over the marsh in spring. Among the smaller birds, the spring dusk and dawn choruses provided by wetland warblers such as Cetti's, moustached and great reed are unforgettable. Neither is the sound of birds restricted to the daytime. At night, listen for the plaintive single note of the scops owl against a backdrop of warblers, crakes and crickets.

The scops owl can be heard in the south of the island too, usually preferring almond groves and olive clumps. Generally speaking, the south is not as rich in birdlife as other parts of the island, the main exception being the **saltpan** habitat of the **Salines de Llevant**, near Colònia de Sant Jord (see p.230). Here, a wide variety of migrant wading birds, wintering duck and small flocks of wintering flamingos and cranes can be seen. The site also has a breeding flock of over a hundred black-winged stilts in summer and the abundance of prey attracts raptors, most frequently marsh harriers, kestrels and ospreys. The pans also host terns and Audouin's gull; this red-billed gull is a Mediterranean specialist and can be chanced upon at many coastal spots but the southern saltpans are favoured.

The country lanes that lattice Mallorca's **central plain**, Es Pla, also have their own distinctive birdlife. In spring and summer, the calls and songs of small birds like serins, corn buntings and Sardinian warblers and the ubiquitous fantailed warbler create a busy backdrop to hot, lazy afternoons. Nightingales seem to be everywhere and their rich song leaves a lasting impression. In the shade of the abundant olive groves, the cryptically-plumaged wryneck can be found all year, often sharing this ancient landscape with the striking hoopoe.

Other fauna

Mallorca's surviving **mammals** are an uninspiring bunch. The wild boar and red fox were eliminated early in the twentieth century, leaving a motley crew of mountain goats, wild sheep, pine martens, genets, weasels and feral cats, as well as commonplace smaller mammals such as hedgehogs, rabbits, hares and shrews.

As far as **reptiles** go, there are four types of snake – all hard to come by – and two species of gecko (or broad-toed lizard), the lowland-living wall gecko and the mountain-dwelling disc-fingered version. With any luck, you'll spot them as ey heat up in the sun, but they move fast since arm gecko is a tasty morsel for many a bird. Off e south coast of Mallorca, the desolate island f Cabrera has a large concentration of the rare, ue-undersided **Lilfords wall lizard**.

Among **amphibians**, Mallorca has a healthy og population, concentrated in its marshlands ut also surviving in its mountain pools (up to round 800m). There are also three types of toad, f which the **Mallorcan midwife toad**, hanging n in the northern corner of the island, is the rest. With no natural predators, its evolution volved a reduction in fecundity (it produces only quarter of the number of eggs laid by its main- nd relative) and the loss of its poison glands.

However, with the introduction of the viperine snake, the resident midwife toads were all but wiped out – only about five hundred pairs remain.

Common **insects** include grasshoppers and cicadas, whose summertime chirping is so evocative of warm Mediterranean nights, as well as over two hundred species of moth and around thirty types of **butterfly**. Some of the more striking butterflies are red admirals, which are seen in winter, and the clouded yellow and painted ladies of spring. One of the more unusu- al species is the two-tailed pasha, a splendidly marked gold-and-bronze butterfly that flits around the coast in spring and late summer, especially in the vicinity of strawberry trees.

Writers on Mallorca

Mallorca has produced few writers of note, but it has been the subject of many foreign jottings, beginning with the well-heeled travellers who nosed around the island in the nineteenth century. The most distinguished of these was George Sand, the partner of Frédéric Chopin, who wintered here in 1838–39. More recently, Mallorca has been used as the backdrop for several English-language thriller writers and has also spawned Tomás Graves, who was born and raised on the island and is fluent in its language and culture.

George Sand

George Sand (1804–76) was the pen name of the French aristocrat Armandine Lucile Aurore Dupin, the Baroness Dudevant. She married the eponymous baron in 1822, and left him nine years later for the literary life of Paris, where she embraced the Republican cause. A prolific author, dramatist and journalist, Sand campaigned against conservatism in its many forms and became a well-known figure in French political circles. She travelled occasionally and one of her excursions, along with her partner, the pianist and composer Frédéric Chopin, was in 1838 to the then backward and remote island of Mallorca. This extract is from Sand's memoir of the time, A Winter in Majorca; *for more, see p.146.*

It is three leagues from Palma to Valldemosa, but three Majorcan leagues, which can't be covered driving fast in under three hours. The road rises imperceptibly for the first two. During the third it enters the mountains and leads up a well-paved slope (possibly a former work of the Carthusian monks), but very narrow, horribly steep, and more dangerous than the rest of the way.

There one has one's first chance to admire the Alpine part of Majorca. But it is not enough that the mountains rise up on either side of the gorge, and that the torrent leaps from rock to rock; only in the heart of winter do these regions take on the wild, untamed aspect that the Majorcans attribute to them. In the month of December, and in spite of recent rains, the torrent was still a delightful stream which glided along among tufts of grass and clusters of flowers; the mountain was in a smiling mood, and the valley in which Valldemosa nestled opened before us like a garden in spring.

To reach the Cartuja you have to leave the coach, for it is impossible for any vehicle to clamber up the stony track that leads to it. It is a fascinating approach with its sudden twists and bends among magnificent trees, and with wonderful views that are unfolded at every step, and increase in beauty the higher one rises. I have seen nothing more pleasing; nor at the same time more melancholy than these prospects where the green holm oak, the carob tree, the pine, the olive, the poplar and the cypress mix their various hues in dense masses of foliage, veritable abysses of verdure amongst which the torrent pursues its course through thickets of gorgeous richness and inimitable attraction. I will never forget a certain bend in the defile from where, turning round, one can see high up on a mountain one of those pretty Arabic-type cottages, half-hidden among the leaves of the prickly pears, and, projecting its silhouette into the air, a great palm tree leaning over the chasm. When the mud and fog of Paris overwhelm me with depression, I shut my eyes and see again, as in a dream, that mountain full of greenery, those bare rocks, and that solitary palm, alone in a rose-coloured sky.

The Valldemosa cordillera rises up in a series of plateaux, becoming narrower and narrower until they form a kind of funnel, surrounded by high mountains and shut in on the north by the slope of the last plateau, at the entrance to which stands the monastery.

The Carthusian monks, through the work of years, have modified the ruggedness of this romantic spot. At the head of the valley where it reaches the hillside, they have made a vast garden, surrounded by walls that do not block the view, and to which a belt of cypress trees, in pyramidal form and disposed irregularly in pairs, give an appearance appropriate to a stage-set graveyard.

This garden, with palm and almond trees,

occupied the whole inclined background of the valley, and rises in a succession of wide terraces on the lower slopes of the mountain. By moonlight, and when its irregularity is masked by the darkness, it could be taken for an amphitheatre carved out for the battles of giants. In the centre and under a group of lovely palms, a stone-built reservoir collects the water from the mountain springs, and distributes it to the lower terraces by means of paved channels, similar to those which irrigate the environs of Barcelona. These works are on too great a scale and too ingenious not to have been the creation of the Moors. They are spread over the whole interior of the island, and he channels that start at the garden of the Carthusian monks, skirt the bed of the torrent and take running water to Palma at all seasons.

The Cartuja, situated at the highest point of this gorge, looks on the north side over an extensive valley which widens out and rises in a gentle slope to the coastal cliffs, whose base is battered and eroded by the sea. One arm of the cordillera points towards Spain, and the others towards the Orient. From this picturesque Carthusian monastery therefore, the sea can be glimpsed or sensed on two sides. Whilst its roar is audible to the north, it can be descried to the south like a line, brilliant line beyond the descending mountain slopes and the immense plain which is revealed to the eye. It is a surpassing picture, framed in the foreground by dark, pine-covered crags; beyond that by the sharply outlined profiles of mountains set off by superb trees; and in the background by the rounded humps of hills, which the setting sun gilds with the warmest shades, and on whose crests one can still distinguish, from a distance of a league, the microscopic outlines of the trees, as fine as the antennae of butterflies, as black and distinct as a trace of Chinese ink on a backdrop of sparkling gold. ...

In accordance with the Carthusian rule, thirteen monks, including the superior, lived in the Cartuja n Valldemosa. It had escaped the decree which n 1836 ordered the demolition of monasteries occupied by less than a dozen persons conjointy; but, like all the others, they had been dispersed and the convent suppressed, to be considered, as it were, the property of the State. The Majorcan government, not knowing what to do with these immense buildings, had decided to let he cells to persons who would care to occupy hem, in the expectation that time and negligence would cause the place to decay and fall down. In spite of the rents being extremely moderate, the villagers in Valldemosa had not chosen to take advantage of the offer, possibly because of their extreme piety and the affection they had felt for the monks, and perhaps also through superstitious fear; this did not prevent them going there to dance on carnival nights, although they did not cease to look very much askance at our irreverent presence among those venerable walls.

Nevertheless, the Cartuja was inhabited during the summer months by middle-class people from Palma who, at that altitude and under the monastery's thick arches, undoubtedly found the air fresher than on the plain or in the city. But with the approach of winter, the cold drove them away, and when we lived in it, the Cartuja had as its only inhabitants, besides myself and my family, the apothecary, the sacristan, and Maria Antonia.

Maria Antonia was a kind of housekeeper who had come from the mainland I believe to get away from squalor and poverty, and she had rented a cell in order to exploit the transient occupants of the Cartuja. Her cell was located next to ours and we made use of it as a kitchen, while she declared herself to be our factotum and help. She had been good-looking and was elegant, clean in appearance and pleasant. She said she came from a good family, had delightful manners, a nice voice, and an ingratiating demeanour. She exercised a very curious sort of hospitality; she would offer her services to the new arrivals and refuse, with an offended air and almost turning pale at the idea, any kind of recompense for her attentions. She did it, she asserted, for the love of God, to be of assistance, and with the sole object of winning the friendship of her neighbours. Her entire furniture consisted of a small folding bed, a foot-warmer, two wicker chairs, a crucifix, and some earthenware crockery, all of which she put at our disposal with great generosity, allowing us to accommodate our new servant, and store our pots and pans, in her dwelling.

But she would immediately take charge of all your belongings, and reserve for herself the best of your finery and food. I have never seen a godly person so fond of her stomach, nor fingers so quick to dip down into a boiling pot without getting burnt, nor a throstle so supple to swallow the coffee and sugar of her dear lodgers, stealthily, whilst she hummed a popular air or a bolero.

It would have been interesting and amusing, if one had been completely disinterested in the matter, to see the good Antonia, Catalina the queer witch-like Valldemosa woman who was our maid, and the *niña* (little girl), a small dishevelled monstrosity who acted as our errand girl, quarrelling among themselves over our food. It was the hour of the Angelus and the three never failed to recite it. The two elders, praying in unison, put their hands into every dish, and the small one, as she answered *Amen*, succeeded in palming some chop or candied fruit with unequalled dexterity. It was quite something to watch and worthwhile pretending not to notice; but when the rains cut communication with Palma and our provisions diminished, the "assistance" of Maria Antonia and her party became less pleasing; and my children and I found ourselves in the role of sentinel and relieving each other, in order to keep a watch on our food stores. I remember once hiding under the headboard of my bed a few packets of biscuits which were earmarked for breakfast the next day; and on another occasion, I had to keep a vulture's eye on some plates of fish in our cooking-stove, so as to scare away those birds of prey who would have left us only the bones.

The sacristan was a lusty young fellow who had possibly served at mass with the Carthusian monks since his childhood; he was now the keeper of the keys of the monastery. There was a scandalous story about him. He was once convicted of and confessed to having seduced a *señorita* who had stayed some months in the Cartuja with her parents. He excused himself on the grounds that the State had only entrusted him with the guardianship of the virgins in the pictures. He was not a good type by any standard, but he put on very pretentious airs. Instead of the semi-Arabic attire used by people of his class, he wore European trousers with braces, which certainly dazzled the girls of the district. His sister was the most beautiful Majorcan girl that I've seen. They didn't live in the monastery. They were rich and proud and had a house in the village; but they made a daily round of the Cartuja and were often in Maria Antonia's cell, who invited them to partake of our provender when she had no appetite herself.

The apothecary was a Carthusian who used to shut himself in his cell, put on his former white robe, and recite his office all alone. As soon as anyone knocked on his door to ask him for some marsh-mallow or couch-grass root (the only specific remedies he possessed), he would quickly hide his habit under his bed and appear in black breeches, stockings and a short pea jacket, the same as worn by the male ballet dancers in Molière's interludes. He was a very mistrustful person who never ceased complaining, and who perhaps prayed for the triumph of Don Carlos and the return of the Holy Inquisition, but he meant no harm to anybody. He sold us his herbs at the price of gold, and consoled himself with these small gains, having been released from his vow of poverty. His cell was a fairly long way from ours, being situated at the entrance to the monastery in a hidden corner, whose door was camouflaged by castor-oil bushes and other medicinal plants of pleasing aspect.

Tomás Graves

Born in 1953, **Tomás Graves**, *the son of Robert (see p.139), lives on Mallorca, where he works as a guitarist, printer and author. His knowledge of – and enthusiasm for – the island and its people permeates every page of* Bread and Oil, *a diverse and intriguing book that describes many aspects of Mallorcan life via its gastronomy. This is an extract from* Bread and Oil, *which was first published in Catalan in 1998.*

Olive cultivation

The vegetation on Majorca's terraced hillsides hardly changes colour with the seasons. There are several shades of evergreen: the dark holm-oak forest, the vivid pines which sprout on any untended terraces, the grey-green olive groves which flash silver when the strong winds turn up the undersides of their leaves; and among the olives, the occasional broad-leaved carob tree.

Our olive groves have drifted into the realms of what some Majorcan farmers derisively call *hobby farming.* We've reached this point because it's not worth a peasant's while to become a registered olive-grower and pay the corresponding social security if he and his family are only going to gather a few sacks of olives in the best of years. It's hardly worth it even to pick up a few subsidies to repair any of the centuries-old stone terraces that collapse. What really subsidizes the continuing existence of the olive groves is our seasonal tourism. Most Majorcans from the *serra* who work in the hotels and restaurants, sign on the dole in November and have all winter to spend looking after their olive groves and go hunting, as well a doing a little moonlighting on the side. If the harvest were in summer, all the olives would rot on the ground.

Spain's olive groves produce forty per cent of the world's olive oil and represent 146,000 permanent jobs as well as temporary labour to the tune of 46 million day's wages a year. Economically speaking, Majorca's share of the oil business is negligible. Not only does the size of the small-holdings make them unprofitable – property is usually divided up *ad absurdam* between heirs – but the local topography limits the kind of mechanization that you see in parts of Andalucia. There's no way you could get a tractor with a tree-shaking attachment up the Moorish steps of the Barranc de Biniaraix, nor could you manoeuvre a crop-dusting plane between those crags. Throughout the Mediterranean, the olive is a crop which, in spite of mechanization, gives work to entire families and is responsible for preserving the social fabric of the mountainous regions, culturally as well as economically. If the olive groves were to disappear, the rural exodus would be catastrophic because no other crop can be cultivated in the mountainous areas. At least, for the moment, no *legal* crop.

Olive cultivation in the *possessions* or large estates was based first on a slave economy, later on serfdom, and then (until the tourist boom) on the exploitation of the fact that an island's work force can't afford to look for work elsewhere. After a couple of decades of plunging olive oil prices (due to bad press and cheap imported sunflower and soya oil) they began to steadily rise in the 1980s, and today a litre of Majorcan oil fetches double what is paid in Andalucia, due to the demand for local produce. But even so, it doesn't begin to pay for the labour-intensive work of picking olives, maintaining the dry-stone terraces, ploughing and pruning the trees in the high groves which are accessible only by foot or donkey.

Olive picking

"The degree of acidity is set by the olive, there's no part of the process at the oil-press that can affect it," explains professional oil-taster Gaspar, shouting over the noise of the newly-imported Italian machinery at the Sóller Co-op oil-mill. "Olive oil must be one of the few products which

has absolutely no additives. You can't mix anything in with it. Every year it's different; some years the acidity is higher, nobody knows exactly why. The weather may have been exactly the same as the year before, the trees are pruned the same way, given the same fertilizer, but the oil is different from one season to the next

"Here on the island, ninety per cent of the olives are picked off the ground. No other fruit is harvested off the floor, it's always better straight from the tree. On the mainland they pull the olives straight off the branches; they're a little greener and the oil they produce has a fruitier smell, a bitterer taste. It's a bit spicy and has a lower acid content; this is the extra virgin oil, the best there is. The green olive – in fact it's neither green nor black but mottled – produces less oil but the quality is better. It's best to beat or comb the tree; you can do it mechanically or with hand-held rakes which don't damage the branches."

It seems that the habit of picking green originated in the northern Mediterranean where the olives had to be harvested before the frost set in. In southern Italy they tend to gather ripe olives from the ground, while in the north they pick them green. Many Majorcan inventors have come up with contraptions to gather olives off the ground, yet whether the principle is suction, a brushing action, or a spiked roller, no mechanical picker seems to be able to distinguish this year's juicy olives from last year's shrivelled ones ... or from sheep's droppings.

"The Majorcans are used to an oil which can reach four or five degrees of acidity and that's what they're after because it's tasty, but it's the musty taste of an olive that's been on the damp ground too long. We're telling the members of our co-op to put their olives in crates instead of in sacks where the air doesn't get to them, where there are bacteria. That's when the olive gets spoiled, it ferments and the acidity increases."

In medieval times when strong olive oil was set aside for preserving food, recipe books would recommend adding honey to counteract the excess acidity. In this century [sic], in the postwar years when even the sharpest oil was better than none, a bit of sugar on your *pa amb oli* would stop the oil grating at the back of your throat.

"Here people pick olives the same way they did a hundred years ago. You could say that if Majorcan oil hasn't the quality of the mainland oil it's partly because here the problem is the terrain; it's not easy to get the olives to the press quickly."

Gathering olives off the ground can be, for someone unaccustomed to this work and to the damp winter climate of the *serra*, an ordeal for the knees and kidneys. Every basketful of four kilos of olives renders a scant litre of oil; not much to show for an hour's work poking about between damp shrubs and under thistles. Many of us who still go for gathering from the ground have found we can save a lot of time by using a strimmer to clear the grass under the trees a week or so before the olives change colour. To go olive picking as a family outing or in order to spend the weekend with friends is a profitable way to commune with nature, each according to his humour. You can work in a group chatting away, but it is equally conducive to solitary meditation.

Why don't we follow the rational northern method of knocking the olives down as soon as they begin to turn colour and thus only have to pick once instead of our weekly pass under the same tree? Well, a Majorcan would say that the only way of ensuring the olive is ripe is to wait for it to fall to the ground... but the hidden argument is that beating or combing the trees not only gives you a crick in the neck, it's also harder work than gathering off the ground. Besides, we've always done it this way and, as they say in the southern US, "if it ain't broke, don't fix it".

The *tafona*, or oil press

The first operation of the traditional oil press, after sifting out any leaves and stones, is to crush the olives on the *jaç*, a flat circular bed about a metre high and three across, fashioned out of a single piece of local stone. A contrivance consisting of a wooden funnel connected to a conical millstone rotates on a vertical axle set in the centre of the stone bed, driven by a blinkered donkey or mule which walks round and round the *jaç*. The sorted olives are tipped into the funnel, the *tremuja*, which feeds them, a few at a time, into the path of the rumbling *trull*. As the olives are crushed to a paste, the *trull* pushes the dark sludge outwards into the gutter which runs around the rim of the *jaç*. From here the virgin oil seeps out of the paste and trickles into a vat.

"The olive contains more water than oil. What flows from the *trull* is pure olive juice, the true virgin olive oil, a mixture of oil and water. When was a little girl I used to go to school i Estellencs," remembers Maria Riera, "and ther was a *tafona* in the village where they'd mak oil. The *tafoners* would let the schoolmistres know the day before a *trullada*, and we'd a troop in with our slices of bread, and they'd toas them over the coals. Then they'd take the toast ed bread with a pair of tongs and dip it in the o which had just come out, and it was so good... was delicious just like that, you didn't even hav to put salt on."

Antoni Pinya explains that "in the *possessions* at the end of the working day when the olive had been crushed and were ready for the ho pressing the next morning, a bottle of virgin o would be collected from the *trull* for the *Senyor* of the estate. After the token bottle had beer given to the landowner, all the paste left on the *trull* would be shovelled into a stone vat, the *esportinador*. Then the *madona* – the overseer's wife – would roll up her sleeve, make a fist an stick it into the paste up to her forearm. As she took out her arm it would leave a good sump hole in the olive paste, into which more virgin o would seep overnight. The next morning, the *tafoners* would toast their bread and dunk it int the oil that had gathered in the sump. This was the *tafoner*'s breakfast, the *rien-ne-va-plus*, the Number One in the world of bread and oil known as *pa amb oli de tafona*."

After the 'cold pressing' comes the hot o 'scalded' pressing. In a traditional *tafona* this is done under the weight of an enormous wooder beam, weighing well over a ton: one end of the beam rests on the ground while the other end is raised and then lowered – by means of a vertical wooden screw, turned by arms of the *tafon ers* – onto the tall stack of circular esparto mats *esportins*, spread with olive paste. As the bean is lowered, one *tafoner* 'scalds' the paste by ladling hot water onto the pile; it seeps down through the mats, drawing the oil out of the paste. Some people still refer to hot-pressed oi as *oli de bigues*, 'beam oil'.

Having pressed the paste under a beam until i will yield no more liquid, the process is still no over. The dry paste is scooped out of the *esportins* and thrown back into the *esportinado* where it is beaten with more hot water. The mats are again spread with this rehydrated paste and submitted once more to the heavy pressure treatment, doused with a continuous flow of boiling water to extract that little bit more. The oil obtained by this pressing is known as 'seconds': the quality is lower than the first hot pressing because the continuous heat destroys the vita-min E content as well as part of the flavour and bouquet.

The traditional way of pressing olives produced several qualities of oil, from the virgin pressing for the immediate use of the landowner's family, right down to the 'thick' oil from the second or third pressing, which was used for making soap, lubricating cart axles and for treating woodwork.

Extract from Bread and Oil: Majorcan Culture's Last Stand *copyright 2000, Tomás Graves.* Bread and Oil *is published by Prospect Books, Totnes, England.*

Books

Most of the following books should be readily available, although one or two are only obtainable in Mallorca. We have given UK and US publishers for each title wherever possible; o/p means out of print.

In the UK, Books on Spain can supply all manner of rare and in- and out-of-print books about Spain. Their comprehensive catalogue includes sections on topics such as travel, the arts, history and culture, plus separate sections (and separate brochures) on the regions, notably the Balearic Islands. Get it free from PO Box 207, Twickenham, TW2 5BQ (☎020/8898 7789, fax 8898 8812, www.books-on-spain.com).

Impressions and travel accounts

Tom Crichton, *Our Man in Majorca* (o/p). The American sailor, adventurer and journalist Tom Crichton was briefly a package-tour representative on Mallorca in the early 1960s. With the encouragement of Robert Graves, he published this account of a comical, disaster-filled fortnight. A book for the sunbed.

Paul Richardson, *Not Part of the Package* (o/p). Richardson spent a year in the heady 1960s observing and enjoying the razzle-dazzle of Ibiza. His idiosyncratic tales are diverting and revealing in equal measure – and, by implication, throw light on the way mass tourism works in the Balearics as a whole.

George Sand, *A Winter in Majorca* (M&N Publishing/Academy Chicago). Accompanied by her lover, Frédéric Chopin, Sand spent the winter of 1838–39 on Mallorca, holing up in the monastery of Valldemossa. These are her recol-

lections, often barbed and sharp-tongued – and very critical of the islanders. Readily available in Valldemossa and Mallorca's better bookshops. Read an extract on p.256.

Gordon West, *Jogging Round Majorca* (o/p). This gentle, humorous account of an extended journey round Mallorca by Gordon and Mary West in the 1920s vividly portrays the island's pre-tourist life and times. The trip had nothing to do with running, but rather "jogging" as in a leisurely progress. West's book lay forgotten for decades until a BBC radio presenter, Leonard Pearcey, stumbled across it in a secondhand bookshop and subsequently read extracts on air. The programmes were very well received, and the book was reprinted in 1994.

History

David Abulafia, *A Mediterranean Emporium: the Catalan Kingdom of Majorca* (Cambridge University Press). Detailed, serious-minded study of medieval Mallorca.

Raymond Carr, *Spain 1808–1975* (Oxford University Press, UK) and *Modern Spain 1875–1980* (Oxford University Press). Two of the best books available on modern Spanish history – concise and well-considered narratives. Of equal standing are Carr's (shorter) 300-page *Spain: A History* (Oxford University Press); and *The Spanish Tragedy: the Civil War in Perspective* (Phoenix, UK).

J.H. Elliott, *Imperial Spain 1469–1716* (Penguin). The best introduction to Spain's "golden age" – academically respected as well as being a gripping yarn. Also see his erudite *The Revolt of the Catalans: A Study in the Decline of Spain 1598–1640* (o/p).

Geoffrey Parker, *The Army of Flanders and the Spanish Road (1567–1659)* (Cambridge University Press). Sounds dry and academic, but this fascinating book gives a marvellous insight into the morals, manners and organization of the Spanish army, then the most feared in Europe.

Hugh Thomas, *The Spanish Civil War* (Penguin/Touchstone). Exhaustively researched, brilliantly detailed account of the war and the complex political manoeuvrings surrounding it, with a section on Mallorca. First published in 1961, it remains easily the best book on the subject.

General background

Mossèn Antoni Alcover, *Folk Tales of Mallorca* (Editorial Moll). The nineteenth-century priest and academic Mossèn Alcover spent decades collecting Mallorcan folk tales and this is a wide selection – almost 400 pages – of them. They range from the intensely religious through to parable and proverb, but many reveal an unpleasant edge to rural island life, both vindictive and mean-spirited. Makes for intriguing background material, but unfortunately particular places on the island are never mentioned or described.

Anthony Bonner (ed.), *Doctor Illuminatus: A Ramon Llull Reader* (Princeton University Press). The Mallorcan scholar and philosopher Ramon Llull wrote lengthy and heavy-going treatises on mysticism and Christian zeal in the thirteenth century that are not for the faint-hearted. His works were some of the first to be written in Catalan. More manageable is *Romancing God: Contemplating the Beloved*, edited by Henry Carrigan Jnr (Paraclete), a 120-page introduction to Llull.

Barbara Catoir, *Miró on Mallorca* (Prestel). Lavishly illustrated book covering Miró's lengthy residence in Cala Major, just outside Palma. There's discussion of the work Miró produced on the island and of his thoughts on the island. Too hagiographical for some tastes.

Carrie B. Douglass, *Bulls, Bullfighting & Spanish Identities* (Arizona University Press). Anthropologist Douglass delves into the symbolism of the bull in the Spanish national psyche, and then goes on to examine the role of the bullfight in some of the many fiestas that encourage it.

Tomás Graves, *Bread & Oil: Majorcan Culture's Last Stand* (Prospect, UK). This intriguing book explores Mallorca via its palate, with sections on what the islanders eat and how the ingredients end up where they do. Entertainingly written by a son of Robert Graves. See p.258 for an extract.

William Graves, *Wild Olives* (o/p). Another son of Robert Graves, William was born in 1940 and spent much of his childhood in Palma and Deià,

sufficient inspiration for these mildly diverting accounts of his Mallorcan contemporaries. The book's real focus, however, is his troubled family life and his difficult relationship with his father. Published in 1995, the centenary of Robert's birth.

John Hooper, *The New Spaniards: A Portrait of the New Spain* (Penguin, UK). Well-constructed and extremely perceptive portrait of post-Franco Spain; an excellent general introduction. Highly recommended.

Janis Mink, *Miró* (Taschen). Beautifully illustrated book that tracks through the artist's life and times. The text is rather ponderous, but there are lots of interesting quotations and, at 96 pages, you're not drowned in detail.

George Orwell, *Homage to Catalonia* (Penguin/Harcourt Brace). Stirring account of Orwell's participation in, and early enthusiasm for, leftist revolution in Barcelona, followed by his growing disillusionment with the factional fighting that divided the Republican forces during the ensuing Civil War.

Miranda Seymour, *Robert Graves: Life on the Edge* (Northcote House, UK). Lengthy account of Robert Graves's personal life with lacklustre commentary on his poetry and novels. Includes much detail on Graves's residence in Deià. Published in 1995, to mark the centenary of Graves's birth.

Fiction

Arturo Barea, *The Forging of a Rebel* (o/p). Superb autobiographical trilogy, taking in the Spanish war in Morocco in the 1920s and Barea's own part in the civil war. Sometimes reprinted in its component titles: *The Forge*, *The Track* and *The Clash*.

Juan Goytisolo, *Marks of Identity, Count Julian, Juan the Landless* (all Serpent's Tail). Born in Barcelona in 1931, Goytisolo became a bitter enemy of the Franco regime and has spent most of his life in exile in Paris and Morocco, widely acclaimed as being one of Spain's leading modern novelists. His most celebrated works confront the whole ambivalent idea of Spain and Spanishness, as in the trilogy of titles listed above. *The Virtues of the Solitary Bird* (Serpent's Tail, 1988) is a deep and powerful study of pain and repression, while *Makbara* (Serpent's Tail, 1980) explores the Arab culture of North Africa in sharp and perceptive style.

Lucia Graves, *A Woman Unknown: Voices from a Spanish Life* (Virago/Counterpoint). Robert Graves's children seem determined to make a literary name for themselves and this is his daughter's effort – thoughtful recollections of life in Mallorca in particular and Spain as a whole. Lucid and interesting in equal measure.

Roderic Jeffries, *An Enigmatic Disappearance* (St Martin's Minotaur). Published in 2000, this is one of the Inspector Alvarez detective novel series that are set in Mallorca. In this particular novel, Alvarez copes with arrogant expats and a disapproving boss to sort out a murder mystery. The author is a Londoner by birth, but is now resident on the island. Other novels in the Alvarez series are *An Artistic Way to Go* and *A Maze of Murders* (both Allison & Busby/St Martin's Minotaur).

Juan Masoliver (ed.), *The Origins of Desire: Modern Spanish Short Stories* (Serpent's Tail). Enjoyable selection of short stories from some of Spain's leading contemporary writers, including Mallorca's own Valentí Puig and Carme Riera.

Ana María Matute, *School of the Sun* (Columbia University Press, US). The loss of childhood innocence on the Balearics, where old enmities are redefined during the Civil War.

Manuel Vázquez Montalbán, *Murder in the Central Committee*, *The Angst-ridden Executive*, *Off Side* (all Serpent's Tail). Riveting tales by Spain's most popular crime thriller writer, a long-time member of the Communist Party and now a well-known journalist resident in Barcelona. Montalbán's great creation is the gourmand private detective Pepe Carvalho. Original and wonderfully entertaining. If this trio of titles whet your appetite, move on to *Southern Seas* (Serpent's Tail) and a world of disillusioned communists, tawdry sex and nouvelle cuisine – key ingredients of post-Franco Spain.

Arturo Pérez-Reverte, *The Fencing Master* (Harvill, UK). Subtle, heavily symbolic novel set in 1860s Madrid that traces the demise of the fencing master, a man in search of the perfect sword thrust. A journalist by profession, Pérez-Reverte is one of Spain's best-selling contemporary authors.

George Scott, *The Bloody Bokhara* (Eyelevel Books, UK). Detective thriller set in modern-day Mallorca, a debut from an American who runs a hotel on the island. It's a fairly good yarn, but somewhat ponderous in expression. Excellent for background information on the island.

Maruja Torres, *Desperately Seeking Julio* (Fourth Estate, US). The Julio is of course the crooner Iglesias (the original Spanish title – "It's Him!" – had no need for names) in this enjoyable romp of a novel. Torres is quite a name in Spain, writing for gossip columns.

Llorenç Villalonga, *The Dolls' Room* (o/p). Subtle if somewhat laboured portrait of nobility in decline in nineteenth-century Mallorca by an island writer. First published in 1956. Several works by Villalonga are in print, but only in Catalan or Spanish. The author's old house in Binissalem is now a museum (see p.134).

Specialist guidebooks

David & Rosamund Brawn, *Walk Mallorca* (Discovery Walking Guides, UK). The Brawns produce the best hiking books about the island – and they are inexpensive too. Directions are almost always easy to follow and the text clear. Each slim booklet detailing the hikes comes with a 1:25,000 map. This particular selection picks hikes from across the island. In the same series are the *Mallorca West Walking Guide*, which focuses on the coast west of Andratx; the *Mallorca Mountains Walking Guide*, covering the Sóller region; and *Mallorca North*, dealing with the Pollença and Alcúdia area. All four are available in Mallorca, but not consistently.

Chris Craggs, *Rock Climbs in Mallorca* (Cicerone, UK). Over 300 pages detailing possible rock climbs across the island.

Lindsay Fisher, *A Layman's History of the Steam Railways of Mallorca* (The King's England Press, UK). The only specialist book on the subject – 68 pages to satisfy trainophiles.

Herbert Heinrich, *Twelve Classic Hikes through Mallorca* (Editorial Moll, Mallorca). Heinrich has published a number of Mallorcan hiking guides in German. This was his first (and best) English volume, a compilation of some of the most enjoyable and less demanding one-day hikes in the Serra de Tramuntana mountains. The descriptions are a bit patchy, but the topographical sketches are extremely helpful. Widely available in Mallorca.

Gaspar Martí, *Walking Tours around the Historical Centre of Palma* (Ajuntament de Palma, Mallorca). Detailed and enjoyable exploration of Palma's historical nooks and crannies. Quality sketches illuminate the text. Published by Palma city council and available in most leading bookshops in the city.

une Parker, *Walking in Mallorca* (Cicerone, UK). Detailed accounts of over seventy Mallorcan hikes to suit almost all levels of fitness, but the text can be hard to fathom and follow.

Flora and fauna

Christopher Grey-Wilson, et al, *Collins Field Guide: Mediterranean Wild Flowers* (Harper Collins, UK). Excellent, comprehensive field guide to flora.

Graham Hearl, *A Birdwatching Guide to Mallorca* (Arlequin, UK). First-rate description of where to see what bird – and how to get there – in every part of the island. There is a handy bird checklist

at the back of the book and the text is sprinkled with useful local maps. The sketches of various birds are, however, not very illuminating – and you'll still need a field guide.

Lars Jonsson, *Birds of Europe* (Helm). As good a field guide as the Collins below, but more specialized.

Killian Mullarney, et al, *Collins Bird Guide* (HarperCollins/Princeton). Excellent field guide to birds – nothing better.

Oleg Polunin, et al, *Flowers of Europe: a Field Guide* (Oxford). First-rate field guide to flora.

Ken Stoba, *Birdwatching in Mallorca* (Cicerone, UK). First published in 1990, this slim book is a competent introduction to Mallorca's birdlife and major birdwatching sites.

Language

Most Mallorcans are bilingual, speaking Castilian (ie Spanish) and *Mallorquín*, their local dialect of the Catalan language, with equal facility.

Català (Catalan) has been the islanders' everyday language since the Reconquest and the subsequent absorption of the island into the medieval Kingdom of Aragón and Catalunya. Castilian, on the other hand, was imposed much later from the mainland as the language of government – and with special rigour by Franco. As a result, Spain's recent move towards regional autonomy has been accompanied by the islanders' assertion of **Catalan** as their official language. The most obvious sign of this has been the change of all the old Castilian town and street names into Catalan versions.

On paper, Catalan looks like a cross between French and Spanish and is generally easy to understand if you know those two, although when spoken it has a very harsh sound and is far harder to come to grips with.

Some background

When **Franco** came to power in 1939, publishing houses, bookshops and libraries were raided and *Català* books destroyed. There was some relaxation in the mid-1940s, but throughout his dictatorship Franco excluded Catalan from the radio, TV, daily press and, most importantly, the schools, which is why many older people cannot read or write *Català* even if they speak it all the time. Mallorca's linguistic picture has been further muddied by the emigration of thousands of mainland

Spaniards to the island, and nowadays it's estimated that Castilian is the dominant language in around forty percent of island households.

Català is spoken by a total of over six million people in the Balearics, Catalunya, part of Aragón, most of Valencia, Andorra and parts of the French Pyrenees; it is thus much more widely spoken than several better-known languages such as Danish, Finnish and Norwegian. It is a Romance language, stemming from Latin and more directly from medieval Provençal. Spaniards in the rest of the country belittle it by saying that to get a *Català* word you just cut a Castilian one in half (which is often true!), but in fact the grammar is much more complicated than Castilian and there are eight vowel sounds, three more than in Castilian.

Getting by in Mallorca

Although Catalan is the preferred **language** of most islanders, you'll almost always get by perfectly well if you speak Castilian (Spanish), as long as you're aware of the use of Catalan in timetables and so forth. Once you get into it, Castilian is one of the easiest languages there is, the rules of pronunciation pretty straightforward and strictly observed. You'll find some basic pronunciation rules below for both Catalan and Castilian, and a selection of words and phrases in both languages. Castilian is certainly easier to pronounce, but don't be afraid to try Catalan, especially in the more out-of-the-way places – you'll generally get a good reception if you at least try communicating in the local language.

Castilian: a few rules

Unless there's an accent, words ending in d, l, r, and z are **stressed** on the last syllable, all others on the second last. All **vowels** are pure and short; combinations have predictable results.

A – somewhere between back and father.

E as in get.

I as in police.

O as in hot.

U as in rule.

CONTEXTS

C is lisped before E and I, hard otherwise: *cerca* is pronounced "thairka".

CH is pronounced as in English.

G is a guttural H sound (like the *ch* in loch) before E or I, a hard G elsewhere: *gigante* is pronounced "higante".

H is always silent.

J is the same sound as a guttural G: *jamón* is pronounced "hamon".

LL sounds like an English Y: *tortilla* is pronounced "torteeya".

N as in English, unless it has a tilde (accent) over it, when it becomes NY: *mañana* sounds like "man-yaana".

QU is pronounced like an English K.

R is rolled, RR doubly so.

V sounds more like B, *vino* becoming "beano".

X has an S sound before consonants, a KS sound before vowels.

Z is the same as a soft C, so *cerveza* is pronounced "thairvaitha".

Catalan: a few rules

With *Català*, don't be tempted to use the few rules of Castilian pronunciation you may know – in particular the soft Spanish Z and C don't apply, so unlike in the rest of Spain it's not "Barthelona" but "Barcelona", as in English.

A as in h**a**t if stressed, as in **a**lone when unstressed.

E varies, but usually as in g**e**t.

I as in pol**i**ce.

IG sounds like the "tch" in the English scratch; *lleig* (ugly) is pronounced "yeah-tch".

O varies, but usually as in h**o**t.

U lies somewhere between p**u**t and r**u**le.

Ç sounds like an English S: *plaça* is pronounced "plassa".

C followed by an E or I is soft; otherwise hard.

G followed by E or I is like the "zh" in Zhivago; otherwise hard.

H is always silent.

J as in the French "Jean".

LL sounds like an English Y or LY, like the "yuh" sound in "million".

N as in English, though before F or V it sometimes sounds like an M.

NY replaces the Castilian Ñ.

QU before E or I sounds like K; before A or O as in "quit".

R is rolled, but only at the start of a word; at the end it's often silent.

T is pronounced as in English, though sometimes it sounds like a D, as in *viatge* or *dotze*.

TX is like the English CH.

V at the start of a word sounds like B; in all other positions it's a soft F sound.

W is pronounced like a B/V.

X is like SH in most words, though in some, like *exit*, it sounds like an X.

Z is like the English Z.

PHRASEBOOKS AND DICTIONARIES

SPANISH/CASTILIAN

Numerous **Spanish phrasebooks** are available in Britain, the most user-friendly being the *Spanish Rough Guide Phrasebook*, laid out dictionary-style for instant access. Both Collins and Cassells publish **dictionaries**. For **teaching yourself** the language, the BBC tape series *España Viva* and *Dígame* are excellent, as is their two-week crash course *Get By in Spanish*. Macmillan's *Breakthrough Spanish* is probably the best of the tape and book home study courses.

CATALAN

The best book for **learning Catalan** is a total immersion course published by the Generalitat de Catalunya called *Digui Digui*, a series of books and tapes that is presented entirely in Catalan; you will, however, need to speak Spanish to take this on. In Britain, the best place to find it is Grant & Cutler, 55 Great Marlborough St, London W1 (☎020/7734 2012). *Teach Yourself Catalan* (Hodder & Stoughton) is less ambitious, but perfectly adequate for most visitors – and it's presented in English. As for English–Catalan **phrasebooks**, the only one currently in print is *Parla Català* (Pia), whilst for a **dictionary** you're limited to the version published by Routledge.

WORDS AND PHRASES

BASICS

	SPANISH	CATALAN
Yes, No, OK	*Sí, No, Vale*	*Si, No, Val*
Please, Thank you	*Por favor, Gracias*	*Per favor, Gràcies*
Where, When	*Dónde, Cuándo*	*On, Quan*
What, How much	*Qué, Cuánto*	*Què, Quant*
Here, There	*Aquí, Allí, Allá*	*Aquí, Allí, Allà*
This, That	*Esto, Eso*	*Això, Allò*
Now, Later	*Ahora, Más tarde*	*Ara, Més tard*
Open, Closed	*Abierto/a, Cerrado/a*	*Obert, Tancat*
With, Without	*Con, Sin*	*Amb, Sense*
Good, Bad	*Buen(o)/a, Mal(o)/a*	*Bo(na), Dolent(a)*
Big, Small	*Gran(de), Pequeño/a*	*Gran, Petit(a)*
Cheap, Expensive	*Barato/a, Caro/a*	*Barat(a), Car(a)*
Hot, Cold	*Caliente, Frío/a*	*Calent(a), Fred(a)*
More, Less	*Más, Menos*	*Més, Menys*
Today, Tomorrow	*Hoy, Mañana*	*Avui, Demà*
Yesterday	*Ayer*	*Ahir*
Day before yesterday	*Anteayer*	*Abans-d'ahir*
Next week	*La semana que viene*	*La setmana que ve*
Next month	*El mes que viene*	*El mes que ve*

GREETINGS AND RESPONSES

	SPANISH	CATALAN
Hello, Goodbye	*Hola, Adiós*	*Hola, Adéu*
Good morning	*Buenos días*	*Bon dia*
Good afternoon/night	*Buenas tardes/noches*	*Bona tarda/nit*
See you later	*Hasta luego*	*Fins després*
Sorry	*Lo siento/discúlpeme*	*Ho sento*
Excuse me	*Con permiso/perdón*	*Perdoni*
How are you?	*¿Cómo está (usted)?*	*Com va?*
I (don't) understand	*(No) Entiendo*	*(No) Ho entenc*
Not at all/You're welcome	*De nada*	*De res*
Do you speak English?	*¿Habla (usted) inglés?*	*Parla anglès?*
I (don't) speak Spanish/Catalan	*(No) Hablo Español*	*(No) Parlo Català*
My name is . . .	*Me llamo . . .*	*Em dic . . .*
What's your name?	*¿Cómo se llama usted?*	*Com es diu?*
I am English	*Soy inglés/esa*	*Sóc anglès/esa*
Scottish	*escocés/esa*	*escocès/esa*
Australian	*australiano/a*	*australià/ana*
Canadian	*canadiense/a*	*canadenc(a)*
American	*americano/a*	*americà/ana*
Irish	*irlandés/esa*	*irlandès/esa*
Welsh	*galés/esa*	*gallès/esa*

HOTELS AND TRANSPORT

	SPANISH	CATALAN
I want	Quiero	Vull (pronounced "fwee")
I'd like	Quisiera	Voldria
Do you know . . . ?	¿Sabe . . . ?	Vostès saben . . . ?
I don't know	No sé	No sé
There is (is there?)	(¿)Hay(?)	Hi ha(?)
Give me . . .	Deme . . .	Doneu-me . . .
Do you have . . . ?	¿Tiene . . . ?	Té . . . ?
. . . the time	. . . la hora	. . . l'hora
. . . a room	. . . una habitación	. . . alguna habitació
. . . with two beds/ double bed	. . . con dos camas/ cama matrimonial	. . . amb dos llits/ llit per dues persones
. . . with shower/bath	. . . con ducha/baño	. . . amb dutxa/bany
for one person (two people)	para una persona (dos personas)	per a una persona (dues persones)
for one night (one week)	para una noche (una semana)	per una nit (una setmana)
It's fine, how much is it?	Está bien, ¿cuánto es?	Esta bé, quant és?
It's too expensive	Es demasiado caro	És massa car
Don't you have anything cheaper?	¿No tiene algo más barato?	En té de més bon preu?
Can one . . . ?	¿Se puede . . . ?	Es pot . . . ?
. . . camp (near) here?	¿ . . . acampar aquí (cerca)?	. . . acampar a la vora?
Is there a hostel nearby?	¿Hay un hostal aquí cerca?	Hi ha un hostal a la vora?
It's not very far	No es muy lejos	No és gaire lluny
How do I get to . . . ?	¿Por dónde se va a . . . ?	Per anar a . . . ?
Left, right, straight on	Izquierda, derecha, todo recto	A l'esquerra, a la dreta, tot recte
Where is . . . ?	¿Dónde está . . . ?	On és . . . ?
. . . the bus station	. . . la estación de autobuses	. . . l'estació de autobuses
. . . the bus stop	. . . la parada	. . . la parada
. . . the railway station	. . . la estación de ferrocarril	. . . l'estació
. . . the nearest bank	. . . el banco más cercano	. . . el banc més a prop
. . . the post office	. . . el correo/ la oficina de correos	. . . l'oficina de correus
. . . the toilet	. . . el baño/aseo/servicio	. . . la toaleta
Where does the bus to . . . leave from?	¿De dónde sale el autobús para . . . ?	De on surt el autobús a . . .?
Is this the train for Barcelona?	¿Es este el tren para Barcelona?	Aquest tren va a Barcelona?
I'd like a (return) ticket to . . .	Quisiera un billete (de ida y vuelta) para . .	Voldria un bitllet (d'anar i tornar) a . . .
What time does it leave (arrive in . . .)?	¿A qué hora sale (llega a . . .)?	A quina hora surt (arriba a . . .)?
What is there to eat?	¿Qué hay para comer?	Què hi ha per menjar?
What's that?	¿Qué es eso?	Què és això? *Continues over*

DAYS OF THE WEEK

	SPANISH	CATALAN
Monday	*lunes*	*dilluns*
Tuesday	*martes*	*dimarts*
Wednesday	*miércoles*	*dimecres*
Thursday	*jueves*	*dijous*
Friday	*viernes*	*divendres*
Saturday	*sábado*	*dissabte*
Sunday	*domingo*	*diumenge*

NUMBERS

	SPANISH	CATALAN
1	*un/uno/una*	*un(a)*
2	*dos*	*dos (dues)*
3	*tres*	*tres*
4	*cuatro*	*quatre*
5	*cinco*	*cinc*
6	*seis*	*sis*
7	*siete*	*set*
8	*ocho*	*vuit*
9	*nueve*	*nou*
10	*diez*	*deu*
11	*once*	*onze*
12	*doce*	*dotze*
13	*trece*	*tretze*
14	*catorce*	*catorze*
15	*quince*	*quinze*
16	*dieciséis*	*setze*
17	*diecisiete*	*disset*
18	*dieciocho*	*divuit*
19	*diecinueve*	*dinou*
20	*veinte*	*vint*
21	*veintiuno*	*vint-i-un*
30	*treinta*	*trenta*
40	*cuarenta*	*quaranta*
50	*cincuenta*	*cinquanta*
60	*sesenta*	*seixanta*
70	*setenta*	*setanta*
80	*ochenta*	*vuitanta*
90	*noventa*	*novanta*
100	*cien(to)*	*cent*
101	*ciento uno*	*cent un*
102	*ciento dos*	*cent dos (dues)*
200	*doscientos*	*dos-cents (dues-centes)*
500	*quinientos*	*cinc-cents*
1000	*mil*	*mil*
2000	*dos mil*	*dos mil*

Glossary

Catalan terms

Ajuntament Town Hall.

Albufera Lagoon (and surrounding wetlands).

Altar major High altar.

Aparcament Parking.

Avinguda (Avgda) Avenue.

Badia Bay.

Barranc Ravine.

Barroc Baroque (see p.272).

Basílica Catholic church with honorific privileges.

Cala Small bay, cove.

Camí Way or road.

Ca'n At the house of (contraction of *casa* and *en*).

Capella Chapel.

Carrer (c/) Street.

Carretera Road, highway.

Castell Castle.

Celler Cellar, or a bar in a cellar.

Claustre Cloister.

Coll Col, mountain pass.

Convent Convent, nunnery or monastery.

Correu Post office.

Coves Caves.

Església Church.

Estany Small lake.

Festa Festival.

Finca Estate or farmhouse.

Font Water fountain or spring.

Gòtic Gothic (p.272).

Illa Island.

Jardí Garden.

Llac Lake.

Mercat Market.

Mirador Watchtower or viewpoint.

Modernisme Literally "modernism", the Catalan form of Art Nouveau, whose most famous exponent was Antoni Gaudí; adjective *modernista*.

Monestir Monastery.

Mozarabe A Christian subject of a medieval Moorish ruler; hence **Mozarabic**, a colourful building style that reveals both Christian and Moorish influences.

Mudéjar A Moorish subject of a medieval Christian ruler. Also a style of architecture developed by Moorish craftsmen working for Christians, characterized by painted woodwork with strong colours and complex geometrical patterns; revived between the 1890s and 1930s and blended with Art Nouveau forms.

Museu Museum.

Nostra Senyora The Virgin Mary ("Our Lady").

Oficina d'Informació Turística Tourist office.

Palau Palace, mansion or manor house.

Parc Park.

Passeig Boulevard; the evening stroll along it.

Pic Summit.

Plaça Square.

Platja Beach.

Pont Bridge.

Port Harbour, port.

Porta Door, gate.

Puig Hill, mountain.

Rambla Avenue or boulevard.

Rei King.

Reial Royal.

Reina Queen.

Reixa Iron screen or grille, usually in front of a window.

Renaixença Rebirth, often used to describe the Catalan cultural revival at the end of the nineteenth and beginning of the twentieth centuries. Architecturally, this was expressed as *modernisme*.

Retaule Retable or reredos, a wooden, ornamental panel behind an altar.

Riu River.

Romeria Pilgrimage or gathering at a shrine.

Salinas Saltpans.

Salt d'aigua Waterfall.

Santuari Sanctuary.

Sant/a Saint.

Serra Mountain range.

Talayot Cone-shaped prehistoric watchtower.

Torrent Stream or river (usually dry in summer).

Urbanització Modern estate development.

Vall Valley.

Art and architectural terms

Ambulatory Covered passage around the outer edge of the choir in the chancel of a church.

Apse Semicircular protrusion at (usually) the east end of a church.

Art Deco Geometrical style of art and architecture popular in the 1930s.

Art Nouveau Style of art, architecture and design based on highly stylised vegetal forms. Popular in the early part of the twentieth century. See also Modernisme on p.271.

Baroque The art and architecture of the Counter-Reformation, dating from around 1600 onwards. Distinguished by its ornate exuberance and (at its best) complex but harmonious spatial arrangement of interiors. Some elements – particularly its gaudiness – remained popular in the Balearics well into the twentieth century.

Caryatid A sculptured female figure used as a column.

Chancel The eastern part of a church, often separated from the nave by a screen or by the choir.

Classical Architectural style incorporating Greek and Roman elements – pillars, domes, colonnades, and so on – at its height in the seventeenth century and revived, as Neoclassical, in the nineteenth.

Churrigueresque Fancifully ornate form of Baroque art named after its leading exponents, the Spaniard José Churriguera (1650–1723) and his extended family.

Cyclopean Prehistoric style of dry stone masonry comprising boulders of irregular form.

Gothic Architectural style of the thirteenth to sixteenth centuries, characterized by pointed arches, rib vaulting, flying buttresses and a general emphasis on verticality.

Nave Main body of a church.

Neoclassical Architectural style derived from Greek and Roman elements – pillars, domes, colonnades, and so on – that was popular in the nineteenth century.

Plateresque Elaborately decorative Renaissance architectural style, named for its resemblance to silversmiths' work (*platería*).

Presbytery The part of the church to the east of the choir and the site of the high altar.

Renaissance Movement in art and architecture developed in fifteenth-century Italy.

Retable Altarpiece.

Romanesque Early medieval architecture distinguished by squat forms, rounded arches and naïve sculpture.

Transept Arms of a cross-shaped church, placed at ninety degrees to nave and chancel.

Triptych Carved or painted work on three panels.

Tympanum Sculpted, usually recessed, panel above a door.

Vault An arched ceiling or roof.

Index

around the world

Alaska ★ Algarve ★ Amsterdam ★ Andalucía ★ Antigua & Barbuda ★ Argentina ★ Auckland Restaurants ★ Australia ★ Austria ★ Bahamas ★ Bali & Lombok ★ Bangkok ★ Barbados ★ Barcelona ★ Beijing ★ Belgium & Luxembourg ★ Belize ★ Berlin ★ Big Island of Hawaii ★ Bolivia ★ Boston ★ Brazil ★ Britain ★ Brittany & Normandy ★ Bruges & Ghent ★ Brussels ★ Budapest ★ Bulgaria ★ California ★ Cambodia ★ Canada ★ Cape Town ★ The Caribbean ★ Central America ★ Chile ★ China ★ Copenhagen ★ Corsica ★ Costa Brava ★ Costa Rica ★ Crete ★ Croatia ★ Cuba ★ Cyprus ★ Czech & Slovak Republics ★ Devon & Cornwall ★ Dodecanese & East Aegean ★ Dominican Republic ★ The Dordogne & the Lot ★ Dublin ★ Ecuador ★ Edinburgh ★ Egypt ★ England ★ Europe ★ First-time Asia ★ First-time Europe ★ Florence ★ Florida ★ France ★ French Hotels & Restaurants ★ Gay & Lesbian Australia ★ Germany ★ Goa ★ Greece ★ Greek Islands ★ Guatemala ★ Hawaii ★ Holland ★ Hong Kong & Macau ★ Honolulu ★ Hungary ★ Ibiza & Formentera ★ Iceland ★ India ★ Indonesia ★ Ionian Islands ★ Ireland ★ Israel & the Palestinian Territories ★ Italy ★ Jamaica ★ Japan ★ Jerusalem ★ Jordan ★ Kenya ★ The Lake District ★ Languedoc & Roussillon ★ Laos ★ Las Vegas ★ Lisbon ★ London ★

in twenty years

ondon Mini Guide ★ London Restaurants ★ Los Angeles ★ Madeira ★
Madrid ★ Malaysia, Singapore & Brunei ★ Mallorca ★ Malta & Gozo ★ Maui
★ Maya World ★ Melbourne ★ Menorca ★ Mexico ★ Miami & the Florida
Keys ★ Montréal ★ Morocco ★ Moscow ★ Nepal ★ New England ★ New
Orleans ★ New York City ★ New York Mini Guide ★ New York Restaurants
★ New Zealand ★ Norway ★ Pacific Northwest ★ Paris ★ Paris Mini Guide
★ Peru ★ Poland ★ Portugal ★ Prague ★ Provence & the Côte d'Azur ★
Pyrenees ★ The Rocky Mountains ★ Romania ★ Rome ★ San Francisco ★
San Francisco Restaurants ★ Sardinia ★ Scandinavia ★ Scotland ★
Scottish Highlands & Islands ★ Seattle ★ Sicily ★ Singapore ★ South Africa,
Lesotho & Swaziland ★ South India ★ Southeast Asia ★ Southwest USA ★
Spain ★ St Lucia ★ St Petersburg ★ Sweden ★ Switzerland ★ Sydney ★
Syria ★ Tanzania ★ Tenerife and La Gomera ★ Thailand ★ Thailand's
Beaches & Islands ★ Tokyo ★ Toronto ★ Travel Health ★ Trinidad &
Tobago ★ Tunisia ★ Turkey ★ Tuscany & Umbria ★ USA ★ Vancouver ★
Venice & the Veneto ★ Vienna ★ Vietnam ★ Wales ★ Washington DC ★
West Africa ★ Women Travel ★ Yosemite ★ Zanzibar ★ Zimbabwe

also look out for our maps, phrasebooks, music guides and reference books

stay in touch

roughnews

Rough Guides' FREE full-colour newsletter

News, travel issues, music reviews, readers' letters and the latest dispatches from authors on the road

If you would like to receive roughnews, please send us your name and address:

62-70 Shorts Gardens
London, WC2H 9AH, UK

4th Floor, 345 Hudson St,
New York NY10014, USA

newslettersubs@roughguides.co.uk

roughnews

Outback
David Leffman

India
Agra-phobia

Letter from Nigeria
What corruption?

Wired World
Rough Guide e-books

On the rails
Trains are special

ROUGH GUIDES

Will you have enough stories to tell your grandchildren?
©2000 Yahoo! Inc.
Yahoo! Travel
Do You Yahoo!?

The ideas expressed in this code were developed by and for independent travellers.

Learn About The Country You're Visiting
Start enjoying your travels before you leave by tapping into as many sources of information as you can.

The Cost Of Your Holiday
Think about where your money goes - be fair and realistic about how cheaply you travel. Try and put money into local peoples' hands; drink local beer or fruit juice rather than imported brands and stay in locally owned accommodation. Haggle with humour and not aggressively. Pay what something is worth to you and remember how wealthy you are compared to local people.

Embrace The Local Culture
Open your mind to new cultures and traditions. Think carefully about what's appropriate in terms of your clothes and the way you behave. You'll earn respect and be more readily welcomed by local people. Respect local laws and attitudes towards drugs and alcohol that vary in different countries and communities. Think about the impact you could have on them.

Exploring The World – The Travellers' Code
Being sensitive to these ideas means getting more out of your travels - and giving more back to the people you meet and the places you visit.

Minimise Your Environmental Impact
Think about what happens to your rubbish - take biodegradable products and a water filter bottle. Be sensitive to limited resources like water, fuel and electricity. Help preserve local wildlife and habitats by respecting rules and regulations, such as sticking to footpaths and not standing on coral.

Don't Rely On Guidebooks
Use your guidebook as a starting point, not the only source of information. Talk to locals, then discover your own adventure!

Be Discreet With Photography
Don't treat people as part of the landscape, they may not want their picture taken. Ask first and respect their wishes.

Tourism Concern works with people the world over to promote tourism that benefits their communities, but we can only carry on our work with the support of people like you. For membership details or to find out how to make your travels work for local people and the environment, visit our website

Tourism Concern
Campaigning for Ethical and Fairly Traded Tourism

www.tourismconcern.org.uk